The Cambridge Pre-GED Program in WRITING

1988 Edition

CAMBRIDGE Adult Education
Prentice Hall Regents, Englewood Cliffs, NJ 07632

The Cambridge Pre-GED Program in

WRITING

Editorial supervision: Tim Foote
Production supervision: Janet Johnston
Manufacturing buyer: Art Michalez

The contributions of Cheryl Moore and Mark Kellar to the development of *The Cambridge Pre-GED Program in Writing* are gratefully acknowledged.

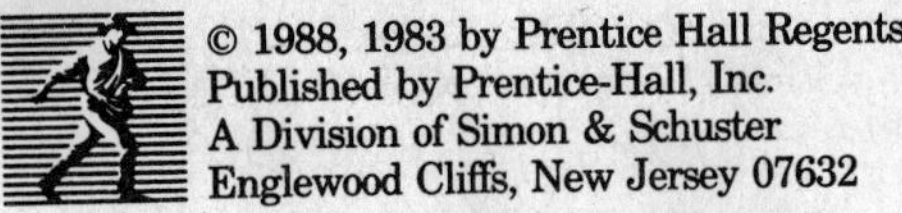

Published by Prentice-Hall, Inc.
A Division of Simon & Schuster
Englewood Cliffs, New Jersey 07632

Printed in the United States of America

10 9 8 7 6 5 4

ISBN 0-13-114240-2

Prentice-Hall International (UK) Limited, *London*
Prentice-Hall of Australia Pty. Limited, *Sydney*
Prentice-Hall Canada Inc., *Toronto*
Prentice-Hall Hispanoamericana, S.A., *Mexico*
Prentice-Hall of India Private Limited, *New Delhi*
Prentice-Hall of Japan, Inc., *Tokyo*
Simon & Schuster Asia Pte. Ltd., *Singapore*
Editora Prentice-Hall do Brasil, Ltda., *Rio de Janeiro*

CONTENTS

PRONOUNS, ADJECTIVES, AND ADVERBS

SENTENCE STRUCTURE, PARAGRAPH STRUCTURE, AND WRITING

INTRODUCTION

The twenty-two units in this book will help you begin your preparation to take the GED, or the High School Equivalency Exam, as it is sometimes called. The Writing Skills Test of the GED has two parts. The first part is made up of 55 multiple-choice questions. The questions cover English usage, sentence structure, and punctuation and spelling. Most of the questions ask you to find and correct errors in sentences. Others ask you to reword sentences so that they are not so awkward. In the second part of the Writing Skills Test you will write a short essay to explain or describe something.

You can use the instruction and practice in this book to help you develop the writing skills you need for success on the test.

This book has several features to help you get the most out of your study. You will find most of them listed in the Contents on pages iii–v.

- The **Pretest** will help you find out about your current skills in writing.

- Each of the three parts of this book begins with the exercise **How Much Do You Know Already?** to help you decide which chapters you should study.

- The three exercises called **Measuring Your Progress** and the **Posttest** help you find out how your skills have improved and which units, if any, you should review.

- Throughout this book there are sets of practice exercises called **Try It** and **Spelling and Usage Hints**, and the **Answers and Explanations** to use to check your work. Among the exercises are several that will help you prepare to write the essay on the GED.

You can use the *Cambridge Pre-GED Exercise Book in Writing* for extra practice as you work through this textbook. The charts on the inside covers of this book and the exercise book show which pages in the exercise book are related to the units in this book.

When you have successfully completed all the units in this book, you will have developed the writing skills you need to continue your preparation for the GED. You will be able to move right into the instruction in Cambridge's GED books because the units on grammar and essay writing build from reviews of the skills you will have learned using this book.

PRETEST

This Pretest will help you plan your work in this book. Answer as many of the items as you can. When you have finished, check your answers on page xii. The chart on page xiv will tell you which exercises you should do next.

PART A

Underline the complete subject in each sentence once. Underline the complete predicate in each sentence twice.

EXAMPLE: The vacant apartment is for rent.

1. My friend Nancy is a computer programmer.
2. The dead battery needs to be recharged.
3. Jose works for a bank in New Haven.
4. The last three racks in the back contain sale items.

PART B

Underline the simple subject in each sentence. If the simple subject is singular, put an **S** in the blank. If the simple subject is plural, put a **P** in the blank.

EXAMPLE: P The condominiums near the water are for sale.

5. ____ Sam and Michelle take turns cooking dinner.
6. ____ Where is the stapler?
7. ____ The apartments in that town are expensive.
8. ____ Dave's new television has remote control.

PART C

Underline the verb that matches the subject in each sentence.

EXAMPLE: The children (want—wants) after-school snacks.

9. Everybody (like—likes) dessert.
10. (Are—Is) you happy about your promotion?
11. Most of the leaves (are—is) raked into piles.
12. Either Pam or Cathy (has—have) an extra ticket.

PART D

Underline the correct verb in each sentence.

EXAMPLE: Robert (has driven—has drove) his car to Florida.

13. Joe (be going—will be going) into the Army soon.
14. We (was waiting—were waiting) for you at the station.

15. I (saw—seen) that movie last week.

16. Maria (gone—went) to the library.

PART E

Underline the correct pronoun in each sentence.

EXAMPLE: Alan and (I—me) went to the mall today.

17. (Them—They) brought the potato salad.

18. He ate by (himself—hisself) at lunch.

19. Terry and Debbie met Bob and (her—she) after work.

20. The mysterious caller was (I—me).

PART F

Underline the correct word in each sentence.

EXAMPLE: This check is (mine—my).

21. The tan car is (hers—her's).

22. The (managers—manager's) are all in a meeting.

23. Which of those (boy's—boys') pranks upset you most?

24. Everyone bought (his—their) ticket yesterday.

PART G

Underline the adjectives in each sentence.

EXAMPLE: These slacks are washable and inexpensive.

25. Janet was wearing a blue and white dress today.

26. The hikers were tired and hungry at the end of the day.

27. A beautiful woman entered the crowded room.

28. I would like a large mug of hot, black coffee.

PART H

Read each pair of sentences. One of the sentences contains a mistake. The other sentence is correct. Circle the letter next to the sentence that is correct.

EXAMPLE: (a) I want these here tools.
(b) I want these tools.

29. (a) The flag is red, white, and blue.
(b) The flag is red white and blue.

30. (a) That there seat is mine.
(b) That seat is mine.

31. (a) The blue and green towel belongs to Peggy.
    (b) The blue, and green towel belongs to Peggy.

32. (a) Them lines are still busy.
    (b) Those lines are still busy.

PART I

Underline the adverbs in each sentence.

EXAMPLE: The mirror <u>quickly</u> fogged up after his shower.

33. Annette patiently explained the problem to Joan.
34. He drove the car very slowly because of the flat tire.
35. I'm truly happy for you.
36. The car alarm whined loudly for fifteen minutes.

PART J

Read each pair of sentences. One of the sentences contains a mistake. The other sentence is correct. Circle the letter next to the sentence that is correct.

EXAMPLE: (a) James ate his ice cream slow.
(b) James ate his ice cream slowly.

37. (a) The subway trains run electricly.
    (b) The subway trains run electrically.

38. (a) Alicia drove to the store quickly.
    (b) Alicia drove to the store quick.

39. (a) Ron plays the organ very good.
    (b) Ron plays the organ very well.

40. (a) David did bad on the exam last year.
    (b) David did badly on the exam last year.

PART K

Read each pair of sentences. One of the sentences contains a mistake. The other sentence is correct. Circle the letter next to the sentence that is correct.

EXAMPLE: (a) Barry is more fat than Bill.
(b) Barry is fatter than Bill.

41. (a) This cheese has the sharpest taste.
    (b) This cheese has the most sharp taste.

42. (a) The shore is cooler than the city.
    (b) The shore is more cool than the city.

43. (a) Of the two sisters, Yvonne is the more intelligent.
    (b) Of the two sisters, Yvonne is the most intelligent.

44. (a) Frank bowls worser than Richard does.
    (b) Frank bowls worse than Richard does.

PART L

For each question there are two sentences. One sentence contains a mistake. The other sentence is correct. Circle the letter next to the sentence that is correct.

EXAMPLE: (a) Lori apologized, but Cathy was still angry. [circled]
(b) Lori apologized but, Cathy was still angry.

45. (a) The beds were made and, the dishes were washed and dried.
    (b) The beds were made, and the dishes were washed and dried.

46. (a) Marian was dieting, but she ate ice cream.
    (b) Marian was dieting, so she ate ice cream.

47. (a) The Night owl, The Bay State, and The Lake Shore Limited are all Amtrak trains.
    (b) The Night Owl, The Bay State, and The Lake Shore Limited, are all Amtrak trains.

48. (a) Neither Art nor Ed is available right now.
    (b) Neither Art or Ed is available right now.

PART M

For each question, there are two sentences. One sentence contains a mistake. The other sentence is correct. Circle the letter next to the sentence that is correct.

EXAMPLE: (a) Robert likes rock music, Marla likes jazz.
(b) Robert likes rock music; Marla likes jazz. [circled]

49. (a) It was almost midnight, but Bobbi still wasn't home.
    (b) It was almost midnight; but Bobbi still wasn't home.

50. (a) Dave is on a winning streak, in fact, he hasn't lost a game all season.
    (b) Dave is on a winning streak; in fact, he hasn't lost a game all season.

51. (a) The computer is down; Irving can fix it.
    (b) The computer is down, Irving can fix it.

52. (a) I heard a noise; and turned on the light.
    (b) I heard a noise and turned on the light.

PART N

For each question, there are two sentences. One sentence contains a mistake. The other sentence is correct. Circle the letter next to the sentence that is correct.

EXAMPLE: (a) The car with racing stripes is parked in my space.

(b) The car is parked in my space with racing stripes.

53. (a) While Fred was still reading, Jan turned the light off.
    (b) While Fred was still reading Jan turned the light off.

54. (a) I saw a woman in the restaurant with a dog.
    (b) I saw a woman with a dog in the restaurant.

55. (a) The Jacksons saw bears driving through Yellowstone.
    (b) Driving through Yellowstone, the Jacksons saw bears.

56. (a) After you finish this, can go home.
    (b) After you finish this, you can go home.

PART O

Read the following paragraph and answer the questions that follow it. The sentences in the paragraph are numbered to help you answer the questions.

(1) Many major cities in the world have underground railroads. (2) For example, in New York there is an extensive subway system. (3) In London the train system is called the Underground. (4) Mexico City, Moscow, Paris, and Washington, D. C., also have underground railroads. (5) Busses are another form of public transportation.

57. Which sentence in the paragraph is the topic sentence?

58. There is one sentence that should not be in the paragraph because it is not on the topic of the paragraph. Which sentence is that?

ANSWER KEY

PART A

1. My friend Nancy is a computer programmer.
2. The dead battery needs to be recharged.
3. Jose works for a bank in New Haven.
4. The last three racks in the back contain sale items.

PART B

5. P Sam and Michelle take turns cooking dinner.
6. S Where is the stapler?
7. P The apartments in that town are expensive.
8. S Dave's new television has remote control.

PART C

9. Everybody likes dessert.
10. Are you happy about your promotion?
11. Most of the leaves are raked into piles.
12. Either Pam or Cathy has an extra ticket.

PART D

13. Joe will be going into the Army soon.
14. We were waiting for you at the station.
15. I saw that movie last week.
16. Maria went to the library.

PART E

17. They brought the potato salad.
18. He ate by himself at lunch.
19. Terry and Debbie met Bob and her after work.
20. The mysterious caller was I.

PART F

21. The tan car is hers.
22. The managers are all in a meeting.
23. Which of those boys' pranks upset you most?
24. Everyone bought his ticket yesterday.

PART G

25. Janet was wearing a blue and white dress today.
26. The hikers were tired and hungry at the end of the day.
27. A beautiful woman entered the crowded room.
28. I would like a large mug of hot, black coffee.

PART H

29. a The flag is red, white, and blue.
30. b That seat is mine.
31. a The blue and green towel belongs to Peggy.
32. b Those lines are still busy.

PART I

33. Annette patiently explained the problem to Joan.
34. He drove the car very slowly because of the flat tire.
35. I'm truly happy for you.
36. The car alarm whined loudly for fifteen minutes.

PART J

37. b The subway trains run electrically.
38. a Alicia drove to the store quickly.
39. b Ron plays the organ very well.
40. b David did badly on the exam last year.

PART K

41. a This cheese has the sharpest taste.
42. a The shore is cooler than the city.
43. a Of the two sisters, Yvonne is the more intelligent.
44. b Frank bowls worse than Richard does.

PART L

45. b The beds were made, and the dishes were washed and dried.
46. a Marian was dieting, but she ate ice cream.
47. a The Night Owl, The Bay State, and The Lake Shore Limited are all Amtrak trains.
48. a Neither Art nor Ed is available right now.

PART M

49. a It was almost midnight, but Bobbi still wasn't home.
50. b Dave is on a winning streak; in fact, he hasn't lost a game all season.
51. a The computer is down; Irving can fix it.
52. b I heard a noise and turned on the light.

PART N

53. a While Fred was still reading, Jan turned the light off.
54. b I saw a woman with a dog in the restaurant.
55. b Driving through Yellowstone, the Jacksons saw bears.
56. b After you finish this, you can go home.

PART O

57. (1)
58. (5)

There are three groups of items on the Pretest. If you missed or did not do one or more of the items in any group, do the exercise called **How Much Do You Know Already?** on the page indicated.

Group	Item Numbers	Exercise Page
Subjects and Verbs	1–16	1
Pronouns, Adjectives, and Adverbs	17–44	119
Sentence Structure, Paragraph Structure, and Writing	45–58	202

Subjects and Verbs

UNIT 1: HOW MUCH DO YOU KNOW ALREADY?

This unit will help you plan your work in Units 2–8. Answer as many of the items as you can. When you have finished, check your answers on page 5. Then in the chart on page 7 circle the number of any item you missed. The chart will tell you which pages to study.

PART A

Underline the complete subject in each sentence once. Underline the complete predicate in each sentence twice.

EXAMPLE: The red brick house on the corner is for sale.

1. The new secretary is a good typist.
2. The boxes on the top shelf contain envelopes.
3. Rick lives in an apartment with his uncle.
4. The leaky old bathroom sink needs to be fixed.
5. The woman behind the counter is the owner of the store.

PART B

Underline the simple subject in each sentence. If the simple subject is singular, put an **S** in the blank. If the simple subject is plural, put a **P** in the blank.

EXAMPLE: __P__ The offices on the third floor of this building are for rent.

6. __P__ Where are my gloves?

7. ____ The man in the white shoes is Brenda's cousin.

8. ____ Here are the tickets for tonight's game.

9. ____ Ben's shiny new car has a flat tire.

10. ____ Do you have change for a dollar?

11. ____ The new album by the Bunnies has several good songs on it.

12. ____ Milt and Earl drive to work together every morning.

13. ____ The apartments in this building have two bedrooms.

14. ____ There is a reward for their capture.

15. ____ The bedroom and the bathroom need to be painted.

PART C

Underline the verb that matches the subject in each sentence.

EXAMPLE: The dog (want—<u>wants</u>) to go outside.

16. Jennifer and Paul (has—have) six children.

17. There (are—is) a note on the refrigerator door.

18. The house with the red shutters (has—have) a vegetable garden.

19. The dog and the cat (fight—fights) all the time.

20. Gail's oldest child (play—plays) the guitar in a band.

21. (Are—Is) you busy right now?

22. I (am—are) worried about my children.

23. Here (are—is) your car keys.

24. The president of the company (work—works) many long hours.

25. (Are—Is) Mr. Filbert in his office?

26. Mathematics (are—is) Terry's favorite subject.

27. Your eyeglasses (are—is) on the table.

28. Our team (play—plays) the Tempos this weekend.

29. The United States (are—is) a member of the United Nations.

30. Two cups (equal—equals) one pint.

31. Few (like—likes) liver.

32. Most of the work (are—is) done.

33. No one (want—wants) any trouble.

34. Something in this refrigerator (are—is) rotten.

35. All of the telephones (are—is) busy at the moment.

36. Everybody (agree—agrees) with me.

37. Neither of the twins (like—likes) to wear matching dresses.

38. Someone (are—is) at the door.

39. One of the tires (are—is) is flat.

40. Some of your cigarettes (are—is) on the floor.

41. Not only Roy but also Kathy (gamble—gambles) at the racetrack.

42. Either Randy or Claude (has—have) an extra umbrella.

43. Neither rain nor snow (are—is) in the forecast.

44. Mercury and Venus (are—is) the closest planets to the sun.

45. Not only Ernie but also his brothers (play—plays) on the team.

PART D

Underline the correct verb in each sentence.

EXAMPLE: Seymour (has ridden—has rode) his motorcycle into town.

46. Floyd (saw—seen) you with Andy last night.

47. We (had ate—had eaten) before the party.

48. You (was—were) sick last week.

49. Matthew (has did—has done) all of Pete's work.

50. Sam (gone—went) to the store.

51. Tom (has known—have known) about the surprise party.

52. Tony (be going—will be going) home soon.

53. We (had driven—had drove) across the country once before.

54. The bride (was gave—was given) away by her father.

55. I (was waiting—were waiting) for your phone call.

ANSWER KEY

PART A

1. The new secretary is a good typist.
2. The boxes on the top shelf contain envelopes.
3. Rick lives in an apartment with his uncle.
4. The leaky old bathroom sink needs to be fixed.
5. The woman behind the counter is the owner of the store.

PART B

6. P Where are my gloves?
7. S The man in the white shoes is Brenda's cousin.
8. P Here are the tickets for tonight's game.
9. S Ben's shiny new car has a flat tire.
10. S Do you have change for a dollar?
11. S The new album by the Bunnies has several good songs on it.
12. P Milt and Earl drive to work together every morning.
13. P The apartments in this building have two bedrooms.
14. S There is a reward for their capture.
15. P The bedroom and the bathroom need to be painted.

PART C

16. Jennifer and Paul have six children.
17. There is a note on the refrigerator door.
18. The house with the red shutters has a vegetable garden.
19. The dog and the cat fight all the time.
20. Gail's oldest child plays the guitar in a band.
21. Are you busy right now?
22. I am worried about my children.
23. Here are your car keys.
24. The president of the company works many long hours.
25. Is Mr. Filbert in his office?
26. Mathematics is Terry's favorite subject.
27. Your eyeglasses are on the table.
28. Our team plays the Tempos this weekend.
29. The United States is a member of the United Nations.
30. Two cups equal one pint.
31. Few like liver.

32. Most of the work is done.
33. No one wants any trouble.
34. Something in this refrigerator is rotten.
35. All of the telephones are busy at the moment.
36. Everybody agrees with me.
37. Neither of the twins likes to wear matching dresses.
38. Someone is at the door.
39. One of the tires is flat.
40. Some of your cigarettes are on the floor.
41. Not only Roy but also Kathy gambles at the racetrack.
42. Either Randy or Claude has an extra umbrella.
43. Neither rain nor snow is in the forecast.
44. Mercury and Venus are the closest planets to the sun.
45. Not only Ernie but also his brothers play on the team.

PART D

46. Floyd saw you with Andy last night.
47. We had eaten before the party.
48. You were sick last week.
49. Matthew has done all of Pete's work.
50. Sam went to the store.
51. Tom has known about the surprise party.
52. Tony will be going home soon.
53. We had driven across the country once before.
54. The bride was given away by her father.
55. I was waiting for your phone call.

In this chart, circle the number of any item you did not answer correctly. The right-hand side of the chart will tell you the unit number to study for any item that you missed.

Item number:	**Unit to study:**
1 2 3 4 5	UNIT 2: Is It a Sentence?
6 7 8 9 10 11 12 13 14 15	UNIT 3: What Is the Simple Subject?
16 17 18 19 20 21 22 23 24 25	UNIT 4: Does the Verb Match the Subject?
26 27 28 29 30	UNIT 5: Is the Noun Singular or Plural?
31 32 33 34 35 36 37 38 39 40	UNIT 6: Is the Pronoun Singular or Plural?
41 42 43 44 45	UNIT 7: Does the Verb Match the Compound Subject?
46 47 48 49 50 51 52 53 54 55	UNIT 8: How Are Verbs Used?

If you answered all the items in this unit correctly, turn to Unit 10 (page 119).

UNIT 2: IS IT A SENTENCE?

Suppose you are sitting on the bus. You see this piece of the newspaper on the floor:

Look at the headlines. What do they tell you? What do they communicate? The headlines give you two pieces of information:

—Wins $1000—

—Mayor Nichols—

Are these pieces of information complete? They're not. They're only fragments of ideas. You don't know **who** won $1000. You don't know **what** Mayor Nichols did. Each headline only gives you a fragment of an idea.

When you write, you want to give your reader complete ideas. You want to tell the reader your main topic—*who* or *what* you are writing about. You also want to tell something about that main topic.

When you write, the best way to give complete ideas is to use **sentences.** A sentence is a group of words. A sentence has a main topic. A sentence says something about that main topic. A sentence gives a complete idea.

LOOKING FOR SUBJECTS

Look at this group of words. Does each group give a complete idea?

scored the winning touchdown

runs the Cozy Bear Motel

is one block north of the shopping mall

In each group of words, something is missing. The words don't tell you

who scored the winning touchdown

who runs the Cozy Bear Motel

what is one block north of the shopping mall

Each word group does not give a complete idea. Each word group is missing a **subject**. A subject tells *who* or *what* is doing something. Or it tells *who* or *what* is being described. The subject is the main topic of a sentence.

If a group of words doesn't have a subject, it is a **fragment.** A fragment is not a sentence. A fragment doesn't give a complete idea.

Here are the word groups with subjects added to them:

Rigger Young scored the winning touchdown.

Lucy Jonson runs the Cozy Bear Motel.

The Town Theater is one block north of the shopping mall.

Now, the three ideas are complete. Now, the three word groups are sentences. Each sentence has a main topic. Each sentence says something about its main topic.

Picking out the subject of a sentence usually is easy. For example, look at this sentence:

The neighbor's dog is sleeping in the hallway.

What is the subject of this sentence? *Who* or *what* is doing something? *Who* or *what* is being described? The neighbor's dog is doing something. It is sleeping in the hallway. The neighbor's dog is the subject of the sentence.

Here is another sentence:

Tom is a good friend.

What is the subject of this sentence? *Who* or *what* is doing something? *Who* or *what* is being described? Tom is being described. He is described as a good friend. Tom is the subject of the sentence.

Most subjects are easy to find. But you can't *always* find the subject in a sentence. There is one kind of sentence in which the subject isn't written.

Look at these sentences. They are instructions from a pay phone:

Pick up the receiver.

Listen for the dial tone.

Are these instructions written in complete sentences? Does each word group have a subject?

These sentences are **commands.** Commands tell you to do something. A command doesn't seem to have a subject. But it does have a subject. The subject is *you.*

> *(You)* pick up the receiver.
>
> *(You)* listen for the dial tone.

The subject of a command is *you.* The subject of a command isn't always written. You don't have to write the subject of a command.

A command is the only kind of sentence that doesn't need a written subject. How can you tell if a group of words is a command? Read it. Does it tell you to do something? If it does, the group of words is a command. The subject of the command is *you.*

Try It: Looking for Subjects

Underline the subject in each sentence. Write in the subject next to commands.

EXAMPLE: Your red sweater is in the dresser.

1. Frederick writes scripts for TV shows.
2. Open the window, please.
3. The mailbox was empty.
4. Will spooned a mound of potatoes onto his plate.
5. Mary's blue van is parked outside.
6. The band stepped onto the stage.
7. The barn door blew off in the storm.
8. Call the police!
9. Carla heard footsteps on the stairs.
10. My vacation seemed very short.

Check your answers on page 18.

LOOKING FOR PREDICATES

Read this story. As you read it, pick out the subject of each sentence.

Mayor Nichols Greets Star

Mayor Nichols met TV actress Carmen Lovelace last night. Miss Lovelace is the star of the hit show "Empire." The 24-year-old actress is in town for a vacation.

Hundreds of the TV star's fans marched in a parade down Center Street. Mayor Nichols gave Miss Lovelace the key to the city. A private party for the star was held at the mayor's home.

Look at the first sentence again. What is the subject?

> Mayor Nichols met TV superstar Carmen Lovelace last night.

Mayor Nichols is the subject. Look at the underlined words in the sentence. What do they tell you? The underlined words tell you what Mayor Nichols did.

Now, look at the second sentence again:

> Miss Lovelace is the star of the hit show "Empire."

The subject of this sentence is Miss Lovelace. What do the underlined words tell you? They tell you something about the subject. They describe the subject. They tell you who Miss Lovelace is.

> Mayor Nichols met TV superstar Carmen Lovelace last night.
>
> Miss Lovelace is the star of the hit show "Empire."

The underlined words in these sentences are **predicates.** A predicate can tell what the subject is doing. Or it can describe the subject. The predicate is the part of the sentence that tells something about the subject.

Look at the next group of words. Does each group give a complete idea?

The young woman in the blue jacket

His cat Leo

The dictionary

In each group of words, something is missing. The words don't tell you anything about the young woman in the blue jacket, his cat Leo, or the dictionary. Each word group is missing a predicate. Each word group does *not* give a complete idea. If a group of words doesn't have a predicate, it isn't a sentence. It's a fragment.

Here are the word groups with predicates added to them:

The young woman in the blue jacket gave me her seat.

His cat Leo likes dog food.

The dictionary is next to the telephone book.

Now, the three ideas are complete. Now, the three word groups are sentences. To be a sentence, a word group must have two main parts. It must have a subject. It must have a predicate.

Finding the predicate of a sentence is usually easy. For example, look at this sentence:

The neighbors' dog is sleeping in the hallway.

What is the predicate of this sentence? Which words tell what the subject is doing? The subject of the sentence is the neighbors' dog. The words is sleeping in the hallway tell what the subject is doing. They are the predicate of the sentence.

Now, look at this sentence:

Tom is a good friend.

What is the predicate of this sentence? Which words describe the subject? The subject of the sentence is Tom. The words is a good friend describe the subject. They are the predicate of the sentence.

Try It: Looking for Predicates

Underline the predicate in each sentence.

1. Karen works at the First County Bank.
2. A small, black bug crawled across his desk.
3. Rick grabbed the telegram out of Rita's hands.

4. The bank is closed on weekends.

5. The stores were filled with last-minute shoppers.

6. John bit into the ham sandwich.

7. Mel hid the gun under the bed.

8. The elevator door opened at the tenth floor.

9. The Board of Health closed down the restaurant.

10. Carol was upset about the election.

Check your answers on page 18.

Try It: Looking for Sentences

Read each group of words. If the groups of words is a sentence, write S in the blank. If the group of words is a fragment, write F in the blank.

EXAMPLE: __F__ The drugstore on the corner.

1. ____ The chair broke.

2. ____ An attractive fifty-year-old woman.

3. ____ Sit down.

4. ____ Worked after dinner.

5. ____ A fried egg.

6. ____ Jack is never late.

7. ____ The four of us.

8. ____ Pick me up at 7:30.

9. ____ I ate dinner with Fred.

10. ____ Lost his money at the racetrack.

Check your answers on page 19.

WHAT MAKES A SENTENCE LOOK LIKE A SENTENCE?

What is wrong with these groups of words?

the restaurant is open until 11 o'clock at night

it has good food

we go there often

Each group of words is a sentence. But the word groups don't *look* like sentences. What's missing from them?

Two things are missing: **capital letters** and **end marks.** Every sentence has to begin with a capital letter. Every sentence has to end with an end mark. A capital letter shows the beginning of a sentence. An end mark shows the end of a sentence.

There are three different end marks:

1. A **period (.)** ends a sentence that tells something.
2. A **question mark (?)** ends a sentence that asks something.
3. An **exclamation point (!)** ends a sentence that expresses surprise or strong feeling.

Look at these sentences:

The restaurant is open until 11 o'clock at night.

It has good food.

We go there often.

Each sentence tells something. It begins with a capital letter and ends with a period.

Look at these sentences:

Is the restaurant open until 11 o'clock at night?

Does it have good food?

Do you go there often?

Each sentence asks something. It begins with a capital letter and ends with a question mark.

Look at these sentences:

I can't believe that the restaurant is open so late!

This food is really good!

Let's go back again!

Each sentence expresses strong feeling. It begins with a capital letter and ends with an exclamation point. (You could use a period if you didn't want to show as much feeling.)

Try It: What Makes a Sentence Look Like a Sentence?

Make each group of words look like a sentence. Rewrite each sentence so that it begins with a capital letter and ends with an end mark. (Some of the sentences have two possible end marks.)

EXAMPLE: would you give Judy a ride to work

Would you give Judy a ride to work?

1. my wife saw your husband this afternoon
2. are you feeling better
3. the hair stylist dyed my hair
4. that's not true
5. is it raining
6. the bus is empty
7. that's great news
8. did she call you
9. we are so excited

10. our TV set doesn't work

Check your answers on page 20.

UNIT REVIEW

In this unit, you have looked at the two main parts of a sentence—the **subject** and the **predicate.** The subject tells *who* or *what* the sentence is about. The predicate shows what the subject did. Or it describes the subject.

Together, the subject and predicate make up a **sentence.** A sentence communicates a complete idea. It has a main topic (the subject). It says something about that main topic (the predicate). In the next units, you will take a closer look at the two main parts of a sentence.

SPELLING AND USAGE HINT: CAPITALIZATION

You have seen that a sentence always begins with a capital letter:

> My sister and her dog live in a city with my aunt.

The first word in the sentence begins with a capital letter. The word is **capitalized.**

Look at this sentence:

> My sister Lou and her dog Spud live in Baltimore with Aunt Jane.

Why are Lou, Spud, Baltimore and Aunt Jane capitalized? These words are capitalized because each one is the name of a specific person, place, or thing.

Look at these sentences. Notice that the name of a specific person, place, or thing is capitalized:

> I met an actress yesterday.
>
> I met the actress Carmen Lovelace yesterday.
>
> He works in a city.
>
> He works in New York City.
>
> There was a fire at a diner.
>
> There was a fire at Joe's Diner.

Call me one day next week.

Call me on Tuesday.

Remember to capitalize

- the first word in a sentence
- the name of a specific person, place, or thing

Try It: Capitalization

Underline the words that should be capitalized.

EXAMPLE: The smiths live next to the department store.

1. Will you call sam tonight?
2. Our cat cleo eats rubber bands.
3. Her cousins live in raleigh, north carolina.
4. My birthday is in august.
5. We went swimming in puffer's lake.
6. I drive a ford mustang.
7. My friend brenda bites her nails.
8. Have you ever been to chicago?
9. We drove to tarrytown for a spaghetti dinner.
10. Her husband jack works at home.

Check your answers on page 20.

ANSWERS AND EXPLANATIONS

Try It: Looking for Subjects

1. **Frederick writes scripts for TV shows.** Frederick is the subject. It tells you *who* writes scripts for TV shows.
2. **Open the window, please.** This sentence is a command. The subject of a command is *you.*
3. **The mailbox was empty.** The mailbox is the subject. It tells you *what* was empty.
4. **Will spooned a mound of potatoes onto his plate.** Will is the subject. It tells you *who* spooned a mound of potatoes onto his plate.
5. **Mary's blue van is parked outside.** Mary's blue van is the subject. It tells you *what* is parked outside.
6. **The band stepped onto the stage.** The band is the subject. It tells you *who* stepped onto the stage.
7. **The barn door blew off in the storm.** The barn door is the subject. It tells you *what* blew off in the storm.
8. **Call the police!** This sentence is a command. The subject of a command is *you.*
9. **Carla heard footsteps on the stairs.** Carla is the subject. It tells you *who* heard footsteps on the stairs.
10. **My vacation seemed very short.** My vacation is the subject. It tells you *what* seemed very short.

Try It: Looking for Predicates

1. **Karen works at the First County Bank.** Works at the First County Bank is the predicate. It tells you what Karen does.
2. **A small, black bug crawled across his desk.** Crawled across his desk is the predicate. It tells you what the bug did.
3. **Rick grabbed the telegram out of Rita's hands.** Grabbed the telegram out of Rita's hands is the predicate. It tells you what Rick did.
4. **The bank is closed on weekends.** Is closed on weekends is the predicate. It describes the bank.
5. **The stores were filled with last-minute shoppers.** Were filled with last-minute shoppers is the predicate. It describes the stores.

6. **John bit into the ham sandwich.** Bit into the ham sandwich is the predicate. It tells you what John did.
7. **Mel hid the gun under the bed.** Hid the gun under the bed is the predicate. It tells you what Mel did.
8. **The elevator door opened at the tenth floor.** Opened at the tenth floor is the predicate. It tells you what the elevator door did.
9. **The Board of Health closed down the restaurant.** Closed down the restaurant is the predicate. It tells you what the Board of Health did.
10. **Carol was upset about the election.** Was upset about the election is the predicate. It describes Carol.

Try It: Looking for Sentences

1. S **The chair broke** is a sentence. It tells you about the chair (the subject). It tells you that the chair broke (the predicate).
2. F **An attractive fifty-year-old woman** is a fragment. It doesn't tell you anything about the attractive fifty-year-old woman. It is missing a predicate.
3. S **Sit down** is a sentence. It is a command. It tells you (the subject) to sit down (the predicate).
4. F **Worked after dinner** is a fragment. It doesn't tell you *who* worked after dinner. It is missing a subject.
5. F **A fried egg** is a fragment. It doesn't tell you anything about the fried egg. It is missing a predicate.
6. S **Jack is never late** is a sentence. It tells you about Jack (the subject). It tells you that he is never late (the predicate).
7. F **The four of us** is a fragment. It doesn't tell you anything about the four of us. It is missing a predicate.
8. S **Pick me up at 7:30** is a sentence. It is a command. It tells you (the subject) to pick me up at 7:30 (the predicate).
9. S **I ate dinner with Fred** is a sentence. It has a subject (I). It tells you that I ate dinner with Fred (the predicate).
10. F **Lost his money at the racetrack** is a fragment. It doesn't tell you *who* lost his money at the racetrack. It is missing a subject.

Try It: What Makes a Sentence Look Like a Sentence?

1. **My wife saw your husband this afternoon.** This sentence tells something. It should begin with a capital letter and end with a period.
2. **Are you feeling better?** This sentence asks something. It should begin with a capital letter and end with a question mark.
3. **The hair stylist dyed my hair.** This sentence tells something. It should begin with a capital letter and end with a period.
4. **That's not true!** or **That's not true.** This sentence could express a strong feeling. It must begin with a capital letter and could end with an exclamation point. (If you wanted to show less feeling, you could end the sentence with a period.)
5. **Is it raining?** This sentence asks something. It should begin with a capital letter and end with a question mark.
6. **The bus is empty.** This sentence tells something. It should begin with a capital letter and end with a period. (If you wanted to show surprise, you could end the sentence with an exclamation point.)
7. **That's great news!** or **That's great news.** This sentence could express a strong feeling. It must begin with a capital letter and could end with an exclamation point. (If you wanted to show less feeling, you could end the sentence with a period.)
8. **Did she call you?** This sentence asks something. It should begin with a capital letter and end with a question mark.
9. **We are so excited!** This sentence expresses strong feeling. It should begin with a capital letter and end with an exclamation point.
10. **Our TV set doesn't work.** This sentence tells something. It should begin with a capital letter and end with a period. (If you wanted to show surprise, you could end the sentence with an exclamation point.)

Try It: Capitalization

1. **Will you call sam tonight?** Sam should be capitalized because it is the name of a specific person.
2. **Our cat cleo eats rubber bands.** Cleo should be capitalized because it is the name of a specific cat.
3. **Her cousins live in raleigh, north carolina.** Raleigh, North Carolina should be capitalized because it is the name of a specific place.

4. **My birthday is in august.** August should be capitalized because it is the name of a specific month.
5. **We went swimming in puffer's lake.** Puffer's Lake should be capitalized because it is the name of a specific lake.
6. **I drive a ford mustang.** Ford Mustang should be capitalized because it is the name of a specific car.
7. **My friend brenda bites her nails.** Brenda should be capitalized because it is the name of a specific person.
8. **Have you ever been to chicago?** Chicago should be capitalized because it is the name of a specific city.
9. **We drove to tarrytown for a spaghetti dinner.** Tarrytown should be capitalized because it is the name of a specific town.
10. **Her husband jack works at home.** Jack should be capitalized because it is the name of a specific person.

UNIT 3: WHAT IS THE SIMPLE SUBJECT?

Suppose that you are in a clothing store. The store is having a special "2 for 1" sale. A customer can buy two items of clothing for the price of one item. Here is a price list of the sale items:

Jacket—$50

Skirt—$35

You could write these sentences to describe the sale:

One jacket costs $50.

Two jackets cost $50.

One skirt costs $35.

Two skirts cost $35.

Look at the first two sentences again. How are they different?

One jacket costs $50.

Two jackets cost $50.

The difference is easy to spot. The sentences have different subjects. The first sentence is about *one* jacket. The second sentence is about *two* jackets.

The subject one jacket is **singular.** It refers to *one* thing. The subject two jackets is **plural.** It refers to *more than one* thing.

What else is different in the sentences?

One jacket costs $50.

Two jackets cost $50.

When the subject changed from singular to plural, the predicate also changed. One jacket costs $50. Two jackets cost $50. The word costs goes with a singular subject. The word cost goes with a plural subject.

In this unit, you will take a closer look at the subject. You will work on finding the key word or words in the subject. The key words tell you if a subject is singular (one) or plural (more than one). Knowing the key words will help you to match the subject to the predicate in a sentence.

FINDING THE SIMPLE SUBJECT

Suppose you are reading your mail. You see this ad:

February 15 Is Winter Sales Day at Carson's!

Here are just some of the great buys:

—Handsome, hand-knit sweaters by Gavin LaPell are on sale for $35.

—Our popular fur-lined hats are only $20.

—Scarves and gloves are 50% off.

—Wool socks in our hosiery department are 40% off.

What does the ad tell you?

The heading tells you that Carson's is having a sale. The sentences under the heading tell you what is on sale. They also describe the things that are on sale.

Look at this sentence:

> Handsome, hand-knit sweaters by Gavin LaPell are on sale for $35.

What is the key word in the subject? Which word tells you exactly what is on sale? The key word in the subject is sweaters. The other words in the subject (handsome, hand-knit, by Gavin LaPell) tell you more about the sweaters. Sweaters is the **simple subject.**

The simple subject is the key word in the subject. It is the most important word in the subject. Without the simple subject, the sentence wouldn't make sense:

> Handsome, hand-knit by Gavin LaPell are on sale for $35.

You could take out some of the other words in the subject. The sentence would still make sense:

> Hand-knit sweaters by Gavin LaPell are on sale for $35.
>
> Sweaters by Gavin LaPell are on sale for $35.
>
> Sweaters are on sale for $35.

You can still see a complete idea. Sweaters are on sale!

What is the simple subject of this sentence?

Our popular fur-lined hats are only $20.

What is the key word in the subject? Which word tells you *what* is only $20? The simple subject is hats. The other words in the subject (our popular fur-lined) tell you more about the hats.

What is the simple subject of this sentence?

Scarves and gloves are 50% off.

What is the key word in the subject? Which word tells you *what* is 50% off? There isn't just *one* key word in this subject. Both the scarves **and** the gloves are 50% off. The simple subject is scarves **and** gloves.

The simple subject is the key word that tells *who* or *what* is doing the action in a sentence. Or it tells *who* or *what* is being described in the sentence. Finding the simple subject usually is easy. But sometimes it can be a little hard. For example, look at this sentence from the ad:

Wool socks in our hosiery department are 40% off.

The complete subject of the sentence is underlined. What is the simple subject? Is it wool socks? Or is it hosiery department?

In some sentences, there may be two or more things that look like a simple subject. The best way to find the simple subject of these sentences is to look at the predicate.

Wool socks in our hosiery department are 40% off.

The predicate of this sentence is are 40% off. To find the simple subject, ask yourself this question:

Who or what is 40% off?

Are the wool socks 40% off? Or is the hosiery department 40% off? The wool socks are 40% off. The simple subject is wool socks. The words hosiery department just tell you where the wool socks are. Hosiery department is not the simple subject. The predicate tells you about the wool socks. The simple subject is wool socks.

To find the simple subject of a sentence, follow these two steps:

1. Find the predicate.
2. Ask "*Who or what?*" before the predicate.

Try It: Finding the Simple Subject

Underline the complete subject of each sentence once. Underline the simple subject of each sentence twice.

EXAMPLE: My youngest son is a doctor.

1. The dresses in the store window are on sale.
2. Your new blue shirt is under the bed.
3. The coat with the brass buttons is expensive.
4. The cashier from the diner lives in our neighborhood.
5. Anna and Rick went to the movies.
6. The windows in the kitchen are open.
7. Her older brother is a good dancer.
8. The sink in the bathroom isn't working.
9. Your red shoes are in the closet.
10. Babe and her husband are my best friends.

Check your answers on page 37.

NOUNS—WORDS THAT NAME

Look at the underlined words in these sentences. What do they have in common?

> Alex lives in Texas.
>
> The car is out of gas.

All of the underlined words *name* something. All of the underlined words are **nouns**. A noun is a word that names a person, a place, a thing, or an idea.

Most sentences contain at least one noun. Many times, the simple subject of a sentence is a noun. For example, look at this sentence:

> A man from the store called today.

What is the simple subject of this sentence? Who called today? A man called. Man is the simple subject. The word man is a noun. It names a person.

Look at the underlined subjects in the next two sentences. How are they different from each other?

The car is out of gas.

The cars are out of gas.

The difference is pretty easy to spot. The first sentence is about *one* car. The second sentence is about *more than one* car.

How can you tell that the sentences are different? The answer to this question is also easy. All you have to do is look at these two words:

car

cars

The first word refers to only *one* car. It is *singular*. The second word refers to *more than one* car. It is *plural*.

With car and cars, it's easy to tell that one is singular and the other is plural. With most nouns, the plural is formed by adding an s to the word.

Sometimes, the spelling of the noun changes a little when the s is added:

The lady wants some help.

The ladies want some help.

The glass is in the sink.

The glasses are in the sink.

(The Spelling and Usage Tips at the end of Units 3, 4, 5, and 6 contain spelling rules to help you with these kinds of nouns.)

Some nouns *don't* have their plurals formed with an s:

The child likes cereal.

The children like cereal.

There is a mouse in my apartment.

There are mice in my apartment.

Such nouns as child and mouse are called **irregular** nouns. That's because their plurals are not formed with an s. They are formed in other ways.

Try It: Nouns—Words That Name

Underline the simple subject of each sentence. Then rewrite the sentence to make the subject plural.

EXAMPLE: Our new neighbor came to our party.
Our new neighbors came to our party.

1. The lake froze.

2. The bedroom light went off.

3. Leroy's son visited Joe.

4. My brother worked at the chemical plant.

5. The store had sales on Labor Day.

6. His sister moved to Toledo.

Check your answers on page 37.

IS THE SIMPLE SUBJECT SINGULAR OR PLURAL?

It's usually pretty easy to tell if a simple subject is singular or plural. That's because a simple subject is usually only one word. For example, look at these sentences:

The phone is out of order.

Onions are on sale at the grocery store.

The simple subject of the first sentence is one word: phone. The word phone is singular. The simple subject of the second sentence is also one word: onions. The word onions is plural.

Now, look at this sentence:

The knife and the fork are on the table.

What is the simple subject of this sentence? The simple subject is made up of two words: knife and fork. Each word stands for only one thing—one knife and one fork. But look at how the words are joined together in the sentence:

The knife and the fork are on the table.

The word and joins the two words together. One knife and one fork are two things. The simple subject is two things. The simple subject is plural.

What is the simple subject of this sentence?

Puerto Rico is an island.

The simple subject is Puerto Rico. The name Puerto Rico has two words in it. But is it singular or plural? Puerto Rico is the name of an island. It's the name of *one* island. The name Puerto Rico is singular even though the name has two words in it.

Some simple subjects are made up of more than one word. It isn't always easy to tell if these subjects are singular or plural. The easiest way to tell is to think about what the subject stands for. Does it stand for one thing? Does it stand for more than one thing? The answer will help you to decide whether the subject is singular or plural.

Try It: Is the Simple Subject Singular or Plural?

Underline the simple subject in each sentence. If the simple subject is singular, put an **S** in the blank. If the simple subject is plural, put a **P** in the blank.

EXAMPLE: __P__ Jack and Mark are great guys.

1. __S__ Your scarf is in the car.
2. __P__ Minneapolis and St. Paul are called the "Twin Cities."
3. __P__ My parents live nearby.
4. __P__ Boxing and football are her favorite sports.
5. __S__ Ocean City is always crowded in August.
6. __P__ Our neighbor's cows got loose yesterday.
7. __P__ Sean and Ann bought a new car.

8. ____ My keys were stolen.

9. ____ Billie Sue works in the hospital.

10. ____ The bus stops at this corner.

Check your answers on page 38.

PRONOUNS AS SUBJECTS

Look at the underlined words in these sentences. What do they have in common?

I am going out.

He works the night shift.

She has black hair.

It is Saturday.

We eat lunch at the diner.

You look tired.

They called the police.

All of the underlined words are subjects. Each word tells who or what is being described. The underlined words have something else in common. They are all **pronouns.**

Pronouns are words that take the place of nouns. Pronouns make sentences simpler. For example, here are some sentences that don't have any pronouns in them:

> Nick picked up the phone. Nick wondered if Nick should call Laurie. Laurie hadn't been very friendly the last time Nick and Laurie had met.

Here are the sentences with pronouns:

> Nick picked up the phone. He wondered if he should call Laurie. She hadn't been very friendly the last time they had met.

Like nouns, pronouns can be singular or plural. Look at these sentences. Are the underlined pronouns singular or plural?

> The woman stepped on the bus. She paid the bus driver.
>
> Nick picked up the phone. He dialed Laurie's number.
>
> The train was late this morning. It is never on time.

These pronouns are singular. The pronoun she refers to one person—the woman. The pronoun he refers to one person—Nick. The pronoun it refers to one thing—the train. She and he always refer to *one* person. It always refers to *one* thing, place, or idea.

Look at these sentences. Are the underlined pronouns singular or plural?

> Wally and I took a vacation. We went to Pittsburgh.
>
> Massachusetts and Rhode Island are states. They are on the East Coast.

These pronouns are plural. The pronoun we refers to more than one person—Wally and I. The pronoun they refers to more than one place—Massachusetts and Rhode Island. We always refers to *more than one* person. They always refers to *more than one* place, person, thing, or idea.

Try It: Pronouns as Subjects

Underline the complete subject in each sentence. Then rewrite the sentence using the correct pronoun in place of the subject.

EXAMPLE: Ron and I did the laundry.

We did the laundry.

1. Anna left an hour ago.

2. A rabbit is under our porch.

3. Mitch and I are thinking about moving.

4. The cars are parked in the lot.

5. Allan and Marcia went to the store.

6. You and I will have a good time.

7. The boy lives with his grandparents.

8. The women cooked dinner.

9. Pedro and Jim drove to Florida.

10. Rhode Island is the smallest state.

Check your answers on page 39.

SUBJECTS THAT ARE HARD TO FIND

Here are some sentences that you've worked with in this unit:

The car is out of gas.

The knife and the fork are on the table.

Wool socks in our hosiery department are 40% off.

You've worked on finding the simple subject in these sentences. Take another look at each sentence. Where is the simple subject in each sentence? Where is the predicate in each sentence?

The car is out of gas.

The knife and the fork are on the table.

Wool socks in our hosiery department are 40% off.

In each sentence, the simple subject comes *before* the predicate. In most sentences, the subject comes before the predicate. This is why the simple subject usually is easy to find. You can guess that the simple subject will be in the beginning of the sentence. You can guess that the simple subject will come before the predicate.

But look at this sentence:

Here are my keys.

What is the subject of this sentence? *Who* or *what* is this sentence about?

It may seem that here is the subject of this sentence. But here doesn't tell *who* or *what* the sentence is about. Which word tells *who* or *what* the sentence is about? The sentence is about the keys. The keys are here. Keys is the simple subject.

Now, look at this sentence. What is the simple subject?

There are five people in the waiting room.

Which word tells *who* or *what* the sentence is about? The sentence is about the people. Five people are in the waiting room. The simple subject is people.

Sentences that start with here or there are different from most sentences. They're different because the subject comes *after* the predicate.

What is the simple subject of this sentence?

Here are Mike and Jim.

The sentence begins with here. The sentence is about Mike and Jim. Both Mike **and** Jim are here. The simple subject is Mike and Jim. The subject Mike and Jim comes after the predicate.

In sentences that start with here or there, the subject usually comes after the predicate. Remember this when you are looking for the subject in a sentence that starts with here or there.

Try It: Subjects That Are Hard to Find

Underline the simple subject in each sentence. If the simple subject is singular, put an **S** in the blank. If the simple subject is plural, put a **P** in the blank.

1. ____ Here comes the bus.
2. ____ There was a fire at the bank last night.
3. ____ Here is your soda.
4. ____ There are pens and pencils in the desk.
5. ____ Here are your shirt and tie.
6. ____ There won't be a parade today.
7. ____ Here are his books.
8. ____ There are plates in the cabinet.

9. ____ Here is your pill.

10. ____ There is a strike at the plant.

Check your answers on page 40.

FINDING THE SIMPLE SUBJECT IN A QUESTION

Most simple subjects are easy to find. That's because most simple subjects are at the beginning of a sentence. Most simple subjects come before the predicate.

Even the simple subject of a sentence that starts with here or there is easy to find. It's easy to find when you know that the simple subject usually comes *after* the predicate in a here/there sentence.

But how do you find the simple subject in a question? Look at this question:

Did Howard find his tie?

Who or *what* is this question about? *Who* or *what* is the subject of this question? Is it Howard? Or is it his tie?

Finding the simple subject of a question is often tricky. It's tricky because the subject is hidden in the predicate. But there's something you can do to make it easier to find the simple subject of a question. You can turn the question into a statement.

Did Howard find his tie?

Howard did find his tie.

Now can you find the simple subject? Can you find *who* or *what* the sentence is about? The sentence is about Howard. Howard is the simple subject of the question.

Here is another question:

Where is Paula?

Turn this question into a statement. What is the simple subject?

Paula is where.

The statement is about Paula. Paula is the simple subject of the question.

The simple subject of a question can be hard to find. But you can make it easier to find by turning the question into a statement. The simple subject of the statement is the simple subject of the question.

Try It: Finding the Simple Subject in a Question

Find the simple subject of each question. First, turn the question into a statement. Write the statement below the question. Find the simple subject of the statement. Then underline the simple subject in the question.

EXAMPLE: Do you have a stamp?

You do have a stamp.

1. Are Kit and Sam looking for her?

2. Did Bill make that table?

3. Can Mike and I come over later?

4. Have Leo and Phil called today?

5. Will they go to the party?

6. Did Carla ask for a raise?

7. What are Steve and you doing?

8. Do the children have school today?

9. Were the plates on the table?

10. Is New York City near Newark?

Check your answers on page 41.

UNIT REVIEW

In this unit, you've worked on two things. First, you've worked on finding the **simple subject** of a sentence. The simple subject is the key word in the subject. It tells you *who* or *what* the sentence is about.

Finding the simple subject is often easy. That's because the simple subject is usually in the first part of the sentence. The simple subject usually comes before the predicate. But sometimes finding the simple subject is harder. It's harder when the sentence begins with here or there. It's harder when you're looking for the subject of a question.

The second thing you've worked on is finding out if the simple subject is **singular** (one) or **plural** (more than one). Usually, it's pretty easy to tell if the simple subject is singular or plural. It's easy, but it's important. It helps you to match the subject to the predicate in a sentence. In the next unit, you'll work on matching the subject to the predicate.

SPELLING AND USAGE HINT: ADDING S TO WORDS THAT END IN S, X, Z, CH, SH

In this unit, you have looked at words that have their plurals formed with an s:

The dog barked all night.

The dog**s** barked all night.

Many words have their plurals formed in this way. But not all words do.

The match won't light if it's wet.

The match**es** won't light if they're wet.

Here is a rule that will help you to add s to some words:

If a word ends in s, x, z, ch, or sh, add es to the word.

Here are some examples:

The dish broke when the waiter tripped.

The dish**es** broke when the waiter tripped.

The glass is on the table.

The glass**es** are on the table.

There's only one exception to this rule. If the word ends in a vowel (a, e, i, o, or u) plus z, double the z before you add es:

We had a spelling quiz.

We had spelling quizzes.

Try It: Adding s to Words That End in s, x, z, ch, sh

Fill in the blank with the plural form of the word in parentheses.

EXAMPLE: Somebody is behind those **bushes** . (bush)

1. He didn't pay any ______________ last year. (tax)
2. Most of the ______________ stop at this corner. (bus)
3. The band played only ______________ . (waltz)
4. Those ______________ are heavy. (box)
5. The light ______________ aren't working. (switch)
6. He made three ______________ on his birthday. (wish)
7. I don't like surprise ______________ . (quiz)
8. There are several ______________ in the park. (bench)
9. Don't drop your cigarette ______________ on the floor. (ash)
10. The ______________ are over at 7:00. (class)

Check your answers on page 42.

ANSWERS AND EXPLANATIONS

Try It: Finding the Simple Subject

1. **The dresses in the store window are on sale.** The simple subject is dresses. Dresses is the key word in the subject that tells you *what* is on sale.
2. **Your new blue shirt is under the bed.** The simple subject is shirt. Shirt is the key word in the subject that tells you *what* is under the bed.
3. **The coat with the brass buttons is expensive.** The simple subject is coat. Coat is the key word in the subject that tells you *what* is expensive.
4. **The cashier from the diner lives in our neighborhood.** The simple subject is cashier. Cashier is the key word in the subject that tells you *who* lives in our neighborhood.
5. **Anna and Rick went to the movies.** The simple subject is Anna and Rick. Anna and Rick are the key words in the subject that tell you *who* went to the movies.
6. **The windows in the kitchen are open.** The simple subject is windows. Windows is the key word in the subject that tells you *what* is open.
7. **Her older brother is a good dancer.** The simple subject is brother. Brother is the key word in the subject that tells you *who* is a good dancer.
8. **The sink in the bathroom isn't working.** The simple subject is sink. Sink is the key word in the subject that tells you *what* isn't working.
9. **Your red shoes are in the closet.** The simple subject is shoes. Shoes is the key word in the subject that tells you *what* is in the closet.
10. **Babe and her husband are my best friends.** The simple subject is Babe and husband. Babe and husband are the key words in the subject that tell you *who* my best friends are.

Try It: Nouns—Words That Name

1. **The lake froze. The lakes froze.** Lake is the key word in the subject that tells you *what* froze. To make lake plural, add s: lakes.

2. **The bedroom light went off. The bedroom lights went off.** Light is the key word in the subject that tells you *what* went off. To make light plural, add s: lights.

3. **Leroy's son visited Joe. Leroy's sons visited Joe.** Son is the key word in the subject that tells you *who* visited Joe. To make son plural, add s: sons.

4. **My brother worked at the chemical plant. My brothers worked at the chemical plant.** Brother is the key word in the subject that tells you *who* worked at the chemical plant. To make brother plural, add s: brothers.

5. **The store had sales on Labor Day. The stores had sales on Labor Day.** Store is the key word in the subject that tells you *what* had sales on Labor Day. To make store plural, add s: stores.

6. **His sister moved to Toledo. His sisters moved to Toledo.** Sister is the key word in the subject that tells you *who* moved to Toledo. To make sister plural, add s: sisters.

Try It: Is the Simple Subject Singular or Plural?

1. S **Your scarf is in the car.** The simple subject is scarf. Since the simple subject names only *one* thing, it is singular.

2. P **Minneapolis and St. Paul are called the "Twin Cities."** The simple subject is Minneapolis **and** St. Paul. Since the simple subject names *more than one* place, it is plural.

3. P **My parents live nearby.** The simple subject is parents. Since the simple subject names *more than one* person, it is plural.

4. P **Boxing and football are her favorite sports.** The simple subject is boxing **and** football. Since the simple subject names *more than one* thing, it is plural.

5. S **Ocean City is always crowded in August.** The simple subject is Ocean City. Since the simple subject names only *one* place, it is singular.

6. P **Our neighbor's cows got loose yesterday.** The simple subject is cows. Since the simple subject names *more than one* thing, it is plural.

7. P **Sean and Ann bought a new car.** The simple subject is Sean **and** Ann. Since the simple subject names *more than one* person, it is plural.

8. P **My keys were stolen.** The simple subject is keys. Since the simple subject names *more than one* thing, it is plural.

9. S **Billie Sue works in the hospital.** The simple subject is Billie Sue. Since the simple subject names only *one* person, it is singular.
10. S **The bus stops at this corner.** The simple subject is bus. Since the simple subject names only *one* thing, it is singular.

Try It: Pronouns as Subjects

1. **Anna left an hour ago. She left an hour ago.** The subject of the first sentence is Anna. The pronoun she takes the place of Anna.
2. **A rabbit is under our porch. It is under our porch.** The subject of the first sentence is a rabbit. The pronoun it takes the place of a rabbit.
3. **Mitch and I are thinking about moving. We are thinking about moving.** The subject of the first sentence is Mitch and I. The pronoun we takes the place of Mitch and I.
4. **The cars are parked in the lot. They are parked in the lot.** The subject of the first sentence is the cars. The pronoun they takes the place of the cars.
5. **Allan and Marcia went to the store. They went to the store.** The subject of the first sentence is Allan and Marcia. The pronoun they takes the place of Allan and Marcia.
6. **You and I will have a good time. We will have a good time.** The subject of the first sentence is you and I. The pronoun we takes the place of you and I.
7. **The boy lives with his grandparents. He lives with his grandparents.** The subject of the first sentence is the boy. The pronoun he takes the place of the boy.
8. **The women cooked dinner. They cooked dinner.** The subject of the first sentence is the women. The pronoun they takes the place of the women.
9. **Pedro and Jim drove to Florida. They drove to Florida.** The subject of the first sentence is Pedro and Jim. The pronoun they takes the place of Pedro and Jim.
10. **Rhode Island is the smallest state. It is the smallest state.** The subject of the first sentence is Rhode Island. The pronoun it takes the place of Rhode Island.

Try It: Subjects That Are Hard to Find

1. S **Here comes the bus.** When the sentence begins with here, the subject comes after the predicate. The key word in the subject is bus. Since bus names only *one* thing, the subject is singular.

2. S **There was a fire at the bank last night.** When the sentence begins with there, the subject comes after the predicate. The key word in the subject is fire. Since fire names only *one* thing, the subject is singular.

3. S **Here is your soda.** When the sentence begins with here, the subject comes after the predicate. The key word in the subject is soda. Since soda names only *one* thing, the subject is singular.

4. P **There are pens and pencils in the desk.** When the sentence begins with there, the subject comes after the predicate. The key words in the subject are pens and pencils. Since pens **and** pencils name *more than one* thing, the subject is plural.

5. P **Here are your shirt and tie.** When the sentence begins with here, the subject comes after the predicate. The key words in the subject are shirt and tie. Since shirt **and** tie name *more than one* thing, the subject is plural.

6. S **There won't be a parade today.** When the sentence begins with there, the subject comes after the predicate. The key word in the subject is parade. Since parade names only *one* thing, the subject is singular.

7. P **Here are his books.** When the sentence begins with here, the subject comes after the predicate. The key word in the subject is books. Since books names *more than one* thing, the subject is plural.

8. P **There are plates in the cabinet.** When the sentence begins with there, the subject comes after the predicate. The key word in the subject is plates. Since plates names *more than one* thing, the subject is plural.

9. S **Here is your pill.** When the sentence begins with here, the subject comes after the predicate. The key word in the subject is pill. Since pill names only *one* thing, the subject is singular.

10. S **There is a strike at the plant.** When the sentence begins with there, the subject comes after the predicate. The key word in the subject is strike. Since strike names only *one* thing, the subject is singular.

Try It: Finding the Simple Subject in a Question

1. **Are Kit and Sam looking for her?** Turn the question into a statement: Kit and Sam are looking for her. The sentence is about Kit and Sam. Kit and Sam is the simple subject.
2. **Did Bill make that table?** Turn the question into a statement: Bill did make that table. The sentence is about Bill. Bill is the simple subject.
3. **Can Mike and I come over later?** Turn the question into a statement: Mike and I can come over later. The sentence is about Mike and I. Mike and I is the simple subject.
4. **Have Leo and Phil called today?** Turn the question into a statement: Leo and Phil called today. The sentence is about Leo and Phil. Leo and Phil is the simple subject.
5. **Will they go to the party?** Turn the question into a statement: They will go to the party. They is the simple subject.
6. **Did Carla ask for a raise?** Turn the question into a statement: Carla did ask for a raise. The sentence is about Carla. Carla is the simple subject.
7. **What are Steve and you doing?** Turn the question into a statement: Steve and you are doing what. The sentence is about Steve and you. Steve and you is the simple subject.
8. **Do the children have school today?** Turn the question into a statement: The children do have school today. The sentence is about the children. Children is the simple subject.
9. **Were the plates on the table?** Turn the question into a statement: The plates were on the table. The sentence is about the plates. Plates is the simple subject.
10. **Is New York City near Newark?** Turn the question into a statement: New York City is near Newark. The sentence is about New York City. New York City is the simple subject.

Try It: Adding s to Words That End in s, x, z, ch, sh

1. **He didn't pay any taxes last year.** Tax ends in x. Add es to make the word plural.
2. **Most of the buses stop at this corner.** Bus ends in s. Add es to make the word plural.
3. **The band only played waltzes.** Waltz ends in z. Add es to make the word plural.
4. **Those boxes are heavy.** Box ends in x. Add es to make the word plural.
5. **The light switches aren't working.** Switch ends in ch. Add es to make the word plural.
6. **He made three wishes on his birthday.** Wish ends in sh. Add es to make the word plural.
7. **I don't like surprise quizzes.** Quiz ends in a vowel (i) plus z. Double the z before you add es.
8. **There are several benches in the park.** Bench ends in ch. Add es to make the word plural.
9. **Don't drop your cigarette ashes on the floor.** Ash ends in sh. Add es to make the word plural.
10. **The classes are over at 7:00.** Class ends in s. Add es to make the word plural.

UNIT 4: DOES THE VERB MATCH THE SUBJECT?

Here are some sentences that you looked at in the last unit:

One jacket costs $50.

Two jackets cost $50.

The first sentence has a singular subject—jacket. The second sentence has a plural subject—jackets.

What else is different in the sentences?

One jacket costs $50.

Two jackets cost $50.

When the subject changed from singular to plural, a word in the predicate also changed. One jacket costs $50. Two jackets cost $50.

Cost is an example of a **verb**. You know that there is a key word in the subject called the simple subject. There is also a key word in the predicate. It's called the verb.

A verb can show an action:

Lee ran to the bus stop.

Sarah forgot my name.

Or a verb can link the subject with words that describe the subject:

I am very tired.

Ralph was angry.

You know that subjects are singular or plural. Verbs are also singular or plural. A singular verb matches a singular subject. A plural verb matches a plural subject. In this unit, you will look at singular and plural verbs.

Try It: Finding the Verb

Underline the verb in each sentence.

EXAMPLE: Her train arrives at 4:30.

1. This milk tastes sour.
2. Ben usually drives Miriam to work.

3. Larry is a lifeguard.

4. Class begins at 8:00.

5. Jenny works at the hospital.

6. Tony lives in Brooklyn.

7. Alice seems upset.

8. Ralph fixes dinner on Thursday nights.

9. John's letter is on the kitchen table.

10. The bank closes early on Saturday.

Check your answers on page 51.

MATCHING SUBJECTS AND VERBS

There's an old saying: "Opposites attract." Remember this when you match subjects and verbs.

Look at these two sentences:

The dog stays outside.

The dogs stay outside.

What is the simple subject of the first sentence? The simple subject is dog. It is singular. But look at the verb. The verb is stays.

You might think that stays is a plural verb. It isn't. It's singular. The rule for singular and plural verbs is just the opposite of the rule for singular and plural nouns. A singular noun does not have an s added to it. But a singular verb *does* have an s added to it.

Now, look at the second sentence again:

The dogs stay outside.

The simple subject is dogs. It is plural. The verb in the sentence is stay. Stay is plural. A plural verb does not have an s added to it.

Look at this sentence. Why is the verb plural?

The woman and her husband own a grocery store.

Woman is singular. Husband is singular. But woman and husband together make up the simple subject. The subject woman and husband is plural. The verb own is plural to match the subject.

Now, look at this sentence. Why is the verb singular?

> Mark Spencer eats hamburgers for lunch.

The simple subject is Mark Spencer. The simple subject is more than one word. But the two words name only one person. The verb is singular because the simple subject is singular.

You have seen that pronouns can take the place of nouns in the subject. Do the pronouns he, she, and it match a singular verb or a plural verb?

> Mark Spencer eats hamburgers for lunch.
> He likes them.
>
> Dana works at Carson's. She works in the men's department.
>
> The dog stays outside. It lives in a doghouse.

He, she, and it are singular pronouns. They match singular verbs.

Do the pronouns we and they match a singular verb or a plural verb?

> Bill and I work near each other. We drive to work together.
>
> The woman and her husband own a store.
> They sell potatoes.

We and they are plural pronouns. They match plural verbs.

Here are two more subject pronouns: I and you. I always refers to one person. You can refer to one or more than one person. You might think that I and you should match singular verbs. But I and you always match plural verbs:

> I need a ride to work.
>
> You look unhappy.

I and you are the only exceptions to the rule for matching subjects and verbs. All other singular subjects match singular verbs.

When you match subjects and verbs, remember the saying, "Opposites attract." Singular subjects do not have s added to them, but singular verbs do.

> The dog stays outside. (singular)

Plural subjects do have s added to them, but plural verbs don't:

The dogs stay outside. (plural)

(Important note: Most verbs are made singular just by adding s to them. But some verbs, like some nouns, have their spellings changed a little when the s is added. The Spelling and Usage Hints for Units 3, 4, 5, and 6 contain spelling rules that can help you to add s to nouns and verbs.)

Try It: Matching Subjects and Verbs

Underline the verb that matches the subject in each sentence.

EXAMPLE: Roses and daisies (grow—grows) in their garden.

1. Bill (drive—drives) a cab.
2. That red-haired lady in the fur hat (live—lives) across the street.
3. I (like—likes) Italian food.
4. He and I (eat—eats) dinner together.
5. Your friend (talk—talks) too much.
6. The man with the long hair (look—looks) like your brother.
7. You and I (think—thinks) alike.
8. He (cook—cooks) dinner for his family.
9. The women in the pool (swim—swims) well.
10. The football players (run—runs) five miles every day.

Check your answers on page 52.

USING THE VERB BE

So far in this unit, you've worked on singular and plural verbs. To form the singular of most verbs, you add an s to the verb.

> They work in a department store. (plural)
>
> He works in a department store. (singular)

But look at the verb in this sentence:

> He is a sales clerk.

What is the subject of this sentence? The subject is he. He is singular. The verb should be singular to match the subject. The verb in the sentence is is. Is it a singular verb?

Is is a form of the verb be. Be is a very important verb. It is also a verb that can be hard to use. It can be hard to use because it has several different forms. Look at the verbs in these sentences:

> I am in the room.
>
> He is in the room.
>
> They are in the room.

Am, is, and are are three forms of the verb be. But they don't look anything like the verb be. Which form is singular? Which is plural?

Here are some rules that can help you to match am, is, and are to the right subjects:

1. Use am only with the subject pronoun I.

   I am on the phone.

2. Use is with any singular noun and with the subject pronouns he, she, and it.

   The book is on the table.

   She is outside the door.

   It is warm in this room.

3. Use are with subjects joined by and, plural nouns, and with the subject pronouns you, we, and they.

   Mark and Steve are good friends.

   The books are on the table.

   We are on our way.

   You are wrong about him.

To use am, is, and are correctly, you have to look at the subject of the sentence. Is the subject singular? If it is, use is as the verb. Is the subject plural? If it is, use are as the verb. Is the subject the pronoun I? If it is, use am as the verb.

Try It: Using the Verb Be

Fill in the blanks. Use the correct form of the verb be. Use am, is, or are.

EXAMPLE: Pete and I __are__ busy tonight.

1. They ______ tired.
2. The fork and the plate ______ on the table.
3. I ______ sorry.
4. There ______ a sale at FoodMart today.
5. He and I ______ engaged.
6. Here ______ your socks.
7. ______ I next?
8. Your new polka dot blouse ______ on the floor.
9. ______ that coat new?
10. The man in the red hat ______ my husband.

Check your answers on page 52.

USING THE VERB HAVE

Look at the verbs in these sentences:

I have a problem.	We have a problem.
He has a problem.	You have a problem.
Sam has a problem.	They have a problem.

The verbs have and has are both forms of the same verb: have. But notice that the singular form of have is has, not haves:

He has a problem. Sam has a problem.

Like be, have is different from other verbs. Its singular is not formed by adding an s to it. But have is an easy verb to use. Just remember to write has when the subject is he, she, it, or a singular noun.

Try It: Using the Verb Have

Fill in the blanks. Use the correct form of the verb have. Use have or has.

1. Martha and her sister ________ the flu.
2. Most large families ________ large bills.
3. Their cousin ________ a rich husband.
4. The van with the blue stripes ________ a flat tire.
5. I ________ a new job.
6. The roof ________ a leak.
7. The tenants in that building ________ high rents.
8. Phil and his boss ________ a lot of fights.
9. They ________ tickets to see The Bonkers.
10. These pills ________ strange side effects.

Check your answers on page 53.

UNIT REVIEW

In this unit, you've worked with **verbs**. You've seen that verbs, like nouns, have **singular** and **plural** forms. You've also seen that the rules for verb singulars and plurals are the opposite of the rules for noun singulars and plurals. The singular of a verb is formed by adding an s to the verb. The plural of a verb does not have an s added to it.

You've also worked with the verbs be and have in this unit. Be is a very important verb, but it can be a hard one to use. It can be hard to use because it has several different forms. The verb have can be tricky to use because its singular is not formed by adding an s to it.

In this unit, you've covered the basics in matching the verb to the subject in a sentence. It's easy to match the verb to the subject when you can tell whether the subject is singular or plural. But it isn't *always* easy to tell whether a subject is singular or plural. In the next unit, you'll work on matching verbs to tricky subjects.

SPELLING AND USAGE HINT: ADDING S TO WORDS THAT END IN Y

When you add an s to a word that ends in y, the spelling of the word usually changes a little. For example, look at the underlined words in these sentences:

The baby is in the crib.

The babies are in the crib.

What happened to the word baby when an s was added to it?

baby + s = babies

The y was changed to i. Then es was added.

To add an s to a word that ends in y, change the y to i and add es:

There is a **fly** in the bedroom.

There are **flies** in the bedroom.

The **city** is too crowded.

The **cities** are too crowded.

There is an exception to this rule. If a vowel (a, e, i, o, or u) comes before the y, just add s:

The **boy** was crying.

The **boys** were crying.

Try It: Adding s to Words That End in y

Fill in the blank with the plural form of the word in parentheses.

1. I locked my ________________ in the car. (key)
2. We had blue ________________ every day of our vacation. (sky)
3. You get three ________________ to hit the ball. (try)
4. We are running out of ________________. (supply)
5. My three children are my three ________________. (joy)
6. She's been dieting for two ________________. (day)
7. Please make five ________________ of this report. (copy)
8. Your friends should be your ________________. (ally)
9. He eats large ________________ of food. (quantity)
10. Jeb shot some ________________ for his dinner. (turkey)

Check your answers on page 54.

ANSWERS AND EXPLANATIONS

Try It: Finding the Verb

1. **This milk tastes sour.** Tastes links the subject (this milk) with a description of the subject (sour). Tastes is a verb.
2. **Ben usually drives Miriam to work.** Drives shows an action. It tells you what the subject (Ben) does. Drives is a verb.
3. **Larry is a lifeguard.** Is links the subject (Larry) with a description of the subject (lifeguard). Is is a verb.
4. **Class begins at 8:00.** Begins shows an action. It tells you what the subject (class) does. Begins is a verb.
5. **Jenny works at the hospital.** Works shows an action. It tells you what the subject (Jenny) does. Works is a verb.
6. **Tony lives in Brooklyn.** Lives shows an action. It tells you what the subject (Tony) does. Lives is a verb.

7. **Alice seems upset.** Seems links the subject (Alice) with a description of the subject (upset). Seems is a verb.
8. **Ralph fixes dinner on Thursday nights.** Fixes shows an action. It tells you what the subject (Ralph) does. Fixes is a verb.
9. **John's letter is on the kitchen table.** Is links the subject (John's letter) with a description of the subject (on the kitchen table). Is is a verb.
10. **The bank closes early on Saturday.** Closes shows an action. It tells you what the subject (the bank) does. Closes is a verb.

Try It: Matching Subjects and Verbs

1. **Bill drives a cab.** The subject (Bill) is singular. A singular subject matches a singular verb (drives).
2. **That red-haired lady in the fur hat lives across the street.** The simple subject (lady) is singular. A singular subject matches a singular verb (lives).
3. **I like Italian food.** The subject pronoun I matches a plural verb (like).
4. **He and I eat dinner together.** The simple subject (he and I) is plural. A plural subject matches a plural verb (eat).
5. **Your friend talks too much.** The simple subject (friend) is singular. A singular subject matches a singular verb (talks).
6. **The man with the long hair looks like your brother.** The simple subject (man) is singular. A singular subject matches a singular verb (looks).
7. **You and I think alike.** The simple subject (you and I) is plural. A plural subject matches a plural verb (think).
8. **He cooks dinner for his family.** The subject (he) is singular. A singular subject matches a singular verb (cooks).
9. **The women in the pool swim well.** The simple subject (women) is plural. A plural subject matches a plural verb (swim).
10. **The football players run five miles every day.** The simple subject (players) is plural. A plural subject matches a plural verb (run).

Try It: Using the Verb Be

1. **They are tired.** The sentence has a plural subject (they). Use are with plural subjects.

2. **The fork and the plate are on the table.** The sentence has a plural subject (fork and plate). Use are with plural subjects.

3. **I am sorry.** The subject of the sentence is I. Use am with the subject pronoun I.

4. **There is a sale at FoodMart today.** The simple subject of the sentence is sale. Sale is a singular noun. Use is with singular subjects.

5. **He and I are engaged.** The sentence has a plural subject (he and I). Use are with plural subjects.

6. **Here are your socks.** The subject of the sentence is socks. Socks is a plural noun. Use are with plural subjects.

7. **Am I next?** Turn the question into a statement: I am next. The subject is I. Use am with the subject I.

8. **Your new polka dot blouse is on the floor.** The subject of the sentence is blouse. Blouse is a singular noun. Use is with singular subjects.

9. **Is that coat new?** Turn the question into a statement: That coat is new. The subject of the question is coat. Coat is a singular noun. Use is with singular subjects.

10. **The man in the red hat is my husband.** The subject of the sentence is man. Man is a singular noun. Use is with singular subjects.

Try It: Using the Verb Have

1. **Martha and her sister have the flu.** The sentence has a plural subject (Martha and sister). Use have with plural subjects.

2. **Most large families have large bills.** The sentence has a plural subject (families). Use have with plural subjects.

3. **Their cousin has a rich husband.** The sentence has a singular subject (cousin). Use has with singular subjects.

4. **The van with blue stripes has a flat tire.** The sentence has a singular subject (van). Use has with singular subjects.

5. **I have a new job.** The subject of the sentence is I. Use have with the subject pronoun I.

6. **The roof has a leak.** The sentence has a singular subject (roof). Use has with singular subjects.

7. **The tenants in that building have high rents.** The sentence has a plural subject (tenants). Use have with plural subjects.

8. **Phil and his boss have a lot of fights.** The sentence has a plural subject (Phil and boss). Use have with plural subjects.
9. **They have tickets to see The Bonkers.** The sentence has a plural subject (they). Use have with plural subjects.
10. **These pills have strange side effects.** The sentence has a plural subject (pills). Use have with plural subjects.

Try It: Adding s to Words That End in y

1. **I locked my keys in the car.** Key ends in a vowel (e) plus y. When a word ends in a vowel plus y, just add s: keys.
2. **We had blue skies every day of our vacation.** Sky ends in y. To make the word plural, change the y to i and add es: skies.
3. **You get three tries to hit the ball.** Try ends in y. To make the word plural, change the y to i and add es: tries.
4. **We are running out of supplies.** Supply ends in y. To make the word plural, change the y to i and add es: supplies.
5. **My three children are my three joys.** Joy ends in a vowel (o) plus y. To make the word plural, just add s: joys.
6. **She's been dieting for two days.** Day ends in a vowel (a) plus y. To make the word plural, just add s: days.
7. **Please make five copies of this report.** Copy ends in y. To make the word plural, change the y to i and add es: copies.
8. **Your friends should be your allies.** Ally ends in y. To make the word plural, change the y to i and add es: allies.
9. **He eats large quantities of food.** Quantity ends in y. To make the word plural, change the y to i and add es: quantities.
10. **Jeb shot some turkeys for his dinner.** Turkey ends in a vowel (e) plus y. To make the word plural, just add s: turkeys.

UNIT 5: IS THE NOUN SINGULAR OR PLURAL?

Here is a sentence that you have seen before. Is the subject singular or plural?

Two jackets cost $50.

It's easy to see that the subject is plural. The word two tells you. But even without two, you would know that the subject is plural:

Jackets cost $50.

The simple subject is jackets. Jackets is the plural form of the word jacket:

jackets = jacket + s

It isn't always so easy to tell whether a noun is singular or plural. For example, look at the next sentences. Try to pick the verb that matches the subject.

Measles (are—is) a painful disease.

His eyeglasses (are—is) in the case.

Our team (are—is) the best in the state.

Fifty dollars (are—is) the price of the radio.

Look at the subject of each sentence. Each subject is tricky. Each subject can give you trouble when you try to match it to a verb. One subject looks plural, but it's really singular. One subject looks as though it stands for only one thing, but it's really plural. The other subjects look as though they stand for more than one thing, but they're really singular. In this unit, you'll work on matching tricky nouns to the right verbs.

SINGULAR NOUNS THAT LOOK PLURAL

Look at this sentence again:

Measles (are—is) a painful disease.

What is the subject of this sentence? The subject is measles. The verb should match the subject measles. Is measles a singular subject or a plural subject?

Measles is a singular subject. It looks like a plural subject, but it's singular. Why is it singular? It's singular because it stands for *one* kind of disease: measles. It stands for one thing even though it looks as though it stands for more than one thing.

Here are some other words that are singular even though they look plural:

athletics	mumps	politics
economics	news	United States
mathematics		

Each of these words looks plural. Each looks as though an s has been added to it to make it plural. But each word is really singular. Each word only stands for one thing.

Mathematics is a hard subject.

(Mathematics is the name of *one* subject. It is singular.)

The United States is a big country.

(United States is the name of *one* country. It is singular.)

Measles is a painful disease.

(Measles is the name of *one* disease. It is singular.)

"PAIR" WORDS

Some words are singular even though they look plural:

Measles is a painful disease.

But look at the subject of this sentence:

His eyeglasses (are—is) in the case.

The subject of the sentence is eyeglasses. Is eyeglasses a singular word or a plural word? It looks plural. But it only stands for one thing.

Eyeglasses is a plural word. Why is it plural if it only stands for one thing? The word eyeglasses is plural because it is a "pair" word.

What is a "pair" word? A "pair" word is a word that is often used with the word pair. For example, look at these sentences:

He has a pair of eyeglasses.

She needs a pair of slacks.

Fred has a new pair of scissors.

When such words as eyeglasses, slacks, and scissors are used alone as subjects, they are plural. They match plural verbs. Here are some other "pair" words:

pants	trousers
sunglasses	tweezers

Most of the time, it's easy to tell if a noun is singular or plural. But sometimes it isn't so easy. Some nouns that look plural are really singular. Some nouns that stand for one thing are really plural.

When you match a verb to a subject, think about the subject. Think about what it stands for. Does it stand for only one thing? Does it stand for more than one thing? Is it a "pair" word? Thinking about the subject will help you match the subject to the right verb.

Try It: Singular Nouns That Look Plural and "Pair" Words

Underline the verb that matches the subject in each sentence.

EXAMPLE: The mumps (are—is) a painful disease.

1. The news (are—is) all over the office.
2. Your trousers (are—is) in the closet.
3. Politics (are—is) often hard to understand.
4. The scissors (are—is) in the drawer.
5. His sunglasses (are—is) brand new.
6. Economics (are—is) a big part of everyday life.
7. Checkers (are—is) a very popular game.

8. Your new pants (are—is) in the washing machine.

9. The United States (has—have) many natural resources.

10. The tweezers (are—is) in the medicine cabinet.

Check your answers on page 63.

NOUNS THAT STAND FOR A GROUP

Look at the subject of this sentence:

Our team (are—is) the best in the state.

The subject of this sentence is team. What is a team? A team is a group of players. The word team stands for a group. Is team a singular word or a plural word? Does it match a singular verb or a plural verb?

The word team is *singular*. A team is made up of more than one player. But you think of a team as *one group* of players. You think of a team as *one single unit*.

There are several words that stand for a group of people or things. Here are some of them:

army	crowd	jury
audience	family	mob
class	herd	public
committee	group	staff
couple		

Each of these words names a collection of people or things. Each word names something that is made up of more than one person or thing. But each word is *singular* because each word stands for *one group*.

The couple is very happy together.
(Couple stands for two people, but you think of the two people as *one* couple. Couple is singular.)

His family lives down the street from me.
(Family stands for a group of people, but you think of the people as *one* family. Family is singular.)

Our team is the best in the state.

(Team stands for a group of players, but you think of the players as *one* team. Team is singular.)

Such words as couple, family, and team are singular because they stand for *one* group. However, there is one time when these words can be *plural*. Look at this sentence:

The couple live in separate apartments.

The subject of this sentence is couple. The verb is live. Is live a singular verb or a plural verb? It's a plural verb. Why is a plural verb being used with couple? A plural verb is being used because, in this sentence, the two people in the couple are *not* acting together. They're acting separately. The sentence tells you they're acting separately. They live in separate apartments.

Most of the time, a word that names a group is singular. That's because most of the time you think of the group as *one* group. But once in a while a word that names a group is plural. It's plural when it refers to a group that is *not* acting together as one single unit.

AMOUNTS AND MEASURES

A word that stands for one group of people or things is singular.

Our team is the best in the state.

In this sentence, the word team stands for one single unit. A team is made up of a group of players. But in this sentence the group is thought of as one single unit.

Now, look at this sentence:

Fifty dollars (are—is) the price of the radio.

What is the subject of this sentence? The subject is fifty dollars. Is the subject singular or plural? Does it match a singular verb or a plural verb?

The subject fifty dollars looks plural. But it's singular. Why is it singular? It's singular because it stands for an amount of *one single thing*. It tells you the price of the radio.

Subjects that name an amount of something usually look plural. But they are really singular if they stand for an amount of one single thing.

Two hours is a long time to wait for a bus.

In this sentence, two hours stands for an amount of time. It is a singular subject.)

Four quarts is enough milk for a week.

(In this sentence, four quarts stands for an amount of milk. It is a singular subject.)

Fifty dollars is the price of the radio.

(In this sentence, fifty dollars stands for an amount of money. It is a singular subject.)

Be careful. Not all subjects that name an amount are singular. For example, look at this sentence:

Thirteen men are in the doctor's office.

The subject of this sentence is thirteen men. Does the subject stand for an amount of one single thing? It doesn't. In this sentence, the subject is plural. It does not stand for an amount of something.

Try It: Nouns That Stand for a Group and Amounts and Measures

Underline the verb that matches the subject in each sentence.

1. The committee (are—is) in a meeting right now.
2. Ten miles (are—is) a long distance to run.
3. Seven people (are—is) in the station wagon.
4. The group (are—is) waiting in the hallway.
5. The audience (are—is) not happy with the show.
6. Two cups (are—is) enough rice for six people.
7. One hundred yards (are—is) the length of a football field.
8. One hundred nails (are—is) in each box.
9. The crowd (are—is) waiting to see the star.

10. The army (has—have) bases all over the world.

11. Our families (get—gets) together once a year for a party.

12. The class (meet—meets) five times a week.

Check your answers on page 64.

UNIT REVIEW

In this unit, you've worked with some tricky subjects. The subjects are tricky because it's sometimes hard to tell if they are singular or plural. It's sometimes hard to match these tricky subjects to the right verbs.

It isn't always easy to match a verb to a subject. But you can make it easier. Think about the subject. Think about what it stands for. Does it stand for only one thing? Does it stand for one single unit? Does it stand for an amount of one single thing? If it does, then the subject is singular. But if it doesn't, it's plural.

SPELLING AND USAGE HINT: ADDING S TO WORDS THAT END IN F OR FE

In the last two Spelling and Usage Hints, you looked at words that change a little when s is added. Those words ended in s, x, z, ch, sh, and y. Some words that end in f or fe also change when s is added:

The life of the firefighter was in danger.

The lives of the firefighters were in danger.

What happened to the word life when an s was added to it?

life + **s** = **lives**

The f was changed to v. Then es was added.

To add an s to a word that ends in f or fe, change the f to v and add es:

The **knife** is in the kitchen.

The **knives** are in the kitchen.

There is a loaf of bread in the refrigerator.

There are loaves of bread in the refrigerator.

There are some words that don't follow this rule. These words end in f, but they don't change when s is added. You'll have to memorize these words.

belief/beliefs	roof/roofs
chef/chefs	chief/chiefs
cliff/cliffs	giraffe/giraffes

Try It: Adding s to Words That End in f or fe

Fill in the blank with the plural form of the word in parentheses.

1. We need some ____________ in the closet. (shelf)
2. Two ____________ equals one whole. (half)
3. Our cat has nine ____________. (life)
4. Both of the ____________ got away. (thief)
5. There is still snow on the ____________ of the stores. (roof)
6. The department ____________ met today to discuss raises. (chief)
7. It's not legal to have two ____________. (wife)
8. ____________ have long necks. (giraffe)
9. The ____________ are turning yellow and red. (leaf)
10. There are ____________ in the woods. (wolf)

Check your answers on page 65.

ANSWERS AND EXPLANATIONS

Try It: Singular Nouns That Look Plural and "Pair" Words

1. **The news is all over the office.** The simple subject is news. News is singular because it stands for *one* thing. The verb is matches the singular subject.
2. **Your trousers are in the closet.** The simple subject is trousers. Trousers is a "pair" word. It is plural. The verb are matches the plural subject.
3. **Politics is often hard to understand.** The simple subject is politics. Politics is singular because it stands for *one* thing. The verb is matches the singular subject.
4. **The scissors are in the drawer.** The simple subject is scissors. Scissors is a "pair" word. It is plural. The verb are matches the plural subject.
5. **His sunglasses are brand new.** The simple subject is sunglasses. Sunglasses is a "pair" word. It is plural. The verb are matches the plural subject.
6. **Economics is a big part of everyday life.** The simple subject is economics. Economics is singular because it stands for *one* thing. The verb is matches the singular subject.
7. **Checkers is a very popular game.** The simple subject is checkers. Checkers is singular because it stands for *one* game. The verb is matches the singular subject.
8. **Your new pants are in the washing machine.** The simple subject is pants. Pants is a "pair" word. It is plural. The verb are matches the plural subject.
9. **The United States has many natural resources.** The simple subject is United States. United States is singular because it stands for *one* country. The verb has matches the singular subject.
10. **The tweezers are in the medicine cabinet.** The simple subject is tweezers. Tweezers is a "pair" word. The verb are matches the plural subject.

Try It: Nouns That Stand for a Group and Amounts and Measures

1. **The committee is in a meeting right now.** The simple subject is committee. Committee is singular because it stands for *one* group of people. The verb is matches the singular subject.
2. **Ten miles is a long distance to run.** Ten miles stands for *one* measure. It is a singular subject. The verb is matches the singular subject.
3. **Seven people are in the station wagon.** The simple subject is people. People is plural because it stands for *more than one* person. The verb are matches the plural subject.
4. **The group is waiting in the hallway.** The simple subject is group. Group is singular because it stands for *one* group of people. The verb is matches the singular subject.
5. **The audience is not happy with the show.** The simple subject is audience. Audience is singular because it stands for *one* group of people. The verb is matches the singular subject.
6. **Two cups is enough rice for six people.** Two cups stands for *one* amount. It is a singular subject. The verb is matches the singular subject.
7. **One hundred yards is the length of a football field.** One hundred yards stands for *one* measure. It is a singular subject. The verb is matches the singular subject.
8. **One hundred nails are in each box.** The simple subject is nails. Nails is plural because it stands for *more than one* nail. The verb are matches the plural subject.
9. **The crowd is waiting to see the star.** The simple subject is crowd. Crowd is singular because it stands for *one* group of people. The verb is matches the singular subject.
10. **The army has bases all over the world.** The simple subject is army. Army is singular because it stands for *one* group of people. The verb has matches the singular subject.
11. **Our families get together once a year for a party.** The simple subject is families. Families is plural because it stands for *more than one* family. The verb get matches the plural subject.
12. **The class meets five times a week.** The simple subject is class. Class is singular because it stands for *one* group of people. The verb meets matches the singular subject.

Try It: Adding s to Words That End in f or fe

1. **We need some shelves in the closet.** To make shelf plural, change the f to v and add es: **shelf** + **s** = **shelves.**
2. **Two halves equals one whole.** To make half plural, change the f to v and add es: **half** + **s** = **halves.**
3. **Our cat has nine lives.** To make life plural, change the f to v and add es: **life** + **s** = **lives.**
4. **Both of the thieves got away.** To make thief plural, change the f to v and add es: **thief** + **s** = **thieves.**
5. **There is still snow on the roofs of the stores.** Roof doesn't follow the rule for adding s to a word that ends in f. Just add **s** to roof: **roofs.**
6. **The department chiefs met today to discuss raises.** Chief doesn't follow the rule for adding s to a word that ends in f. Just add **s** to chief: **chiefs.**
7. **It's not legal to have two wives.** To make wife plural, change the f to v and add es: **wife** + **s** = **wives.**
8. **Giraffes have long necks.** Giraffe doesn't follow the rule for adding s to a word that ends in f. Just add **s** to giraffe: **giraffes.**
9. **The leaves are turning yellow and red.** To make leaf plural, change the f to v and add es: **leaf** + **s** = **leaves.**
10. **There are wolves in the woods.** To make wolf plural, change f to v and add es: **wolf** + **s** = **wolves.**

UNIT 6: IS THE PRONOUN SINGULAR OR PLURAL?

Here are some sentences that you looked at earlier in this book:

I am going out.

He works the night shift.

We eat lunch at the diner.

The subjects of these sentences are pronouns. Earlier in this book, you worked with the subject pronouns I, you, he, she, it, we, and they. You worked on matching these subject pronouns to the right verbs.

I, you, he, she, it, we, and they are the most common subject pronouns. But they are not the only pronouns that can be used as subjects in a sentence. Look at these sentences:

Everyone (like—likes) the new boss.

Each (like—likes) the new boss.

All of the workers (like—likes) the new boss.

The subjects of these sentences are all pronouns. Each pronoun takes the place of a noun.

Such pronouns as everyone, each, and all are often used as subjects in sentences. They often cause problems. They cause problems because it's often hard to tell if they are singular or plural. In this unit, you will take a closer look at pronouns. You'll look at ways to match pronouns to the right verbs.

–ONE, –BODY, AND –THING WORDS

Look at this sentence again:

Everyone (like—likes) the new boss.

The subject of this sentence is everyone. Is everyone singular or plural? You might think that everyone is plural. After all, it stands for all the people in a group.

But everyone is *not* a plural subject. It's singular. It matches a singular verb. Why is everyone singular? To answer this question, take a closer look at the word:

every**one**

The word everyone ends with one. Words that end with one are singular. Words that end with body or thing also are singular.

Everyone likes the new boss.

(The subject pronoun everyone ends with one. It is singular, and it matches the singular verb likes.)

Is anybody home?

(The subject pronoun anybody ends with body. It is singular, and it matches the singular verb is.)

Everything is ready for the party.

(The subject pronoun everything ends with thing. It is singular, and it matches the singular verb is.)

When you see such words as someone, anybody, and everything, think about the ending of the word. One, body, and thing are all singular words. Any word that ends in one, body, or thing also is singular.

Try It: –One, –Body, and –Thing Words

Read each sentence. See if the verb matches the subject. If the verb does not match the subject, rewrite the sentence. Change the verb so that it matches the subject.

EXAMPLE: Nothing work in that old car.

Nothing works in that old car.

1. Everybody have something to do.

2. No one want the new job.

3. There is something in this bag for you.

4. Everyone is at the party tonight.

5. Is anybody ready for the trip?

Check your answers on page 74.

MATCHING VERBS WITH OTHER PRONOUNS

Look at the next sentence. Which verb matches the subject?

Each (like—likes) the new boss.

The subject of this sentence is each. Each is a pronoun. Is it singular or plural?

Each is singular. In this sentence, each stands for each separate person in a group. Each person likes the new boss.

There is a group of pronouns like each. These pronouns are always singular. That's because they stand for each separate person or thing in a group. They stand for each *one* in a group. Here are some pronouns that are always singular:

each   either   neither   another

Each likes the new boss.

(The subject each is singular. It stands for each *one* in a group.)

Either is a good plan.

(The subject either is singular. It stands for either *one* of the plans.)

Neither is a bad plan.

(The subject neither is singular. It stands for neither *one* of the plans.)

It's pretty easy to remember that the words each, either, neither, and another are always singular. But these words often cause problems when they are used as subjects. They cause problems because they usually don't appear by themselves in the subject. They usually appear with other words. For example, look at this sentence:

Each of the workers (like—likes) the new boss.

The sentence begins with the word each. Each is singular. But is it the simple subject of this sentence? Is it the key word in the subject? What about the word workers? The word workers is plural. Is workers the subject, or is each the subject?

To answer this question, take a closer look at the sentence:

Each of the workers (like—likes) the new boss.

Of the workers is a phrase. It is a part of the complete subject. It tells you something about the subject. But the key word in the subject is each. The simple subject is each.

Such words as of, in, and at often appear in the complete subject of a sentence. These words are at the beginning of phrases. The phrases tell you something about the subject. But they don't contain the simple subject.

Either of the plans is good.

(In this sentence, either is the simple subject. Of the plans is a phrase that tells you something about the subject.)

Each of the workers likes the new boss.

(In this sentence, each is the simple subject. Of the workers is a phrase that tells you something about the subject.)

The words each, either, neither, and another are always singular when they are subjects. They always match singular verbs. But some pronouns are always plural. Look at this sentence:

Both of the workers (like—likes) the new boss.

What is the simple subject of this sentence? The simple subject is both. Is the word both singular or plural?

To answer this question, think about the word both. You use the word both to talk about more than one person or thing. You use the word both to show that you are talking about two people or things. The word both is plural. It matches a plural verb.

Here is a list of pronouns that are always plural:

both   many   few   several

Few of the jackets are cheap.

(The subject few is plural. It stands for more than one jacket.)

Many are very expensive.

(The subject many is plural. It stands for more than one thing.)

Try It: Matching Verbs with Other Pronouns

Underline the verb that matches the subject in each sentence. Make sure that the verb correctly matches the *simple* subject.

1. Few (know—knows) his real name.

2. Neither of us (like—likes) his cooking.

3. Each of his relatives (are—is) very proud of him.

4. Many of the items (are—is) on sale.

5. Another of the groups (want—wants) more money.

6. Both of his friends (has—have) new cars.

7. Neither (has—have) a lot of money.

8. Either of the mixes (make—makes) a good cake.

Check your answers on page 75.

SUBJECTS THAT CAN BE SINGULAR OR PLURAL

You've looked at a few different kinds of pronouns in this unit. Some of the pronouns are always singular:

Everyone likes the new boss.

Each of the workers likes the new boss.

Some of them are always plural:

Both of the workers like the new boss.

But look at the subject in these two sentences:

All of the workers (like—likes) the new boss.

All of the work (are—is) done.

What word is the subject of each sentence? The subject of each sentence is all. Is the word all singular or plural? Does it match a singular verb or a plural verb?

The word all is a very tricky subject. It's tricky because it can be *either* singular *or* plural.

How can you tell if all is singular or plural in a sentence? Look at the first sentence again:

All of the workers (like—likes) the new boss.

The simple subject is all. Of the workers is a phrase that tells you something about the subject. You know that the phrase does not give you the simple subject. But, in this sentence, the phrase is very important. It tells you whether the simple subject (all) is singular or plural.

In this sentence, what does the pronoun all stand for? It stands for the workers. Workers is a plural word. In this sentence, the word all is plural to match the plural word workers.

All of the workers like the new boss.

Now, look at the second sentence again:

All of the work (are—is) done.

The simple subject is all. Is all singular or plural in this sentence? What does all stand for in this sentence? Look at the phrase that follows all. The phrase is of the work. In this sentence, all stands for work. Is the word work singular or plural? It's singular. Therefore, all is singular in this sentence. It matches a singular verb.

All of the work is done.

Here is a list of pronouns that are like all. These pronouns can be either singular or plural. It depends on what the pronoun stands for in a sentence.

all	any	half	most
none	part	some	

When these pronouns stand for *one* person or thing, they are singular. When they stand for *more than one* person or thing, they are plural.

Some of the cake is gone.

(In this sentence, some stands for cake. Cake is a singular word. Therefore, some is singular in this sentence. It matches the singular verb is.)

Some of the cakes are gone.

(In this sentence, some stands for cakes. Cakes is a plural word. Therefore, some is plural in this sentence. It matches the plural verb are.)

Try It: Subjects That Can Be Singular or Plural

Underline the verb that matches the subject in each sentence.

1. None of these apartments (are—is) empty.
2. Half of the class (are—is) absent today.
3. Most of the train (are—is) full.
4. Some of the children (has—have) the measles.
5. Any of your friends (are—is) welcome.
6. None of the food (are—is) good.
7. All of the neighbors (own—owns) cars.
8. Part of her letter (are—is) about you.
9. Most of the potatoes (are—is) rotten.
10. Some of my money (are—is) in the bank.

Check your answers on page 75.

UNIT REVIEW

In this unit, you've taken a close look at matching some subject pronouns to the right verbs. Pronouns that end with the words one, body, or thing are always singular. They always match singular verbs. Each, either, neither, and another are also pronouns that are always singular. When they are subjects, they match singular verbs. Some pronouns are always plural, and they match plural verbs. Both, many, few, and several are always plural. Other pronouns can be *either* singular *or* plural. It depends on the words that the pronoun stands for in the sentence. All, any, half, most, none, part, and some can be either singular or plural.

Matching subject pronouns to the right verbs can be tricky. Sometimes it's hard to tell if the pronoun is singular or plural. Sometimes it's hard to tell if the pronoun is really the subject. But you can make the job easier. First, make sure that you find the word in the sentence that is the simple subject. If that word is a pronoun, think about it. Does it end with one, body, or thing? If it does, then it's singular. Is it one of the other singular pronouns? Is it one of the plural pronouns? If it can be either singular or plural, what word does it stand for in the sentence? Thinking about these questions and answering them will help you to match pronouns to the right verbs.

SPELLING AND USAGE HINT: ADDING S TO WORDS THAT END IN O

You have seen how words that end in s, x, z, ch, sh, y, and f change when s is added. Now look at these words. They end in o. Do the words change when s is added?

Slice a tomato for our salad.

Slice some tomatoes for our salad.

Our radio doesn't work.

Our radios don't work.

One of the words changed when s was added (tomato, tomatoes). But the other word did not change (radio, radios). Here are two rules to help you decide whether or not the word should change:

If a word ends in a consonant plus o, add es to make the word plural.

tomat**o**, tomat**oes** hero, her**oes**

If a word ends in a vowel plus o, just add s.

radio, **radios** **zoo**, **zoos**

There are some words that don't follow these rules. These words end in a consonant plus o. But they are made plural just by adding s:

auto, autos Eskimo, Eskimos

piano, pianos two, twos

Try It: Adding s to Words That End in o

Fill in the blank with the plural form of the word in parentheses.

1. I went to several ________________ this year. (rodeo)

2. We had mashed ________________ for dinner. (potato)

3. The ______________ hit the submarine. (torpedo)

4. All of the ______________ were tuned to WXYZ. (radio)

5. We took a tour of the movie ______________ . (studio)

6. Some Eskimos live in ______________ . (igloo)

7. Fineway's sells used ______________ . (piano)

8. Several ______________ hit the town last year. (tornado)

9. Big Al buys and sells used ______________ . (auto)

10. The children walked in ______________ . (two)

Check your answers on page 76.

ANSWERS AND EXPLANATIONS

Try It: –One, –Body, and –Thing Words

1. **Everybody has something to do.** The subject is everybody. Everybody is singular. The verb has matches the singular subject.
2. **No one wants the new job.** The subject is no one. No one is singular. The verb wants matches the singular subject.
3. **There is something in this bag for you.** The subject is something. Something is singular. The verb is matches the singular subject.
4. **Everyone is at the party tonight.** The subject is everyone. Everyone is singular. The verb is matches the singular subject.
5. **Is anybody ready for the trip?** The subject is anybody. Anybody is singular. The verb is matches the singular subject.

Try It: Matching Verbs with Other Pronouns

1. **Few know his real name.** The simple subject is few. Few refers to *more than one* person. It is plural. The verb know matches the plural subject.
2. **Neither of us likes his cooking.** The simple subject is neither. Neither refers to neither *one* of us. It is singular. The verb likes matches the singular subject.
3. **Each of his relatives is very proud of him.** The subject is each. Each refers to each *one* of his relatives. It is singular. The verb is matches the singular subject.
4. **Many of the items are on sale.** The subject is many. Many refers to *more than one* item. It is plural. The verb are matches the plural subject.
5. **Another of the groups wants more money.** The subject is another. Another refers to another *one* of the groups. It is singular. The verb wants matches the singular subject.
6. **Both of his friends have new cars.** The subject is both. Both refers to *more than one* person. It is plural. The verb have matches the plural subject.
7. **Neither has a lot of money.** The subject is neither. Neither refers to neither *one* of the people. It is singular. The verb has matches the singular subject.
8. **Either of the mixes makes a good cake.** The subject is either. Either refers to either *one* of the mixes. It is singular. The verb makes matches the singular subject.

Try It: Subjects That Can Be Singular or Plural

1. **None of these apartments are empty.** The simple subject none stands for apartments. Apartments is a plural word. Therefore, none is plural in this sentence. The verb are matches the plural subject.
2. **Half of the class is absent today.** The simple subject half stands for class. Class is a singular word. Therefore, half is singular. The verb is matches the singular subject.
3. **Most of the train is full.** The simple subject most stands for train. Train is a singular word. Therefore, most is singular in this sentence. The verb is matches the singular subject.
4. **Some of the children have the measles.** The simple subject some stands for children. Children is a plural word. Therefore, some is plural. The verb have matches the plural subject.

5. **Any of your friends are welcome.** The simple subject any stands for friends. Friends is a plural word. Therefore, any is plural. The verb are matches the plural subject.
6. **None of the food is good.** The simple subject none stands for food. Food is a singular word. Therefore, none is singular. The verb is matches the singular subject.
7. **All of the neighbors own cars.** The simple subject all stands for neighbors. Neighbors is a plural word. Therefore, all is plural. The verb own matches the plural subject.
8. **Part of her letter is about you.** The simple subject part stands for letter. Letter is a singular word. Therefore, part is singular. The verb is matches the singular subject.
9. **Most of the potatoes are rotten.** The simple subject most stands for potatoes. Potatoes is a plural word. Therefore, most is plural. The verb are matches the plural subject.
10. **Some of my money is in the bank.** The simple subject some stands for money. Money is a singular word. Therefore, some is singular. The verb is matches the singular subject.

Try It: Adding s to Words That End in o

1. **I went to several rodeos this year.** Rodeo ends in a vowel (e) plus o. Add s to the word.
2. **We had mashed potatoes for dinner.** Potato ends in a consonant (t) plus o. Add es to the word.
3. **The torpedoes hit the submarine.** Torpedo ends in a consonant (d) plus o. Add es to the word.
4. **All of the radios were tuned to WXYZ.** Radio ends in a vowel (i) plus o. Just add s to the word.
5. **We took a tour of the movie studios.** Studio ends in a vowel (i) plus o. Add s to the word.
6. **Some Eskimos live in igloos.** Igloo ends in a vowel (o) plus o. Just add s to the word.
7. **Fineway's sells used pianos.** Piano is an exception to the o rule. Just add s to the word.
8. **Several tornadoes hit the town last year.** Tornado ends in a consonant (d) plus o. Add es to the word.
9. **Big Al sells used autos.** Auto is an exception to the o rule. Just add s to the word.
10. **The children walked in twos.** Twos is an exception to the o rule. Just add s to the word.

UNIT 7: DOES THE VERB MATCH THE COMPOUND SUBJECT?

Here is a sentence you have seen before. What is the subject?

The knife and the fork are on the table.

This sentence is about two things: the knife and the fork. The subject is the knife and the fork. It is a compound subject.

Earlier in this book, you worked with compound subjects. A compound subject is a subject that is made up of two or more parts. Most of the time, it's pretty easy to match a compound subject to the right verb. But sometimes it isn't so easy. In this unit, you'll take a closer look at matching verbs and compound subjects.

FINDING COMPOUND SUBJECTS

Take another look at this sentence:

The knife and the fork are on the table.

The subject of this sentence is the knife and the fork. It is a compound subject. A compound subject is a subject that is made up of two or more parts. In this sentence, the two parts are knife and fork. The knife is on the table. The fork is on the table. Together, the knife *and* the fork are on the table.

To be a compound, a subject has to be made up of more than one part. But a subject also needs something else to be a compound. It needs a connecting word. It needs a word that connects the parts of the compound together.

What is the connecting word in this compound subject?

The knife and the fork are on the table.

The connecting word is and. The word and comes between the two subject parts. The word and tells you that the subject is a compound subject.

The word and is often used to connect the parts of a compound subject. But it isn't the *only* word that can be used. Look at these sentences:

Either George or Phil has a key.

Neither Hank nor Richie has a key.

Not only George but also Phil has a key.

The underlined pairs of words are connecting words. They are used to connect the parts of a compound subject. Along with and, they are the *only* words that can be used to connect the parts of a compound subject. You can't use any other words.

Some sentences may seem as though they have a compound subject. For example, look at this sentence:

> George, along with Phil, has a key.

What is the subject of this sentence? At first, it looks as though there is a compound subject. It looks as though both George and Phil are subjects in this sentence. But take a closer look at the sentence. Can you find any of the connecting words? Does the word and connect George and Phil? It doesn't. Do the connecting words either/or, neither/nor, or not only/but also appear in the sentence? They don't. Without any of these connecting words, a subject can't be a compound. This sentence does *not* have a compound subject.

If the subject isn't a compound, then what *is* the subject? To find out, take another look at the sentence:

> George, along with Phil, has a key.

Along with Phil is a phrase. It adds information to the sentence. But it does *not* name the subject. The words along with cannot be used to connect the parts of a compound subject. The only words that can be used to make a compound subject are and, either/or, neither/nor, and not only/but also. In this sentence, George is the subject. Phil follows the words along with. Phil is *not* the subject.

Here are some other sentences that look as though they have a compound subject:

> The pie, as well as the cake, was delicious.
>
> (The subject of this sentence is pie. The words as well as cannot be used to connect the parts of a compound subject.)
>
> Mr. Sims, together with his wife, was at the meeting.
>
> (The subject of this sentence is Mr. Sims. The words together with cannot be used to connect the parts of a compound subject.)
>
> In addition to the window, the door does not lock.
>
> (The subject of this sentence is door. The words in addition to cannot be used to connect the parts of a compound subject.)

If you think a sentence has a compound subject, look at it carefully. Make sure that the subject *is* a compound. Remember that there are only four ways to connect the parts of a compound subject. The parts of a compound subject can only be connected with these words:

and   either/or

neither/nor   not only/but also

Try It: Finding Compound Subjects

Look at the following sentences. If the sentence has a compound subject, put a **C** in the blank next to it. If it does not have a compound subject, put an **N** in the blank.

EXAMPLE: C Not only my boots but also my shoes have holes in the soles.

1. ____ Either Eddie or Steve has your radio.
2. ____ Both the train and the bus were late this morning.
3. ____ The shirt, as well as the skirt, was on sale.
4. ____ Neither the bartender nor the bouncer looks friendly.
5. ____ Winston, along with his family, is in Jamaica this week.
6. ____ The manager, together with the coaches, was fired.
7. ____ Not only Clem but also his brother owns a truck.
8. ____ The duck and the rabbit were gifts from my uncle.
9. ____ Sadie, in addition to Wilma, wants a raise.
10. ____ The dog, as well as the cat, needs a bath.

Check your answers on page 84.

MATCHING VERBS WITH COMPOUND SUBJECTS

Look at the next sentences. How are they the same? How are they different?

The knife and the fork are on the table.

Either the knife or the fork is on the table.

Neither the knife nor the fork is on the table.

Not only the knife but also the fork is on the table.

Each sentence has a compound subject. In each sentence, the parts of the compound are the same: knife and fork. But different connecting words are used for each compound. The word and is used in the first sentence. Either/or is used in the second sentence. Neither/nor is used in the third sentence. Not only/but also is used in the last sentence.

Do you notice anything else that's different in the sentences? Look at the first two sentences again:

The knife and the fork are on the table.

Either the knife or the fork is on the table.

The parts of the compound subject are the same in each sentence. But the verbs are different. In the first sentence, the subject matches a plural verb. But, in the second sentence, the subject matches a *singular* verb.

Earlier in this book, you worked on finding out if a compound subject is singular or plural. A compound subject that is connected by the word and is always plural. It always matches a plural verb.

The knife **and** the fork are on the table.

But compound subjects that are connected by either/or, neither/nor, or not only/but also are different. They aren't always plural. They can be either singular *or* plural.

How can you tell if one of these compound subjects is singular or plural? To find out, you have to take a closer look at the parts of the compound. Look at this sentence again:

Either the knife **or** the fork is on the table.

The two parts of the compound are knife and fork. They are connected by the words either/or. The verb in the sentence is singular (is). Why is it singular?

17

1 breath ✗
2 Captain ✓
3 Ceiling ✓
4 Competition ✓
5 Con ✗ CONCEIVABLE
6 Condition. ✓
7 Conferance ✗
8 Confident ✓
9 Conquer ✓
10 ~~Concious~~ Conscience ✓
11 Conscientious ✓
12 Concious ✗
13 Consequence ✓
14 Consequently ✓
15 Considerable. ✓
16 Consistency ✓
17 Consistent ✓
18 Continual ✓
19 Continuous ✓
20 Controlled. ✓

Good

The verb is singular because it matches the part of the compound subject that is *closer* to it. Which part of the compound subject is closer to the verb? Fork is closer to the verb. Fork is a singular word. The verb is is singular to match fork.

When a compound subject is connected by either/or, neither/nor, or not only/but also, the verb should match the part of the compound subject that is closer to it. If the subject part is singular, then the verb should be singular. If the subject part is plural, then the verb should be plural.

> **Either** the food **or** the drinks are free.
>
> (The parts of the compound subject are connected by either/or. The plural verb are matches the part of the compound subject that is closer to it (drinks).)
>
> **Either** the drinks **or** the food is free.
>
> (The parts of the compound subject are connected by either/or. The singular verb is matches the part of the compound subject that is closer to it (food).)

Try It: Matching Verbs with Compound Subjects

Underline the verb that matches the compound subject in each sentence. Make sure to look at the words that connect the parts of the compound subject.

EXAMPLE: Neither Larry nor his cousins (know—knows) Joe.

1. Margo and her parents (visit—visits) each other often.
2. Either the cups or the glasses (are—is) in the dishwasher.
3. Neither the cake nor the cookies (taste—tastes) good.
4. Not only Sheila but also her children (are—is) sick.
5. Either the windows or the door (are—is) open.
6. Vern and Fred (need—needs) a ride to work.
7. Not only stores but also a restaurant (are—is) in the mall.

8. Either my husband or my daughter (are—is) home now.

9. Neither my cats nor my dog (like—likes) my girlfriend.

10. Your gloves and my scarf (are—is) on the table.

Check your answers on page 85.

UNIT REVIEW

In this unit, you've worked on matching compound subjects to the right verbs. Matching a compound subject to the right verb can be tricky. But you can make it easier by following these steps:

1. Make sure that the subject *is* a compound. Remember, only the words and, either/or, neither/nor, and not only/but also can be used to connect the parts of a compound subject.
2. Look at the word that connects the subject parts. If the word is and, the subject is always plural. It should match a plural verb.
3. If the connecting words are either/or, neither/nor, or not only/but also, look for the subject part that is closer to the verb. Then match the verb to the closer subject part.

SPELLING AND USAGE HINT: I BEFORE E RULE

Sometimes, rules can help you remember how to spell words correctly. One helpful rule is the i before e rule. The i before e rule can often help you decide whether to use ie or ei in a word.

Use ei after the letter c.

Use ie after all other letters.

You may have heard the rule put this way:

Use i before e except after c.

Here are some examples of ie and ei words:

I believe you.

Can I have a piece of cake?

Did you receive my package yet?

The salesman gave me a receipt.

The i before e rule can help you with most words that have ie or ei in them. However, there are a few exceptions to the rule.

One exception is when the vowels make an ay sound:

How much do you weigh?

He is a good neighbor.

Use e before i when the vowels make an ay sound.

Another exception is when the c stands for an sh sound:

We visited the ancient ruins.

Is he a very efficient worker?

Use i before e when c stands for an sh sound.

Here are some other exceptions to the i before e rule:

either, foreign, height, neither, weird

The i before e rule doesn't work all the time. But it works most of the time. Use it to check your spelling of ie and ei words.

Try It: I Before E Rule

Underline the correctly spelled word in each sentence.

EXAMPLE: Please be (patient—pateint).

1. There's a crack in the (ceiling—cieling).
2. You can bring a (freind—friend) to my party.
3. I'll be home (either—iether) at 6:00 or 6:30.
4. The police caught the (theif—thief) minutes after the robbery.
5. There is an (anceint—ancient) curse on this land.
6. Did you (receive—recieve) my letter?
7. I never read movie (reveiws—reviews).

8. They have (eight—ieght) children.

9. This car has a (deisel—diesel) engine.

10. The quarterback ran up the (feild—field) with the ball.

Check your answers on page 85.

ANSWERS AND EXPLANATIONS

Try It: Finding Compound Subjects

1. __C__ **Either Eddie or Steve has your radio.** The parts of the subject are connected with either/or. The subject is compound.

2. __C__ **Both the train and the bus were late this morning.** The parts of the subject are connected with and. The subject is compound.

3. __N__ **The shirt, as well as the skirt, was on sale.** The words as well as do not connect a compound subject.

4. __C__ **Neither the bartender nor the bouncer looks friendly.** The parts of the subject are connected with neither/nor. The subject is compound.

5. __N__ **Winston, along with his family, is in Jamaica this week.** The words along with do not connect a compound subject.

6. __N__ **The manager, together with the coaches, was fired.** The words together with do not connect a compound subject.

7. __C__ **Not only Clem but also his brother owns a truck.** The parts of the subject are connected with not only/but also. The subject is compound.

8. __C__ **The duck and the rabbit were gifts from my uncle.** The parts of the subject are connected with and. The subject is compound.

9. __N__ **Sadie, in addition to Wilma, wants a raise.** The words in addition to do not connect a compound subject.

10. __N__ **The dog, as well as the cat, needs a bath.** The words as well as do not connect a compound subject.

Try It: Matching Verbs with Compound Subjects

1. **Margo and her parents visit each other often.** The compound subject is joined by and. It is plural. The verb visit matches the plural subject.
2. **Either the cups or the glasses are in the dishwasher.** The compound subject is joined by either/or. The plural verb are matches the part of the compound subject that is closer to it (glasses).
3. **Neither the cake nor the cookies taste good.** The compound subject is joined by neither/nor. The plural verb taste matches the part of the compound that is closer to it (cookies).
4. **Not only Sheila but also her children are sick.** The compound subject is joined by not only/but also. The plural verb are matches the part of the compound that is closer to it (children).
5. **Either the windows or the door is open.** The compound subject is joined by either/or. The singular verb is matches the part of the compound that is closer to it (door).
6. **Vern and Fred need a ride to work.** The compound subject is joined by and. It is plural. The verb need matches the plural subject.
7. **Not only stores but also a restaurant is in the mall.** The compound subject is joined by not only/but also. The singular verb is matches the subject part that is closer to it (restaurant).
8. **Either my husband or my daughter is home now.** The compound subject is joined by either/or. The singular verb is matches the subject part that is closer to it (daughter).
9. **Neither my cats nor my dog likes my girlfriend.** The compound subject is joined by neither/nor. The verb likes matches the subject part that is closer to it (dog).
10. **Your gloves and my scarf are on the table.** The compound subject is joined by and. It is plural. The verb are matches the plural subject.

Try It: I Before E Rule

1. **There's a crack in the ceiling.** Use ei after c.
2. **You can bring a friend to my party.** Use i before e except after c.
3. **I'll be home either at 6:00 or 6:30.** Either is an exception to the i before e rule.

4. **The police caught the thief minutes after the robbery.** Use i before e except after c.
5. **There is an ancient curse on this land.** Use ie when c stands for an sh sound.
6. **Did you receive my letter?** Use ei after c.
7. **I never read movie reviews.** Use i before e except after c.
8. **They have eight children.** Use ei when the vowels make an ay sound.
9. **This car has a diesel engine.** Use i before e except after c.
10. **The quarterback ran up the field with the ball.** Use i before e except after c.

UNIT 8: HOW ARE VERBS USED?

In the last few units, you've worked on matching subjects and verbs. A singular verb matches a singular subject. A plural verb matches a plural subject.

He works on the night shift.

They work on the night shift.

The verbs in these two sentences are different. The first verb (works) is singular. It matches the singular subject he. The second verb (work) is plural. It matches the plural subject they.

Now, look at these two sentences:

He worked on the night shift.

They worked on the night shift.

The verbs in these two sentences are the same. What does each verb tell you?

The verbs tell you *when* the action in the sentences happened. In these sentences, the verb worked tells you that the action happened in the past.

You already know that the verb is a very important part of a sentence. The verb tells you what is happening. It *also* tells you *when* the action happened. In this unit, you'll take a close look at how to use verbs to tell *when* something happened.

CHANGING A VERB TO SHOW TIME

Look at the next sentences. How are they alike? How are they different?

He works on the night shift.

He worked on the night shift.

He will work on the night shift.

The sentences are the same except for one thing. Each verb names the same action: work. But the verbs don't look exactly the same. In each sentence, the verb looks a little different.

Each sentence shows a different **verb tense.** What is a verb tense? A verb tense is a *form* of a verb. It's a form that shows *when* the action in the sentence happened. A verb tense shows time.

There are three basic ways to show time with verbs. There are three basic verb tenses. You can show that something is happening *now*. To do this, you use the present tense.

He works on the night shift.

(The verb works is in the present tense. It shows that he *now* works on the night shift.)

You can show that something happened *before.* To do this, you use the past tense.

He worked on the night shift.

(The verb worked is in the past tense. It shows that he *used to* work on the night shift.)

You can show that something will happen *later.* To do this, you use the future tense.

He will work on the night shift.

(The verb will work is in the future tense. It shows that he *will* work on the night shift *in the future.*)

How do you use the three basic verb tenses? How do you change a verb to show *when* the action in a sentence happened? To answer these questions, take a closer look at the verb work.

VERB:	work
PRESENT TENSE:	works (singular) work (plural)
PAST TENSE:	worked
FUTURE TENSE:	will work

There are two forms of the verb work in the present tense. The first one is singular. It has an s added to it: works. It matches singular subjects. The second form is plural: work. It doesn't have anything added to it or changed in it.

Now look at the past tense form of work: worked. How is it different from the present tense? It has ed added to it. To show that a regular verb is in the past tense, you add a d or ed to it. You add a d when the regular verb ends with an e.

I liked the show.

(The verb like ends with an e. To form the past tense, you add a d to it: like + d = liked.)

You add ed to all other regular verbs.

He worked on the night shift.

They worked on the night shift.

(The verb worked is the past tense of work: work + ed = worked.)

Look at the last two sentences again. In the first sentence, the subject is he. He is a singular subject. In the second sentence, the subject is they. They is a plural subject. But the verb is exactly the same in both sentences. In both sentences, the verb is worked.

The present tense is the only verb tense that has singular and plural forms. You don't have to worry about matching subjects and verbs in the past or future tense. There's only one past tense form of a verb. There's only one future tense form. Each past and future tense form matches both singular and plural verbs.

There is only one exception to this. The exception is with the verb be. Look at these sentences:

He is in the kitchen.

He was in the kitchen.

They are in the kitchen.

They were in the kitchen.

The subject of the first two sentences is singular: he. The first sentence is in the present tense. The singular verb is matches the singular subject he. The second sentence is in the past tense. The verb in the second sentence is was.

Now look at the last two sentences again. The subject of these two sentences is plural: they. The first sentence is in the present tense. The plural verb are matches the plural subject they. The second sentence is in the past tense. The verb in the second sentence is were.

Was is the *singular* past tense form of be. Were is the *plural* past tense form of be. Were matches all plural subjects. It also matches the subject you. Be is the only verb that has a singular and plural form in the past tense. And other verbs only have one form in the past tense. All verbs (even be) only have one form in the future tense:

He will work on the night shift.

They will work on the night shift.

These two sentences are in the future tense. In the future tense, the main verb does not change. However, the word will is put before the main verb. Together, will and the main verb show that the action will happen in the future. Together, will and the main verb form the future tense.

Try It: Changing a Verb to Show Time

Underline the verb in each sentence. Then tell if it is in the present, past, or future tense. If the verb is in the present tense, put **PR** in the blank next to the sentence. If the verb is in the past tense, put a **P** in the blank next to the sentence. If the verb is in the future tense, put an **F** in the blank next to the sentence.

EXAMPLE: PR Howard calls Rita every day.

1. ____ Sam waited outside for his brother.
2. ____ I will cook dinner later.
3. ____ Roy Owens lives on Hamburg Street.
4. ____ The car will be in the driveway.
5. ____ Everybody hated the new law.
6. ____ Louie and Gus enjoyed the ballet.
7. ____ Her friends will meet us at the bus stop.
8. ____ You were in the car with Stella.
9. ____ Those hot dogs look very good.
10. ____ The crackers in that box were stale.

Check your answers on page 103.

USING IRREGULAR VERBS

To show that a regular verb is in the past tense, you add a d or ed to it:

I like the show. (present tense)

I liked the show. (past tense)

He works on the night shift. (present tense)

He worked on the night shift. (past tense)

Like and work are **regular** verbs. A regular verb is any verb that has its past tense formed with a d or ed. It's easy to form the past tense of a regular verb. But not all verbs are regular verbs. Look at the verb in this sentence:

I see the problem.

The verb in this sentence is see. See is in the present tense. How would you change it to the past tense? Would you add a d? Or would you do something else?

Here is the same sentence in the past tense:

I saw the problem.

The verb in this sentence is saw. Saw is the past tense of the verb see. But you didn't form the past tense by adding a d or ed to the verb. That's because the verb see is an **irregular** verb.

An irregular verb is any verb that does not have its past tense formed with a d or ed. Irregular verbs have their past tense formed in irregular ways.

I see the problem. (present tense)

I saw the problem. (past tense)

He is in the kitchen. (present tense)

He was in the kitchen. (past tense)

There are a lot of irregular verbs. Here is a list of common irregular verbs:

IRREGULAR VERB	PAST TENSE
become	became
do	did
drink	drank
drive	drove
eat	ate
fall	fell
give	gave
go	went
have	had
know	knew
ride	rode
run	ran
see	saw
speak	spoke
take	took
throw	threw
write	wrote

There are more irregular verbs like the ones in the list. As you can see, irregular verbs have their past tense formed in many different ways. There aren't any rules to help you form the past tense of irregular verbs. You just have to memorize how the past tense of an irregular verb is formed.

But memorizing the irregular verbs probably won't be hard. That's because you probably know most of the irregular verbs already. Take another look at the verbs in the list. You probably use many of them in everyday speaking. You've probably already memorized most of the irregular verbs.

If you're not sure whether a verb is regular or irregular, there's something you can do. You can look up the verb in a dictionary. If the verb is irregular, the dictionary will give you the past tense of the verb.

Try It: Using Regular and Irregular Verbs

Rewrite these sentences. Change the verb tense from present to past. Some of the verbs are regular verbs, and some are irregular.

1. I walk to work.

2. Carlos has a headache.

3. The cars need gas.

4. The Bongo Club is empty on Wednesday nights.

5. They are wrong.

6. Don only dances with Dawn.

7. That man drives a black sedan.

8. We talk at lunchtime.

9. They drink too much soda.

10. I am tired.

Check your answers on page 103.

USING HAVE AS A HELPING VERB

So far in this unit, you've worked with the three basic verb tenses. You've worked with the present tense, the past tense, and the future tense. These three verb tenses are the most common verb tenses. But they're not the only verb tenses. There are other ways that you can change verbs to show time.

Look at these three sentences:

He works on the night shift.

He worked on the night shift.

He has worked on the night shift.

You've seen the first two sentences before. The first sentence is in the present tense. The second sentence is in the past tense. But look at the third sentence. How is it different from the first two sentences? What does this verb show about time?

The third sentence has a helping verb in it. The helping verb is has. Has is a singular verb. It is the present tense of the verb have. The verb have is often used as a helping verb. This means that it is often used with another verb in a sentence.

Together, the helping verb have and the main verb form a verb tense. What does this verb tense show about time? To answer this question, take a look at these sentences:

He worked on the night shift for five years.

He has worked on the night shift for five years.

The verb in the first sentence is in the past tense. The action in the first sentence happened in the past. He used to work on the night shift, but he doesn't anymore.

Now, look at the second sentence again. The helping verb have is in the present tense. It is singular to match the singular subject. This verb tense tells you that the action started in the past. But it tells you something else, too. It tells you that the action *is still happening* in the present. He used to work on the night shift, and he still does.

I lived in that house for a year.

(I used to live there, but I don't anymore.)

I have lived in that house for a year.

(I have lived there for a year, and I *still* live there.)

You can use the present tense of have together with the main verb to show something else. You can use it to show an action that has taken place at an *unknown* time in the past.

Gloria has stopped smoking cigarettes.

(The helping verb has and the main verb stopped show that the action has taken place at an unknown time in the past.)

Gloria stopped smoking cigarettes last month.

(In this sentence, the helping verb is not used because the sentence tells *when* the action took place in the past.)

You can also use the helping verb had with a main verb. Had is the past tense of have. You can use had to show an action that happened *before* something else in the past. For example, look at these sentences:

Henry walked ten miles yesterday.

He had walked twelve miles the day before that.

Both of these sentences are about something that happened in the past. The helping verb had is used with the main verb to show what had happened first.

Will have can also be used as a helping verb. Will have is the future tense of the verb have. You can use will have with a main verb to show an action that *will* happen before something else *in the future*. For example, look at these sentences:

I have not cleaned my kitchen yet.

But I will have cleaned my kitchen by next Monday.

The first sentence tells you that something hasn't happened yet. I haven't cleaned my kitchen yet. The second sentence tells you that the kitchen will get cleaned by a certain time in the future. It will get cleaned by next Monday. The helping verb will have is used with the main verb to show that the cleaning will have happened by a certain time in the future.

You can use the present, past, and future tenses of have as a helping verb. You use the helping verb together with a main verb. But what does the main verb look like? What *form* is the main verb in? To answer these questions, take another look at some of the sentences:

He has worked on the night shift for five years.

I have lived in that house for a year.

He had walked twelve miles the day before that.

Look at the main verb in each sentence. The main verbs are work, live, and walk. Each main verb has a d or ed added to it.

The main verbs in these sentences are in a form called the **past participle.** With regular verbs, the past participle is formed the same way that the past tense is formed. You form the past participle of a regular verb by adding a d or ed to it.

But the past participle of an *irregular* verb isn't always the same as the past tense. For example, look at these sentences:

I saw the problem.

(Saw is the past tense of the verb see).

I have seen the problem.

(Seen is the past participle of the verb see.)

Here is a list of irregular verbs with their past tense and past participle forms:

IRREGULAR VERB	PAST TENSE	PAST PARTICIPLE
be	was, were	been
become	became	become
do	did	done
drink	drank	drunk
drive	drove	driven
eat	ate	eaten
fall	fell	fallen
give	gave	given
go	went	gone
have	had	had
know	knew	known
ride	rode	ridden
run	ran	run
see	saw	seen
speak	spoke	spoken
take	took	taken
throw	threw	thrown
write	wrote	written

(If you're not sure whether a verb is regular or irregular, look up the verb in a dictionary. If the verb is irregular, the dictionary will give you the past tense and the past participle of the verb.)

As you can see, the past participles of irregular verbs are formed in many different ways. It's important to know the difference between the past tense and the past participle of a verb. Don't use the past tense with the helping verb have. Use the past participle with the helping verb have.

> I have took Charlie to the dentist.
>
> (The verb is this sentence is WRONG. Took is the past tense of take. You need to use the past participle with the helping verb have.)
>
> I have taken Charlie to the dentist.
>
> (The verb in this sentence is RIGHT. Taken is the past participle of take.)
>
> I took Charlie to the dentist.
>
> (The verb in this sentence is RIGHT. If you don't use the helping verb have, use the past tense of the verb.)

Have is an important helping verb. It's important because you can use it to show three different verb tenses:

IF YOU USE:	YOU SHOW:
has or have + past participle (Use has with singular subjects. Use have with plural subjects.)	• an action that started in the past and is still going on, or • an action that happened at an unknown time in the past
had + past participle	• an action that happened before something else in the past
will have + past participle	• an action that will happen before something else in the future

Try It: Using Have as a Helping Verb

Here are some sentences in the present tense. Change each sentence by adding the helping verb has or have to it. Make sure that the helping verb matches the subject. Also make sure to change the main verb into the past participle form.

EXAMPLE: Bill works at Carson's.
Bill has worked at Carson's.

1. The cats miss their owner.

2. Rita does the dishes.

3. I eat breakfast.

4. Jimmy lives in Yorkville.

5. Boris knows her secrets.

6. The men cook dinner.

7. I am sick.

8. The road is closed.

9. Pete has our ladder.

10. Our neighbors are away.

Check your answers on page 104.

Try It: Using the Past Participle

Underline the correct verb form in each sentence.

1. I (have saw—have seen) Carla in the parking lot.
2. Bonnie (has ridden—has rode) horses for many years.
3. Dora (had knew—had known) the answer before Jerry.
4. I (will have spoke—will have spoken) to him by next week.
5. Steve (has fallen—has fell) in love again.
6. Bertha and I (have drank—have drunk) all of the punch.

Check your answers on page 105.

USING BE AS A HELPING VERB

You have seen that have can be used as a helping verb. Have is an important helping verb. You use it with the past participle of another verb to form different verb tenses.

The verb be is another important helping verb. You've worked with be earlier in this book. You know that be has many different forms. Here are the forms of be in the present, past, and future tenses:

PRESENT TENSE:	am (with I) is (singular) are (plural)
PAST TENSE:	was (singular) were (plural)
FUTURE TENSE:	will be

You can use be as a helping verb in two ways. One way is to use be with the past participle of a main verb. Look at this sentence:

Mary was taken to the show by Slim.

In this sentence, was is a helping verb. It is used with the past participle of the verb take (taken). Together, what do the helping verb and the main verb tell you? They tell you that the subject of the sentence is *not* doing the action in the sentence. Look at the subject of the sentence again. The subject is Mary. What does the sentence say about Mary? It says that Mary was taken to the show. Mary did not do the taking. Someone else did. Slim did.

Slim took Mary to the show.

(The verb is in the past tense. The subject Slim is doing the action in the sentence.)

Mary was taken to the show by Slim.

(In this sentence, the helping verb be is used with the past participle of take. That's because the subject Mary is *not* doing the action.)

If you use be as a helping verb, make sure that you use the past participle of the main verb. Don't use the past tense.

Mary was took to the show by Slim.

(The verb in this sentence is WRONG. The past participle of take should be used.)

Mary was taken to the show by Slim.

(The verb in this sentence is RIGHT. Taken is the past participle of take.)

You can use the helping verb be with a past participle. You can also use be in another way. Look at this sentence:

He is going to work.

In this sentence, is is a helping verb. Look at the main verb that it is used with: going. Going is the verb go with ing added to it. You can add ing to any verb and use it with the helping verb be. You can use these verbs together to show something that is happening right at a particular time.

He is going to work.

(Is going shows what the subject is doing *right now.*)

I was washing the dishes when you called.

(Was washing shows what the subject was doing right when you called.)

They will be leaving in ten minutes.

(Will be leaving shows what the subject will be doing in ten minutes.)

When you use be as a helping verb, remember a few things. Remember to change the verb into the present, past, or future tense. If be is in the present or past tense, remember to match it to the subject.

I be working late tomorrow.

(The verb in this sentence is WRONG. The helping verb be should be in the future tense. The sentence is about something that will be happening tomorrow.)

I will be working late tomorrow.

(The verb in this sentence is RIGHT. Will be is the future tense of be.)

You was seen at the movies.

(The verb in this sentence is WRONG. The subject you matches were, not was.)

You were seen at the movies.

(The verb in this sentence is RIGHT. Were matches the subject you.)

Try It: Using Be as a Helping Verb

In each sentence, the verb be is used as a helping verb. If the be verb is not in its correct form, rewrite the sentence. Put the be verb in its correct form.

1. Paul and Peter is being foolish.

2. The employees be given raises next week.

3. Val be working now.

4. You is shaking.

5. The accident be reported to the police last night.

6. The car were driven by Alex.

7. Maura was drinking my soda.

8. It be raining now.

9. The house were bought by an older couple.

10. They be coming to the party tomorrow.

Check your answers on page 105.

UNIT REVIEW

In this unit, you've taken a close look at verbs. The verb is probably the most important part of a sentence. The verb tells you what is going on in a sentence. The verb also tells you *when* the action in the sentence is taking place. The **tense** of the verb shows when the action is taking place. A verb tense shows time.

You've seen that there are three basic verb tenses: present, past, and future. You've looked at how to form each tense. You've also looked at some irregular verbs—verbs that have their past tense formed in different ways. You've seen how helping verbs can be used in verb tenses. You can use the helping verb have with the past participle of a main verb to show different verb tenses. You can also use the verb be as a helping verb.

There are a lot of things to remember when you use verbs. You have to remember to put the verb in the right tense. You have to remember to make sure that the verb matches the subject. If you use helping verbs, you have to make sure that the right form of the helping verb is used. You also have to make sure that the right form of the main verb is used. There are a lot of steps to follow when you use verbs. But the steps are important. They help you to make sure that the verb stands *exactly* for what you want to say in a sentence.

SPELLING AND USAGE HINT: ADDING ED TO WORDS THAT END IN Y

You have seen that verbs have different forms. The past tense form of regular verbs is made by adding ed:

They work on the night shift.

They worked on the night shift.

Sometimes, the verb changes a little when ed is added. Look at these sentences:

They try hard.

They tried hard.

How does the verb try change when ed is added?

try + **ed** = **tried**

The y is changed to i. Then ed is added.

You have added the ending s to words that end in y:

The baby is in the crib.

The **babies** are in the crib.

The rule for adding ed is similar. To add ed to a word that ends in y, change the y to i and add ed:

We carry the groceries home in a cart.

We **carried** the groceries home in a cart.

If a vowel comes before the y, just add ed:

The children **play** in the park nearby.

The children **played** in the park nearby.

Try It: Adding ed to Words That End in y

Fill in the blank with the past tense form of the verb in parentheses.

1. Bill ________________ the report for his boss. (copy)
2. Quinn ________________ for his driving test. (study)
3. The dog ________________ its owner's commands. (obey)
4. Rob ________________ to catch the last train. (hurry)
5. Tim ________________ his high-school teacher. (marry)
6. The faucet ________________ water onto the wall. (spray)

7. Pat _______________ during the entire movie. (cry)

8. Vern _______________ me by cracking his knuckles. (annoy)

9. Ted _______________ the eggs in butter. (fry)

10. Peggy _______________ for the sales job. (apply)

Check your answers on page 106.

ANSWERS AND EXPLANATIONS

Try It: Changing a Verb to Show Time

1. __P__ **Sam waited outside for his brother.** Waited is the past tense form of wait.
2. __F__ **I will cook dinner later.** Will cook is the future tense form of cook.
3. __PR__ **Roy Owens lives on Hamburg Street.** Lives is the singular present tense form of live.
4. __F__ **The car will be in the driveway.** Will be is the future tense form of be.
5. __P__ **Everybody hated the new law.** Hated is the past tense form of hate.
6. __P__ **Louie and Gus enjoyed the ballet.** Enjoyed is the past tense form of enjoy.
7. __F__ **Her friends will meet us at the bus stop.** Will meet is the future tense form of meet.
8. __P__ **You were in the car with Stella.** Were is the plural past tense form of be.
9. __PR__ **Those hot dogs look very good.** Look is the plural present tense form of look.
10. __P__ **The crackers in that box were stale.** Were is the plural past tense form of be.

Try It: Using Regular and Irregular Verbs

1. **I walk to work. I walked to work.** Walk is a regular verb. Its past tense is formed by adding ed.

2. **Carlos has a headache. Carlos had a headache.** Have is an irregular verb. Its past tense form is had.
3. **The cars need gas. The cars needed gas.** Need is a regular verb. Its past tense is formed by adding ed.
4. **The Bongo Club is empty on Wednesday nights. The Bongo Club was empty on Wednesday nights.** Be is an irregular verb. Its singular past tense form is was.
5. **They are wrong. They were wrong.** Be is an irregular verb. Its plural past tense form is were.
6. **Don only dances with Dawn. Don only danced with Dawn.** Dance is a regular verb. Its past tense is formed by adding ed.
7. **That man drives a black sedan. That man drove a black sedan.** Drive is an irregular verb. Its past tense form is drove.
8. **We talk at lunchtime. We talked at lunchtime.** Talk is a regular verb. Its past tense is formed by adding ed.
9. **They drink too much soda. They drank too much soda.** Drink is an irregular verb. Its past tense form is drank.
10. **I am tired. I was tired.** Be is an irregular verb. Its singular past tense is was.

Try It: Using Have as a Helping Verb

1. **The cats miss their owner. The cats have missed their owner.** The helping verb have matches the plural subject cats. The past participle of miss is missed.
2. **Rita does the dishes. Rita has done the dishes.** The helping verb has matches the singular subject Rita. The past participle of do is done.
3. **I eat breakfast. I have eaten breakfast.** The helping verb have matches the subject I. The past participle of eat is eaten.
4. **Jimmy lives in Yorkville. Jimmy has lived in Yorkville.** The helping verb has matches the singular subject Jimmy. The past participle form of live is lived.
5. **Boris knows her secrets. Boris has known her secrets.** The helping verb has matches the singular subject Boris. The past participle form of know is known.
6. **The men cook dinner. The men have cooked dinner.** The helping verb have matches the plural subject men. The past participle form of cook is cooked.
7. **I am sick. I have been sick.** The helping verb have matches the subject I. The past participle form of be is been.

8. **The road is closed. The road has been closed.** The helping verb has matches the singular subject road. The past participle form of be is been.
9. **Pete has our ladder. Pete has had our ladder.** The helping verb has matches the singular subject Pete. The past participle form of have is had.
10. **Our neighbors are away. Our neighbors have been away.** The helping verb have matches the plural subject neighbors. The past participle form of be is been.

Try It: Using the Past Participle

1. **I have seen Carla in the parking lot.** The past participle form of see is seen.
2. **Bonnie has ridden horses for many years.** The past participle form of ride is ridden.
3. **Dora had known the answer before Jerry.** The past participle form of know is known.
4. **I will have spoken to him by next week.** The past participle form of speak is spoken.
5. **Steve has fallen in love again.** The past participle form of fall is fallen.
6. **Bertha and I have drunk all of the punch.** The past participle form of drink is drunk.

Try It: Using Be as a Helping Verb

1. **Paul and Peter are being foolish.** The verb be should be in its present tense form. Are matches the plural subject Paul and Peter. Together with being, it shows what the subject is doing right now.
2. **The employees will be given raises next week.** The verb be should be in its future tense form. Together with given, it shows a future action.
3. **Val is working now.** The verb be should be in its present tense form. Is matches the singular subject Val. Together with working, it shows what the subject is doing right now.
4. **You are shaking.** The verb be should be in its present tense form. Are matches the subject you. Together with shaking, it shows what the subject is doing right now.
5. **The accident was reported to the police last night.** The verb be should be in its past tense form. Was matches the singular

subject accident. Was is used with reported to show that the subject did not perform the action.

6. **The car was driven by Alex.** The verb be should be in its past tense form. Was matches the singular subject car. Was is used with driven to show that the subject did not perform the action.
7. **Maura was drinking my soda.** The verb be should be in its past tense form. Was matches the singular subject Maura. Together with drinking, it shows an action that was going on in the past.
8. **It is raining now.** The verb be should be in its present tense form. Is matches the singular subject it. Together with raining, it shows an action that is happening right now.
9. **The house was bought by an older couple.** The verb be should be in its past tense form. Was matches the singular subject house. Was is used with bought to show that the subject did not perform the action.
10. **They will be coming to the party tomorrow.** The verb be should be in its future tense form. Together with coming, it shows an action that will be happening in the future.

Try It: Adding ed to Words That End in y

1. **Bill copied the report for his boss.** Copy ends in y. Change the y to i and add ed.
2. **Quinn studied for his driving test.** Study ends in y. Change the y to i and add ed.
3. **The dog obeyed its owner's commands.** Obey ends in a vowel (e) plus y. Just add ed.
4. **Rob hurried to catch the last train.** Hurry ends in y. Change the y to i and add ed.
5. **Tim married his high-school teacher.** Marry ends in y. Change the y to i and add ed.
6. **The faucet sprayed water onto the wall.** Spray ends in a vowel (a) plus y. Just add ed.
7. **Pat cried during the entire movie.** Cry ends in y. Change the y to i and add ed.
8. **Vern annoyed me by cracking his knuckles.** Annoy ends in a vowel (o) plus y. Just add ed.
9. **Ted fried the eggs in butter.** Fry ends in y. Change the y to i and add ed.
10. **Peggy applied for the sales job.** Apply ends in y. Change the y to i and add ed.

UNIT 9: MEASURING YOUR PROGRESS

In the first part of this book, you have looked at the two main parts of a sentence—the subject and the predicate. You have worked on these things:

- finding the subject and the predicate of a sentence
- finding the simple subject of a sentence
- deciding if the simple subject is singular or plural
- finding the verb in a sentence
- matching the verb with the subject
- forming and using verb tenses

In the Spelling and Usage Hints, you have worked on capitalizing nouns, forming noun plurals, spelling words with ie and ei, and adding ed to verbs.

This unit will help you to see how much you have learned so far with this book. Complete all the parts of this unit. After you have finished, check your answers. The answer section tells you what pages to turn to for review. You should review the pages for any items that you do not answer correctly.

PART A

Underline the complete subject in each sentence once. Underline the complete predicate in each sentence twice.

EXAMPLE: The oldest hotel in town is the Dinkler Arms.

1. The mayor led the parade down Center Street.

2. His father's hobby is watching television.

3. The green van on the corner belongs to Rod.

4. The citizens of Bowlers Field voted against the bill.

5. My wife works for an insurance company.

6. The furnace is in the basement.

7. Our neighbor Ted Barnes writes soft drink ads.

8. The cheapest watch in the store costs fifty dollars.

9. The swimmer in the fourth lane is winning the race.

10. Traffic on Route 40 was at a halt.

11. A large bat flew across the ceiling.

12. The angry mob trapped him in the alley.

PART B

Underline the simple subject in each sentence. If the simple subject is singular, put an **S** in the blank. If the simple subject is plural, put a **P** in the blank.

EXAMPLE: ___P___ Here are the maps for our trip.

13. ____ Darlene lost her ring on the bus.

14. ____ It snowed yesterday.

15. ____ There is a dove outside her window.

16. ____ Are the potatoes in the oven?

17. ____ Here are two hamburgers for your lunch.

18. ____ Whom did Anita marry?

19. ____ The neighborhood dogs chased after the butcher.

20. ____ Bud and I waited nervously in her living room.

21. ____ The nurses on the night shift work with Dr. Hans.

22. ____ Lee's coat and tie are hanging on the door.

23. ____ The smoke from their cigars floated through the room.

24. ____ He wants to be president of the company.

PART C

Read each sentence. Underline the simple subject once and the verb twice. Then see if the verb matches the subject. If the subject and the verb don't match, rewrite the sentence. Change the verb so that it matches the subject.

EXAMPLE: The photographs in this album is very old.

The photographs in this album are very old.

25. My new car have radial tires.

26. The suitcase with the clear handles belong to Milton.

27. Jack McDuff and Liz Johnson is police officers.

28. The telephones in the office is out of order.

29. My sisters lives in Hoboken.

30. I bowls with my friends on Monday nights.

31. He drive a cab.

32. The lot behind the new apartments is covered with trash.

33. I is tired of Melvin's practical jokes.

34. We has tickets for the fight.

35. The cashiers in the grocery store work six days a week.

36. Sharp, shiny stones covers the path to the lake.

PART D

Underline the verb that matches the subject in each sentence.

EXAMPLE: The public usually (has—have) the last word.

37. The jury (believe—believes) her story.
38. These scissors (are—is) very sharp.
39. The news about them (are—is) grim.
40. The United States (are—is) part of North America.
41. Two pints (equal—equals) one quart.
42. The committee always (meet—meets) on Thursdays.
43. Six hours (are—is) a long time to wait for a bus.
44. Something (are—is) wrong.
45. Everybody (want—wants) to go home.
46. No one (live—lives) in that house.
47. Both of her children (are—is) in elementary school.
48. Each of the suspects (has—have) a motive.
49. Several of the seats (are—is) empty.
50. Some of the employees (has—have) the flu.
51. Part of the quilt (are—is) finished.
52. None of the hotels (has—have) any empty rooms.
53. All of the milk (are—is) sour.
54. Your skirt and my pants (are—is) on the bed.
55. Not only Bert but also his sisters (work—works) at the factory.
56. Either the map or the road signs (are—is) wrong.
57. Neither the coffee nor the candies (give—gives) me more energy.

58. Either the pipes or the furnace (need—needs) repair.

59. Neither my parents nor my brother (like—likes) my wife.

60. Frieda, together with her sons, (run—runs) a gift shop.

PART E

Underline the correct verb in each sentence.

EXAMPLE: I (did—done) the dishes last night.

61. Jeno (has spoken—have spoken) to the boss about him.

62. The office (was closed—were closed) yesterday.

63. I (has made—have made) plans for this evening.

64. Mark and I (are going—be going) to the movies.

65. The hunters (search—searched) for deer yesterday.

66. The sky (are turning—is turning) dark gray.

67. We (have knew—have known) others like you.

68. The cat (fed—was fed) by the neighbors.

69. The night watchman (had been—has been) at his desk before the crime occurred.

70. Max (had became—had become) a foreman before Alex.

71. We (be taking—will be taking) a vacation soon.

72. The food (was ate—was eaten) by Bernie.

73. Arnold (has written—has wrote) a letter to the manager.

74. Ralph (be hiding—is hiding) in the closet.

75. I (am living—be living) on Fulton Street.

76. Five employees (was fired—were fired) yesterday.

77. Clarence (worked—works) at the Tasty Diner until last year.

78. I (has received—have received) your letter.

79. The winning horse (was ridden—was rode) by Sue Parker.

80. The party (had ended—has ended) before we got there.

PART F

Read each sentence. Underline any words that should be capitalized in each sentence.

EXAMPLE: uncle floyd is a practical joker.

81. My parents are from new mexico.

82. The mars hotel is closed in the wintertime.

83. Our grandchildren live in salt lake city, utah.

84. I saw ann marie at the store yesterday.

85. Joe burton lives across the street.

86. Her cat bitsy ran away.

87. They can see mt. snow from their living-room window.

88. He crossed the atlantic ocean in a canoe.

89. His brother works at the jackson city zoo.

90. The reporter questioned maloney.

PART G

Fill in the blanks with the plural form of the noun in parentheses.

EXAMPLE: Buy some __tomatoes__ for the sauce. (tomato)

91. Larry keeps his ________________ in the tool box. (wrench)

92. The _______________ wouldn't stop crying. (baby)

93. The music store is having a sale on _______________. (stereo)

94. There are two _______________ to get to my house. (way)

95. _______________ by Gavin LaPell are on sale. (scarf)

96. The dogs chased after the _______________. (fox)

97. Jones only completed two _______________ in the entire game. (pass)

98. The _______________ were given medals. (hero)

99. No _______________ were lost in the fire. (life)

100. Her _______________ are very long. (eyelash)

PART H

Underline the word in parentheses that is spelled correctly.

EXAMPLE: Bart (received—recieved) a promotion.

101. Don (beleived—believed) Margo's story.

102. The mirror broke into a thousand (peices—pieces).

103. Did the sales clerk give you a (receipt—reciept)?

104. Our (neighbors—nieghbors) are away this weekend.

105. The (preist—priest) stood before the altar.

PART I

Fill in the blank with the past tense form of the verb in parentheses.

EXAMPLE: Joe ____fried____ bacon for our breakfast. (fry)

106. The clothes _______________ quickly in the hot sun. (dry)

107. Ralph ______________ that he had hit the car. (deny)

108. Phyllis ______________ reading on the porch. (enjoy)

109. Everyone ______________ about Mike. (worry)

110. Rick ______________ his daughter in his arms. (carry)

ANSWER KEY

Part A

1. The mayor led the parade down Center Street.
2. His father's hobby is watching television.
3. The green van on the corner belongs to Rod.
4. The citizens of Bowlers Field voted against the bill.
5. My wife works for an insurance company.
6. The furnace is in the basement.
7. Our neighbor Ted Barnes writes soft drink ads.
8. The cheapest watch in the store costs fifty dollars.
9. The swimmer in the fourth lane is winning the race.
10. Traffic on Route 40 was at a halt.
11. A large bat flew across the ceiling.
12. The angry mob trapped him in the alley.

Part B

13. S Darlene lost her ring on the bus.
14. S It snowed yesterday.
15. S There is a dove outside her window.
16. P Are the potatoes in the oven?
17. P Here are two hamburgers for your lunch.
18. S Whom did Anita marry?
19. P The neighborhood dogs chased after the butcher.
20. P Bud and I waited nervously in her living room.
21. P The nurses on the night shift work with Dr. Hans.
22. P Lee's coat and tie are hanging on the door.
23. S The smoke from their cigars floated through the room.
24. S He wants to be president of the company.

Part C

25. My new car has radial tires.
26. The suitcase with the clear handles belongs to Milton.
27. Jack McDuff and Liz Johnson are police officers.
28. The telephones in the office are out of order.
29. My sisters live in Hoboken.
30. I bowl with my friends on Monday nights.
31. He drives a cab.
32. The lot behind the new apartments is covered with trash.
33. I am tired of Melvin's practical jokes.
34. We have tickets for the fight.
35. The cashiers in the grocery store work six days a week.
36. Sharp, shiny stones cover the path to the lake.

Part D

37. The jury believes her story.
38. These scissors are very sharp.
39. The news about them is grim.
40. The United States is part of North America.
41. Two pints equals one quart.
42. The committee always meets on Thursdays.
43. Six hours is a long time to wait for a bus.
44. Something is wrong.
45. Everybody wants to go home.
46. No one lives in that house.
47. Both of her children are in elementary school.
48. Each of the suspects has a motive.
49. Several of the seats are empty.
50. Some of the employees have the flu.
51. Part of the quilt is finished.
52. None of the hotels have any empty rooms.
53. All of the milk is sour.
54. Your skirt and my pants are on the bed.
55. Not only Bert but also his sisters work at the factory.
56. Either the map or the road signs are wrong.
57. Neither the coffee nor the candies give me more energy.
58. Either the pipes or the furnace needs repair.
59. Neither my parents nor my brother likes my wife.
60. Frieda, together with her sons, runs a gift shop.

Part E

61. Jeno has spoken to the boss about him.
62. The office was closed yesterday.
63. I have made plans for this evening.
64. Mark and I are going to the movies.
65. The hunters searched for deer yesterday.
66. The sky is turning dark gray.
67. We have known others like you.
68. The cat was fed by the neighbors.
69. The night watchman had been at his desk before the crime occurred.
70. Max had become a foreman before Alex.
71. We will be taking a vacation soon.
72. The food was eaten by Bernie.
73. Arnold has written a letter to the manager.
74. Ralph is hiding in the closet.
75. I am living on Fulton Street.
76. Five employees were fired yesterday.
77. Clarence worked at the Tasty Diner until last year.
78. I have received your letter.
79. The winning horse was ridden by Sue Parker.
80. The party had ended before we got there.

Part F

81. My parents are from New Mexico.
82. The Mars Hotel is closed in the wintertime.
83. Our grandchildren live in Salt Lake City, Utah.
84. I saw Ann Marie at the store yesterday.
85. Joe Burton lives across the street.
86. Her cat Bitsy ran away.
87. They can see Mt. Snow from their living-room window.
88. He crossed the Atlantic Ocean in a canoe.
89. His brother works at the Jackson City Zoo.
90. The reporter questioned Maloney.

Part G

91. Larry keeps his wrenches in the tool box.
92. The babies wouldn't stop crying.
93. The music store is having a sale on stereos.
94. There are two ways to get to my house.
95. Scarves by Gavin LaPell are on sale.

96. **The dogs chased after the foxes.**
97. **Jones only completed two passes in the entire game.**
98. **The heroes were given medals.**
99. **No lives were lost in the fire.**
100. **Her eyelashes are very long.**

Part H

101. **Don believed Margo's story.**
102. **The mirror broke into a thousand pieces.**
103. **Did the sales clerk give you a receipt?**
104. **Our neighbors are away this weekend.**
105. **The priest stood before the altar.**

Part I

106. **The clothes dried quickly in the hot sun.**
107. **Ralph denied that he had hit the car.**
108. **Phyllis enjoyed reading on the porch.**
109. **Everyone worried about Mike.**
110. **Rick carried his daughter in his arms.**

In this chart, circle the number of any item you did not answer correctly. The right-hand side of the chart will tell you the pages to review for any item that you missed. Review the pages for any item that you missed before you go on to the next unit.

Item number:	Pages to study:
1 2 3 4 5 6 7 8 9 10 11 12	UNIT 2: Is It a Sentence? (pages 8–21)
13 14 15 16 17 18 19 20 21 22 23 24	UNIT 3: What Is the Simple Subject? (pages 22–42)
25 26 27 28 29 30 31 32 33 34 35 36	UNIT 4: Does the Verb Match the Subject? (pages 43–54)
37 38 39 40 41 42 43 44	UNIT 5: Is the Noun Singular or Plural? (pages 55–65)
45 46 47 48 49 50 51 52 53	UNIT 6: Is the Pronoun Singular or Plural? (pages 66–76)
54 55 56 57 58 59 60	UNIT 7: Does the Verb Match the Compound Subject? (pages 77–86)
61 62 63 64 65 66 67 68 69 70 71 72 73 74 75 76 77 78 79 80	UNIT 8: How Are Verbs Used? (pages 87–106)
81 82 83 84 85 86 87 88 89 90	SPELLING AND USAGE HINT: Capitalization (pages 16–17)
91 92 93 94 95 96 97 98 99 100	SPELLING AND USAGE HINTS: Adding s to Words (pages 35–36, 50–51, 61–62, 73–74)
101 102 103 104 105	SPELLING AND USAGE HINT: I Before E Rule (pages 82–84)
106 107 108 109 110	SPELLING AND USAGE HINT: Adding ed to Words (pages 101–103)

Pronouns, Adjectives, and Adverbs

UNIT 10: HOW MUCH DO YOU KNOW ALREADY?

This unit will help you plan your work in Units 11–15. Answer as many of the items as you can. When you have finished, check your answers on page 124. Then in the chart on page 126 circle the number of any item you missed. The chart will tell you which pages to study.

PART A

Underline the correct pronoun in each sentence.

EXAMPLE: Jane and (<u>I</u>—me) ate lunch together this afternoon.

1. Wally and Steve met (her—she) at the restaurant.
2. (Them—They) walked along the river bank.
3. My brothers and (I—me) drove to the lake last Saturday.
4. Buy something for the children and (you—yourself) with this money.
5. (Her—She) found ten dollars in an old tin can.
6. Richard gave (I—me) his phone number.
7. I told (me—myself) not to worry.
8. (Us—We) waited in line for an hour.
9. I gave the address to Dave and (her—she).
10. The police officer questioned (us—we) about the fire.
11. The person in the mirror was (I—me).

12. You and (us—we) should get together soon.

13. He made (himself—hisself) a chocolate milk shake.

14. (He—Him) always wore a black scarf.

15. The guide led (them—they) through the cave.

PART B

Underline the correct word in each sentence.

EXAMPLE: This hat is (<u>mine</u>—my).

16. (Marcuses—Marcus's) motorcycle is parked outside.

17. This is (your—yours) last chance.

18. The team won (its—their) first game.

19. That monkey is (their—theirs).

20. Not only Melba but also her daughters wear (her—their) hair short.

21. The (childrens—children's) toys are in their bedroom.

22. That man is (mine—my) brother.

23. The (churches'—churches's) bells could be heard all over town.

24. Everyone wants (his—their) dinner now.

25. Some of the customers want (his—their) money back.

26. The two (dog's—dogs') bowls are empty.

27. The blue scarf is (hers—her's).

28. Each of the men signed (his—their) name to the contract.

29. The (owners—owner's) of that store went bankrupt.

30. Either Ed or Pete has quit (his—their) job.

PART C

Underline the adjectives in each sentence.

EXAMPLE: The <u>old</u> man fixed the <u>broken</u> car.

31. Paul and I had a cold soda before lunch.

32. The blue and green parrot is in the big cage.

33. Everyone thinks he is a great player.

34. The water felt good after a long, hot day.

35. He is happy about his new job.

PART D

Read each pair of sentences. One of the sentences contains a mistake. The other sentence is correct. Circle the letter next to the sentence that is correct.

EXAMPLE: (a) I need these here books.
(b) I need these books.

36. (a) The black and white dog belongs to Fred.
(b) The black, and white dog belongs to Fred.

37. (a) Them new video games are fun.
(b) Those new video games are fun.

38. (a) Her hair is long black and shiny.
(b) Her hair is long, black, and shiny.

39. (a) I met this here man at the movies.
(b) I met a man at the movies.

40. (a) That there gun is loaded.
(b) That gun is loaded.

PART E

Underline the adverbs in each sentence.

EXAMPLE: I walked quickly to the front of the room.

41. Mike looked angrily at the customer.

42. Hal drives his car very fast.

43. Bernice quietly listened to the radio.

44. Richard sounded very happy about his trip.

45. The telephone rang loudly for several minutes.

PART F

Read each pair of sentences. One of the sentences contains a mistake. The other sentence is correct. Circle the letter next to the sentence that is correct.

EXAMPLE: (a) Henry watched his weight carefully.
(b) Henry watched his weight careful.

46. (a) Edna sang the song fantastically.
    (b) Edna sang the song fantasticly.

47. (a) This candy tastes too sweet.
    (b) This candy tastes too sweetly.

48. (a) Vinnie plays the piano very good.
    (b) Vinnie plays the piano very well.

49. (a) Barnes moves very quick for a big man.
    (b) Barnes moves very quickly for a big man.

50. (a) Felix felt bad about his mistake.
    (b) Felix felt badly about his mistake.

PART G

Read each pair of sentences. One of the sentences contains a mistake. The other sentence is correct. Circle the letter next to the sentence that is correct.

EXAMPLE: (a) Rick is more thin than Sally.
(b) Rick is thinner than Sally.

51. (a) Of the two secretaries, Howard types more fastly.
    (b) Of the two secretaries, Howard types faster.

52. (a) Jeanette has the loudest voice in the choir.
    (b) Jeanette has the most loud voice in the choir.

53. (a) Eugene plays the piano worse than Tony does.
    (b) Eugene plays the piano worser than Tony does.

54. (a) Phil thinks that pigs are the more intelligent of all animals.
    (b) Phil thinks that pigs are the most intelligent of all animals.

55. (a) The ring is more expensive than the watch.
    (b) The ring is expensiver than the watch.

56. (a) The sofa is more heavier than the table.
    (b) The sofa is heavier than the table.

57. (a) Tanya is more gracefuller than the other dancers.
    (b) Tanya is more graceful than the other dancers.

58. (a) Helene is the bestest cook in our town.
    (b) Helene is the best cook in our town.

59. (a) Fran's skin is softer than a baby's.
    (b) Fran's skin is more soft than a baby's.

60. (a) Of the two players, Jackson is the more powerful hitter.
    (b) Of the two players, Jackson is the most powerful hitter.

ANSWER KEY

PART A

1. Wally and Steve met her at the restaurant.
2. They walked along the river bank.
3. My brothers and I drove to the lake last Saturday.
4. Buy something for the children and yourself with this money.
5. She found ten dollars in an old tin can.
6. Richard gave me his phone number.
7. I told myself not to worry.
8. We waited in line for an hour.
9. I gave the address to Dave and her.
10. The police officer questioned us about the fire.
11. The person in the mirror was I.
12. You and we should get together soon.
13. He made himself a chocolate milk shake.
14. He always wore a black scarf.
15. The guide led them through the cave.

PART B

16. Marcus's motorcycle is parked outside.
17. This is your last chance.
18. The team won its first game.
19. That monkey is theirs.
20. Not only Melba but also her daughters wear their hair short.
21. The children's toys are in their bedroom.
22. That man is my brother.
23. The churches' bells could be heard all over town.
24. Everyone wants his dinner now.
25. Some of the customers want their money back.
26. The two dogs' bowls are empty.
27. The blue scarf is hers.
28. Each of the men signed his name to the contract.
29. The owners of that store went bankrupt.
30. Either Ed or Pete has quit his job.

PART C

31. Paul and I had a cold soda before lunch.
32. The blue and green parrot is in the big cage.
33. Everyone thinks he is a great player.
34. The water felt good after a long, hot day.
35. He is happy about his new job.

PART D

36. a The black and white dog belongs to Fred.
37. b Those new video games are fun.
38. b Her hair is long, black, and shiny.
39. b I met a man at the movies.
40. b That gun is loaded.

PART E

41. Mike looked angrily at the customer.
42. Hal drives his car very fast.
43. Bernice quietly listened to the radio.
44. Richard sounded very happy about his trip.
45. The telephone rang loudly for several minutes.

PART F

46. a Edna sang the song fantastically.
47. a This candy tastes too sweet.
48. b Vinnie plays the piano very well.
49. b Barnes moves very quickly for a big man.
50. a Felix felt bad about his mistake.

PART G

51. b Of the two secretaries, Howard types faster.
52. a Jeanette has the loudest voice in the choir.
53. a Eugene plays the piano worse than Tony does.
54. b Phil thinks that pigs are the most intelligent of all animals.
55. a The ring is more expensive than the watch.
56. b The sofa is heavier than the table.
57. b Tanya is more graceful than the other dancers.
58. b Helene is the best cook in our town.
59. a Fran's skin is softer than a baby's.
60. a Of the two players, Jackson is the more powerful hitter.

In this chart, circle the number of any items you did not answer correctly. The right-hand side of the chart will tell you the unit number to study for any item that you missed.

Item number:	Unit to study:
1 2 3 4 5 6 7 8 9 10 11 12 13 14 15	UNIT 11: Is the Pronoun Right?
16 17 18 19 20 21 22 23 24 25 26 27 28 29 30	UNIT 12: Does the Word Show Possession?
31 32 33 34 35 36 37 38 39 40	UNIT 13: Is the Adjective Right?
41 42 43 44 45 46 47 48 49 50	UNIT 14: Is the Adverb Right?
51 52 53 54 55 56 57 58 59 60	UNIT 15: How Do You Use Words to Compare?

If you answered all the items in this unit correctly, turn to Unit 17 (page 202).

UNIT 11: IS THE PRONOUN RIGHT?

Look at the underlined words in these sentences. What do they have in common?

> I have met Phyllis before.
>
> He sold Sheila a car.
>
> She called Harry last night.
>
> We saw Peter and Ann at the laundromat.
>
> They gave Marta and me a ride to work.

All of the underlined words are pronouns. All of the underlined words are subjects. I, he, she, we, and they are called **subject pronouns**. You worked with subject pronouns earlier in this book. A subject pronoun is a pronoun that can be used as a subject in a sentence. When you want to use a pronoun as a subject, you use a subject pronoun.

Now, look at the underlined words in these sentences. What do they have in common?

> Phyllis has met me before.
>
> He sold her a car.
>
> She called him last night.
>
> We saw them at the laundromat.
>
> They gave us a ride to work.

All of the underlined words are pronouns. They can take the place of nouns:

> He sold Sheila a car.
>
> He sold her a car.

Take another look at the next two sentences. What else do the underlined pronouns have in common?

> He **sold** her a car.
>
> She **called** him last night.

In both sentences, the underlined pronouns come after the verb. They don't name the subject. They are part of the predicate. They are the *objects* of the action in the sentences. Me, him, her, us, and them are called **object pronouns**.

In this unit, you will look at object pronouns. You will work on knowing when to use object pronouns in a sentence.

CHOOSING THE RIGHT PRONOUN

In the first part of this book, you did a lot of work with subjects and verbs. You worked on finding the simple subject in a sentence. The simple subject is the word that tells you who or what the sentence is about.

Jane met Nick last night.

In this sentence, Jane is the simple subject. It tells you who the sentence is about.

You also worked with subject pronouns earlier in this book. Pronouns are words that can take the place of nouns in a sentence. You use a subject pronoun to take the place of a noun subject.

She met Nick last night.

In this sentence, the pronoun she is the subject. The pronoun she is used in place of Jane.

The sentence tells you that she met somebody last night. Met is the verb in the sentence. It is the word that tells you what she did.

The sentence also tells you whom she met. She met Nick. In the sentence, Nick is the object. In a sentence, an object is a person or thing that is the receiver of the subject's action. Nick is the person that she met. Nick is the object.

There are pronouns that can replace noun subjects. There are also pronouns that can replace noun objects. Look at these sentences:

She met Nick last night.

She met him last night.

The pronoun him replaces Nick in the second sentence. Him is an object pronoun. It can be used in place of the object noun Nick.

Here is a list of subject and object pronouns:

Subject Pronouns	**Object Pronouns**
(pronouns that tell who or what did the action)	(pronouns that tell who or what received the action)
I	me
you	you
he/she/it	him/her/it
we	us
they	them

(Notice that you and it can be subject or object pronouns. You don't have to worry about using you and it incorrectly.)

Pronouns are words that often are used in sentences. Most of the time, it's easy to use pronouns. It's usually easy to tell when to use a subject pronoun and when to use an object pronoun. But sometimes pronouns cause trouble. For example, look at this sentence:

Alma and me walked to the park.

What is the subject of this sentence? This sentence has a compound subject: Alma and me. Look at the pronoun me. Is it a subject pronoun or an object pronoun? It's an object pronoun. It shouldn't be used as a subject pronoun. The subject pronoun I should be used in this sentence.

Alma and I walked to the park.

Now, look at this sentence:

Jackie invited she and I to the party.

Who is the subject of this sentence? Jackie is the subject. What did Jackie do? Jackie invited some people to the party. The people that were invited are the *objects* in this sentence. They are the receivers of the action. The sentence says that Jackie invited she and I to the party. She and I are subject pronouns. They shouldn't be used in this sentence. Object pronouns should be used instead.

Jackie invited her and me to the party.

If you have trouble deciding which pronoun to use, think about the sentence. Does the pronoun name the subject? If it does, then it should be a subject pronoun. Does the pronoun name an object in the sentence? Does it name a receiver of the action? If it does, then it should be an object pronoun.

Try It: Choosing the Right Pronoun

Each sentence contains one or more pronouns. If the wrong pronoun is used in a sentence, rewrite the sentence. Use the right pronoun.

EXAMPLE: Ted gave he the job.

Ted gave him the job.

1. Jack and me found the dog in the woods.

2. Her and I have dated for three years.

3. Ralph drove Ed and I to work.

4. Maria and him are away on vacation.

5. The boss asked me a lot of questions.

6. Either you or us should leave.

7. I met Gail and he at the movies.

8. Ken and he left for the day.

9. Both them and us are happy about it.

10. The traffic made Henry and she late for work.

Check your answers on page 136.

USING PRONOUNS AFTER BE

Take another look at the next sentences. Do you notice anything about where the object pronouns are?

> She met him last night.
>
> Jackie invited her and me to the party.
>
> We saw them at the laundromat.

In each sentence, the object pronouns come *after* the verb. That's because the pronouns show who is receiving the action in the sentence. A pronoun that comes after a verb is usually an object pronoun.

But look at the next two sentences. Which sentence has the right pronoun in it?

> The man in that picture is me.
>
> The man in that picture is I.

The first sentence *looks* like the right one. The pronoun follows the verb. Me is an object pronoun.

But, because of a special grammar rule, the first sentence is *wrong*. The second sentence has the right pronoun in it. Take another look at the second sentence:

The man in that picture is I.

The verb in the sentence is a form of be. As you have seen, the verb be usually breaks the rules! Whenever a pronoun follows a form of the verb be, the pronoun should be a *subject* pronoun. This is because the pronoun renames the subject (man=I).

Using a subject pronoun after a be verb may sound strange to you. Most people would say "It's me" instead of "It's I," for example. However, the rule says to use a subject pronoun after a be verb.

Try It: Using Pronouns After Be

Underline the correct pronoun in each sentence. Remember to use a subject pronoun if the pronoun follows be.

1. The man outside is (he—him).
2. The nurse asked (them—they) to wait.
3. Jane's best friend was (I—me).
4. We sent (her—she) some flowers.
5. They told (us—we) jokes.
6. The people behind you were Ned and (her—she).
7. Your first customers will be (us—we).
8. I will call (he—him) later.
9. The couple in the car is (them—they).
10. The waiter gave (I—me) the check.

Check your answers on page 136.

USING REFLEXIVE PRONOUNS

Look at these sentences. How are they different?

Rob likes him.

Rob likes himself.

In the first sentence, Rob likes another person (him). In the second sentence, Rob likes Rob. The pronoun himself tells you that the person who receives the action is also the person who does the action. The pronoun himself refers back to the subject Rob.

A pronoun that refers back to the subject is called a **reflexive pronoun**. The underlined words in the following sentences are reflexive pronouns:

I saw myself in the mirror.

You saw yourself in the mirror.
(when you is one person)

He saw himself in the mirror. (not hisself)

She saw herself in the mirror.

It saw itself in the mirror.

We saw ourselves in the mirror.

You saw yourselves in the mirror.
(when you is more than one person)

They saw themselves in the mirror.
(not theirselves)

Reflexive pronouns that stand for *one* person or thing end in self. Reflexive pronouns that stand for *more than one* person or thing end in selves.

Only use a reflexive pronoun when the pronoun *receives* the action. Don't use a reflexive pronoun as a subject:

Leonard and myself applied for the job.

(This sentence is WRONG. The pronoun should be a subject pronoun.)

Leonard and I applied for the job.

(This sentence is RIGHT.)

Also, make sure that you use a reflexive pronoun only when the subject of the sentence is also receiving the action.

The noise gave himself a headache.

(This sentence is WRONG. The subject is noise. The noise is not receiving the action. A reflexive pronoun should *not* be used. An object pronoun should be used.)

The noise gave him a headache.

(This sentence is RIGHT.)

Try It: Using Reflexive Pronouns

Each sentence contains one or more pronouns. If the wrong pronoun is used in a sentence, rewrite the sentence. Use the right pronoun. If a sentence has a reflexive pronoun, make sure it is in the right form.

1. Bill and I gave yourselves the money yesterday.
2. My friend and myself are taking a trip.
3. Harry and you should prepare yourselves for some bad news.
4. The boss gave hisself a big raise.
5. I saw me on TV last week.

Check your answers on page 137.

UNIT REVIEW

In this unit, you have looked at three kinds of pronouns: subject, object, and reflexive. Subject pronouns can tell who or what *did* the action. Subject pronouns are used in the subject. Subject pronouns also follow a be verb in a sentence. Object pronouns can tell who or what *received* the action. Object pronouns are used in the predicate. Reflexive pronouns also tell who or what *received* the action. They show that the person (or thing) who did the action also received the action. Reflexive pronouns are used in the predicate.

There is another kind of pronoun. It shows possession or ownership. In the next unit, you will look at pronouns that show possession.

SPELLING AND USAGE HINT: DOUBLING CONSONANTS WITH ED AND ING

You have seen that letters can be added to the end of a word. You have made words plural by adding an s. Look at the underlined words. What endings are added to them?

They **ask** too much of us.

He asked about the price.

That man is asking for change.

You **look** nice.

They looked angry.

I am looking for Harry.

The endings ed and ing are added to these words.

Sometimes the spelling of the word changes a little when ed or ing is added:

We plan to move soon.

They planned to go out.

I am planning a trip.

What happened to the word plan when ed was added to it? What happened when ing was added?

plan + **ed** = **planned**

plan + **ing** = **planning**

Another n was added. The final consonant, n, was doubled.

When should you double the final consonant before adding ed or ing? Double the final consonant when a single vowel (a, e, i, o, u, or y) comes before the consonant in a one-syllable word:

pl–a–n	plan**n**ed	plan**n**ing
r–u–b	rub**b**ed	rub**b**ing
h–o–p	hop**p**ed	hop**p**ing

Don't double the last consonant if another consonant or two vowels comes before it:

wi–s–h	wis**h**ed	wis**h**ing
l–oo–k	loo**k**ed	loo**k**ing

There is an exception to this rule. Never double w or x.

row	rowed	rowing
tax	taxed	taxing

Try It: Doubling Consonants with ed and ing

Complete each sentence by adding the ending given to the word in parentheses.

EXAMPLE: The waiter ___dropped___ the tray. (drop + ed)

1. Melvin angrily ______________ up the letter. (rip + ed)
2. Someone is ______________ on the window. (tap + ing)
3. Dana ______________ Luke's sideburns. (trim + ed)
4. That man is ______________ at Laura. (grin + ing)
5. Mayor Nichols ______________ the star. (greet + ed)
6. It ______________ in the mountains yesterday. (snow + ed)
7. It just ______________ raining. (stop + ed)
8. Ralph is ______________ on his car today. (work + ing)
9. Frank is ______________ the floor. (mop + ing)
10. The movie is ______________. (start + ing)

Check your answers on page 138.

ANSWERS AND EXPLANATIONS

Try It: Choosing the Right Pronoun

1. **Jack and I found the dog in the woods.** Jack and I are the subjects of the sentence. The object pronoun me should not be used in the subject. The subject pronoun I belongs in the subject.
2. **She and I have dated for three years.** She and I are the subjects of the sentence. The object pronoun her should not be used in the subject. The subject pronouns she and I belong in the subject.
3. **Ralph drove Ed and me to work.** Ed and me are the objects of the verb drove. The subject pronoun I should not be used as an object. The object pronoun me should be used as an object.
4. **Maria and he are away on vacation.** Maria and he are the subjects of the sentence. The object pronoun him should not be used in the subject. The subject pronoun he belongs in the subject.
5. **The boss asked me a lot of questions.** This sentence is correct as it is. The object pronoun me is the object of the verb asked.
6. **Either you or we should leave.** You and we are the subjects of the sentence. The object pronoun us should not be used in the subject. The subject pronoun we belongs in the subject.
7. **I met Gail and him at the movies.** Gail and him are the objects of the verb met. The subject pronoun he should not be used as an object. The object pronoun him should be used as an object.
8. **Ken and he left for the day.** This sentence is correct as it is. Ken and the subject pronoun he are the subjects of the sentence.
9. **Both they and we are happy about it.** They and we are the subjects of the sentence. The object pronouns them and us should not be used in the subject. The subject pronouns they and we belong in the subject.
10. **The traffic made Henry and her late for work.** Henry and her are the objects of the verb made. The subject pronoun she should not be used as an object. The object pronoun her should be used as an object.

Try It: Using Pronouns After Be

1. **The man outside is he.** The subject pronoun he is used because the pronoun follows the verb is. The pronoun he renames the subject man.

2. **The nurse asked them to wait.** The object pronoun them is used because the pronoun is the object of the verb asked.
3. **Jane's best friend was I.** The subject pronoun I is used because the pronoun follows the verb was. The pronoun I renames the subject friend.
4. **We sent her some flowers.** The object pronoun her is used because the pronoun is the object of the verb sent.
5. **They told us jokes.** The object pronoun us is used because the pronoun is the object of the verb told.
6. **The people behind you were Ned and she.** The subject pronoun she is used because the pronoun follows the verb were. The pronoun she (with Ned) renames the subject people.
7. **Your first customers will be we.** The subject pronoun we is used because the pronoun follows the verb will be. The pronoun we renames the subject customers.
8. **I will call him later.** The object pronoun him is used because the pronoun is the object of the verb will call.
9. **The couple in the car is they.** The subject pronoun they is used because the pronoun follows the verb is. The pronoun they renames the subject couple.
10. **The waiter gave me the check.** The object pronoun me is used because the pronoun is the object of the verb gave.

Try It: Using Reflexive Pronouns

1. **Bill and I gave you the money yesterday.** The subject of the sentence is Bill and I. Bill and I did not get the money. The reflexive pronoun yourselves should not be used. The object pronoun you should be used.
2. **My friend and I are taking a trip.** The subject of the sentence is friend and I. The reflexive pronoun myself should not be used in the subject. The subject pronoun I belongs in the subject.
3. **Harry and you should prepare yourselves for some bad news.** This sentence is correct as it is. The subject of the sentence is Harry and you. Harry and you are also receiving the action, so the reflexive pronoun yourselves should be used.
4. **The boss gave himself a big raise.** The subject of the sentence is boss. The boss is also receiving the action, so the reflexive pronoun himself should be used. Hisself is not a standard word.
5. **I saw myself on TV last week.** The subject of the sentence is I. The subject I is also receiving the action, so the reflexive pronoun myself should be used.

Try It: Doubling Consonants with ed and ing

1. **Melvin angrily ripped up the letter.** Rip is a one-syllable word. It ends with one vowel plus a consonant (i–p). Double the final consonant when you add the ending.
2. **Someone is tapping on the window.** Tap is a one-syllable word. It ends with one vowel plus a consonant (a–p). Double the final consonant when you add the ending.
3. **Dana trimmed Luke's sideburns.** Trim is a one-syllable word. It ends with one vowel plus a consonant (i–m). Double the final consonant when you add the ending.
4. **That man is grinning at Laura.** Grin is a one-syllable word. It ends with one vowel plus a consonant (i–n). Double the final consonant when you add the ending.
5. **Mayor Nichols greeted the star.** Greet ends with *two* vowels plus a consonant (ee–t). *Don't* double the final consonant.
6. **It snowed in the mountains yesterday.** Snow ends in w. *Don't* double the final consonant.
7. **It just stopped raining.** Stop is a one-syllable word. It ends with a vowel plus a consonant (o–p). Double the final consonant when you add the ending.
8. **Ralph is working on his car today.** Work ends with *two* consonants. *Don't* double the final consonant.
9. **Frank is mopping the floor.** Mop is a one-syllable word. It ends with a vowel plus a consonant (o–p). Double the final consonant when you add the ending.
10. **The movie is starting.** Start ends with *two* consonants. *Don't* double the final consonant.

UNIT 12: DOES THE WORD SHOW POSSESSION?

Look at the next two sentences. How are they alike? How are they different?

This wallet belongs to Hank.

This is Hank's wallet.

Both sentences tell you the same thing. They tell you whom a wallet belongs to. But the sentences use different words to tell you this.

This wallet belongs to Hank.

This is Hank's wallet.

In the second sentence, the word Hank's shows you that the wallet belongs to Hank. Hank's is the **possessive form** of the word Hank.

A noun is a word that names a person, place, thing, or idea. The possessive form of a noun shows that something belongs to that person, place, thing, or idea. In this unit, you will take a close look at forming the possessive of nouns. You'll also work on using possessive pronouns.

FORMING NOUN POSSESSIVES

Think back to the sentences about Hank and the wallet. What happened to the word Hank in the second sentence?

This wallet belongs to Hank.

This is Hank's wallet.

Something was added to the word Hank. Something was added to change Hank into the possessive form.

Hank Hank's

To change a singular noun into its possessive form, you add 's to the noun. The mark before the s (') is called an **apostrophe**. You always use an apostrophe to show the possessive form of a noun.

This is Hank's wallet.

The dog's toys are in the yard.

The bus's windows are broken.

The tricky part of forming the possessive of a noun is using the apostrophe. Look at these two sentences:

The dog's toys are in the yard.

The dogs' toys are in the yard.

What is the difference between the two underlined words? In the first word, the apostrophe comes before the s: dog's. In the second word, the apostrophe comes *after* the s: dogs'. The two words look almost exactly alike. But there's a big difference between them. The word dog's tells you that *one* dog owns the toys. The word dogs' tells you that *more than one* dog owns the toys.

Earlier in this book, you looked at forming noun plurals. For most nouns, you form the plural by adding an s to the word:

one dog   two dogs

When you form the possessive of a noun, the place where you put the apostrophe is important. It tells you whether the noun is singular or plural.

one dog's toys   two dogs' toys

There are three basic rules for forming the possessive of a noun. If you know the rules, you can form the possessive of *any* noun. Here are the three rules:

1. To form the possessive of any singular noun, add an apostrophe (') and s to the noun.

   dog, dog's   Hank, Hank's   class, class's   Chris, Chris's

2. To form the possessive of a plural noun that ends in s, just add an apostrophe:

   dogs, dogs'   classes, classes'

3. Some nouns have irregular plural forms. Some plural nouns do not end in s. To form the possessive of a plural noun that does not end in s, add an apostrophe and s to the noun.

   children, children's   mice, mice's

Here is another way to think about forming possessives:

- Add an ' to plural nouns that end in s.
- Add an 's to all other nouns.

Remember that you use an apostrophe when you form the *possessive* of a noun. Don't use an apostrophe to form a noun plural.

The boy's ran down the street.

(The underlined word is WRONG. In this sentence, you need the plural form of the word boy. All you have to do is add an s to the word.)

The boys ran down the street.

(The underlined word in this sentence is RIGHT. Boys is the plural of the word boy.)

Try It: Forming Noun Possessives

Fill in the blank with the correct possessive form of each noun.

EXAMPLE: This book belongs to Morris. This is Morris's book.

1. This coat belongs to Betty. This is _______________ coat.
2. This lunchroom belongs to the employees.
   This is the _______________ lunchroom.
3. This car belongs to Sam. This is _______________ car.
4. These mittens belong to the children.
   These are the _______________ mittens.
5. This bike belongs to my son.
   This is my _______________ bike.
6. This union belongs to the teachers.
   This is the _______________ union.
7. This office belongs to the boss.
   This is the _______________ office.
8. These boots belong to the fishermen.
   These are the _______________ boots.
9. This bowl belongs to the cats.
   This is the _______________ bowl.
10. These seats belong to the women.
    These are the _______________ seats.

Check your answers on page 150.

USING POSSESSIVE PRONOUNS

So far in this unit, you've worked on forming the possessive of nouns:

This wallet belongs to Hank.

This is Hank's wallet.

Pronouns are words that take the place of nouns. Pronouns also have possessive forms. Look at these two sentences:

This wallet belongs to him.

This is his wallet.

His is the possessive form of the pronoun him. It shows whom the wallet belongs to.

Many pronouns have two different possessive forms. One form is used when the thing that is owned is named after the pronoun. The other form is used when the thing that is owned is *not* named after the pronoun. Look at these sentences:

This book belongs to me.

This is my book.

This book is mine.

Both my and mine are possessive forms. They stand for the same person: me. My is used when the thing that is owned (the book) is named after the pronoun. Mine is used when the thing is *not* named after the pronoun.

Here are the possessive pronoun forms:

This book belongs to me.
This is my book.
This book is mine.

This book belongs to you.
This is your book.
This book is yours.

This book belongs to her.
This is her book.
This book is hers.

This book belongs to them.
This is their book.
This book is theirs.

This book belongs to us.
This is our book.
This book is ours.

This book belongs to him.
This is his book.
This book is his.

This book belongs to it.
This is its book.

When you form the possessive of a noun, you always use an apostrophe. But you do *not* use an apostrophe with the possessive forms of pronouns.

> The coat in the closet is her's.
>
> (The pronoun in this sentence is WRONG. Don't use an apostrophe with a possessive pronoun.)
>
> The coat in the closet is hers.
>
> (The pronoun in this sentence is RIGHT.)

Try It: Using Possessive Pronouns

Fill in the blanks with the correct possessive pronouns.

EXAMPLE: This snake belongs to me.

It is ___my___ snake. This snake is ___mine___.

1. This apartment belongs to them.

   This is _________ apartment. This apartment is _________.

2. This farm belongs to us.

   This is _________ farm. This farm is _________.

3. This collar belongs to it.

   This is _________ collar.

4. This necklace belongs to her.

   This is _________ necklace. This necklace is _________.

5. This newspaper belongs to you.

   This is _________ newspaper. This newspaper is _________.

6. This glass belongs to him.

   This is __________ glass. This glass is __________.

7. This job belongs to me.

   This is __________ job. This job is __________.

Check your answers on page 151.

CHOOSING THE RIGHT POSSESSIVE PRONOUN

How would you rewrite this sentence?

Hank lost Hank's wallet.

You would probably write this:

Hank lost his wallet.

You don't need to repeat the word Hank after the verb. Your reader would know that the pronoun his stands for Hank.

Look at these sentences. Which word does the pronoun stand for in each sentence?

Teresa saves her money.

The workers park their cars in the lot.

In the first sentence, the pronoun her stands for Teresa. In the second sentence, the pronoun their stands for workers.

Earlier in this book, you worked on matching subjects to the right verbs. Singular verbs match singular subjects. Plural verbs match plural subjects.

Teresa saves her money.

The workers park their cars in the lot.

Possessive pronouns are like subjects and verbs. There are singular and plural possessive pronouns. Possessive pronouns should match the word that they stand for in a sentence.

Teresa saves her money.

In this sentence, the possessive pronoun her stands for Teresa. Teresa is a woman's name. It is singular. The singular possessive pronoun her matches Teresa.

The workers park their cars in the lot.

In this sentence, the possessive pronoun their stands for workers. Workers is a plural word. The plural possessive pronoun their matches workers.

It's usually easy to match a verb to a subject. Likewise, it's usually easy to match a pronoun to the word that it stands for. But it isn't always easy. In Units 5, 6, and 7 of this book, you worked on matching verbs to subjects like these:

Our team is the best in the state.

Everyone likes the new boss.

Either of the plans is good.

Some of the cakes are gone.

These subjects can be hard to match because it isn't always easy to tell if they are singular or plural. It can be hard to match verbs to these subjects. It can also be hard to match possessive pronouns to them.

The team missed (its—their) plane.

Everyone knew (her—his—their) job.

Either of the plans had (its—their) good points.

In Units 5, 6, and 7, you worked on how to match these kinds of subjects to the right verbs. You follow the same steps for matching these words to the right possessive pronouns.

Use the information that follows to review the steps for matching. If you have trouble with a step, you may want to review it some more. Go back to the unit that shows how to match the words to the right verbs. Remember, if you know the rules for matching subjects and verbs, you know the rules for matching subjects and possessive pronouns.

1. Remember that these words are usually singular (see Unit 5). They match singular pronouns:

army	committee	family	mob	staff
audience	couple	group	public	
class	jury	herd	team	

The team missed its plane.

2. These words are singular even though they look plural (see Unit 5):

athletics	mathematics	mumps	politics
economics	measles	news	United States

The United States sent its troops to the area.

3. These words are plural even though they may stand for one thing (see Unit 5):

eyeglasses pants trousers scissors

The trousers are missing their buttons.

4. These words are always singular and take singular pronouns (see Unit 6):

everyone	everybody	everything
someone	somebody	something
no one	nobody	nothing
anyone	anybody	anything

Everyone knew his job.

(NOTE: Look at the example. The sentence doesn't tell you whether the word everyone refers to every man or every woman. If you can't tell whether a word stands for every man or every woman, use the pronouns he, him, his, and himself. This may not be fair to women, but it's usually accepted as a rule.)

5. These words are always singular and take singular pronouns (see Unit 6):

each	another	either	much
one	other	neither	

Either of the plans had its good points.

6. These words are always plural and take plural pronouns (see Unit 6):

both few many several

Both of the plans had their good points.

7. These words may be singular or plural (see Unit 6):

all	any	most	none
some	part	half	

When one of these words stands for a singular word, it is singular.

All of the building has lost its hot water.

When it stands for a plural word, it is plural.

None of the apartments have lost their heat.

8. If a compound is joined by and, the pronoun is plural (see Unit 7).

   Anita and Max live with their parents.

9. If a compound is joined by either/or, neither/nor, or not only/but also, the pronoun matches with the compound part that is closer to it (see Unit 7).

   Either Max or Anita lives with her parents.
   Neither Anita nor Max lives with his parents.
   Not only Max but also his sisters live with their parents.

Try It: Choosing the Right Possessive Pronoun

Underline the correct pronoun in each sentence.

EXAMPLE: The dog and the cats want (its—their) food.

1. Everything is in (its—their) place.
2. Rita and Joey gave (its—their) pet bird away.
3. Either Jean or Ann lost (her—their) gloves.
4. The jury reached (its—their) decision.
5. Several of the customers wanted (its—their) money back.
6. Part of the cake is missing (its—their) icing.
7. The news has (its—their) bright side.
8. Not only Matt but also his sons drink (his—their) coffee black.
9. These pants have holes in (its—their) pockets.
10. None of the people like (its—their) food.
11. The committee presented (its—their) plan to the president.
12. The measles left (its—their) mark on the young boy.

13. The scissors have lost (its—their) sharpness.

14. Someone left (his—their) keys on the table.

15. Each wants (his—their) share of the profits.

16. Many lost (his—their) homes in the flood.

17. Half of the workers received increases in (his—their) pay.

18. Clare and Jim bought (his—their) refrigerator at Norton's Store.

19. Neither Pat nor Steve likes (his—their) job.

20. Much of the ice has melted in (its—their) tray.

Check your answers on page 152.

UNIT REVIEW

In this unit, you've worked on two things. First, you've worked on how to put a noun into its **possessive** form. Plural nouns that end in s get an apostrophe. All other nouns get an apostrophe (') and s.

The second thing you've worked on is **possessive pronouns**. You've seen that some possessive pronouns have two different forms. One form is used when the pronoun stands by itself (This mug is mine.). The other form is used when the pronoun goes with a noun (This is my mug.). You've also worked on matching pronouns to the words they stand for.

SPELLING AND USAGE HINT: CONTRACTIONS

You have seen that apostrophes are used with nouns to show possession:

Mark's brother is in the army.

Apostrophes can be used in other ways. Another way that apostrophes can be used is in **contractions**. A contraction is a shorter way of writing words that are often together. Here are some contractions. Notice where the apostrophe goes:

Word Pair	Contraction
I am	I'm
you are	you're
he is	he's
she is	she's
it is	it's
we are	we're
they are	they're

The apostrophe takes the place of the letter that is left out:

I am = I'm

In this unit, you have looked at possessive pronouns. Some possessive pronouns sound just like contractions. As you know, however, they mean very different things.

Possessive Pronoun	Contraction
your (belonging to you)	you're (you are)
its (belonging to it)	it's (it is) (it has)
their (belonging to them)	they're (they are)

Possessive pronouns never have apostrophes in them. However, contractions always have apostrophes.

When you write a contraction, think of the two words that it stands for. That will help you catch mistakes.

The dogs buried they're (they are) bones.

(This contraction is WRONG. They're stands for they are. You don't need they are in this sentence. You need the possessive pronoun their.)

The dogs buried their bones.

(This sentence is RIGHT.)

Try It: Contractions

Underline the correct word in each sentence.

EXAMPLE: (Their—They're) late for work.

1. (Your—You're) sister called me.
2. (Their—They're) waiting for you.
3. This book is missing (its—it's) cover.
4. (Your—You're) going to get a raise.
5. (Its—It's) twelve o'clock.
6. The Taylors invited the neighbors to (their—they're) party.
7. (Its—It's) cold outside today.
8. I like (your—you're) hat.
9. (Their—They're) too busy to go out.
10. (Its—It's) bowls are in the kitchen.

Check your answers on page 153.

ANSWERS AND EXPLANATIONS

Try It: Forming Noun Possessives

1. **This coat belongs to Betty. This is Betty's coat.** Betty is a singular noun. Add an apostrophe (') and s to make the singular noun possessive.
2. **This lunchroom belongs to the employees. This is the employees' lunchroom.** Employees is a plural noun that ends in s. Just add an apostrophe to make the plural noun possessive.
3. **This car belongs to Sam. This is Sam's car.** Sam is a singular noun. Add an apostrophe (') and s to make the singular noun possessive.
4. **These mittens belong to the children. These are the children's mittens.** Children is a plural noun, but it does not end in s. Add an apostrophe and s to make the noun possessive.

5. **This bike belongs to my son. This is my son's bike.** Son is a singular noun. Add an apostrophe and s to make the singular noun possessive.
6. **This union belongs to the teachers. This is the teachers' union.** Teachers is a plural noun that ends in s. Just add an apostrophe to make the plural noun possessive.
7. **This office belongs to the boss. This is the boss's office.** Boss is a singular noun. Add an apostrophe and s to make the singular noun possessive.
8. **These boots belong to the fishermen. These are the fishermen's boots.** Fishermen is a plural noun, but it does not end in s. Add an apostrophe and s to make the noun possessive.
9. **This bowl belongs to the cats. This is the cats' bowl.** Cats is a plural noun that ends in s. Just add an apostrophe to make the plural noun possessive.
10. **These seats belong to the women. These are the women's seats.** Women is a plural noun, but it does not end in s. Add an apostrophe and s to make the noun possessive.

Try It: Using Possessive Pronouns

1. **This apartment belongs to them. This is their apartment. This apartment is theirs.** Their and theirs are possessive forms of the pronoun them. Use their when the thing that is owned (the apartment) is named after the pronoun. Use theirs when the thing is not named after the pronoun.
2. **This farm belongs to us. This is our farm. This farm is ours.** Our and ours are possessive forms of the pronoun us. Use our when the thing that is owned (the farm) is named after the pronoun. Use ours when the thing is not named after the pronoun.
3. **This collar belongs to it. This is its collar.** Its is the possessive form of the pronoun it.
4. **This necklace belongs to her. This is her necklace. This necklace is hers.** Her and hers are possessive forms of the pronoun her. Use her when the thing that is owned (the necklace) is named after the pronoun. Use hers when the thing is not named after the pronoun.
5. **This newspaper belongs to you. This is your newspaper. This newspaper is yours.** Your and yours are possessive forms of the pronoun you. Use your when the thing that is owned (the newspaper) is named after the pronoun. Use yours when the thing is not named after the pronoun.

6. **This glass belongs to him. This is his glass. This glass is his.** His is the possessive form of the pronoun him.

7. **This job belongs to me. This is my job. This job is mine.** My and mine are possessive forms of the pronoun me. Use my when the thing that is owned (the job) is named after the pronoun. Use mine when the thing is not named after the pronoun.

Try It: Choosing the Right Possessive Pronoun

1. **Everything is in its place.** Everything is singular. The singular pronoun its matches everything.
2. **Rita and Joey gave their pet bird away.** The compound subject is connected by and. Therefore, the subject is plural. The plural pronoun their matches the plural subject.
3. **Either Jean or Ann lost her gloves.** The compound subject is connected by either/or. The pronoun her matches the compound part that is closer to it—the singular noun Ann.
4. **The jury reached its decision.** Jury is singular. It stands for one group of people. The singular pronoun its matches jury.
5. **Several of the customers wanted their money back.** Several is plural. The pronoun their matches several.
6. **Part of the cake is missing its icing.** In this sentence, part stands for the singular noun cake. Therefore, part is singular. The singular pronoun its matches part.
7. **The news has its bright side.** News is singular. The singular pronoun its matches news.
8. **Not only Matt but also his sons drink their coffee black.** The compound subject is connected by not only/but also. The pronoun their matches the subject part that is closer to it—the plural noun sons.
9. **These pants have holes in their pockets.** Pants is plural. The plural pronoun their matches pants.
10. **None of the people like their food.** In this sentence, none stands for the plural noun people. Therefore, none is plural. The plural pronoun their matches none.
11. **The committee presented its plan to the president.** Committee is singular. It stands for one group of people. The pronoun it matches committee.
12. **The measles left its mark on the young boy.** Measles is singular. The singular pronoun its matches measles.
13. **The scissors have lost their sharpness.** Scissors is plural. The plural pronoun their matches scissors.

14. **Someone left his keys on the table.** Someone is singular. The singular pronoun his matches someone.

15. **Each wants his share of the profits.** Each is singular. The singular pronoun his matches each.

16. **Many lost their homes in the flood.** Many is plural. The plural pronoun their matches many.

17. **Half of the workers received increases in their pay.** In this sentence, half stands for the plural noun workers. Therefore, half is plural. The plural pronoun their matches half.

18. **Clare and Jim bought their refrigerator at Norton's Store.** The compound subject is joined by and. Therefore, it is plural. The plural pronoun their matches the compound subject.

19. **Neither Pat nor Steve likes his job.** The compound subject is joined by neither/nor. The singular pronoun his matches the compound part that is closer to it—the singular noun Steve.

20. **Much of the ice has melted in its tray.** Much is singular. The singular pronoun its matches much.

Try It: Contractions

1. **Your sister called me.** Your is a possessive pronoun. It tells you *whose* sister called me.

2. **They're waiting for you.** They're stands for they are: They are waiting for you.

3. **This book is missing its cover.** Its is a possessive pronoun. It tells you that the cover belongs to the book.

4. **You're going to get a raise.** You're stands for you are: You are going to get a raise.

5. **It's twelve o'clock.** It's stands for it is: It is twelve o'clock.

6. **The Taylors invited the neighbors to their party.** Their is a possessive pronoun. It tells you *whose* party the neighbors were invited to.

7. **It's cold outside today.** It's stands for it is: It is cold outside today.

8. **I like your hat.** Your is a possessive pronoun. It tells you *whose* hat I like.

9. **They're too busy to go out.** They're stands for they are: They are too busy to go out.

10. **Its bowls are in the kitchen.** Its is a possessive pronoun. It tells you *whose* bowls are in the kitchen.

UNIT 13: IS THE ADJECTIVE RIGHT?

Here is an ad you have seen before. Notice the underlined words in the ad:

February 15 Is Winter Sales Day at Carson's!

Here are just some of the great buys:

—Handsome, hand-knit sweaters by Gavin LaPell are on sale for $35.

—Our popular fur-lined hats are only $20.

—All scarves and gloves are 50% off.

—Wool socks in our hosiery department are 40% off.

Now imagine if the underlined words were changed like this:

February 15 Is Winter Sales Day at Carson's!

Here are just some of the lousy buys:

—Ugly, machine-made sweaters by Gavin LaPell are $35.

—Our unpopular overpriced hats are $20.

—Few scarves and gloves are 50% off.

—Rubber socks in our hosiery department are 40% off.

Only the underlined words were changed in the ad. But, as you can see, the two ads are very different. Nobody would want to buy these clothes!

The underlined words in the ads are **adjectives**. Adjectives are words that describe people, places, things, or ideas. Adjectives are very important to the meaning of sentences.

Look at the adjective in this sentence. What does it describe?

Handsome sweaters by Gavin LaPell are on sale for $35.

The adjective handsome describes the sweaters. The adjective tells *what kind* of sweaters are on sale. Adjectives also tell *which* and *how many*:

Our fur-lined hats are only $20.

(The adjective tells *which* hats are only $20.)

All scarves and gloves are 50% off.

(The adjective tells *how many* scarves and gloves are 50% off.)

In the last two units, you have looked at nouns and pronouns. In this unit, you will look at words that describe nouns and pronouns. You will look at adjectives.

FINDING ADJECTIVES

Most of the time, it's easy to find the adjectives in a sentence. Adjectives usually go in front of the words they describe:

Handsome sweaters are on sale.

Our fur-lined hats are only $20.

In both of these sentences, the adjective comes before the word it describes. But sometimes adjectives go after verbs. Look at this sentence:

Ralph is angry.

In Unit 4, you worked with verbs. You saw that a verb can link a subject to a description of the subject. A verb can link a subject to an adjective.

A verb that links a subject to an adjective is a **linking verb**. The linking verbs are underlined in these sentences. They link subjects to adjectives:

The water feels cold.

(The adjective cold tells how the water feels.)

You seem upset.

(The adjective upset tells how you seem.)

The house looks beautiful.

(The adjective beautiful tells how the house looks.)

The baby is tired and hungry.

(The adjectives tired and hungry tell what the baby is.)

Try It: Finding Adjectives

Underline the adjectives in each sentence.

EXAMPLE: The yellow car ran off the road.

1. My gray winter coat is at the cleaner's.
2. Seymour feels sick about his job.
3. We ate breakfast at the new diner.
4. Icy rain fell on the joggers.
5. A dim lamp lit the room.
6. The coat is washable.
7. She wore a black, feathered hat to the party.
8. The news sounds bad.
9. The dentist pulled out two teeth.
10. The car is old and rusty.

Check your answers on page 163.

USING COMMAS WITH ADJECTIVES

Look at the next sentences. What happens when the two adjectives are put together in one sentence?

Our beautiful sweaters are on sale.

Our washable sweaters are on sale.

Our beautiful, washable sweaters are on sale.

A comma comes between the two adjectives when they are put together.

Using one adjective to describe something is easy. You don't have to worry about using commas. But when you put two or more adjectives together, you have to think about commas. You have to think about whether or not to use them.

Most of the time, you use a comma with two or more adjectives. For example, look at these sentences:

> Our beautiful, washable sweaters are on sale.
>
> The sweaters are beautiful, washable, and inexpensive.

You use the commas to separate the adjectives. Don't put a comma after the last adjective in the group. Don't put a comma between an adjective and the word that it describes.

There are two times when you don't use a comma to separate two adjectives. The first time is when the word and already comes between the adjectives. When the word and separates two adjectives, don't use a comma.

> The sweaters are blue, and green.
>
> (The comma in this sentence is WRONG. The word and already separates the adjectives blue and green. A comma is not needed.)
>
> The sweaters are blue and green.
>
> (This sentence is RIGHT.)

However, you *should* use commas when and is used with more than two adjectives.

> The sweaters are beautiful, washable, and inexpensive.

The other time that you don't need a comma is when one of the two adjectives can be thought of as part of the noun. For example, look at this sentence:

> The brown turtleneck sweaters are for sale.

Both brown and turtleneck are adjectives. But you can think of the word turtleneck as being part of the noun sweaters. In a sentence like this, you don't need a comma between the two adjectives.

Try It: Using Commas with Adjectives

Read each sentence. See if commas are used correctly. If commas are not used correctly, rewrite the sentence. Put commas where they belong in the sentence.

EXAMPLE: My green, blue, and orange, tie is missing.
My green, blue, and orange tie is missing.

1. These peaches are juicy ripe and sweet.

2. Sue put catsup on her scrambled, eggs.

3. These green beans are fresh, and delicious.

4. My brother is tall, dark, and handsome.

5. The house is dark cold and empty.

6. The brown, gray, and black, cat scratched at the door.

7. Greta wore a striped, dress.

8. Rick seems nervous, and afraid.

Check your answers on page 163.

USING THIS, THAT, THESE, AND THOSE

Look at these two sentences. How are they different?

This house is for sale.

That house is for sale.

The sentences are different because these two words are different:

this

that

This and that are adjectives. They are singular. They are used to point out a person or a thing. They point out which person or which thing the speaker means. This is used to point to a person or a thing near the speaker. That is used to point to a person or a thing farther away from the speaker.

Here are two more adjectives:

these

those

These and those are plural adjectives. Like this, these is used to point to people or things that are near the speaker.

This house is for sale.

These houses are for sale.

Like that, those is used to point to people or things that are farther away from the speaker.

That house is for sale.

Those houses are for sale.

It's usually easy to use the adjectives this, that, these, and those. But sometimes these words are not used correctly. For example, look at these sentences:

This here food is good.

That there dress is pretty.

The words this and that already tell you if the person or thing is near or farther away. The words here and there aren't needed. Don't use here or there with this, that, these, or those.

This food is good.

That dress is pretty.

Here is another problem sentence:

Them tomatoes are ripe.

The word them is an object pronoun. It isn't a word that points to something. Don't use them in place of these or those.

These tomatoes are ripe.

Those tomatoes are ripe.

Use this, that, these, or those to point to people or things. However, don't use them in place of the words a or an.

There was this song on the radio about pigs.

(In this sentence, the word this is WRONG. The word a should be used.)

There was a song on the radio about pigs.

(The sentence is RIGHT.)

Try It: Using This, That, These, and Those

Read each sentence. Check to see if the words this, that, these, and those are used correctly. If a word is not used correctly, rewrite the sentence.

1. This scissors are very sharp.

2. Bring me that there book.

3. Them dishes are dirty.

4. This pants are too short.

5. Them coats are expensive.

6. That there hat is mine.

7. There was this man on the bus yesterday.

8. Most of those fruit tastes good.

Check your answers on page 164.

UNIT REVIEW

In this unit, you've worked with adjectives. Adjectives are words that describe people, places, things, or ideas. Adjectives can go before the words they describe. Adjectives can also go after linking verbs.

You've seen how to use commas with more than one adjective. You've also seen how to use the adjectives this, that, these, and those correctly.

In this unit, you've looked at words that describe nouns and pronouns—adjectives. In the next unit, you'll look at words that describe verbs—adverbs.

SPELLING AND USAGE HINT: PREFIXES

You have seen that letters can be added to a word. For example, you have made nouns plural by adding an s. You have put verbs in the past tense by adding ed. When you add letters to a word, you give the word a different meaning. When you add an s to a noun, you show that you mean *more than one*. When you add ed to a verb, you show that the verb is in the past tense.

Letters that are added to the *beginning* of a word are called **prefixes**. Look at these words. The prefixes are underlined. Notice that prefixes give the words different meanings:

happy, unhappy

like, dislike

write, rewrite

game, pregame

Here are some commonly used prefixes:

Prefix	Meaning	Examples
co–	with	copilot, cooperate
dis–	opposite of	disrespectful, dissimilar
il–	not	illegal, illegible
im–	not	improper, immoral
ir–	not	irregular, irrational
mis–	wrong	misplace, misspell
un–	not	uninvited, unnecessary

Now, look at this word:

immoral

The last letter of the prefix is m (im–). The first letter of the base word is m (–moral). **Both** letters belong in the word.

Here are some other words with double letters. One letter is from the prefix. The other letter is from the base word:

co + operate = cooperate
dis + similar = dissimilar
il + legal = illegal
ir + regular = irregular
mis + spell = misspell
un + necessary = unnecessary

Don't make a common spelling mistake. Remember to use both letters.

Try It: Prefixes

Read each sentence. See if the words are spelled correctly. If words are not spelled correctly, rewrite the sentence.

EXAMPLE: One word is mispelled.

One word is misspelled.

1. Carla is responsible, but her brother is iresponsible.

2. Sometimes Bill is very imature.

3. We need your coperation to get this project done.

4. Dino feels unwanted and uneeded.

5. The boss is disatisfied with my work.

6. The Smiths are very uneighborly.

Check your answers on page 164.

ANSWERS AND EXPLANATIONS

Try It: Finding Adjectives

1. **My gray winter coat is at the cleaner's.** The adjectives gray and winter describe the coat.
2. **Seymour feels sick about his job.** The adjective sick describes Seymour. The linking verb feels links the subject Seymour to the adjective sick.
3. **We ate breakfast at the new diner.** The adjective new describes the diner.
4. **Icy rain fell on the joggers.** The adjective icy describes the rain.
5. **A dim lamp lit the room.** The adjective dim describes the lamp.
6. **The coat is washable.** The adjective washable describes the coat. The linking verb is links the subject coat to the adjective washable.
7. **She wore a black, feathered hat to the party.** The adjectives black and feathered describe the hat.
8. **The news sounds bad.** The adjective bad describes the news. The linking verb sounds links the subject news to the adjective bad.
9. **The dentist pulled out two teeth.** The adjective two tells how many teeth were pulled.
10. **The car is old and rusty.** The adjectives old and rusty describe the car. The linking verb is links the subject car to the adjectives old and rusty.

Try It: Using Commas with Adjectives

1. **These peaches are juicy, ripe, and sweet.** When the word and is used with *three or more* adjectives, separate the adjectives with commas.
2. **Sue put catsup on her scrambled _ eggs.** Don't use a comma to separate an adjective (scrambled) from a noun (eggs).
3. **These green beans are fresh _ and delicious.** Don't use a comma when *two* adjectives are separated by the word and.
4. **My brother is tall, dark, and handsome.** This sentence is correct as it is. When the word and is used with *three or more* adjectives, separate the adjectives with commas.
5. **The house is dark, cold, and empty.** When the word and is used with *three or more* adjectives, separate the adjectives with commas.

6. **The brown, gray, and black cat scratched at the door.** Use commas to separate three adjectives joined by and. However, don't use a comma after the last adjective in the group. A comma is never used to separate an adjective (black) from a noun (cat).
7. **Greta wore a striped dress.** Don't use a comma to separate an adjective (striped) from a noun (dress).
8. **Rick seems nervous and afraid.** Don't use a comma when two adjectives are separated by the word and.

Try It: Using This, That, These, and Those

1. **These scissors are very sharp.** The noun scissors is plural. The plural adjective these matches the plural noun.
2. **Bring me that book.** Don't use there with that.
3. **Those dishes are dirty.** Them is an object pronoun. It doesn't belong in this sentence. The adjective those (or these) belongs in the sentence.
4. **These pants are too short.** The noun pants is plural. The plural adjective these matches the plural noun.
5. **Those coats are expensive.** Them is an object pronoun. It doesn't belong in this sentence. The adjective those (or these) belongs in this sentence.
6. **That hat is mine.** Don't use there with that.
7. **There was a man on the bus yesterday.** Don't use this in place of a.
8. **Most of that fruit tastes good.** Fruit is a singular noun. The singular adjective that matches the singular noun.

Try It: Prefixes

1. **Carla is responsible, but her brother is irresponsible.**
   Ir + responsible = irresponsible
2. **Sometimes Bill is very immature.** Im + mature = immature
3. **We need your cooperation to get this project done.**
   Co + operation = cooperation
4. **Dino feels unwanted and unneeded.**
   Un + needed = unneeded.
5. **The boss is dissatisfied with my work.**
   Dis + satisfied = dissatisfied
6. **The Smiths are very unneighborly.**
   Un + neighborly = unneighborly

UNIT 14: IS THE ADVERB RIGHT?

Read these two stories. Pay close attention to the underlined words:

A man entered the building early yesterday. He walked slowly down the hall. He went up to the last door in the hall. He knocked quietly on the door. No one answered. The man politely knocked again. This time, the door opened.

"I have a message for you," the man said warmly to the very surprised person inside.

A man entered the building late yesterday. He walked quickly down the hall. He went up to the last door in the hall. He knocked loudly on the door. No one answered. The man rudely knocked again. This time, the door opened.

"I have a message for you," the man said coldly to the very surprised person inside.

Each story is about the same thing. Each story has the same subjects and verbs. Only the underlined words have been changed. But did you notice a difference between the two stories? Because of the underlined words, the two stories are different.

The underlined words are **adverbs**. Adverbs are like adjectives. They shape the meaning of sentences. They describe other words in the sentence.

In this unit, you'll take a look at adverbs. You'll see when to use adverbs instead of adjectives. You'll work on ways to avoid mistakes when you use adverbs.

LOOKING FOR ADVERBS

Look at this sentence again. What does the underlined word describe?

He walked slowly down the hall.

The underlined word is an adverb. The adverb slowly describes the verb walked. It tells *how* the man walked.

Adverbs can show how something is done. Adverbs can also tell *when* and *where* something is done.

A man entered the building early yesterday.

(The adverb yesterday tells *when* the man entered the building.)

He went up to the last door in the hall.

(The adverb up tells *where* the man went.)

Adverbs can also describe adjectives and other adverbs:

. . . the man said warmly to the very surprised person inside.

(The adverb very describes the adjective surprised. It shows *how* surprised the person inside was.)

A man entered the building early yesterday.

(The adverb early describes the adverb yesterday. It tells *when* the man entered the building yesterday.)

Try It: Looking for Adverbs

In each sentence, underline the adverbs once. Underline the word that the adverb describes twice.

EXAMPLE: The doctor listened closely to my heart.

1. Wilma entered the room quietly.
2. George politely asked the man a question.
3. Jean whispered softly into his ear.
4. Mel shops wisely.
5. Frank stared at the very pretty woman.
6. The bomb squad examined the ticking box carefully.
7. Mickey hit the ball hard into left field.
8. That candidate speaks foolishly about the economy.
9. We went to the movies yesterday.
10. The protesters marched peacefully.

Check your answers on page 175.

TURNING ADJECTIVES INTO ADVERBS

In the last unit, you worked with adjectives. Adjectives are words that describe nouns and pronouns.

Marla has a beautiful voice.

The adjective in this sentence is beautiful. Beautiful is used to describe Marla's voice.

Now, look at this sentence:

Marla sings beautifully.

What does the word beautifully describe? It describes how Marla sings. Beautifully is an adverb.

Look at the adjective and the adverb again. What is the difference between the two words?

beautiful

beautifully

The adverb is almost the same as the adjective. The only difference is the ly at the end of the word.

Most of the time, it's easy to turn an adjective into an adverb. All you have to do is add ly to the end of the adjective.

His car is slow.

His car moves slowly.

His car has a loud rattle.

His car rattles loudly.

Sometimes, you have to change the ending of the adjective a little before you add ly. Here are some spelling tips that can help you to turn adjectives into adverbs:

1. If an adjective ends in le, drop the e and add y.

   reasonab**le** + **y** = reasonab**ly**

   That is a reasonable price for a pair of pants.
   (adjective)

   Those pants are priced reasonably.
   (adverb)

2. If an adjective ends in ll, just add y.

   full + **y** = **fully**

He has a full understanding of the subject.
(adjective)

He understands the subject fully.
(adverb)

3. You have worked with nouns and verbs that end in y. You have changed the y to i before you added s or ed. If an adjective ends in y, change the y to i and add ly.

easy + **ly** = **easily**

This is an easy task.
(adjective)

Walter completed the task easily.
(adverb)

4. If the adjective ends in ic, add ally.

This is an electric toothbrush.
(adjective)

This toothbrush works electrically.
(adverb)

5. Some adjectives change their spelling when they are made into adverbs.

That's a true story.
(adjective)

I'm truly sorry.
(adverb)

The dictionary can also help you change an adjective into its adverb form. If you're not sure how to spell the adverb, look up the adjective. The adverb form will be listed with the adjective.

These five tips are for times when the adverb and adjective have different forms. But look at these sentences:

This magazine arrives monthly.

This is a monthly magazine.

In the first sentence, monthly is used as an adverb. It describes the verb arrives. It tells *when* the magazine arrives. In the second sentence, monthly is used as an adjective. It describes the noun magazine. It tells *what kind* of magazine. The word monthly can be used as both an adverb and an adjective. Here are some other words like monthly:

Adverb	Adjective
He left early.	He took an early train.
She shops daily.	She reads the daily newspaper.

They are paid weekly.	They receive a weekly paycheck.
They get raises yearly.	They get yearly raises.
He drives fast.	He drives a fast car.
We work hard.	We are hard workers.
He stayed up late.	He watched the late movie.

You don't have to change the adjective form to make these words adverbs.

Try It: Turning Adjectives into Adverbs

Fill in the blank in each sentence with the adverb form of the adjective in parentheses.

EXAMPLE: Willy sang ___happily___ to himself. (happy)

1. The child ________________ stroked the cat. (gentle)
2. Martin screamed ________________ for the police. (shrill)
3. Tom eats too ________________. (fast)
4. Everyone ________________ prepared for the party. (busy)
5. That newspaper is published ________________. (daily)
6. The new detergent works ________________. (fantastic)
7. Bob is ________________ right. (probable)
8. Wanda sighed ________________. (heavy)
9. He ________________ fell off the ladder. (accidental)
10. Leon tries too ________________ to win. (hard)

Check your answers on page 176.

ADVERB OR ADJECTIVE?

In the last unit, you worked with adjectives. Adjectives are words that describe nouns and pronouns:

Marla has a beautiful voice.

Adverbs are words that describe verbs, adjectives, or other adverbs.

Maria sings beautifully.

One problem with using adjectives and adverbs is deciding which kind of word to use. For example, look at the next sentence:

The thief ran away from the bank (quick—quickly).

Which is the right word to use? Is it the adjective quick? Or is it the adverb quickly? To answer these questions, you have to figure out what the word is supposed to describe. In the sentence, what is the word supposed to describe?

The thief ran away from the bank (quick—quickly).

The word is supposed to describe how the thief ran. Ran is a verb. The word that describes it should be an adverb:

The thief ran away from the bank quickly.

Now, look at this sentence:

She stopped for a (quick—quickly) lunch.

Which word should be used in this sentence? The word is supposed to describe lunch. In this sentence, lunch is a noun. The word that describes the noun should be an adjective:

She stopped for a quick lunch.

The way to decide whether to use an adjective or an adverb is to look at the word that is being described. Is the word a noun or pronoun? If it is, then the describing word should be an *adjective*. Is it a verb, an adjective, or an adverb? If it is, then the describing word should be an *adverb*.

Try It: Adverb or Adjective?

Choose the correct word in each sentence.

EXAMPLE: Seymour is a very (serious—seriously) person.

1. That is a very (sad—sadly) story.

2. The woman nodded her head (sad—sadly).

3. Spiro is a very (honest—honestly) man.

4. I (honest—honestly) don't know the answer.

5. I took a (quick—quickly) shower.

6. I got ready (quick—quickly).

7. He always says (kind—kindly) things about people.

8. He speaks (kind—kindly) about people.

9. Alice smiled (bright—brightly) at her daughter.

10. These scarves come in (bright—brightly) colors.

Check your answers on page 177.

PROBLEMS WITH ADVERBS AND ADJECTIVES

Look at the next sentence. Which word is correct?

The accident was not (serious—seriously).

In the last unit, you did some work with linking verbs. A linking verb is a verb that can link the subject to a description of the subject. In this sentence, was is a linking verb. It links the subject accident to a description of the accident. The word that describes the noun accident should be an adjective.

The accident was not serious.

The verb be is often used as a linking verb. Here are some other verbs that often are used as linking verbs:

appear	grow	smell
become	look	sound
feel	seem	taste

When these verbs are used as linking verbs, the describing words that follow them should be adjectives.

They grew tired at the party.

In this sentence, grew acts as a linking verb. It links the subject they with a description. The adjective tired describes the subject.

However, the verbs in the list aren't *always* linking verbs. Look at this sentence:

The new plants grew (quick—quickly).

Which word is correct? What is the word describing? In this sentence, grew is *not* a linking verb. In this sentence, grew stands for an action. It tells you what the plants did. The word that follows grew tells you *how* the plants grew. It describes the verb. In this sentence, the adverb quickly is correct.

The new plants grew quickly.

The best way to decide whether or not to use an adjective or an adverb is to think about the sentence. Is the verb acting as a linking verb? If it is, the word that follows it should be an *adjective*. Is the verb showing an action? If it is, the word that follows it should be an *adverb*.

Now, look at these two sentences:

Byron is a bad singer.

Byron sings badly.

Bad is an adjective. It describes the noun singer. It tells *what kind* of singer Byron is. Badly is an adverb. It describes the verb sings. It tells *how* Byron sings. Sometimes, the words bad and badly are used incorrectly. Just remember that bad is an adjective. It should be used to describe nouns and pronouns. Badly is an adverb. It should be used to describe verbs and adjectives.

Here are two more troublesome words:

Jennifer is a good cook.

Jennifer cooks well.

Good is an adjective. It describes the noun cook. It tells *what kind* of cook Jennifer is. Well is an adverb. It describes the verb cooks. It tells *how* Jennifer cooks. Keep in mind that good is an adjective. Well is an adverb.

There is one time when well can be used as an adjective. When well describes a person's health, it can be used as an adjective.

Phil feels well.

When well means healthy, it is used as an adjective. It is used instead of good.

If you can't decide whether to use an adjective or an adverb, just remember this:

- Adjectives describe people, places, and things (nouns or pronouns).
- Adverbs describe actions (all verbs except linking verbs).
- Adverbs describe other describing words (adjectives and adverbs).

Try It: Problems with Adverbs and Adjectives

Underline the correct word in each sentence.

1. Mr. Degas is a (good—well) teacher.
2. Marco has felt (bad—badly) since last night.
3. Kim types (bad—badly).
4. The patient isn't feeling very (good—well).
5. He seems very (happily—happy) this morning.
6. That dress looks (good—well) on her.
7. Liz works (good—well) with others.
8. The ball was hit (bad—badly).
9. He looked (quick—quickly) at the picture.
10. Your perfume smells (good—well).

Check your answers on page 177.

UNIT REVIEW

In this unit, you've looked at adjectives and adverbs. You've seen that adverbs describe different kinds of words than adjectives do. Adjectives describe nouns and pronouns. Adverbs describes verbs, adjectives, and other adverbs.

You have also seen that adverbs can be formed from adjectives. You have worked on forming and using adverbs. You have also seen that some adjectives and adverbs have the same form. You have worked with bad, badly, good, and well.

Adjectives and adverbs can *describe* people, places, things, and actions. But they can also be used to *compare* people, places, things, and actions. In the next unit, you will see how to make comparisons.

SPELLING AND USAGE HINT: ADDING ING TO WORDS THAT END IN E

In the last Spelling and Usage Hint, you saw that a *prefix* can be added to the beginning of a word. A *suffix* can be added to the end of a word. In this unit, you worked with the suffix ly. You saw that sometimes letters are dropped when you add ly:

true + ly = truly

Here is another suffix: ing. Sometimes ing is simply added to the end of a word:

You look tired.

I was looking for you.

But other times, a letter is dropped before ing is added:

Please type this letter.

He is typing the letter.

Notice that type ends in e. If a word ends in a consonant plus e, drop the e and add ing.

Sometimes I drive to work.

I am driving to work today.

If a word ends in a vowel plus e, just add ing:

I can't see clearly.

I am seeing double.

Of course, be does not follow this rule:

You are being foolish.

Try It: Adding ing to Words That End in e

Fill in the blank with the ing form of the word in parentheses.

EXAMPLE: Terry is ___receiving___ an award. (receive)

1. Felix is ______________ popcorn. (make)
2. Matt is ______________ me to the movies. (take)
3. My daughter is ______________ in Houston. (live)
4. Dan's dog is ______________ your cat. (bite)
5. Stan has been ______________ our ladder. (use)
6. Rick and Ruby went ______________ last weekend. (canoe)
7. I was just ______________ your shoes. (admire)
8. Bill's directions were ______________. (confuse)
9. The tenants were ______________ from the fire. (flee)
10. Joe is ______________ on his trombone. (practice)

Check your answers on page 178.

ANSWERS AND EXPLANATIONS

Try It: Looking for Adverbs

1. **Wilma entered the room quietly.** The adverb quietly describes the verb entered. It tells *how* Wilma entered the room.
2. **George politely asked the man a question.** The adverb politely describes the verb asked. It tells *how* George asked the question.
3. **Jean whispered softly into his ear.** The adverb softly describes the verb whispered. It tells *how* Jean whispered.
4. **Mel shops wisely.** The adverb wisely describes the verb shops. It tells *how* Mel shops.

5. **Frank stared at the very pretty woman.** The adverb very describes the adjective pretty. It tells *how* pretty the woman was.
6. **The bomb squad examined the ticking box carefully.** The adverb carefully describes the verb examined. It tells *how* the bomb squad examined the box.
7. **Mickey hit the ball hard into left field.** The adverb hard describes the verb hit. It tells *how* Mickey hit the ball.
8. **That candidate speaks foolishly about the economy.** The adverb foolishly describes the verb speaks. It tells *how* the candidate speaks about the economy.
9. **We went to the movies yesterday.** The adverb yesterday describes the verb went. It tells *when* we went to the movies.
10. **The protesters marched peacefully.** The adverb peacefully describes the verb marched. It tells *how* the protesters marched.

Try It: Turning Adjectives into Adverbs

1. **The child gently stroked the cat.** To form an adverb from an adjective that ends in le, drop the e and add y: gentle + y = gently.
2. **Martin screamed shrilly for the police.** To form an adverb from an adjective that ends in ll, just add y: shrill + y = shrilly.
3. **Tom eats too fast.** The word fast does not change when it's used as an adverb. The adjective and adverb forms of the word are the same.
4. **Everyone busily prepared for the party.** To form an adverb from an adjective that ends in y, change the y to i and add ly: busy + ly = busily.
5. **That newspaper is published daily.** The word daily does not change when it's used as an adverb. The adjective and adverb forms of the word are the same.
6. **The new detergent works fantastically.** To form an adverb from an adjective that ends in ic, add ally: fantastic + ally = fantastically.
7. **Bob is probably right.** To form an adverb from an adjective that ends in le, drop the e and add y: probable + y = probably.
8. **Wanda sighed heavily.** To form an adverb from an adjective that ends in y, change the y to i and add ly: heavy + ly = heavily.
9. **He accidentally fell off the ladder.** To form an adverb from most adjectives, just add ly: accidental + ly = accidentally.

10. **Leon tries too hard to win.** The word hard does not change when it's used as an adverb. The adjective and adverb forms of the word are the same.

Try It: Adverb or Adjective?

1. **That is a very sad story.** The adjective sad describes the noun story.
2. **The woman nodded her head sadly.** The adverb sadly describes the verb nodded.
3. **Spiro is a very honest man.** The adjective honest describes the noun man.
4. **I honestly don't know the answer.** The adverb honestly describes the verb know.
5. **I took a quick shower.** The adjective quick describes the noun shower.
6. **I got ready quickly.** The adverb quickly describes the verb got.
7. **He always says kind things about people.** The adjective kind describes the noun things.
8. **He speaks kindly about people.** The adverb kindly describes the verb speaks.
9. **Alice smiled brightly at her daughter.** The adverb brightly describes the verb smiled.
10. **These scarves come in bright colors.** The adjective bright describes the noun colors.

Try It: Problems with Adverbs and Adjectives

1. **Mr. Degas is a good teacher.** The adjective good describes the noun teacher. It tells you *what kind* of teacher Mr. Degas is.
2. **Marco has felt bad since last night.** In this sentence, the verb has felt acts as a linking verb. It links the subject Marco with a description. The adjective bad describes the noun Marco.
3. **Kim types badly.** The adverb badly describes the verb types. It tells you *how* Kim types.
4. **The patient isn't feeling very well.** The word well is used as an adjective to describe the patient's health.

5. **He seems very happy this morning.** In this sentence, the verb seems acts as a linking verb. It links the subject he with a description. The adjective happy describes the pronoun he.
6. **That dress looks good on her.** In this sentence, the verb looks acts as a linking verb. It links the subject dress with a description. The adjective good describes the noun dress.
7. **Liz works well with others.** The adverb well describes the verb works. It tells you *how* Liz works.
8. **The ball was hit badly.** The adverb badly describes the verb hit. It tells you *how* the ball was hit.
9. **He looked quickly at the picture.** The adverb quickly describes the verb looked. It tells you *how* he looked.
10. **Your perfume smells good.** In this sentence, the verb smells acts as a linking verb. It links the subject perfume with a description. The adjective good describes the noun perfume.

Try It: Adding ing to Words That End in e

1. **Felix is making popcorn.** If a word ends in a consonant plus e, drop the e and add ing: make + ing = making.
2. **Matt is taking me to the movies.** If a word ends in a consonant plus e, drop the e and add ing: take + ing = taking.
3. **My daughter is living in Houston.** If a word ends in a consonant plus e, drop the e and add ing: live + ing = living.
4. **Dan's dog is biting your cat.** If a word ends in a consonant plus e, drop the e and add ing: bite + ing = biting.
5. **Stan has been using our ladder.** If a word ends in a consonant plus e, drop the e and add ing: use + ing = using.
6. **Rick and Ruby went canoeing last weekend.** If a word ends in a vowel (o) plus e, just add ing: canoe + ing = canoeing.
7. **I was just admiring your shoes.** If a word ends in a consonant plus e, drop the e and add ing: admire + ing = admiring.
8. **Bill's directions were confusing.** If a word ends in a consonant plus e, drop the e and add ing: confuse + ing = confusing.
9. **The tenants were fleeing from the fire.** If a word ends in a vowel (e) plus e, just add ing: flee + ing = fleeing.
10. **Joe is practicing on his trombone.** If a word ends in a consonant plus e, drop the e and add ing: practice + ing = practicing.

UNIT 15: HOW DO YOU USE WORDS TO COMPARE?

In the last two units, you've worked with adjectives and adverbs. Adjectives and adverbs are describing words. You use them to describe other things in a sentence.

His car is fast.

(The word fast is an adjective. It describes the subject car.)

Harold works quickly.

(The word quickly is an adverb. It describes the verb works.)

Most of the time, adjectives and adverbs are used to describe things. But they can be used in other ways. For example, look at these sentences:

His car is faster than my car.

Harold works more quickly than Steve.

In these sentences, faster and more quickly are used to compare things. In the first sentence, his car and my car are compared. In the second sentence, the way Harold works and the way Steve works are compared.

When you use an adjective or an adverb to compare things, you have to change the form of the adjective or adverb. With some of them, you add an er or est ending. With others, you put the words more or most in front of them.

In this unit, you will look at using adjectives and adverbs to compare things. You'll take a close look at how to change the form of a word when you use it to compare.

ADDING ER OR EST TO COMPARE

Look at the next sentences. How are they alike? How are they different?

Ralph is older than Ed.

Ed is older than Carlos.

Ralph is the oldest of the three men.

In each of the first two sentences, the ages of two men are being compared. In the first sentence, Ralph's age is being compared with Ed's age. In the second sentence, Ed's age is being compared with Carlos's age. In the third sentence, the ages of all three men are being compared.

Look at the adjectives in the sentences. How are they different?

> Ralph is older than Ed.
>
> Ed is older than Carlos.
>
> Ralph is the oldest of the three men.

In each sentence, a form of the adjective old is used. In the first two sentences, two men are being compared. In the first two sentences, er is added to the word old: older. In the last sentence, the ages of all three men are being compared. In the last sentence, est is added to the word old: oldest.

When you use an adjective or adverb to compare things, you have to change the form of the adjective or adverb. With some adjectives and adverbs, you add an ending to the word. You add either an er ending or an est ending.

But when do you add er? When do you add est? The ending that you add usually depends on the number of things that are being compared. If two things are being compared, you *always* add an er ending.

> Ralph is older than Ed.
>
> Potatoes are cheaper than tomatoes.
>
> Mary works later than Marge.

If three or more things are being compared *together* as one group, you add an est ending.

> Ralph is the oldest of the three men.
>
> (Three men are being compared *together*. The est ending is used.)
>
> Potatoes are the cheapest thing in the store.
>
> (Everything in the store is being compared *together*. The est ending is used.)
>
> Of all the people at work, Mary works the latest.
>
> (All the people at work are being compared *together*. The est ending is used.)

You have to be careful abut using the est ending. Sometimes, you don't use est even though it may seem that you are comparing more than two things. Look at these sentences:

> Ralph is the oldest of the three men.
>
> Ralph is older than the other men.

In the first sentence, the three men are one group. Ralph is one of the three men. He is a part of the group.

Look at the second sentence again. Is Ralph part of the group? Or does the sentence tell you something else?

> Ralph is older than the other men.

Ralph's age is being compared with the other men's ages. In this sentence, Ralph's age stands apart from the other men's ages. All the ages are *not* being compared together. If one person or thing is separated from the group, you use the er ending, not the est ending.

> Potatoes are cheaper than anything else in the store.

What is being compared in this sentence? The price of potatoes is being compared with the price of everything else in the store. All the prices are *not* being compared together. The price of potatoes stands apart from the price of everything else. That's why er, not est, is added to cheap.

Now, look at this sentence. Why is later used instead of latest?

> Mary works later than all the other people.

In this sentence, Mary is being compared with all the other people. Mary stands apart from all the other people. The er ending is added to the adverb late in this sentence.

Notice that in all these sentences, the word than is used in the comparison:

> Ralph is older than the other men.
>
> Potatoes are cheaper than anything else in the store.
>
> Mary works later than all the other people.

When than is used in a comparison, it separates the parts of the comparison into two groups. That's why the er form of the word is used.

When you are deciding whether to use an er or est ending, remember these things:

1. If two things are being compared, use the er ending. Don't use the est ending when only two things are being compared.

   Ralph is the oldest of the two men.

   (The adjective in this sentence is WRONG. Only two men are being compared. The er ending should be used.)

   Ralph is the older of the two men.

   (The adjective in this sentence is RIGHT. Use the er ending to compare two people or things.)

2. If more than two things are being compared *together,* use the est ending.

   Ralph is the oldest of the three men.

   (The adjective in this sentence is RIGHT. The ages of the three men are being compared *together*. The est ending should be used.)

3. If one person or thing is separated from a group with the word than, use the er ending, not the est ending.

   Ralph is older than the other men.

   (The adjective in this sentence is RIGHT. Ralph's age stands apart from the other men's ages. The er ending should be used.)

Try It: Adding er or est to Compare

Underline the correct adjective or adverb in each sentence.

EXAMPLE: Leo is (younger—youngest) than Max and I.

1. I can carry the (heavier—heaviest) of the three packages.
2. Of the five players, Schwartz is the (faster—fastest).
3. Madge is the (happier—happiest) of the two sisters.
4. That dog is the (bigger—biggest) of all the dogs in the pound.
5. Of the two fighters, Gomez punches the (harder—hardest).
6. Betty Jean is the (smarter—smartest) child in her class.

7. Tony is the (richer—richest) of her four boyfriends.

8. Mount Everest is the (taller—tallest) mountain in the world.

9. Jimbo drives the (older—oldest) of the two cars.

10. Charlie likes the (uglier—ugliest) of the two jackets.

Check your answers on page 190.

USING MORE OR MOST TO COMPARE

So far, you've looked at when to use er and when to use est to compare people or things. You use the er ending when you are comparing two people or things. You use the est ending when you are comparing more than two things together.

> Ralph is the older of the two men.
>
> Ralph is the oldest of the three men.

You don't always add er or est when you compare people or things. Sometimes, you use the words more or most. For example, look at these sentences:

> Ralph is the more interesting of the two men.
>
> Ralph is the most interesting of the three men.

In these sentences, the words more and most are used instead of the er and est endings. You use more and most the same way that you use er and est. When you are comparing two people or things, you always use the word more.

> Ralph is the more interesting of the two men.
>
> (In this sentence, two men are being compared. Use more in front of the adjective.)

When you are comparing more than two people or things together in a group, you use most.

> Ralph is the most interesting of the three men.
>
> (In this sentence, three men are being compared together. Ralph is one of the three men. Use most when you compare more than two people or things together in a group.)

Try It: Using More or Most to Compare

Underline the correct word in each sentence.

1. Helga is the (more—most) beautiful of the two women.
2. Of all the people I know, John drives the (more—most) carefully.
3. He bought the (more—most) expensive ring in the store.
4. Stanley is the (more—most) sensitive of the four brothers.
5. That shirt is the (more—most) colorful of all the shirts in the store.
6. Of the two waiters, Vern is the (more—most) patient.
7. Gloria is the (more—most) helpful cashier in the supermarket.
8. "Weenie's" is the (more—most) popular diner in town.
9. Compared with his brother Jake, Archie is (more—most) understanding.
10. The Grover is the (more—most) economical of the two cars.

Check your answers on page 191.

PUTTING WORDS IN THE RIGHT FORM

Look at these two sentences:

> Nurses' Aspirin is cheaper than Miracle Aspirin.
>
> Correctal Aspirin is more expensive than Miracle Aspirin.

In each sentence, the underlined words are used to compare two kinds of aspirin. In the first sentence, an er ending is added to the word cheap. In the second sentence, the word more is put before the word expensive. Why are the words cheap and expensive treated differently?

The answer to this question lies in the number of syllables that the word contains. A syllable is a word part. When you say a word that has more than one syllable, you can almost hear little breaks in the word. For example, think about the word expensive:

ex–pen–sive

The word expensive has three syllables. It is made up of three smaller parts.

Now, think about the word cheap. How many parts do you hear in cheap?

cheap

The word cheap only has one syllable. There aren't any breaks in the word.

If a word contains only one syllable, you add an er or est ending to use the word when you compare.

> Nurses' Aspirin is cheaper than Miracle Aspirin.
> Nurses' Aspirin is the cheapest of the three brands.
>
> (The adjective cheap contains only one syllable. Add er or est to it when you use it to compare.)
>
> Tony runs faster than Jethro.
>
> (The adverb fast contains only one syllable. Add er or est to it when you use it to compare.)

If a word contains three or more syllables, you put more or most in front of the word. You also use more or most with any adverb that is formed with an ly ending.

> Correctal Aspirin is more expensive than Miracle Aspirin.
> Correctal Aspirin is the most expensive of the three brands.
>
> (The adjective expensive contains three syllables. Use more or most with it when you use it to compare.)
>
> Harold works more quickly than Steve.
>
> (The adverb quickly is formed by adding ly to the word quick. Use more or most with any adverb that is formed with an ly ending.)

You add er or est to a word that has one syllable. You use more or most with a word that has more than two syllables and with most adverbs. But what about adjectives that contain two syllables? Do you add an ending to them? Or do you use more or most?

There is no simple answer to these questions. Sometimes, you add an ending to a two-syllable adjective. Sometimes, you use more or most. For example, look at these sentences:

> Tom is happier than Jerry is.
>
> But Tom is more foolish than Jerry is.

In the first sentence, the adjective happy is used to compare two people. The word happy contains two syllables: hap–py. When you use happy to compare, you add er or est to it.

But look at the second sentence. The adjective foolish is used to compare the two people. The word foolish also contains two syllables: fool–ish. But you don't add er or est when you use foolish to compare. Instead, you put more or most in front of it.

There aren't any rules that can help you with words that have two syllables. Some words, like happy, have endings added to them. With other words, like foolish, you use more or most. The dictionary can help you if you're not sure how to use a word to compare. If the word has an ending added to it, the endings will be listed next to the word.

Now, look at this sentence. What is wrong with the underlined words?

This is the most happiest day of my life.

In this sentence, the word happy is being used to compare things. When you use happy to compare, you should add er or est to it. In this sentence, est is added: happiest.

But look at the word that comes before happy. The word is most. The word most should not be in this sentence. You only need to use one of the ways to compare. You should not use both ways.

This is the happiest day of my life.

This sentence is correct. The est ending is added to the word happy. Most is not needed. When you use adjectives and adverbs to compare, remember to use only one of the ways to compare things. If the word takes an er or est ending, do not use more or most with it.

Try It: Putting Words in the Right Form

Fill in the blank with the correct form of the word in parentheses.

EXAMPLE: The Blue Goose is the most expensive restaurant in the city. (expensive)

1. These shoes are ________________ than my other pair. (small)

2. Ralph drives ________________ than any other bus driver. (slowly)

3. "The Zookeeper" is the ____________________ show on TV. (interesting)

4. Lee is the ____________________ of the five children. (old)

5. Irv hits the ball ____________________ than Roger. (hard)

6. Robbie is the ____________________ of my three sons. (tall)

7. Well's Cough Syrup is ____________________ than Command Cough Syrup. (powerful)

8. Jane speaks ____________________ than anyone else I know. (softly)

9. The kitchen is the ____________________ of the three rooms. (warm)

10. Clarence thinks that he is the ____________________ person alive. (intelligent)

Check your answers on page 192.

USING IRREGULAR ADJECTIVES AND ADVERBS

Why are these verbs called "irregular" verbs?

drive	drove	driven
eat	ate	eaten

These verbs are called "irregular" verbs because their past and past participle forms aren't made in the regular way. Now look at these adjectives and adverbs. Why are they called "irregular"?

good	bad
well	badly

These words are "irregular" because you don't use er, est, more, or most with them when you use them to compare. These words have different forms when they are used to compare.

good	better	best
well	better	best
bad	worse	worst
badly	worse	worst

There isn't any rule for forming irregular adjectives and adverbs. However, you probably know the forms already. Remember that the words good, well, bad, and badly are irregular. When you use them to compare, use better, best, worse, or worst.

Try It: Using Irregular Adjectives and Adverbs

Rewrite each sentence, using the correct form of the adjective or adverb.

EXAMPLE: Josepha sings more badly than Ulna.

Josepha sings worse than Ulna.

1. Clayton feels worser than Linda does.

2. Jay types more well than Bob does.

3. That was the baddest movie I've ever seen.

4. This ice cream tastes gooder than those lima beans.

5. Quinn Dexter is the bestest player on the team.

6. The Yellow Jackets are the worse team in the league.

7. Willy drives more badly than Sam.

8. Reggie's is the worstest restaurant in town.

Check your answers on page 193.

UNIT REVIEW

In this unit, you have worked on how to use adjectives and adverbs to compare people and things. You've seen that the way to change the adjective or adverb depends on how many things you are comparing. When you are comparing *two* people or things, you used the er ending or the word more. When you were comparing *more than two* people or things together in a group, you used the est ending or the word most.

The form of the adjective or adverb also depends on the number of syllables it contains. If the word contains one syllable, always use the er or est ending. If the word contains three or more syllables, use more or most with it. Also use more or most with any adverb that is formed with an ly ending.

You've also looked at irregular adjectives and adverbs. The words good, well, bad, and badly are irregular. When you use good or well to compare, use better or best. When you use bad or badly to compare, use worse or worst.

SPELLING AND USAGE HINT: ADDING ER AND EST TO WORDS THAT END IN Y

In this unit, you saw that the endings er and est can be added to adjectives and adverbs. These endings are added when you make comparisons.

Most of the time, the er or est ending is simply added to the word:

> Joe is tall.
>
> Joe is tall**er** than Mike.
>
> Joe is the tall**est** person in the class.

But sometimes you have to change the adjective or adverb a little before you add er or est:

> Yesterday was sunny.
> Today is sunn**ier** than yesterday.

Here is a rule for adding er/est to words that end in y:

> When the word ends in a consonant plus y, change the y to i before you add er/est.
>
> lazy, lazier, laziest
>
> ugly, uglier, ugliest
>
> When the word ends in a vowel plus y, just add er/est.
>
> gray, grayer, grayest
>
> gay, gayer, gayest

Try It: Adding er and est to Words That End in y

Fill in the blank with the correct form of the word in parentheses.

EXAMPLE: Cookies are ___tastier___ than crackers. (tasty)

1. The air on the West Coast seems ______________ than the air on the East Coast. (dry)
2. The first test was ______________ than the second test. (easy)
3. Monday is always the ______________ day at work. (busy)
4. Tim is the ______________ person I know. (lucky)
5. Of the five pieces of furniture, the sofa is the ______________. (heavy)
6. Judy's hair is ______________ than Val's. (wavy)
7. That is the ______________ idea Howard's ever had. (crazy)
8. The sky is ______________ today than it was yesterday. (gray)

Check your answers on page 194.

ANSWERS AND EXPLANATIONS

Try It: Adding er or est to Compare

1. **I can carry the heaviest of the three packages**. Three packages are being compared. Because *more than two* things are being compared *together*, you should add est to the adjective heavy.
2. **Of the five players, Schwartz is the fastest**. Five players are being compared. Because *more than two* people are being compared *together*, you should add est to the adjective fast.
3. **Madge is the happier of the two sisters**. Two sisters are being compared. Because *two* people are being compared, you should add er to the adjective happy.
4. **That dog is the biggest of all the dogs in the pound**. All of the dogs are being compared. Because *more than two* things are being compared *together*, you should add est to the adjective big.

5. **Of the two fighters, Gomez punches the harder**. Two fighters are being compared. Because *two* people are being compared, you should add er to the adverb hard.
6. **Betty Jean is the smartest child in her class**. All of the children in Betty Jean's class are being compared. Because *more than two* people are being compared *together*, you should add est to the adjective smart.
7. **Tony is the richest of her four boyfriends**. Four boyfriends are being compared. Because *more than two* people are being compared *together*, you should add est to the adjective rich.
8. **Mount Everest is the tallest mountain in the world**. All of the mountains in the world are being compared. Because *more than two* things are being compared *together*, you should add est to the adjective tall.
9. **Jimbo drives the older of the two cars**. Two cars are being compared. Because *two* things are being compared, you should add er to the adjective old.
10. **Charlie likes the uglier of the two jackets**. Two jackets are being compared. Because *two* things are being compared, you should add er to the adjective ugly.

Try It: Using More or Most to Compare

1. **Helga is the more beautiful of the two women**. Two women are being compared. Because *two* people are being compared, you should use more with the adjective beautiful.
2. **Of all the people I know, John drives the most carefully**. All of the people I know are being compared. Because *more than two* people are being compared *together*, you should use most with the adverb carefully.
3. **He bought the most expensive ring in the store**. All of the rings in the store are being compared. Because *more than two* things are being compared *together*, you should use most with the adjective expensive.
4. **Stanley is the most sensitive of the four brothers**. Four brothers are being compared. Because *more than two* people are being compared *together*, you should use most with the adjective sensitive.
5. **That shirt is the most colorful of all the shirts in the store.** All of the shirts in the store are being compared. Because *more than two* things are being compared *together,* you should use most with the adjective colorful.
6. **Of the two waiters, Vern is the more patient.** Two waiters are being compared. Because *two* people are being compared, you should use more with the adjective patient.

7. **Gloria is the most helpful cashier in the supermarket.** All of the cashiers in the supermarket are being compared. Because *more than two* people are being compared *together,* you should use most with the adjective helpful.

8. **"Weenie's" is the most popular diner in town.** All of the diners in town are being compared. Because *more than two* things are being compared *together,* you should use most with the adjective popular.

9. **Compared with his brother Jake, Archie is more understanding.** Two brothers are being compared. Because *two* people are being compared, you should use more with the adjective understanding.

10. **The Grover is the more economical of the two cars.** Two cars are being compared. Because *two* things are being compared, you should use more with the adjective economical.

Try It: Putting Words in the Right Form

1. **These shoes are smaller than my other pair.** Small is a one-syllable word. You add er or est when you use a one-syllable word to compare. Since *two* pairs of shoes are being compared, you should add er to the adjective small.

2. **Ralph drives more slowly than any other bus driver.** Slowly is an adverb. You use more or most with adverbs that are formed with an ly ending. Since Ralph is *separated* from the other bus drivers, you should use more with the adverb slowly.

3. **"The Zookeeper" is the most interesting show on TV.** The word interesting has more than two syllables (in-ter-est-ing). You add more or most when you use a word with more than two syllables to compare. Since *more than two* shows are being compared *together,* you should use most with the adjective interesting.

4. **Lee is the oldest of the five children.** Old is a one-syllable word. You add er or est when you use a one-syllable word to compare. Since *more than two* children are being compared *together,* you should add est to the adjective old.

5. **Irv hits the ball harder than Roger.** Hard is a one-syllable word. You add er or est when you use a one-syllable word to compare. Since *two* actions are being compared, you should add er to the adverb hard.

6. **Robbie is the tallest of my three sons.** Tall is a one-syllable word. You add er or est when you use a one-syllable word to compare. Since *more than two* sons are being compared *together,* you should add est to the adjective tall.

7. **Well's Cough Syrup is more powerful than Command Cough Syrup.** The word powerful has more than two syllables (pow-er-ful). You add more or most when you use a word with more than two syllables to compare. Since *two* things are being compared, you should use more with the adjective powerful.

8. **Jane speaks more softly than anyone else I know.** Softly is an adverb. You use more or most with adverbs that are formed with an ly ending. Since Jane is *separated* from anyone else I know, you should use more with the adverb softly.

9. **The kitchen is the warmest of the three rooms.** Warm is a one-syllable word. You add er or est when you use a one-syllable word to compare. Since *more than two* rooms are being compared *together,* you should add est to the adjective warm.

10. **Clarence thinks that he is the most intelligent person alive.** The word intelligent has more than two syllables (in-tel-li-gent). You add more or most when you use a word with more than two syllables to compare. Since *more than two* people are being compared *together,* you should use most with the adjective intelligent.

Try It: Using Irregular Adjectives and Adverbs

1. **Clayton feels worse than Linda does.** Two people are being compared. Worse is the correct form of the adjective bad to use when *two* people are being compared.

2. **Jay types better than Bob does.** Two actions are being compared. Better is the correct form of the adverb well to use when *two* actions are being compared.

3. **That was the worst movie I've ever seen.** More than two things are being compared. Worst is the correct form of the adjective bad to use when *more than two* things are being compared.

4. **This ice cream tastes better than those lima beans.** Two things are being compared. Better is the correct form of the adjective good to use when *two* things are being compared.

5. **Quinn Dexter is the best player on the team.** All of the players on the team are being compared *together.* Best is the correct form of the adjective good to use when *more than two* people are being compared.

6. **The Yellow Jackets are the worst team in the league.** All of the teams in the league are being compared *together.* Worst is the correct form of the adjective bad to use when *more than two* things are being compared.

7. **Willy drives worse than Sam.** The ways that two people drive are being compared. Worse is the correct form of the adverb badly to use when *two* actions are being compared.
8. **Reggie's is the worst restaurant in town.** All of the restaurants in town are being compared *together.* Worst is the correct form of the adjective bad to use when *more than two* things are being compared.

Try It: Adding er and est to Words That End in y

1. **The air on the West Coast seems drier than the air on the East Coast.** Since two things are being compared, the er ending should be used. Change the y to i when you add er: dry + er = drier.
2. **The first test was easier than the second test.** Since two things are being compared, the er ending should be used. Change the y to i when you add er: easy + er = easier.
3. **Monday is always the busiest day at work.** Since more than two things are being compared, the est ending should be used. Change the y to i when you add est: busy + est = busiest.
4. **Tim is the luckiest person I know.** Since more than two people are being compared, the est ending should be used. Change the y to i when you add est: lucky + est = luckiest.
5. **Of the five pieces of furniture, the sofa is the heaviest.** Since more than two things are being compared, the est ending should be used. Change the y to i when you add est: heavy + est = heaviest.
6. **Judy's hair is wavier than Val's.** Since two things are being compared, the er ending should be used. Change the y to i when you add er: wavy + er = wavier.
7. **That is the craziest idea Howard's ever had.** Since more than two things are being compared, the est ending should be used. Change the y to i when you add est: crazy + est = craziest.
8. **The sky is grayer today than it was yesterday.** Since two things are being compared, the er ending should be used. Since gray ends in a vowel (a) plus y, the word doesn't change when you add er: gray + er = grayer.

UNIT 16: MEASURING YOUR PROGRESS

In Units 11–15, you have taken a closer look at many important parts of a sentence. You have worked on these things:

- using subject and object pronouns
- showing possession with nouns and pronouns
- identifying adjectives and adverbs
- forming adverbs from adjectives
- deciding whether to use an adjective or an adverb
- making comparisons with adjectives and adverbs

In the Spelling and Usage Hints, you have worked on these things:

- spelling words that have ed or ing added to them
- choosing between contractions and pronouns that sound alike (you're/your, it's/its, they're/their)
- spelling words that contain prefixes
- adding er and est to words that end in y

This unit will help you to see how much you have learned from your work in Units 11–15. Complete all the parts in this unit. After you have finished, check your answers. A chart at the end of the answer key tells you what pages to turn to for review. You should review the pages for any item that you do not answer correctly.

PART A

Underline the correct pronoun in each sentence.

EXAMPLE: Rick and (I—me) found five dollars on the sidewalk.

1. Marvin gave (he—him) good advice.

2. (Her—She) lives near the post office.

3. The person in that picture is (I—me).

4. I saw (them—they) at the bus stop.

5. I bought (me—myself) a birthday present.

6. Ned gave Joe and (us—we) directions to his house.

7. My brother and (I—me) usually visit each other once a week.

8. Jim asked (her—herself) for a date.

9. Prepare (you—yourself) for some bad news.

10. (Us—We) play basketball after work.

PART B

Underline the correct word in each sentence.

EXAMPLE: That is (Phil's—Phils') hat.

11. This scarf is (your—yours).

12. (Chrises—Chris's) records are at my house.

13. Someone left (his—their) keys on the table.

14. (Our—Ours) house is next to the gas station.

15. Each of the workers signed (his—their) name to the agreement.

16. None of the employees lost (his—their) job.

17. The sandwich in this bag is (yours—your's).

18. Neither Ralph nor Ned likes (his—their) coffee black.

19. This radio is (mine—my).

20. Everyone wants (his—their) own team to win.

PART C

Read each sentence. Check to see if the adjectives are used correctly. If the adjectives are not used correctly, rewrite the sentence to make them correct. Remember to check the commas.

EXAMPLE: We studied grammar spelling and capitalization

We studied grammar, spelling, and capitalization.

21. That restaurant is crowded noisy, and expensive.

22. I'm wearing my blue and brown pants to the party.

23. I want to buy this here coat.

24. The bear was strong mean and hungry.

25. The Colts' colors are blue and white.

PART D

Read each sentence. Each sentence contains an underlined word. Check to see if the underlined word should be an adjective or an adverb. If the wrong word is used, rewrite the sentence. Use the correct adjective or adverb form.

EXAMPLE: Your cologne smells well.

Your cologne smells good.

26. A long vacation sounds beautiful.

27. Karen feels badly about her mother.

28. He runs too slow to be a sprinter.

29. This soup tastes bad.

30. Stan works good with others.

PART E

Underline the correct words in the next sentences.

EXAMPLE: Harry can type (faster—fastest) than anyone else.

31. You can use the (sharper—sharpest) of the three pencils.
32. Eddie is the (smarter—smartest) of the two men.
33. Tuna salad is the (deliciousest—most delicious) thing on the menu.
34. Trudy ordered the (more expensive—most expensive) dinner on the menu.
35. Of the two dancers, Homer is the (more graceful—most graceful).
36. Buzzsaw Wilson is the (hardest—most hardest) puncher in boxing.
37. Chester is a (worse—worser) checker player than I am.
38. That was the (best—bestest) movie I've seen in months.
39. My old jacket is (bigger—more big) than my new one.
40. Use the (newer—newest) of the two machines.

PART F

Read each sentence. Some sentences contain words that are spelled incorrectly. Others contain words that are used incorrectly. If a sentence contains a word that is spelled or used incorrectly, rewrite the sentence. Make the word correct.

EXAMPLE: They're team lost by seven points.

Their team lost by seven points.

41. Its a good day for the picnic.

42. The old dog waged its tail.

43. One of these words is mispelled.

44. They're giving the kittens away.

45. She is prettyer than her sister.

46. Don likes the sillyest shows on TV.

47. Can't you find you're coat?

48. Do you feel like stoping for lunch?

49. It's ilegal to serve liquor to minors.

50. It's becomeing cloudy outside.

ANSWER KEY

PART A

1. Marvin gave him good advice.
2. She lives near the post office.
3. The person in that picture is I.
4. I saw them at the bus stop.
5. I bought myself a birthday present.
6. Ned gave Joe and us directions to his house.
7. My brother and I usually visit each other once a week.
8. Jim asked her for a date.
9. Prepare yourself for some bad news.
10. We play basketball after work.

PART B

11. This scarf is yours.
12. Chris's records are at my house.
13. Someone left his keys on the table.
14. Our house is next to the gas station.
15. Each of the workers signed his name to the agreement.
16. None of the employees lost their job.
17. The sandwich in this bag is yours.
18. Neither Ralph nor Ned likes his coffee black.
19. This radio is mine.
20. Everyone wants his own team to win.

PART C

21. That restaurant is crowded, noisy, and expensive.
22. I'm wearing my blue and brown pants to the party.
23. I want to buy this coat.
24. The bear was strong, mean, and hungry.
25. The Colts' colors are blue and white.

PART D

26. A long vacation sounds beautiful.
27. Karen feels bad about her mother.
28. He runs too slowly to be a sprinter.
29. This soup tastes bad.
30. Stan works well with others.

PART E

31. You can use the sharpest of the three pencils.
32. Eddie is the smarter of the two men.
33. Tuna salad is the most delicious thing on the menu.
34. Trudy ordered the most expensive dinner on the menu.
35. Of the two dancers, Homer is the more graceful.
36. Buzzsaw Wilson is the hardest puncher in boxing.
37. Chester is a worse checker player than I am.
38. That was the best movie I've seen in months.
39. My old jacket is bigger than my new one.
40. Use the newer of the two machines.

PART F

41. It's a good day for a picnic.
42. The old dog wagged its tail.

43. One of these words is misspelled.
44. They're giving the kittens away.
45. She is prettier than her sister.
46. Don likes the silliest shows on TV.
47. Can't you find your coat?
48. Do you feel like stopping for lunch?
49. It's illegal to serve liquor to minors.
50. It's becoming cloudy outside.

In this chart, circle the number of any item that you did not answer correctly. The right-hand side of the chart will tell you the pages to review for any item that you missed. Review the pages for any item that you missed before you go on to the next unit.

Item number:	Pages to study:
1 2 3 4 5 6 7 8 9 10	UNIT 11: Is the Pronoun Right? (pages 127–138)
11 12 13 14 15 16 17 18 19 20	UNIT 12: Does the Word Show Possession? (pages 139–153)
21 22 23 24 25	UNIT 13: Is the Adjective Right? (pages 154–164)
26 27 28 29 30	UNIT 14: Is the Adverb Right? (pages 165–178)
31 32 33 34 35 36 37 38 39 40	UNIT 15: How Do You Use Words to Compare? (pages 179–194)
41 42 43 44 45 46 47 48 49 50	SPELLING AND USAGE HINTS (pages 134–135, 149–150, 161–162, 174–175, 189–190)

Sentence Structure, Paragraph Structure, and Writing

UNIT 17: HOW MUCH DO YOU KNOW ALREADY?

This unit will help you plan your work in Units 18–21. Answer as many of the items as you can. When you have finished, check your answers on page 206. Then in the chart on the same page circle the number of any item you missed. The chart will tell you which pages to study.

PART A

For each question, there are two sentences. One sentence contains a mistake. The other sentence is correct. Circle the letter next to the sentence that is correct.

EXAMPLE: (a) Sam ran to the bus stop but, the bus had already left.

(b) Sam ran to the bus stop, but the bus had already left.

1. (a) Neither Luke nor Harry came to work today.
   (b) Neither Luke or Harry came to work today.
2. (a) Raoul was hungry, but he ate something.
   (b) Raoul was hungry, so he ate something.
3. (a) The doors were unlocked and, the windows were wide open.
   (b) The doors were unlocked, and the windows were wide open.
4. (a) Not only Jean but also Tina wanted to ask Fred to the dance.
   (b) Jean but also Tina wanted to ask Fred to the dance.
5. (a) All of the lights are on in the house, yet no one is home.
   (b) All of the lights are on in the house, so no one is home.

6. (a) Norma either plays softball or goes fishing on Saturday afternoons.

   (b) Norma either plays softball nor goes fishing on Saturday afternoons.

7. (a) Ben opened the door, and stepped into the room.

   (b) Ben opened the door and stepped into the room.

8. (a) We need some groceries, or all of the stores are closed.

   (b) We need some groceries, but all of the stores are closed.

9. (a) The dog, the cat, and the gerbil, are all named "Creature."

   (b) The dog, the cat, and the gerbil are all named "Creature."

10. (a) Mr. Nesbit and Ms. Clark met to discuss the sales plans.

    (b) Mr. Nesbit, and Ms. Clark met to discuss the sales plans.

PART B

For each question, there are two sentences. One sentence contains a mistake. The other sentence is correct. Circle the letter next to the sentence that is correct.

EXAMPLE: (a) [circled] Our team is playing well this year; in fact, we've won all of our games.

(b) Our team is playing well this year, in fact, we've won all of our games.

11. (a) Lucy has lived; and worked in Brockton for five years.

    (b) Lucy has lived and worked in Brockton for five years.

12. (a) It was getting late, Howard still wasn't home.

    (b) It was getting late; Howard still wasn't home.

13. (a) Marge wasn't sleeping well; in fact, she could only sleep for three hours every night.

    (b) Marge wasn't sleeping well; in fact she could only sleep for three hours every night.

14. (a) Joe doesn't have enough money for a vacation; on the other hand, he can't get time off from work.

    (b) Joe doesn't have enough money for a vacation; besides, he can't get time off from work.

15. (a) We had planned to go to the park this weekend; however, it might rain.

    (b) We had planned to go to the park this weekend however, it might rain.

16. (a) Hank's train was late; for example, he wasn't on time for work.

    (b) Hank's train was late; therefore, he wasn't on time for work.

17. (a) Steve slammed the book on the desk; and kicked the chair.

    (b) Steve slammed the book on the desk and kicked the chair.

18. (a) It hasn't rained very much this summer; as a result, the crops aren't growing very well.

    (b) It hasn't rained very much this summer; for example, the crops aren't growing very well.

19. (a) This is a very tall building; in fact it's the tallest building in this city.

    (b) This is a very tall building; in fact, it's the tallest building in this city.

20. (a) The keys are on the table; the car is parked outside.

    (b) The keys are on the table, the car is parked outside.

PART C

For each question, there are two sentences. One sentence contains a mistake. The other sentence is correct. Circle the letter next to the sentence that is correct.

EXAMPLE: (a) The car is parked by the curb with the new tires.

(b) The car with the new tires is parked by the curb.

21. (a) After he finishes, can go home.

    (b) After he finishes, he can go home.

22. (a) Although the sky is gray and cloudy, it's not supposed to rain.
    (b) Although the sky is gray and cloudy it's not supposed to rain.

23. (a) Until we find the key, no one may leave.
    (b) Until we find the key no one may leave.

24. (a) I saw a woman in the diner with a gold tooth.
    (b) I saw a woman with a gold tooth in the diner.

25. (a) There is a bus on the street with a flat tire.
    (b) There is a bus with a flat tire on the street.

PART D

Read the following paragraph and answer the questions that follow it. The sentences in the paragraph are numbered to help you answer the questions.

> (1) Having a pet can teach a child responsibility and caring. (2) If it is a child's duty to feed the family pet, that child gets a lesson in taking responsibility. (3) Some kinds of dogs are better with children than others. (4) A child who nurses a pet through an injury or illness learns how it feels to care.

26. Which sentence in the paragraph is the topic sentence?

27. There is one sentence that should not be in the paragraph because it is not on the topic of the paragraph. Which sentence is that?

ANSWER KEY

PART A		PART B		PART C	PART D
1. **a**	6. **a**	11. **b**	16. **b**	21. **b**	26. **1**
2. **b**	7. **b**	12. **b**	17. **b**	22. **a**	27. **3**
3. **b**	8. **b**	13. **a**	18. **a**	23. **a**	
4. **a**	9. **b**	14. **b**	19. **b**	24. **b**	
5. **a**	10. **a**	15. **a**	20. **a**	25. **b**	

In this chart, circle the number of any items you did not answer correctly. The right-hand side of the chart will tell you the unit number to study for any item that you missed.

Item Number:	**Unit to study:**
1 2 3 4 5 6 7 8 9 10	UNIT 18: How Are Compounds Used?
11 12 13 14 15 16 17 18 19 20	UNIT 19: How Are Compound Sentences Put Together?
21 22 23 24 25	UNIT 20: How Are Phrases and Fragments Used?
26 27	UNIT 21: What Makes a Good Paragraph?

(If you answered all the items in this unit correctly, you have completed your work in this book.)

UNIT 18: HOW ARE COMPOUNDS USED?

In Unit 2 of this book, you took a close look at the sentence. What is a sentence? A sentence is a group of words. It gives a complete idea about something.

Fred will drive to Las Vegas.

This group of words is a sentence. It gives a complete idea about somebody.

When you write, you use sentences. You use sentences to give your reader a clear and complete idea. You use sentences to let your reader know exactly what you mean.

Every sentence that you write contains a complete idea. Sometimes, ideas have a lot in common. Sometimes, you can *combine* two sentences into one. One of the basic ways to combine ideas is to use **compounds**.

Earlier in this book, you worked with compound subjects. In this unit, you'll take a closer look at compounds. You'll work with compound subjects. You'll also work with compound verbs. And you'll take a look at putting two sentences together to form a compound sentence.

BUILDING COMPOUND SUBJECTS AND COMPOUND VERBS

Look at these two sentences. How are they alike?

Fred will drive to Las Vegas.
Ethel will drive to Las Vegas.

These two sentences are separate. The first sentence tells you about Fred. The second sentence tells you about Ethel. But Fred and Ethel have something in common. They both will do the same thing. They both will drive to Las Vegas. You could put the two sentences together like this:

Fred and Ethel will drive to Las Vegas.

Fred and Ethel is a **compound subject**. A compound subject is a subject made up of two or more simple subjects linked together.

Fred and Ethel will drive to Las Vegas.

In this sentence, what word links the two parts of the compound subject? The word and links the two parts of the compound subject: Fred **and** Ethel.

In Unit 7 of this book, you matched compound subjects to the right verbs. What other words can be used to connect the parts of a compound subject?

Fred will drive to Las Vegas.
Or Ethel will drive to Las Vegas.

Either Fred or Ethel will drive to Las Vegas.

Fred won't drive to Las Vegas.
Ethel won't drive to Las Vegas.

Neither Fred nor Ethel will drive to Las Vegas.

Fred will drive to Las Vegas.
Ethel will also drive to Las Vegas.

Not only Fred but also Ethel will drive to Las Vegas.

The words either/or, neither/nor, and not only/but also are used to connect the parts of a compound subject. As you can see, the meaning of the sentence depends on which connecting words are used.

Putting subjects together in a compound is one basic way to combine ideas in a sentence. But it isn't the only way. Look at the next two sentences. What do they have in common?

Harry talks in his sleep.

Harry walks in his sleep.

Both sentences have the same subject: Harry. Each sentence tells you something that Harry does. Each tells you something that Harry does in his sleep. You could combine the ideas in the two sentences like this:

Harry talks and walks in his sleep.

Talks and walks is a **compound verb**. A compound verb is two or more verbs joined together with a connecting word. Each part of a compound verb is linked to the same subject:

Harry talks and walks in his sleep.

You can use the same connecting words with compound verbs as you use with compound subjects.

Harry talks in his sleep.
Or Harry walks in his sleep.

Harry either talks or walks in his sleep.

Harry doesn't talk in his sleep.
Harry doesn't walk in his sleep.

Harry neither talks nor walks in his sleep.

Harry talks in his sleep.
Harry also walks in his sleep.

Harry not only talks but also walks in his sleep.

Linking subjects or verbs together in a compound isn't hard. However, be careful with the connecting words that you use in a compound. Be careful how you use the connecting words either/or, neither/nor, and not only/but also. Look at this sentence:

Neither Hank or Gus went to the rodeo.

This sentence has a compound subject. But something is wrong with it. Look at the words that are used to connect the parts of the compound:

Neither Hank or Gus went to the rodeo.

The word or doesn't belong with the word neither. Or belongs with either. Neither goes with nor. When you put things together in a compound, take a close look at the connecting words. Only use the connecting words that belong to the same pair.

Here's another problem with using connecting words:

Wendell runs but also plays basketball.

The connecting words but also are part of a pair. They go with not only. But not only is missing from the sentence. Both parts of the pair belong in the sentence.

Wendell not only runs but also plays basketball.

Try It: Building Compound Subjects and Compound Verbs

Combine the two sentences. Use the connecting words that follow the sentences in parentheses.

EXAMPLE: Wally lived in Cedar Rapids.
Elaine lived in Cedar Rapids. (and)

Wally and Elaine lived in Cedar Rapids.

1. Victor washed the car. Victor waxed the car. (not only/but also)

2. Becky cooked all day. Becky cleaned all day. (and)

3. Sally worked at Carson's Store. Liz worked at Carson's Store. (neither/nor)

4. Sean lives in Hooterville. Sean works in Hooterville. (not only/but also)

5. Frank will drive you to work. Carla will drive you to work. (either/or)

6. Dave walks to work. Dave drives to work. (neither/nor)

7. Charles types. Charles files. (and)

8. Harvey will help you. Harold will help you. (either/or)

9. Roger went to the beach. Phil went to the beach. (neither/nor)

10. Woody will see us later. Esther will see us later. (and)

Check your answers on page 217.

BUILDING COMPOUND SENTENCES

Up to now, you've worked with compound subjects and compound verbs. You know that you can join subjects and verbs together when they have something in common.

> Fred will drive to Las Vegas.
> Ethel will drive to Las Vegas.
>
> Fred and Ethel will drive to Las Vegas.

Now, look at these two sentences:

> The phone rang.
>
> Trudy answered it.

Each sentence tells you about something that happened. The sentences have different subjects and different verbs. But they do have something in common. The two things that happened are connected with each other. You could write the two sentences like this:

> The phone rang, and Trudy answered it.

This new sentence is a **compound sentence**. A compound sentence is made up of two parts. Each part has a subject and a verb. Each part can stand on its own as a complete sentence. But the two parts are joined together because they have something in common.

Look at the next sentence. What are the two parts that make up the compound?

> Ted went to the movies, but Kim stayed home.

Each part of this compound sentence has a subject and a verb. Each part can stand on its own as a complete sentence.

> Ted went to the movies.
>
> Kim stayed home.

But the two ideas have a lot in common. They can be combined into one compound sentence.

Take another look at the next two sentences. How are the parts of the compounds joined together?

> The phone rang, and Trudy answered it.
>
> Ted went to the movies, but Kim stayed home.

In each sentence, there is a word that connects the two parts together. In the first sentence, the word is and. In the second sentence, the word is but. And and but are two connecting words that you can use in compound sentences. Here are some others:

or	nor	so	yet
either/or	neither/nor	not only/but also	

When you use these connecting words, make sure you also put a comma between the two parts of the compound sentence.

Carla seems fine, yet she is really upset.

I not only want more money, but I also need it.

You should leave now, or you will be late.

Bill's car broke down, so he walked to work.

Try It: Building Compound Sentences

Each of the following pairs of sentences has something in common. Join them together in a compound sentence. Use the connecting word in parentheses. (Remember to put a comma between the two parts of the compound sentence.)

EXAMPLE: Tony is my brother. Angela is my sister. (and)

Tony is my brother, and Angela is my sister.

1. Pat burned the dinner. We went to the diner. (so)

2. The joke was funny. No one laughed. (but)

3. Rudy was tired. He finished his job. (yet)

4. Rita will stay home with the children. Joe will take them to the park. (either/or)

5. You can pick me up. I can take the bus. (or)

Check your answers on page 218.

USING COMMAS WITH COMPOUNDS

Look at these three sentences. How are they different from one another?

> Gary and his dog went for a walk.
>
> I ran home and called her.
>
> The milk was sour, so we brought it back.

The first sentence has a compound subject. The second sentence has a compound verb. The third sentence is a compound sentence.

How is the third sentence different from the other two?

> The milk was sour, so we brought it back.

In the third sentence, a comma is used. Commas are used in compound sentences. They are used to separate the parts of the compound sentence. The comma comes before the connecting word.

However, commas are *not* used to connect two parts of a compound subject or a compound verb.

> Gary and his dog went for a walk.

Gary and his dog is a compound *subject*. This sentence is not a compound *sentence*. A comma is not needed in it.

There is only one time that you use commas in a compound subject or verb. That's when the compound is made up of three or more parts. For example, look at this sentence:

> Manny, Moe, and Jack are his best friends.

This sentence contains a compound subject. The compound subject is Manny, Moe, and Jack. It is made up of three parts. Use commas to separate the parts of a compound subject or compound verb *only* when it is made up of three or more parts.

> They danced, sang, and laughed all night.
>
> (The compound verb is made up of three parts. Therefore, commas are used to separate the parts.)
>
> They danced and sang all night.
>
> (In this sentence, the compound verb is made up of only two parts. A comma is *not* used to separate the parts.)

Using commas with compounds can be a little tricky. But it can be easy if you think about what kind of compound is in the sentence. If you don't know whether to use a comma, take a close look at the compound. Is it a compound subject or a compound verb? If it is, you shouldn't use a comma unless there are more than two parts to the compound. Is it a compound sentence? If it is, then you should use a comma. You should put the comma before the connecting word.

Try It: Using Commas with Compounds

Read each sentence. Decide whether the sentence needs commas in it. If it does, rewrite the sentence. Put the commas in the right place.

EXAMPLE: The bus didn't come so I was late for work.

The bus didn't come, so I was late for work.

1. Steve dusted and mopped the house.

2. Lenny lost his wallet but he found his keys.

3. June Mike and Teresa bought raffle tickets from Bud.

4. Clark whistled and sang in the shower.

5. I'll stay with friends or I'll rent a room at a motel.

6. Donald typed copied and filed the report.

Check your answers on page 218.

UNIT REVIEW

In this unit, you've taken a close look at compounds. A compound is a basic way to combine ideas in a sentence. A **compound subject** is two or more subjects combined together in one sentence. A **compound verb** is two or more verbs combined together in one sentence. A **compound sentence** is two sentences that are combined into one.

You also worked on one way to put the parts of a compound sentence together. You use a connecting word to put the parts together. You also put a comma before the connecting word. In the next unit, you will work on some other ways to join the parts of a compound sentence together.

SPELLING AND USAGE HINT: HOMONYMS

Some words sound alike but mean different things. For example, look at the following words. Say each word aloud.

accept	except	
to	too	two
than	then	
affect	effect	
whether	weather	

These pairs of words are called **homonyms**. Homonyms are words that sound alike but are spelled differently. They also mean different things. Homonyms can cause trouble when you write. It's easy to mix them up because they sound the same.

Here is a list of commonly confused homonyms. Study the meaning and spelling of each word.

accept: to take willingly; to approve

except: to leave out; but

The committee accepted Johnson's plan.

Jean remembered everything except her toothbrush.

to: a preposition of direction

two: the number 2

too: also; more than is needed; very

Allan drove to the airport.

There are only two tickets left.

Melvin called earlier, and his wife called, too.

than: a word used in comparisons

then: a word used to show time

Carol is taller than Jim.

It was sunny until noon; then it began to rain.

affect: to influence; to have an effect on

effect: a result

The noise affected his hearing.

The effects of the tornado could be seen all over town.

whether: if

weather: the condition of the air and atmosphere

I'm not sure whether Jack is at home or at work today.

The weather was beautiful all week.

Try It: Homonyms

Read each sentence. If a word is used incorrectly, rewrite the sentence.

EXAMPLE: There are too empty seats in the front row.

There are two empty seats in the front row.

1. Mildred excepted the award.

2. First he knocked on the door, and than he opened it.

3. I'm going away this weekend and next weekend, two.

4. No one knows how the news will effect Clarence.

5. There are too supermarkets in that shopping mall.

6. The weather is warmer today then it was yesterday.

7. To much sun affects her skin.

Check your answers on page 219.

ANSWERS AND EXPLANATIONS

Try It: Building Compound Subjects and Compound Verbs

1. **Victor not only washed but also waxed the car.** The two sentences have the same subject: Victor. They can be combined with a compound verb. The connecting words not only/but also join the verbs washed and waxed.
2. **Becky cooked and cleaned all day.** The two sentences have the same subject: Becky. They can be combined with a compound verb. The connecting word and joins the verbs cooked and cleaned.
3. **Neither Sally nor Liz worked at Carson's Store.** The two sentences have the same verb: worked. They can be combined with a compound subject. The connecting words neither/nor join the subjects Sally and Liz.
4. **Sean not only lives but also works in Hooterville.** The two sentences have the same subject: Sean. They can be combined with a compound verb. The connecting words not only/but also join the verbs lives and works.
5. **Either Frank or Carla will drive you to work.** The two sentences have the same verb: will drive. They can be combined with a compound subject. The connecting words either/or join the subjects Frank and Carla.
6. **Dave neither walks nor drives to work.** The two sentences have the same subject: Dave. They can be combined with a compound verb. The connecting words neither/nor join the verbs walks and drives.
7. **Charles types and files.** The two sentences have the same subject: Charles. They can be combined with a compound verb. The connecting word and joins the verbs types and files.
8. **Either Harvey or Harold will help you.** The two sentences have the same verb: will help. They can be combined with a compound subject. The connecting words either/or join the subjects Harvey and Harold.
9. **Neither Roger nor Phil went to the beach.** The two sentences have the same verb: went. They can be combined with a compound subject. The connecting words neither/nor join the subjects Harvey and Harold.
10. **Woody and Esther will see us later.** The two sentences have the same verb: will see. They can be combined with a compound subject. The connecting word and joins the subjects Woody and Esther.

Try It: Building Compound Sentences

1. **Pat burned the dinner, so we went to the diner.** The connecting word so joins the two parts of the compound sentence. A comma belongs before the connecting word so.
2. **The joke was funny, but no one laughed.** The connecting word but joins the two parts of the compound sentence. A comma belongs before the connecting word but.
3. **Rudy was tired, yet he finished his job.** The connecting word yet joins the two parts of the compound sentence. A comma belongs before the connecting word yet.
4. **Either Rita will stay home with the children, or Joe will take them to the park.** The connecting words either/or join the two parts of the compound sentence. A comma belongs before the connecting word or.
5. **You can pick me up, or I can take the bus.** The connecting word or joins the two parts of the compound sentence. A comma belongs before the connecting word or.

Try It: Using Commas with Compounds

1. **Steve dusted and mopped the house.** This sentence has a compound verb: dusted and mopped. A comma is not needed to separate a compound verb that has only two parts.
2. **Lenny lost his wallet, but he found his keys.** This is a compound sentence. The parts of the compound are joined with the connecting word but. A comma should be placed before but.
3. **June, Mike, and Teresa bought raffle tickets from Bud.** This sentence has a compound subject: June, Mike, and Teresa. The compound subject has three parts. Therefore, commas are used to separate the parts.
4. **Clark whistled and sang in the shower.** This sentence has a compound verb: whistled and sang. A comma is not needed to separate a compound verb that has only two parts.
5. **I'll stay with friends, or I'll rent a room at a motel.** This is a compound sentence. The parts of the compound are joined with the connecting word or. A comma should be placed before or.
6. **Donald typed, copied, and filed the report.** This sentence has a compound verb: typed, copied, and filed. The compound verb has three parts. Therefore, commas are used to separate the parts.

Try It: Homonyms

1. **Mildred accepted the award.** Except means "to leave out" or "but." Excepted is not correct in this sentence. The correct word, accepted, means "took willingly."
2. **First he knocked on the door, and then he opened it.** Than is a word used in comparisons. Than is not correct in this sentence. The correct word, then, is a word used to show time.
3. **I'm going away this weekend and next weekend, too.** Two means "the number 2." Two is not correct in this sentence. The correct word, too, means "also."
4. **No one knows how the news will affect Clarence.** Effect means "a result." Effect is not correct in this sentence. The correct word, affect, means "to have an effect on."
5. **There are two supermarkets in that shopping mall.** Too means "more than is needed" or "also." Too is not correct in this sentence. The correct word, two, means "the number 2."
6. **The weather is warmer today than it was yesterday.** Then is a word used to show time. Then is not correct in this sentence. The correct word, than, is a word used in comparisons.
7. **Too much sun affects her skin.** To is a preposition. It shows direction. To is not correct in this sentence. The correct word, too, means "more than is needed" in this sentence.

UNIT 19: HOW ARE COMPOUND SENTENCES PUT TOGETHER?

You worked with this sentence in the last unit:

Ted went to the movies, but Kim stayed home.

You know that this sentence is a compound sentence. It is made up of two parts. Each part could stand on its own as a complete sentence. But the two parts are joined together because they have something in common.

In the last unit, you worked on one way to join the parts of a compound sentence together. But there are other ways. Look at these sentences:

Ted went to the movies; Kim stayed home.

Ted went to the movies; however, Kim stayed home.

Each of these sentences is a compound sentence. In this unit, you'll work on using these different ways to put the parts of a compound sentence together.

USING SEMICOLONS WITH COMPOUNDS

Look at the underlined marks in the next two sentences. How are they different?

I saw him, but he didn't see me.

I saw him; he didn't see me.

You know what the mark in the first sentence is. It's a comma. You've been using commas throughout this book. But take a look at the mark in the second sentence. It's not a comma. It's a **semicolon**. Like the comma and the period, the semicolon is a punctuation mark. It has its own uses.

One of the uses of a semicolon is in compound sentences. You know that you can use a comma and a connecting word to connect the parts of a compound sentence. You can also use a semicolon.

I saw him; he didn't see me.

When you use a semicolon, you don't need a connecting word. A semicolon can connect the parts of a compound sentence by itself. However, when you use a semicolon, be careful. Make sure that it is connecting the parts of a compound *sentence*. Don't use semicolons to connect two parts of a compound subject or a compound verb.

Nancy left the store; walked to the post office.

(The semicolon in this sentence is WRONG. Don't use a semicolon to connect the parts of a compound verb.)

Nancy left the store and walked to the post office.

(This sentence is RIGHT.)

Here is another problem to watch out for:

I tried to start the car, the battery was dead.

In this sentence, a comma is used to connect the two parts of a compound sentence. This sentence is WRONG. A comma can't be used by itself to connect the parts of a compound sentence. If a comma is used to connect the parts of a compound sentence, a connecting word must follow it. Only a semicolon can be used by itself.

I tried to start the car, but the battery was dead.

I tried to start the car; the battery was dead.

Try It: Using Semicolons in Compounds

Read each sentence. Make sure that the commas and semicolons are used correctly. If they aren't used correctly, rewrite the sentence.

EXAMPLE: Pete went home early, Mark stayed late.

Pete went home early; Mark stayed late.

1. I went to the window; and saw her in the yard.

2. This house was built in 1810, it is the oldest building in town.

3. I heard a shot; and screamed for help.

4. I waited an hour for her, but she never arrived.

5. The man in the blue suit, and the woman in the denim jacket are my cousins.

6. The apartment is too small but we can't afford to move.

7. Irving has a large family, he has ten children.

8. Mr. Vega was a tough boss, but he was fair to everyone.

9. Claude and Phillip are Jerry's sons.

10. The sky was cloudy, it was ready to pour.

Check your answers on page 228.

USING CONNECTING WORDS WITH SEMICOLONS

Look at this compound sentence:

> Not all birds can fly; penguins can't get off the ground.

What do the ideas in the two parts of the compound have in common? How are they related? The first part gives a statement. The second part gives an example of the statement. You could show how the two parts fit together in this way:

> Not all birds can fly; for example, penguins can't get off the ground.

In this sentence, for example is used to connect the two ideas together. It is used with a semicolon.

You know that you can use a semicolon by itself to connect the two parts of a compound sentence. But you can also use a connecting word with a semicolon. The connecting word can show what the two parts have in common. It can show how the two parts are related.

Here is a list of some common connecting words that can be used with semicolons. They are used to show the links that ideas have to each other.

however—shows a contrast between ideas

> You aren't getting a raise; however, you are getting a promotion.

still—shows a contrast between ideas

> James is a skilled, hard-working man; still, he can't get a job.

nevertheless—shows a contrast between ideas

> The rules aren't fair; nevertheless, you must obey them.

besides—shows that the second idea is being added to the first

> It's too late to go out; besides, I don't have much money.

for example—shows that the second idea is an example of the first

> There are many good restaurants in town; for example, The Tavern has great food.

for instance—shows that the second idea is an example of the first

> Maddy has had lots of trouble with his car; for instance, the car's muffler fell out last week.

therefore—shows that the second idea is the result of the first

> I don't have a driver's license; therefore, I can't be a cab driver.

thus—shows that the second idea is the result of the first

> Stan forgot to turn off the oven; thus, dinner was burned.

consequently—shows that the second idea is the result of the first

> Bruce was always late for work; consequently, he was fired.

The connecting word comes after the semicolon. A comma comes after the connecting word.

> You aren't getting a raise; **however**, you are getting a promotion.

Try It: Using Connecting Words with Semicolons

Choose the connecting word that best combines the two sentences. Use the connecting word to combine the two sentences. Remember to use the correct punctuation.

EXAMPLE: Sales were good last year. Sales are poor this year. (for example—however)

Sales were good last year; however, sales are poor this year.

1. Charles doesn't like beef. He ate a hamburger. (besides—nevertheless)

2. Not all snakes are dangerous. Garter snakes can't hurt you. (for example—thus)

3. I have never ridden a horse. I have ridden a donkey. (for instance—however)

4. The drive to the beach is too long. The weather isn't very nice today. (besides—however)

5. John's headache is gone. He is feeling better. (therefore—still)

6. I'm not hungry. I will eat dinner. (therefore—still)

7. Mack goes on trips often. He went to New York City last Saturday. (consequently—for instance)

8. All of the hotels in town are full. We will have to stay somewhere else. (for example—thus)

Check your answers on page 229.

UNIT REVIEW

In the last two units, you've looked at many different ways to join sentences in a compound. You know that you can join sentences in a compound when they have something in common.

Al lives in Texas. His family lives in New Mexico.

What are some of the ways to join these two sentences?

Al lives in Texas, but his family lives in New Mexico.

Al lives in Texas; his family lives in New Mexico.

Al lives in Texas; however, his family lives in New Mexico.

All of these sentences are correct. You can join sentences any of these ways. Just follow these rules:

1. Make sure that the sentences belong together. Don't put ideas together if they don't have anything in common.

   The newspaper is on the table, and it's raining outside.

   (These sentences should *not* be joined together. The ideas don't have any connection.)

2. Make sure each part of the compound is a complete sentence. Make sure each part can stand on its own.

   Burt can use the car; however, not today.

   (This sentence is WRONG. Not today is not a complete sentence. It can't stand on its own.)

   Burt can use the car; however, he can't use it today.

   (This sentence is RIGHT. Burt can use the car and he can't use it today can both stand on their own as complete sentences.)

3. Make sure that the connecting words show the right connection between the ideas.

   I'm going out; for example, I'll be back in an hour.

   (This sentence is WRONG. I'll be back in an hour isn't an example of I'm going out.)

   I'm going out; however, I'll be back in an hour.

   (The connecting word in this sentence is RIGHT.)

4. Make sure that punctuation is used correctly. Use a comma before the connecting words and, or, but, yet, so, and nor. Use a semicolon and a comma with such connecting words as however and for example. Remember that the semicolon comes before the connecting word and the comma comes after it.

   Francine is a good worker, however; Wilma is much better.

   (The connection in this sentence is WRONG. The semicolon should come before the connecting word. The comma should come after the connecting word.)

   Francine is a good worker; however, Wilma is much better.

   (The connection in this sentence is RIGHT.)

SPELLING AND USAGE HINT: MORE ON HOMONYMS

In the last Spelling and Usage Hint, you looked at homonyms. You saw that some words sound alike but are spelled differently. Now look at the words below. The words in the first column are contractions. (A contraction is two words joined into one.) The words in the second and third columns sound like the contractions:

it's	its	
you're	your	
they're	their	there
who's	whose	

Study the meanings of these words to avoid confusing them.

it's: contraction for it is or it has

its: possessive pronoun

It's Monday. (It is Monday.)

It's been a long time. (It has been a long time.)

The bar lost its liquor license.

you're: contraction for you are

your: possessive pronoun

You're late. (You are late.)

Your brother is on the phone.

they're: contraction for they are

their: possessive pronoun

there: word used to point out a place or to start a sentence

> They're not home tonight. (They are not home tonight.)
>
> Their union is very powerful.
>
> There is someone at the door.

who's: contraction form of who is or who/has

whose: possessive pronoun

> Who's calling me? (Who is calling me?)
>
> Who's been here? (Who has been here?)
>
> Whose sweater is this?

Try It: More on Homonyms

Read each sentence. If a word is used incorrectly, rewrite the sentence.

EXAMPLE: Whose on the phone?
Who's on the phone?

1. The company laid off many of it's employees.

2. Call the doctor if your sick.

3. They're daughter was born last Friday morning.

4. Who's taken your keys?

5. The dog is barking because its hungry.

6. Your brother called while you were out.

7. Their is some money in my savings account.

8. Who's sweater are you wearing?

9. You're opinions are very different from theirs.

10. There apartment was damaged in the fire.

Check your answers on page 230.

ANSWERS AND EXPLANATIONS

Try It: Using Semicolons in Compounds

1. **I went to the window and saw her in the yard.** This sentence has a compound verb: went and saw. A semicolon should *not* be used to connect the parts of a compound verb.
2. **This house was built in 1810; it is the oldest building in town.** This is a compound sentence. The parts of the compound sentence are *not* joined by a connecting word. A semicolon is needed to connect the parts of the compound sentence.
3. **I heard a shot and screamed for help.** This sentence has a compound verb: heard and screamed. A semicolon should *not* be used to connect the parts of a compound verb.
4. **I waited an hour for her, but she never arrived.** This sentence is correct as it is. It is a compound sentence. The parts of the compound sentence are joined by the connecting word but. A comma is placed before the connecting word.
5. **The man in the blue suit and the woman in the denim jacket are my cousins.** This sentence has a compound subject: man and woman. A comma should *not* be used to connect the parts of a compound subject.
6. **The apartment is too small, but we can't afford to move.** This is a compound sentence. The parts of the compound sentence are joined by the connecting word but. A comma should be placed before the connecting word.
7. **Irving has a large family; he has ten children.** This is a compound sentence. The parts of the compound sentence are *not* joined by a connecting word. A semicolon is needed to connect the parts of the compound sentence.

8. **Mr. Vega was a tough boss, but he was fair to everyone.** This sentence is correct as it is. It is a compound sentence. The parts of the compound are joined by the connecting word but. A comma is used before the connecting word.

9. **Claude and Phillip are Jerry's sons.** This sentence is correct as it is. Claude and Phillip is a compound subject. A comma is *not* needed to separate the parts of a compound subject.

10. **The sky was cloudy; it was ready to pour.** This is a compound sentence. The parts of the compound are *not* joined by a connecting word. A semicolon is needed to connect the parts of the compound sentence.

Try It: Using Connecting Words with Semicolons

1. **Charles doesn't like beef; nevertheless, he ate a hamburger.** The connecting word nevertheless shows a contrast between the ideas in the compound. A semicolon belongs before the connecting word; a comma belongs after it.

2. **Not all snakes are dangerous; for example, garter snakes can't hurt you.** The connecting words for example show that the second idea is an example of the first. A semicolon belongs before the connecting words; a comma belongs after the words.

3. **I have never ridden a horse; however, I have ridden a donkey.** The connecting word however shows a contrast between the ideas in the compound. A semicolon belongs before the connecting word; a comma belongs after the word.

4. **The drive to the beach is too long; besides, the weather isn't very nice today.** The connecting word besides shows that the second idea is being added to the first. A semicolon belongs before the connecting word; a comma belongs after it.

5. **John's headache is gone; therefore, he is feeling better.** The connecting word therefore shows that the second idea is the result of the first. A semicolon belongs before the connecting word; a comma belongs after it.

6. **I'm not hungry; still, I will eat dinner.** The connecting word still shows a contrast between the ideas in the compound. A semicolon belongs before the connecting word; a comma belongs after it.

7. **Mack goes on trips often; for instance, he went to New York City last Saturday.** The connecting words for instance show that the second idea is an example of the first. A semicolon belongs before the connector; a comma belongs after it.

8. **All of the hotels in town are full; thus, we will have to stay somewhere else.** The connecting word thus shows that the second idea is the result of the first. A semicolon belongs before the connecting word; a comma belongs after it.

Try It: More on Homonyms

1. **The company laid off many of its employees.** It's is a contraction for it is or it has. It's is not correct in this sentence. The correct word, its, is a possessive pronoun.
2. **Call the doctor if you're sick.** Your is a possessive pronoun. Your is not correct in this sentence. The correct word, you're, is the contraction for you are.
3. **Their daughter was born last Friday morning.** They're is the contraction for they are. They're is not correct in this sentence. The correct word, their, is a possessive pronoun.
4. **Who's taken your keys?** This sentence is correct as it is. The word who's is the contraction for who has in this sentence. Your is a possessive pronoun.
5. **The dog is barking because it's hungry.** Its is a possessive pronoun. Its is not correct in this sentence. The correct word, it's, is the contraction for it is in this sentence.
6. **Your brother called while you were out.** This sentence is correct as it is. The word your is a possessive pronoun.
7. **There is some money in my savings account.** Their is a possessive pronoun. Their is not correct in this sentence. The correct word, there, is a word used to start a sentence.
8. **Whose sweater are you wearing?** Who's is a contraction for who is or who has. Who's is not correct in this sentence. The correct word, whose, is a possessive pronoun.
9. **Your opinions are very different from theirs.** You're is the contraction for you are. You're is not correct in this sentence. The correct word, your, is a possessive pronoun.
10. **Their apartment was damaged in the fire.** There is a word used to point out a place or to start a sentence. There is not correct in this sentence. The correct word, their, is a possessive pronoun.

UNIT 20: HOW ARE PHRASES AND FRAGMENTS USED?

In the last two units, you worked on a basic way to combine ideas in a sentence. You worked on putting ideas together in compounds.

John likes peanuts.
Mary likes peanuts.

John and Mary like peanuts.

Warren wanted a new shirt.
He didn't have enough money.

Warren wanted a new shirt, but he didn't have enough money.

Using compounds is one way to combine ideas in a sentence. It's one way to show how ideas fit together. It's one way to show that ideas have something in common. But there are other ways to combine ideas in a sentence. Look at these examples:

Henry works overtime.
Henry works in the grocery store.

Henry works overtime in the grocery store.

Henry works overtime.
Henry needs money.

Henry works overtime because he needs money.

In this unit, you'll take a closer look at some ways to combine ideas in a sentence.

USING PREPOSITIONAL PHRASES

Look at the underlined words in this sentence. What do they tell you?

The store on the corner sells fresh vegetables.

The underlined words tell you more about the store. They tell you where the store is. They describe the store.

Earlier in this book, you looked at words that describe—adjectives and adverbs. Groups of words can also act as adjectives or adverbs. They can describe nouns and verbs. They can build up sentences by supplying more information about nouns and verbs.

Look at this sentence again:

The store on the corner sells fresh vegetables.

The underlined words make up a **prepositional phrase**. A **phrase** is a group of words without a subject or verb. A prepositional phrase is a group of words that describes the noun or verb nearest to it. It begins with a **preposition** and ends with a noun. A preposition is a kind of linking word. It shows how a noun is related to a verb or another noun.

The underlined words in these sentences are prepositional phrases.

The man with the baseball hat is my brother.

(The prepositional phrase with the baseball hat tells you *which* man is my brother.)

The woman in the photograph is Delores.

(The prepositional phrase in the photograph tells you *which* woman is Delores.)

We drove to the farm.

(The prepositional phrase to the farm tells you *where* we drove.)

I live above the bank.

(The prepositional phrase above the bank tells you *where* I live.)

With, in, to, and above are all prepositions. Here are some other common prepositions:

across	after	at	before
between	by	for	from
near	of	over	through
under	until	up	within

It's usually easy to use prepositional phrases. It's usually easy to decide which preposition to use. However, you have to be careful about where you put the prepositional phrase in the sentence. Suppose you wanted to combine the ideas in these two sentences:

A man knocked on my door.
The man had a mustache.

You could use a prepositional phrase. But where would you put the phrase?

A man knocked on my door with a mustache.

A man with a mustache knocked on my door.

A prepositional phrase describes the noun or verb that is closest to it. Look at the first sentence again. Which noun or verb is closest to the phrase?

A man knocked on my door with a mustache.

Door is closest to the phrase. Does the door have a mustache? It doesn't. The phrase is in the wrong place.

Now look at the second sentence. Which noun or verb is closest to it?

A man with a mustache knocked on my door.

Man is closest to the phrase. Does the man have a mustache? He does. The phrase is in the right place.

Try It: Using Prepositional Phrases

For each item there are two sentences. Make the second sentence a prepositional phrase and combine the two sentences.

EXAMPLE: The yellow car belongs to George. The yellow car is in the parking lot.

The yellow car in the parking lot belongs to George.

1. The cat jumped onto my leg. The cat has sharp claws.

2. The clown is in the circus. He has a polka-dot tie.

3. The millionaire's daughter was kidnapped. Terrorists kidnapped her.

4. There is a jar on the shelf. The jar contains pickles.

5. The suit belongs to my father. The suit is in the closet.

6. The bird is eating a worm. The bird has blue feathers.

7. There is a box on the table. The box contains cereal.

8. The house was cleaned. Clara cleaned the house.

Check your answers on page 240.

USING FRAGMENTS

In the beginning of this unit, you looked at this sentence:

Henry works overtime because he needs money.

The underlined words add information to the main idea. They tell why Henry works overtime.

Look at the underlined words again. How are they different from a prepositional phrase?

Henry works overtime because he needs money.

A prepositional phrase doesn't have a subject and a verb. But because he needs money has a subject (he) and a verb (needs).

Because he needs money has a subject and a verb. But is it a sentence? Can it stand on its own as a complete thought?

Because he needs money.

This group of words doesn't express a complete idea. Something important is missing. The words don't say *what* he does because he needs money. This group of words is incomplete by itself. It is a **fragment.**

You worked with fragments in the first part of this book. You looked at fragments that were missing a subject or a verb. There is another kind of fragment. It *does* have a subject and a verb. It looks and sounds a lot like a sentence. But there is one word in the fragment that keeps it from being a sentence:

because he needs money

The word because is a connecting word. It is used to connect two ideas together. But when it is used, the idea that follows it becomes a fragment. It cannot stand by itself as a sentence. It needs to be connected to a sentence.

Look at this fragment:

as soon as they are finished

Do you get a complete idea from this? You don't. They are finished could stand as a complete sentence. It has a subject (they) and a verb (are finished). But the connecting words as soon as turn the sentence into a fragment. The fragment doesn't tell you what is going to happen as soon as they are finished. The fragment can't stand by itself.

We will clean up as soon as they are finished.

Now is the sentence complete? Does it give you a complete idea? It does. We will clean up is a complete sentence. It has a subject (we). It has a verb (will clean). There is no connecting word in front of this sentence. It isn't a fragment. The fragment as soon as they are finished is added to the complete sentence. It adds more information to the sentence. The fragment tells you *when* we will clean up.

Here is a list of connecting words. You can use these words to combine ideas in a sentence.

after	although	as	because
before	even though	as though	since
as soon as	though	as if	so that
until	unless	if	

Remember that these connecting words begin fragments. They have to be connected to a complete sentence.

Unless he wants it.

(This is a FRAGMENT. It cannot stand on its own. It needs to be connected to a sentence.)

He shouldn't get it unless he wants it.

(This is a SENTENCE. He shouldn't get it can stand on its own as a complete sentence. The fragment is added to it.)

Try It: Using Fragments

Underline the fragment in each sentence.

1. I'll call you after the show is over.
2. Ralph left at seven so that he wouldn't be late.

3. Dinner will be served as soon as Tom gets home.

4. The team lost the game even though it played well.

5. Harry sang while Joe played the guitar.

6. Judy acts as if she owns the world.

7. The children can play outside until it gets dark.

8. I'm going to throw this away unless you want it.

Check your answers on page 240.

PUTTING A SENTENCE AND A FRAGMENT TOGETHER

What's the difference between these two sentences?

We were late because the traffic was heavy.

Because the traffic was heavy, we were late.

In the first sentence, the fragment comes after the main sentence. In the second sentence, the fragment comes *before* the main sentence. But both sentences mean the same thing.

Most of the time, a fragment can come before *or* after the main sentence. But what happens when the fragment comes *before* the main sentence?

Because the traffic was heavy, we were late.

A comma is used to make it clear where the fragment ends and the main sentence begins. You don't need a comma when the fragment comes after the main sentence. The connecting word makes it clear that the ideas are separate.

We were late because the traffic was heavy.

When you put a fragment together with a sentence, there are a couple of things you should keep in mind. The first thing is to make sure that one of the parts *is* a complete sentence. Don't put two fragments together. They won't make a complete sentence.

Because it is a holiday, since the banks are closed.

(This is NOT a sentence. Because it is a holiday is a fragment. Since the banks are closed is also a fragment. One of the fragments should be changed into a sentence.)

Because it is a holiday, the banks are closed.

(This IS a sentence. The banks are closed can stand as a complete sentence.)

Here is another problem to watch out for:

Because the traffic was heavy, so we were late.

The word because is a connecting word. It connects the fragment to the main sentence. But the word so also is a connecting word. It's used to connect two sentences together in a compound.

You don't need both connecting words in the sentence. You should use one word or the other, but not both.

Because the traffic was heavy, we were late.

The traffic was heavy, so we were late.

Try It: Putting a Sentence and a Fragment Together

Read each sentence. If the sentence is put together incorrectly, rewrite it. Make it correct. Remember to put a comma between the fragment and the main sentence part when the fragment comes first.

EXAMPLE: Since he left early; therefore, he didn't finish the job.

Since he left early, he didn't finish the job.

or

He left early; therefore, he didn't finish the job.

1. Even though it was late, but we went to Bill's house.

2. Unless the economy improves the plant will be closed.

3. Although the plumber came yesterday yet the pipes are still broken.

4. Since the typewriter broke because Peter dropped it.

5. Milton brought his camera so that he could take pictures.

Check your answers on page 241.

UNIT REVIEW

In this unit, you've taken a look at some ways to connect ideas together in a sentence. First, you looked at using **prepositional phrases**. You saw that prepositional phrases describe nouns and verbs. A preposition is a word (such as with or to) that shows the link between a noun and a verb or another noun.

You also worked with using **fragments** in this unit. A fragment has a subject and a verb, but it is not a sentence. It's not a sentence because the first word of a fragment is a connecting word. In order to be used correctly, a fragment must be connected to a main sentence.

Compounds, prepositional phrases, and fragments are all important ways to connect ideas together in a sentence. They are important because they help to make ideas clearer. You use them to show that ideas have something in common. You use them to show *what* ideas have in common. You use them to build sentences that make sense.

SPELLING AND USAGE REVIEW: CAPITALIZATION AND PUNCTUATION

Throughout this book, you have worked on capitalization and punctuation rules. In Unit 2, you saw that capital letters and end marks make a sentence "look" like a sentence. You also worked with some capitalization and punctuation rules in that unit. In Unit 12, you worked on using apostrophes to form the possessive of nouns. You also worked with apostrophes and contractions in that unit. In Unit 13, you worked on using commas with lists of adjectives. In Unit 18, you worked on using commas with compounds. You worked with compounds and semicolons in Unit 19. And, in this unit, you've worked on using commas with fragments.

The capitalization and punctuation rules that you've worked on in this book are basic and important. The next exercise will give you a chance to see how well you use the rules. If you miss any of the items in the exercise, don't worry. The answer section will tell you where you can turn to in this book to review the rule.

Try It: Capitalization and Punctuation

Read each sentence. See if the capital letters and punctuation marks are used correctly. If they are not, rewrite the sentence. Put in any capital letters or punctuation marks that are missing. Take out any capital letters or punctuation marks that don't belong in the sentence.

EXAMPLE: Mike said that i might get a raise.

Mike said that I might get a raise.

1. She's lived on Main street all her life.

2. It was the middle of July and, it was hot.

3. The kittens are black white and gray.

4. I did'nt think it was funny.

5. Rob went to Buffalo last Thursday.

6. What is his name

7. We'd like to help; however we can't.

8. After Carol leaves, we can watch TV.

9. Mikes mother works in a laundromat.

10. The white car, and the blue truck belong to Herman.

11. I can drive you to the store or you can walk there.

12. The rain didn't stop, the game was canceled.

Check your answers on page 242.

ANSWERS AND EXPLANATIONS

Try It: Using Prepositional Phrases

1. **The cat with sharp claws jumped onto my leg.** The prepositional phrase with sharp claws tells you *which* cat jumped onto my leg. The phrase belongs close to the word it describes—the noun cat.
2. **The clown with a polka-dot tie is in the circus.** The prepositional phrase with a polka-dot tie tells you *which* clown is in the circus. The phrase belongs close to the word it describes—the noun clown.
3. **The millionaire's daughter was kidnapped by terrorists.** The prepositional phrase by terrorists tells you *who* kidnapped the millionaire's daughter. The phrase belongs close to the word it describes—the word kidnapped.
4. **There is a jar of pickles on the shelf.** The prepositional phrase of pickles tells you *which* jar is on the shelf. The phrase belongs close to the word it describes—the noun jar.
5. **The suit in the closet belongs to my father.** The prepositional phrase in the closet tells you *where* the suit is. The phrase belongs close to the word it describes—the noun suit.
6. **The bird with blue feathers is eating a worm.** The prepositional phrase with blue feathers tells you *which* bird is eating a worm. The phrase belongs close to the word it describes—the noun bird.
7. **There is a box of cereal on the table.** The prepositional phrase of cereal tells you *which* box is on the table. The phrase belongs close to the word it describes—the noun box.
8. **The house was cleaned by Clara.** The prepositional phrase by Clara tells you who cleaned the house. The phrase belongs close to the word it describes—the word cleaned.

Try It: Using Fragments

1. **I'll call you after the show is over.** After the show is over is a fragment. It begins with the connecting word after. It cannot stand on its own as a sentence.
2. **Ralph left at seven so that he wouldn't be late.** So that he wouldn't be late is a fragment. It begins with the connecting words so that. It cannot stand on its own as a sentence.

3. **Dinner will be served as soon as Tom gets home.** As soon as Tom gets home is a fragment. It begins with the connecting words as soon as. It cannot stand on its own as a sentence.
4. **The team lost the game even though it played well.** Even though it played well is a fragment. It begins with the connecting words even though. It cannot stand on its own as a sentence.
5. **Harry sang while Joe played the guitar.** While Joe played the guitar is a fragment. It begins with the connecting word while. It cannot stand on its own as a sentence.
6. **Judy acts as if she owns the world.** As if she owns the world is a fragment. It begins with the connecting words as if. It cannot stand on its own as a sentence.
7. **The children can play outside until it gets dark.** Until it gets dark is a fragment. It begins with the connecting word until. It cannot stand on its own as a sentence.
8. **I'm going to throw this away unless you want it.** Unless you want it is a fragment. It begins with the connecting word unless. It cannot stand on its own as a sentence.

Try It: Putting a Sentence and a Fragment Together

1. **Even though it was late, we went to Bill's house.** or **It was late, but we went to Bill's house.** The first sentence has a fragment and a main sentence. Since the fragment comes before the main sentence, a comma is used. The second sentence is a compound sentence. Both parts of the compound could stand alone as sentences. A comma is needed before the connecting word but.
2. **Unless the economy improves, the plant will be closed.** The fragment unless the economy improves comes before the main sentence. A comma belongs after a fragment when it comes before the main sentence.
3. **Although the plumber came yesterday, the pipes are still broken.** or **The plumber came yesterday, yet the pipes are still broken.** The first sentence has a fragment and a main sentence. Since the fragment comes before the main sentence, a comma is used. The second sentence is a compound sentence. Both parts of the compound could stand alone as sentences. A comma is needed before the connecting word yet.
4. **The typewriter broke because Peter dropped it.** This sentence has a fragment (because Peter dropped it) and a main sentence (the typewriter broke). A comma is not needed because the fragment comes after the main sentence.

5. **Milton brought his camera so that he could take pictures.** This sentence has a fragment (so that he could take pictures) and a main sentence (Milton brought his camera). A comma is not needed because the fragment comes after the main sentence.

Try It: Capitalization and Punctuation

1. **She's lived on Main Street all her life.** The words Main Street are capitalized because they name a specific street. (See Unit 2, pages 16–17.)
2. **It was the middle of July, and it was hot.** The comma comes *before* the connecting word in a compound sentence. (See Unit 18, pages 213–214.)
3. **The kittens are black, white, and gray.** When three or more adjectives are listed together, use commas to separate them. (See Unit 13, pages 156–158.)
4. **I didn't think it was funny.** In a contraction, the apostrophe takes the place of the missing letter. The missing letter in didn't is between the n and t (did not). (See Unit 12, pages 149–150.)
5. **Rob went to Buffalo last Thursday.** This sentence is correct as it is. Buffalo is the name of a specific place. Thursday is the name of a specific day of the week. (See Unit 2, pages 16–17.)
6. **What is his name?** A question mark should end a question. (See Unit 2, pages 14–16.)
7. **We'd like to help; however, we can't.** When you use a word like however to connect two parts of a compound sentence, put a semicolon before the word and a comma after it. (See Unit 19, pages 220–222.)
8. **After Carol leaves, we can watch TV.** This sentence is correct as it is. When a fragment comes before the main sentence, put a comma between the fragment and the main sentence. (See Unit 20, pages 236–238.)
9. **Mike's mother works in a laundromat.** To form the possessive of a singular noun, add an apostrophe and s to the noun (Mike + 's = Mike's). (See Unit 12, pages 139–143.)
10. **The white car and the blue truck belong to Herman.** Don't put a comma between two parts of a compound subject (car and truck). (See Unit 18, pages 213–214.)
11. **I can drive you to the store, or you can walk there.** In this sentence, the word or connects two sentences in a compound sentence. A comma belongs before or. (See Unit 18, pages 213–214.)
12. **The rain didn't stop; the game was canceled.** Don't use a comma by itself to connect two parts of a compound sentence. Use a semicolon instead. (See Unit 19, pages 220–222.)

UNIT 21: WHAT MAKES A GOOD PARAGRAPH?

In the last three units you worked on combining ideas to make one sentence out of two. You put related subjects and verbs together to build compound subjects and compound verbs. You built compound sentences by joining related sentences. By adding phrases and fragments to sentences, you created sentences made up of several related ideas. The underlined words in the following sentence show some of the ways ideas can be combined.

> Ted and Peter went to the movies, but Mark worked at his father's store.

Ted and Peter is a compound subject. The , but joins the two parts of this compound sentence. The words at his father's store add an idea to the sentence in a prepositional phrase.

In this unit you will look at how sentences with related ideas are grouped together into paragraphs. You will also be able to practice writing paragraphs.

BUILDING PARAGRAPHS—TOPIC SENTENCES

A **paragraph** is a group of sentences. All the sentences in a paragraph are about the same **topic**. Many paragraphs contain a **topic sentence** that announces the topic. In the following paragraph the topic sentence is underlined. What is the topic?

> New car prices have gone up steadily since the 1930s. In the '30s many new cars cost only $500. By 1960 new car prices were up to about $3000. Today you will pay $10,000 or more for the average new car.

The topic sentence lets you know that the whole paragraph is about how new car costs have changed since 1930. The next three sentences give examples. The examples demonstrate that costs have risen steadily, as the topic sentence says.

The following paragraph about the results of two surveys needs a topic sentence. What sentence could fill in the blank to make a good topic sentence?

> ______________________. A 1987 survey showed that 78% of working people wish they had a different job. Another recent survey reported that 87% of all workers do not like their jobs.

Here are a couple of possibilities for a topic sentence:

> Recent surveys show that most workers are not happy with their jobs.

Two surveys report discontent among workers.

The first topic sentence above is the better one. It tells exactly what the paragraph is about. The second one is not as exact. Workers could feel discontent about many things—taxes, benefits, working hours, and so on. The second topic sentence doesn't make it clear that the workers' discontent is about their jobs.

Try It: Building Paragraphs—Topic Sentences

Underline the topic sentence in the following paragraph.

1. My two closest friends commute to the city to work. Helen drives a city bus on a downtown route. Jose is a teller at the main branch of the First National Bank.

Read paragraphs 2 and 3 and the three topic sentences that follow. In the blank by the paragraph, write the letter of the topic sentence that would fit each paragraph. (One of the topic sentences should not be used.)

____ 2. Teenagers who used their incomes for entertainment once made up the largest group of minimum-wage earners. Now many people who can earn only the minimum wage support whole families.

____ 3. Since 1938, when it was established, the amount of the minimum wage has risen. Coverage has been extended to include many types of workers the original law did not protect.

Topic Sentences

A. The purpose of the minimum wage has changed since 1938.

B. The characteristics of the minimum-wage earner have changed.

C. The amount and coverage of the minimum wage have increased over time.

Check your answers on page 255.

BUILDING PARAGRAPHS—SUPPORTING SENTENCES

All the sentences in a good paragraph are about the same topic. A good paragraph is unified—made one—by being about one topic. The topic sentence announces the topic of a paragraph. All the other sentences—**supporting sentences**—give examples, details, or reasons that support the idea in the topic sentence.

The topic sentence is underlined in the following paragraph. One of the sentences in the paragraph does not belong there. It is "off topic." Which sentence doesn't belong?

> Some older cameras are difficult to operate. Many older cameras cannot be operated without light meters. Others are hard to focus. A modern camera with a built-in meter and an automatic focus costs about $20.

The topic of the paragraph is the difficulty of operating some older cameras. The second and third sentences give examples of that idea. However, the last sentence in the paragraph is off topic. It discusses a *modern* camera and its *cost.* In fact it seems to describe a camera that would be *easy* to operate. With the last sentence, the paragraph is not unified—it is not about one topic. Without the last sentence, the paragraph would be unified.

Is the following paragraph unified?

> Not everyone who knows about the dangers of cigarette smoking is a nonsmoker. Many informed people continue to smoke. The price of a pack of cigarettes varies from state to state. Smoking is even increasing among some groups although they know the hazards.

The paragraph is not unified. The third sentence—about the price of a pack of cigarettes—does not belong in the paragraph. The topic sentence announces that the paragraph is about smokers who know the dangers of smoking—not price. The second and fourth sentences give examples of the idea in the topic sentence.

The "price" sentence could be the topic sentence for another paragraph. What supporting sentences could be added to this new topic sentence to make a unified paragraph?

> The price of a pack of cigarettes varies from state to state.

To continue the paragraph, it would be necessary to write supporting sentences about varying cigarette prices. The following is a unified paragraph about prices.

> The price of a pack of cigarettes varies from state to state. It is not the cost of the cigarettes themselves that differs. The difference is in the amount of tax a state charges on cigarettes. Some states tax cigarettes heavily; others apply only low taxes.

Try It: Building Paragraphs—Supporting Sentences

Make each of the following paragraphs a unified paragraph. In each paragraph, cross out any sentence that does not belong.

1. Movie studios do not produce many movies today. They spend their money to make a few high-budget movies. The last movie I saw was too expensive. Studios prefer to finance a few movies that will bring in a high profit rather than several low-profit movies.

2. Natural events can be as destructive as bombs. Whole cities can be leveled by a volcano or an earthquake. A tidal wave can wipe out an entire island. One atom bomb destroyed Hiroshima.

In the blank next to each topic sentence, write the letters of the two supporting sentences that best support the topic sentence.

Topic Sentences

____ 3. My first minimum-wage job was in a mailroom.

____ 4. I now need a wage higher than the minimum wage.

Supporting Sentences

A. My financial reponsibilities have increased recently.

B. My duty was to stuff envelopes with advertising brochures.

C. Like a lot of people, I cannot make it on the minimum wage.

D. It was an easy way to earn money, but it was boring.

Check your answers on page 255.

WRITING TOPIC SENTENCES

So far in this unit you have seen that a paragraph is made up of a topic sentence and supporting sentences. You have also seen that paragraphs should be unified. In this part of the unit, you will take the first step toward writing paragraphs on your own.

To write a paragraph's topic sentence, you first need to have a clear idea about the topic and the purpose of the paragraph. Suppose you are going to write a paragraph about how difficult it is to be a parent. Before you write the topic sentence, make a note of the topic and the purpose of the paragraph:

Topic: Problems of Being a Parent

Purpose: To list some examples of the problems parents have.

The topic sentence should mention the topic and imply the purpose.

> It will *mention* the problems of parents—the topic.
>
> It will *imply*, in some way, that the supporting sentences will list examples of those problems—the purpose.

Here are two possible topic sentences:

> Topic Sentences:
>
> Parents face many problems raising their families.
>
> Bringing up children presents problems to any parent.

Either sentence would be a good topic sentence. Each mentions parents, problems, and children. (In the first topic sentence, *families* means *children.*) Each sentence would also lead a reader to expect to find some problems named in the supporting sentences.

Sometimes when you are planning to write a paragraph, you may know what the supporting sentences will say. You may not have a clear idea of your topic or purpose, however. Before you try to write a topic sentence, note down the paragraph's topic and purpose. Doing that should help you think more clearly about what the topic sentence should say.

Suppose you need a topic sentence for these supporting sentences:

> Look the car over before you buy it. Have a mechanic check it. Compare its price to the prices of similar used cars.

You could write these notes for the paragraph's topic and purpose:

> Topic: Used Car Buying Hints
>
> Purpose: To list three steps to take before buying a used car.

When you write the topic sentence, *mention* the topic and *imply* the purpose of the paragraph:

> Topic sentence: There are three things you should do before you buy a used car.

The first part of the topic sentence—There are three things you should do—*implies* that the supporting sentence will list the three steps. The second part of the topic sentence—before you buy a used car—*mentions* the topic.

Try It: Writing Topic Sentences

Think about the paragraph topics and purposes listed below. Write one topic sentence for each set.

1. Topic: Reasons to Get a GED.

   Purpose: To list three reasons people have for getting a GED.

   Topic Sentence: ______________________________

   ____

2. Topic: Rising Prices for Necessities

   Purpose: To give some examples of prices for necessary items that have gone up.

   Topic Sentence: ______________________________

   ____

Read the supporting sentences that follow. Make a note of their topic and purpose. Then write a topic sentence.

3. Supporting sentences: In Japan the school year is about 240 days long. Japanese students—even first graders—spend 2 hours a day doing homework. Many Japanese students attend extra classes to prepare for examinations.

   Topic: ______________________________

   Purpose: ______________________________

   Topic Sentence: ______________________________

   ____

Check your answers on pages 255–256.

WRITING SUPPORTING SENTENCES

If you write a paragraph without planning, it is easy to write a paragraph that is not unified. Each sentence you write can give you new ideas, but those ideas may not belong in your paragraph. If you take a moment before writing to jot down the ideas you want to mention in your supporting sentences, you will write a unified paragraph more easily.

Suppose you are writing a paragraph with the following topic, purpose, and topic sentence:

> Topic: My Favorite Kind of TV Show.
>
> Purpose: To give three reasons I like suspense mysteries.
>
> Topic sentence: I like suspense mysteries more than anything else on television.

You want to give three reasons for your tv show preference. Jot down your reasons on three separate lines:

> Supporting sentence notes:
>
> 1. The suspense is exciting.
> 2. I like to guess what will happen next.
> 3. I like to try to solve the mystery.

Each of those three notes mentions a good reason for liking suspense mysteries. Supporting sentences stating those reasons, together with the topic sentence, will create a unified paragraph:

> I like suspense mysteries more than anything else on television. I like the excitement I feel when the suspense has me on the edge of my seat. It is fun to try to figure out what will happen next. I like to try to solve mysteries before the solutions are shown.

Try It: Writing Supporting Sentences

Read the following notes about a paragraph's topic, purpose, and three supporting sentences.

> Topic: Car Owners' Expenses
>
> Purpose: To list three expenses car owners have.
>
> Supporting sentence notes:
>
> 1. Insurance.
> 2. Fuel.
> 3. Repairs.

Now, complete this paragraph by writing the three supporting sentences. (The topic sentence is written for you.)

People who own cars have many expenses. ______________________

____

____

____

____

____

Check your answer on page 256.

USING TRANSITION WORDS

In Unit 19 you used connecting words to join the two parts of a compound sentence. Connecting words show how the two parts of a sentence are related. In paragraphs, **transition words** show how the ideas in different sentences are related. Transition words help a reader move or pass from one idea to another.

You have read the paragraph about suspense mysteries. Transition words are included in the version below. They are underlined.

> I like suspense mysteries more than anything else on television. I like the excitement I feel when the suspense has me on the edge of my seat. It is <u>also</u> fun to try to figure out what will happen next. <u>Most of all</u>, I like to try to solve mysteries before the solutions are shown.

<u>Also</u> relates the second and third sentences. It shows that the excitement (in the second sentence) and the fun (in the third sentence) are two separate and equal reasons for the writer's preference for suspense mysteries. <u>Most of all</u> shows that the last reason is the most important one of all.

Transition words are not always necessary, but they can help a paragraph read more smoothly. More important, they show how ideas relate to each other.

There are many transitions words. Some of them you can use in paragraphs that list examples are these:

To show addition	To show example
also	for example
another	for instance
in addition	one of the
most of all	one kind of

Try It: Using Transition Words

Add transition words from the lists on page 250 to the blanks in each of the following paragraphs.

1. Kate can be difficult sometimes. ________________, she usually insists that everybody do things her way. She is ________________ not very sensitive to the feelings of others.

2. Attending night classes involves some hardships for me. ________________, I cannot go home to eat after work if I want to get to class on time. ________________, I have to pay a babysitter to feed and watch my children.

3. I have plans for myself when I get my GED. ________________ plans I have is to take some college courses. ________________ thing I want to do is apply for that job I could not get without a diploma.

Check your answers on page 256.

WRITING PARAGRAPHS

In this unit, you have written topic sentences and supporting sentences by referring to notes that helped you plan your writing. You have also added transition words to supporting sentences. Now you can bring all your skills together to write complete paragraphs.

Follow these steps to write a unified paragraph:

Step 1. Make a note about the topic of your paragraph.
Step 2. Make a note about your purpose in writing the paragraph.
Step 3. Make a note for each supporting sentence. Be sure that each supporting sentence you plan is on the topic.
Step 4. Write the topic sentence. Mention the topic and imply the purpose of the paragraph.
Step 5. Write each supporting sentence. Use transition words if possible.

Study the following example. It shows all the steps in writing a unified paragraph.

Topic: Cold Remedies

Purpose: To list two examples of cold remedies that are useless or harmful.

Supporting sentence notes:

1. Mouthwashes kill germs but don't fight colds.

2. Cough medicines and cold tablets—habit-forming.

Paragraph:

Many cold remedies available today are useless or harmful. Some mouthwashes may kill germs, but they do not fight colds. Some cough medicines and cold tablets contain drugs that can be habit forming.

Try It: Writing Paragraphs

Use the lines printed below to plan and write a paragraph that lists three reasons you like or do not like something. The thing you decide to write about will be your topic. Be sure that you have three different reasons for liking or not liking that thing. You may find it helpful to refer to the example above as you do your planning.

Topic: ______________________________

Purpose: ______________________________

____

Supporting sentence notes:

1. ______________________________
2. ______________________________
3. ______________________________

Paragraph:

____

____

____

____

____

____

There is no entry in the answer key for this **Try It**. You may wish to ask another person to comment on the planning you did and the paragraph you wrote.

UNIT REVIEW

In this unit you have looked at the parts of a good **paragraph**, a group of sentences on the same **topic**. You have seen that many paragraphs have a **topic sentence** that explains exactly what the paragraph is about. **Supporting sentences** build paragraphs by giving examples, details, or reasons to support the idea in the topic sentence. **Transition words** are used in supporting sentences to show how the ideas in a paragraph relate to each other and to help the reader pass easily from one idea to another.

You have practiced writing topic sentences, supporting sentences, and paragraphs. You followed notes you made about the topic, purpose, and supporting sentences for each paragraph.

By working through this unit, you have laid a good foundation for mastering the kind of writing you will do when you take the GED. As you continue your preparation for the GED, you will write short essays that explain or describe something. Those essays will be made up of paragaphs that you will write based on a plan. You will use the same techniques to write essays that you have used to write paragraphs in this unit.

WRITING HINT: KEEPING A JOURNAL

A **journal** is a written daily record. Many people set aside a special notebook as a journal. In it they write—sometimes every day—about their experiences and thoughts, or about events in their lives. A lot of people find that writing in a journal helps them work through problems or uncomfortable feelings. Some people keep their journals for years as a sort of "written scrapbook" of their lives.

Keeping a journal helps people improve their writing. Writing is a skill. With any skill, practice brings improvement. The more you write (and try to write well), the better you will write.

Many people who are preparing for the GED keep journals. They do it to practice writing and for the pleasure it gives them. If you do not already have the practice of keeping a journal, this would be a good time to start.

What kind of things do people write in their journals? Look at these examples:

> I wish I had a different job. Loading trucks is back-breaking work and I am sick of it. I also am tired of working nights. I never get to see much of my kids because I have to sleep when they're up. That's no kind of family life. This has to change.

> It would make my heart glad if Jim would talk to me about the things he feels. He looks worried. I don't know whether I can help him or not, but what I don't like is feeling cut off. When he doesn't tell me what's going on, I feel like he doesn't want me around.

> I'm going to buy that used pickup I saw at the garage. It's in good enough shape that I can fix it up for next to nothing. Then I'll be able to do some odd jobs to make some extra money. If I spend a little money to buy that truck, I can make money so I can pay off my bills.

As you can see, you can write about anything you want in a journal. A journal is for you—no one else needs to read it.

The best part about keeping a journal is that there are no rules. You don't have to write on an assigned topic; you don't have to write a certain number of paragraphs or pages. You can just write whatever you want.

Here are some suggestions for keeping a journal.

1. Use a special notebook for your journal. Write only your journal entries in that book.

2. Record the date of each of your journal entries.

3. If possible, write every day, even if it's only a sentence or two. That way, you develop the habit of writing.

4. Write at about the same time every day. That also helps you develop the habit of writing.

When you write in your journal, you should concentrate most on saying what you want to say. Don't worry so much about grammar, spelling, punctuation, and paragraphs. The main point is to express your thoughts. Of course, you shouldn't ignore everything you know about good writing. The better you write, the better you express yourself. But, keep your eye on the purpose—to practice writing, to express your thoughts, and to enjoy doing both.

Try It: Keeping a Journal

Start keeping a journal today. Find a notebook you like—one that will last a long time—and set it aside as your journal. Write "Journal of (Your Name)" on the first page. On the next page enter today's date. Then spend a few minutes—maybe 5 minutes to start—making your first entry. If you can't decide what to write, you could write about why you are starting to keep a journal.

Write in your journal every day, if possible. Soon you may find yourself spending a lot of pleasurable time recording your thoughts and experiences. You will soon begin to see improvement in your writing, too. That is a benefit you will appreciate when you take the GED.

There is no entry in the answer key for this **Try It.**

ANSWERS AND EXPLANATIONS

Try It: Building Paragraphs—Topic Sentences

1. **My two closest friends commute to the city to work.** The topic sentence mentions two friends who work in the city. The next two sentences discuss Helen's and Jose's city jobs.
2. **B.** The paragraph explains that minimum-wage earners were once teenagers but now are people who support families. This shows a change in the characteristics of minimum-wage earners.
3. **C.** The two sentences in the paragraph discuss (1) the rise in the amount of the minimum wage and (2) the extension of its coverage.

Note: Neither paragraph discusses the *purpose* of the minimum wage (choice **A**).

Try It: Building Paragraphs—Supporting Sentences

1. **The last movie I saw was too expensive.** The paragraph is about why studios produce few movies today. This sentence states the writer's opinion of the charge for admission to a movie. It is "off topic."
2. **One atom bomb destroyed Hiroshima.** The paragraph is about destructive *natural* events. An atom bomb is not a natural event. The topic sentence mentions bombs only to show how destructive natural events can be.
3. **B, D.** Both sentences describe the writer's first minimum-wage job in a mailroom.
4. **A, C.** Each sentence gives a reason the writer needs a wage higher than minimum wage.

Try It: Writing Topic Sentences

1. Suggested answers: **People have a variety of reasons for getting a GED.** Or, **There are many reasons people get GEDs.** Your topic sentence may be different, but it should *mention* the topic, reasons to get a GED, and *imply* that the supporting sentences will list some reasons.
2. Suggested answers: **The prices of necessary items have gone up.**

Or, **Items that are necessary cost more now than before.** Your topic sentence may be different, but it should *mention* the topic, necessary items' higher prices, and *imply* that the supporting sentences will list some examples.

3. Suggested answer: Topic: **Time Japanese Students Spend on Education.** Purpose: **To list three examples of the amount of time Japanese students spend on education.** Topic sentence: **Japanese students spend long hours on education.** The wording of your answer will be different, but it should express the same ideas the suggested answer does.

Try It: Writing Supporting Sentences

Suggested answer: **Most states require car owners to buy insurance. Every car owner has to buy gasoline. When repairs are necessary, car owners have to pay for parts and labor.** The wording of your supporting sentences will be different, but they should discuss these three expenses:
(1) insurance, (2) fuel, and (3) repairs.

Try It: Using Transition Words

1. The words in the first blank should show example: **For example** or **For instance**. The word in the second blank should show addition: **also**.
2. The words in the first blank should show example: **For example** or **For instance**. The words in the second blank should show addition: **In addition**.
3. The words in the first blank should show example: **One of the**. In the second blank, the word should show addition: **Another**.

UNIT 22: MEASURING YOUR PROGRESS

In the last part of this book, you've worked on combining ideas in sentences and on building paragraphs. In addition, you've reviewed punctuation and capitalization rules. In the Spelling and Usage Hints, you've worked with some groups of commonly confused words.

This unit will help you to see how much you have learned in the last few units. Complete all the parts in this unit. After you have finished, check your answers. The answer section tells you what pages to turn to for review. You should review the pages for any items that you do not answer correctly.

PART A

For each question, there are two sentences. One sentence contains a mistake. The other sentence is correct. Circle the letter next to the sentence that is correct.

EXAMPLE: (a) Tina put on lipstick, and combed her hair.
(b) Tina put on lipstick and combed her hair. [(b) circled]

1. (a) Neither Joe or Steve answered his phone last night.
   (b) Neither Joe nor Steve answered his phone last night.
2. (a) Our team's star player was injured, so we lost the game.
   (b) Our team's star player was injured; however, we lost the game.
3. (a) The salt was in the refrigerator, and the milk was in the cabinet.
   (b) The salt was in the refrigerator and the milk was in the cabinet.
4. (a) Rebecca signed the check, and handed it to Dr. Robbins.
   (b) Rebecca signed the check and handed it to Dr. Robbins.
5. (a) The liquor store, but also the grocery store sells beer.
   (b) Not only the liquor store but also the grocery store sells beer.

6. (a) Lauren wanted to invite Jack to the party, but she was afraid to call him.

   (b) Lauren want to invite Jack to the party, however she was afraid to call him.

7. (a) Matt opened the window, and cried for help.

   (b) Matt opened the window and cried for help.

8. (a) You can pay with cash, or you can use a credit card.

   (b) You can pay with cash or you can use a credit card.

9. (a) Steve wanted to buy a stereo, so he couldn't even afford the speakers.

   (b) Steve wanted to buy a stereo, but he couldn't even afford the speakers.

10. (a) Milk eggs sugar and flour are the main ingredients in the cake.

    (b) Milk, eggs, sugar, and flour are the main ingredients in the cake.

11. (a) Mike either walks to work or takes the bus.

    (b) Mike either walks to work nor takes the bus.

12. (a) Dishwashing soap, and paper towels are on sale at Fish's Market.

    (b) Dishwashing soap and paper towels are on sale at Fish's Market.

PART B

For each question, there are two sentences. One sentence contains a mistake. The other sentence is correct. Circle the letter next to the sentence that is correct.

13. (a) They talked and laughed until morning.

    (b) They talked; and laughed until morning.

14. (a) The phone rang; Martin was calling us again.

    (b) The phone rang, Martin was calling us again.

15. (a) We usually eat hot dogs on Thursday night; however this Thursday night we're having hamburgers.

    (b) We usually eat hot dogs on Thursday night; however, this Thursday night we're having hamburgers.

16. (a) We've driven the van on many long trips; for instance, last month we drove it from Oregon to Mexico.

    (b) We've driven the van on many long trips, for instance, last month we drove it from Oregon to Mexico.

17. (a) Marge bought Rick and herself tickets to the circus; however Rick couldn't go.

    (b) Marge bought Rick and herself tickets to the circus; however, Rick couldn't go.

18. (a) Joe forgot to set his alarm clock; for example, he overslept.

    (b) Joe forgot to set his alarm clock; therefore, he overslept.

19. (a) It might rain today, or it might snow.

    (b) It might rain today or it might snow.

20. (a) I don't want to eat dinner at home tonight; on the other hand, there isn't any food in the house.

    (b) I don't want to eat dinner at home tonight; besides, there isn't any food in the house.

21. (a) The elevator wasn't working; we had to walk up ten flights of stairs.

    (b) The elevator wasn't working, we had to walk up ten flights of stairs.

22. (a) Tom was in the shower, he didn't hear the doorbell ring.

    (b) Tom was in the shower; he didn't hear the doorbell ring.

23. (a) Joe loves pizza, in fact, he eats it every day.

    (b) Joe loves pizza; in fact, he eats it every day.

24. (a) Mr. Jordon is in a meeting; please call back later.

    (b) Mr. Jordon is in a meeting, please call back later.

PART C

Decide whether each of the following sentences is written correctly. If a sentence is incorrect, rewrite it. Make sure that commas are used correctly.

25. After Jonson left the committee voted.

26. Under the table, the woman dropped her napkin.

27. Carol saw our cat on the way to class this morning.

28. As soon as we have decided we'll call you.

29. He met his friend in the diner.

30. Full of office supplies, Kim picked up the box.

31. While you were out Mr. Thomas called.

32. On the wall, Rick spotted a roach.

PART D

Decide whether the capitalization and punctuation are correct in each sentence. If the capitalization and punctuation are not correct, rewrite the sentence.

33. Leo asked me if I would drive him to work

34. He doesn't know what he wants.

35. The restaurant is out of turkey, however, you can get chicken.

36. Alice dyed her hair green, pink, and yellow, for Halloween.

37. I've never seen the Pacific ocean, but I have seen the Atlantic ocean.

38. I'm not ready now, but I will be ready in an hour.

39. Maryland Pennsylvania and New York have been Mel's home.

40. His mothers house is for sale.

PART E

Underline the correct word in each sentence.

EXAMPLE: He bet (to—too—two) dollars on the favorite.

41. (Who's—Whose) going to do the dishes?
42. Carol drives a truck better (than—then) Alex.
43. Do you know if (your—you're) mother is coming?
44. The actor gladly (accepted—excepted) the award.
45. They are taking (their—there) time.

PART F

Use the following lines to plan and write a paragraph that lists three reasons you like or dislike a certain kind of television show. The kind of television show you write about will be your topic. Be sure you have three reasons for liking or disliking that kind of show.

Topic: ____________________

Purpose: ____________________

____

Supporting sentence notes:

1. ____________________
2. ____________________
3. ____________________

Paragraph:

____

____

____

____

____

ANSWER KEY

PART A

1. **b** Neither Joe nor Steve answered his phone last night.
2. **a** Our team's star player was injured, so we lost the game.
3. **a** The salt was in the refrigerator, and the milk was in the cabinet.
4. **b** Rebecca signed the check and handed it to Dr. Robbins.
5. **b** Not only the liquor store but also the grocery store sells beer.
6. **a** Lauren wanted to invite Jack to the party, but she was afraid to call him.
7. **b** Matt opened the window and cried for help.
8. **a** You can pay with cash, or you can use a credit card.
9. **b** Steve wanted to buy a stereo, but he couldn't even afford the speakers.
10. **b** Milk, eggs, sugar, and flour are the main ingredients in the cake.
11. **a** Mike either walks to work or takes the bus.
12. **b** Dishwashing soap and paper towels are on sale at Fish's Market.

PART B

13. **a** They talked and laughed until morning.
14. **a** The phone rang; Martin was calling us again.
15. **b** We usually eat hot dogs on Thursday night; however, this Thursday night we're having hamburgers.
16. **a** We've driven the van on many long trips; for instance, last month we drove it from Oregon to Mexico.
17. **b** Marge bought Rick and herself tickets to the circus; however, Rick couldn't go.
18. **b** Joe forgot to set his alarm clock; therefore, he overslept.
19. **a** It might rain today, or it might snow.
20. **b** I don't want to eat dinner at home tonight; besides, there isn't any food in the house.
21. **a** The elevator wasn't working; we had to walk up ten flights of stairs.
22. **b** Tom was in the shower; he didn't hear the doorbell ring.
23. **b** Joe loves pizza; in fact, he eats it every day.
24. **a** Mr. Jordon is in a meeting; please call back later.

PART C

25. After Jonson left, the committee voted.
26. The woman dropped her napkin under the table.
27. On the way to class this morning, Carol saw our cat.
28. As soon as we have decided, we'll call you.

29. He met his friend in the diner.
30. Kim picked up the box full of office supplies.
31. While you were out, Mr. Thomas called.
32. Rick spotted a roach on the wall.

PART D

33. Leo asked me if I would drive him to work.
34. He doesn't know what he wants.
35. The restaurant is out of turkey; however, you can get chicken.
36. Alice dyed her hair green, pink, and yellow for Halloween.
37. I've never seen the Pacific Ocean, but I have seen the Atlantic Ocean.
38. I'm not ready now, but I will be in an hour.
39. Maryland, Pennsylvania, and New York have been Mel's home.
40. His mother's house is for sale.

PART E

41. Who's going to do the dishes?
42. Carol drives a truck better than Alex.
43. Do you know if your mother is coming?
44. The actor gladly accepted the award.
45. They are taking their time.

PART F

Ask another person to comment on the planning you did for your paragraph and on the paragraph you wrote.

The chart on the next page will show you the pages that you need to review.

In this chart, circle the number of any item you did not answer correctly. The right-hand side of the chart will tell you the pages to review for any item that you missed. Review the pages for any item that you missed.

Item number:	**Pages to study:**
1 3 4 5 7 8 9 10 11 12 19 38 39	UNIT 18: How Are Compounds Used? (pages 207–219)
2 6 13 14 15 16 17 18 20 21 22 23 24 35	UNIT 19: How Are Compound Sentences Put Together? (pages 220–230)
25 26 27 29 30 31 32	UNIT 20: How Are Phrases and Fragments Used? (pages 231–242)
33	What Makes a Sentence Look Like a Sentence? (pages 14–16)
34	Contractions (pages 149–150)
36	Using Commas with Adjectives (pages 156–158)
37	Capitalization (pages 16–17)
40	Forming Noun Possessives (pages 139–143)
41 42 43 44 45	SPELLING AND USAGE HINTS: Homonyms (pages 215–216, 226–228)

If you want further practice in paragraph writing, review Unit 21: What Makes a Good Paragraph? (pages 243–256).

POSTTEST

This Posttest will help you decide whether you should review parts of this book or continue on in your GED preparation. Answer as many of the items as you can. When you have finished, check your answers on page 271. The chart on page 274 will tell you which units you should review, if any.

PART A

Underline the complete subject in each sentence once. Underline the complete predicate in each sentence twice.

EXAMPLE: The runner in the pink jersey is winning the race.

1. The man in the navy jacket is the owner of the team.
2. The dirty clothes are in the laundry basket.
3. His new bicycle is very lightweight.
4. My son is just like his father.

PART B

Underline the simple subject in each sentence. If the simple subject is singular, put an __S__ in the blank. If the simple subject is plural, put a __P__ in the blank.

EXAMPLE: __S__ It rained last night.

5. ____ There is a large prize available in this week's drawing.
6. ____ Are the hamburgers on the grill?
7. ____ Here is the sandwich you ordered.
8. ____ Sharon and I watched the baseball game on television.

PART C

Read each sentence. Underline the simple subject once and the verb twice. Then see if the verb matches the subject. If the subject and the verb don't match, rewrite the sentence. Change the verb so that it matches the subject.

EXAMPLE: The jokes in this book is very funny.
The jokes in this book are very funny.

9. We has presents for the bride and groom.
10. My new apartment has air conditioning.
11. He ride a bus to work.
12. Running and jogging is good aerobic exercises.

PART D

Underline the verb that matches the subject in each sentence.

EXAMPLE: Some of the employees (has—have) computer terminals.

13. This pair of slacks (are—is) a size eight.
14. The files on it (are—is) classified top secret.
15. The team always (practice—practices) on Wednesdays.
16. Everybody (has—have) plans for Saturday.
17. None of the apartments (has—have) large kitchens.
18. No one (want—wants) that to happen again.
19. Neither Diane nor Susan (drink—drinks) coffee.
20. Either the antifreeze or the transmission fluid (are—is) leaking.
21. Not only John but also his brother (play—plays) a guitar in the band.

PART E

Underline the correct verb in each sentence.

EXAMPLE: I (am working—be working) at the factory.

22. Jan and I (are going—be going) to the store.
23. Two new employees (was hired—were hired) today.
24. The fans (wait—waited) for tickets yesterday.
25. Don (has known—have known) about the party since Monday.

PART F

Read each sentence. Underline any words that should be capitalized in each sentence.

EXAMPLE: My brother lives in san francisco, california.

26. My aunt emily is a great cook.
27. Jim is from buffalo.
28. Her horse trigger has spirit.
29. He sailed across the pacific ocean by himself.

PART G

Fill in the blanks with the plural form of the noun in parentheses.

EXAMPLE: Peel some potatoes for dinner. (potato)

30. My________________are over for today. (class)

31. We have plenty of ________________ for our trip. (supply)
32. The________________need sharpening. (knife)
33. The________________are from our garden. (tomato)

PART H

Underline the word in parentheses that is spelled correctly.

EXAMPLE: I don't (beleive—believe) you.

34. Phil always saves his (receipts—reciepts).
35. It is not polite to ask someone's (weight—wieght).
36. May I have another (peice—piece) of candy?
37. Our new (neighbors—nieghbors) are very friendly.

PART I

Fill in the blank with the past tense form of the verb in parentheses.

EXAMPLE: He tried to please everyone. (try)

38. The children________________softball all afternoon. (play)
39. Bob________________Susan last June. (marry)
40. Marlene makes great________________chicken. (fry)
41. We________________seeing you again. (enjoy)

PART J

Underline the correct pronoun in each sentence.

EXAMPLE: Keith and (I—me) went to the movies last night.

42. His boss gave (he—him) a large raise.
43. Bill showed (us—we) how to use the new computer.
44. (Us—We) have too much work to do.
45. (Them—They) gave us a ride home.

PART K

Underline the correct word in each sentence.

EXAMPLE: (Their—They're) always early.

46. Overall, the (classes—class's) grades are improving.
47. This coat is (your—yours).
48. Each of the citizens cast (his—their) vote at the polls.
49. This car is (mine—my).

PART L

Read each sentence. Check to see if the adjectives are used correctly. If the adjectives are not used correctly, rewrite the sentence to make them correct. Remember to check the commas.

EXAMPLE: We studied social studies science and literature.
We studied social studies, science, and literature.

50. The choir is wearing red and black outfits.
51. That city is crowded noisy, and dirty.
52. I want to see that there movie.
53. The child is tired and cranky.

PART M

Read each sentence. Each sentence contains an underlined word. Check to see if the underlined word should be an adjective or an adverb. If the wrong word is used, rewrite the sentence. Use the correct adjective or adverb form.

EXAMPLE: He feels badly about the accident.

He feels bad about the accident.

54. She walks too slow when she wears high heels.
55. His muffler sounds loud.
56. He dances beautiful.
57. Jenny plays good with other children.

PART N

Underline the correct words in the next sentences.

EXAMPLE: Joan is the (smarter—smartest) of the two sisters.

58. Barbara is a (worse—worser) cook than I am.
59. Clayton can run (faster—fastest) than anyone else.
60. He bought the (more expensive—most expensive) suit in the store.
61. This light is the (brighter—brightest) of the pair.

PART O

Read each sentence. The sentences contain words that are spelled or used incorrectly. If a sentence contains a word that is spelled or used incorrectly, rewrite the sentence. Make the word correct.

EXAMPLE: Your late. You're late.

62. He couldn't help grining when she agreed to marry him.

63. Its the first day of spring today.

64. Sara felt unloved and uneeded.

65. I enjoy liveing in this part of town.

66. Saturday is the busyest day at the laundromat.

PART P

For each question there are two sentences. One sentence contains a mistake. The other sentence is correct. Circle the letter next to the sentence that is correct.

EXAMPLE: (a) Jeff picked up the phone, and called the police.
(b) Jeff picked up the phone and called the police.

67. (a) The Carlsons wanted to buy a house, so they couldn't afford the high mortgage payments.
(b) The Carlsons wanted to buy a house, but they couldn't afford the high mortgage payments.

68. (a) Don wore a white shirt, and a striped tie.
(b) Don wore a white shirt and a striped tie.

69. (a) Neither Jo nor Amy was home today.
(b) Neither Jo or Amy was home today.

70. (a) Tomatoes basil garlic and oil are the main ingredients in the sauce.
(b) Tomatoes, basil, garlic, and oil are the main ingredients in the sauce.

PART Q

For each question there are two sentences. One sentence contains a mistake. The other sentence is correct. Circle the letter next to the sentence that is correct.

71. (a) We wanted to visit Aunt Esther; however, she wasn't home.
(b) We wanted to visit Aunt Esther however, she wasn't home.

72. (a) Don hates lima beans, in fact, he never eats them.
(b) Don hates lima beans; in fact, he never eats them.

73. (a) Jeff went to one movie, Frank went to another.
(b) Jeff went to one movie; Frank went to another.

74. (a) We pushed and pulled the car until it was out of the mud.
(b) We pushed, and pulled the car until it was out of the mud.

PART R

Decide whether each of the following sentences is written correctly. If a sentence is incorrect, rewrite it. Make sure that commas are used correctly.

75. Chris saw a duck driving home from work.
76. While we were on vacation our car had a flat tire.
77. On the street, Ron found a dollar bill.
78. Under the stairs, the baseball rolled.

PART S

Decide whether the capitalization and punctuation are correct in each sentence. If the capitalization and punctuation are not correct, rewrite the sentence.

79. David told me all about his vacation.
80. My friend Sharon and her dog king lived in new milford.
81. His sisters car has front-wheel drive.
82. Theyr'e waiting for us.
83. Those red, green, and yellow, sweaters look like stoplights.

PART T

Underline the correct word in each sentence.

EXAMPLE: (<u>Whose</u>—Who's) socks are these?

84. The (whether—weather) report predicted rain for today.
85. His sore throat (affected—effected) his voice.
86. (Their—There) is one piece of pie left.
87. (Its—It's) payday this Friday.

PART U

88. Use the lines below to plan and write a paragraph that lists three reasons you like or dislike your current job or a job you have had. The job you write about will be your topic. Be sure you have three reasons for liking or disliking that job.

Topic: ____

Purpose: ____

____

Supporting sentence notes:

1. ______________________________

2. ______________________________

3. ______________________________

Paragraph:

____

____

____

____

____

ANSWER KEY

PART A

1. The man in the navy jacket is the owner of the team.
2. The dirty clothes are in the laundry basket.
3. His new bicycle is very lightweight.
4. My son is just like his father.

PART B

5. **S** There is a large prize available in this week's drawing.
6. **P** Are the hamburgers on the grill?
7. **S** Here is the sandwich you ordered.
8. **P** Sharon and I watched the baseball game on television.

PART C

9. We have presents for the bride and groom.
10. My new apartment has air conditioning.
11. He rides a bus to work.
12. Running and jogging are good aerobic exercises.

PART D

13. This pair of slacks is a size eight.
14. The files on it are classified top secret.
15. The team always practices on Wednesdays.
16. Everybody has plans for Saturday.

17. None of the apartments have large kitchens.
18. No one wants that to happen again.
19. Neither Diane nor Susan drinks coffee.
20. Either the antifreeze or the transmission fluid is leaking.
21. Not only John but also his brother plays a guitar in the band.

PART E

22. Jan and I are going to the store.
23. Two new employees were hired today.
24. The fans waited for tickets yesterday.
25. Don has known about the party since Monday.

PART F

26. My Aunt Emily is a great cook.
27. Jim is from Buffalo.
28. Her horse Trigger has spirit.
29. He sailed across the Pacific Ocean by himself.

PART G

20. My classes are over for today.
31. We have plenty of supplies for our trip.
32. The knives need sharpening.
33. The tomatoes are from our garden.

PART H

34. Phil always saves his receipts.
35. It is not polite to ask someone's weight.
36. May I have another piece of candy?
37. Our new neighbors are very friendly.

PART I

38. The children played softball all afternoon.
39. Bob married Susan last June.
40. Marlene makes great fried chicken.
41. We enjoyed seeing you again.

PART J

42. His boss gave him a large raise.
43. Bill showed us how to use the new computer.
44. We have too much work to do.
45. They gave us a ride home.

PART K

46. Overall, the class's grades are improving.
47. This coat is yours.
48. Each of the citizens cast his vote at the polls.
49. This car is mine.

PART L

50. The choir is wearing red and black outfits.
51. That city is crowded, noisy, and dirty.
52. I want to see that movie.
53. The child is tired and cranky.

PART M

54. She walks too slowly when she wears high heels.
55. His muffler sounds loud.
56. He dances beautifully.
57. Jenny plays well with other children.

PART N

58. Barbara is a worse cook than I am.
59. Clayton can run faster than anyone else.
60. He bought the most expensive suit in the store.
61. This light is the brighter of the pair.

PART O

62. He couldn't help grinning when she agreed to marry him.
63. It's the first day of spring today.
64. Sara felt unloved and unneeded.
65. I enjoy living in this part of town.
66. Saturday is the busiest day at the laundromat.

PART P

67. b The Carlsons wanted to buy a house, but they couldn't afford the high mortgage payments.
68. b Don wore a white shirt and a striped tie.
69. a Neither Jo nor Amy was home today.
70. b Tomatoes, basil, garlic, and oil are the main ingredients in the sauce.

PART Q

71. a We wanted to visit Aunt Esther; however, she wasn't home.
72. b Don hates lima beans; in fact, he never eats them.
73. b Jeff went to one movie; Frank went to another.
74. a We pushed and pulled the car until it was out of the mud.

PART R

75. Driving home from work, Chris saw a duck.
76. While we were on vacation, our car had a flat tire.
77. Ron found a dollar bill on the street.
78. The baseball rolled under the stairs.

PART S

79. David told me all about his vacation.
80. My friend Sharon and her dog King lived in New Milford.
81. His sister's car has front-wheel drive.
82. They're waiting for us.
83. Those red, green, and yellow sweaters look like stoplights.

PART T

84. The weather report predicted rain for today.
85. His sore throat affected his voice.
86. There is one piece of pie left.
87. It's payday this Friday.

PART U

88. Ask another person to comment on the planning you did for your paragraph and on the paragraph you wrote.

There are three groups of items on the Posttest. If you missed or did not do one or more of the items in any group, review the units that cover that group. If you got all of the items correct, you are probably ready to go on to further GED preparation.

Group	Item Numbers	Exercise Page
Subjects and Verbs	1–41	8–103
Pronouns, Adjectives, and Adverbs	42–66	127–194
Sentence Structure, Paragraph Structure, and Writing	67–88	207–256

GRADE 1

Spiral to Infinity Steve Allen

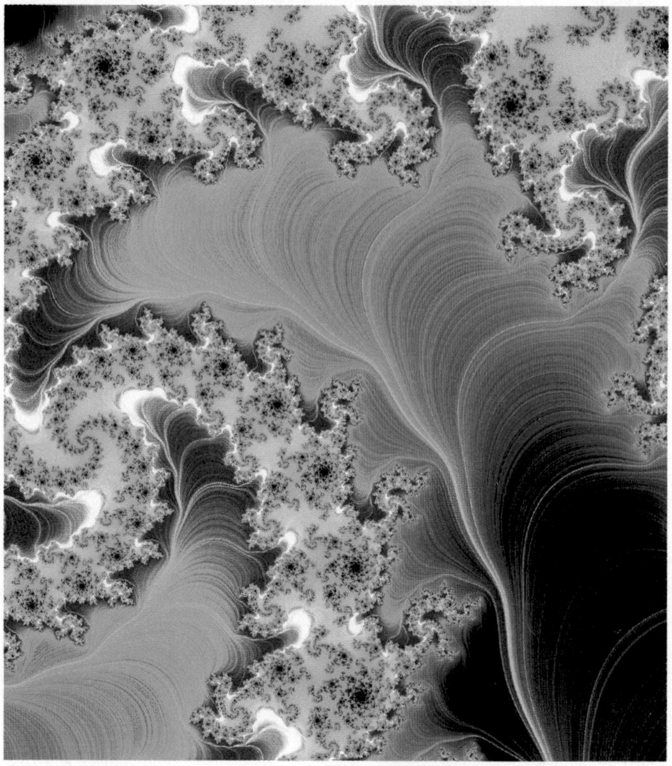

"Fractal images are often made up of small images-within-images, constantly repeating and going smaller and smaller."– **Steve Allen**

Differentiation and Intervention Guide

Investigations

IN NUMBER, DATA, AND SPACE®

Glenview, Illinois • Boston, Massachusetts
Chandler, Arizona • Upper Saddle River, New Jersey

The Investigations curriculum was developed by TERC, Cambridge, MA.

This material is based on work supported by the National Science Foundation ("NSF") under Grant No.ESI-0095450. Any opinions, findings, and conclusions or recommendations expressed in this material are those of the author(s) and do not necessarily reflect the views of the National Science Foundation.

ISBN-13: 978-0-328-62338-9

ISBN-10: 0-328-62338-5

5 6 7 8 9 10 V063 14 13 12

Contents

About This Guide

Overview

The *Differentiation and Intervention Guide* is a flexible and versatile component that supplements the *Investigations* curriculum units. An Intervention, Practice, and Extension activity is provided for every Investigation. The differentiation activities presented in this guide can be used anytime after the session referenced, such as during Math Workshops, or outside of math time. In addition, a Quiz is available to use as a formative assessment after an Investigation is completed.

Teachers may also assign multiple activities for an Investigation to a single student. For example, after a student completes the Practice activity, it may be appropriate for that student to work on the Extension activity. Similarly, Practice and Extension activities can also be used to reinforce and extend Intervention suggestions, either during the Investigation or later in the unit.

Within each curriculum unit, a feature titled "Differentiation: Supporting the Range of Learners" appears regularly. This feature offers ideas for Intervention, Extension, and ELL related to the content of that session. The *Differentiation and Intervention Guide* expands many of these existing Intervention and Extension suggestions by providing teaching suggestions and/or student masters. The *Differentiation and Intervention Guide* also provides additional Practice activities for all students.

Curriculum Unit 3, p. 22

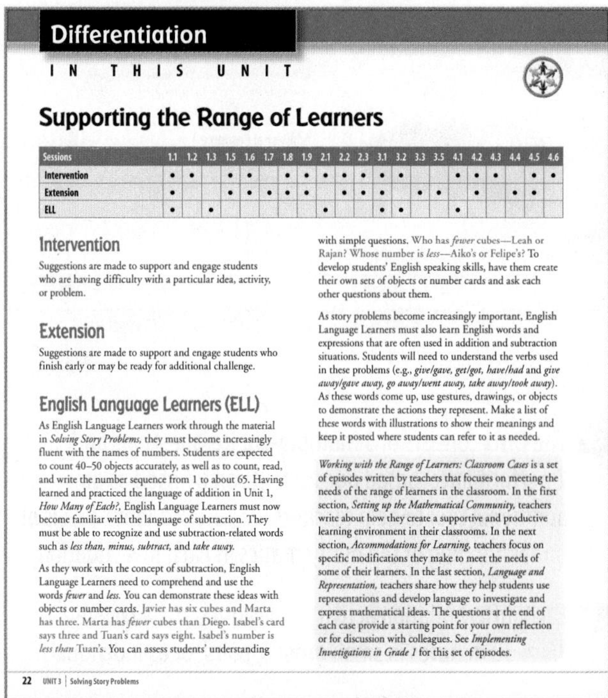

Differentiation

IN THIS UNIT

Supporting the Range of Learners

Sessions	1.1	1.2	1.3	1.5	1.6	1.7	1.8	1.9	2.1	2.2	2.3	3.1	3.2	3.3	3.5	4.1	4.2	4.3	4.4	4.5	4.6
Intervention	•	•		•	•		•	•	•	•	•	•	•			•	•	•		•	•
Extension	•			•	•	•	•	•		•	•	•		•	•		•		•	•	
ELL	•		•						•			•	•			•					

Intervention

Suggestions are made to support and engage students who are having difficulty with a particular idea, activity, or problem.

Extension

Suggestions are made to support and engage students who finish early or may be ready for additional challenge.

English Language Learners (ELL)

As English Language Learners work through the material in *Solving Story Problems,* they must become increasingly fluent with the names of numbers. Students are expected to count 40–50 objects accurately, as well as to count, read, and write the number sequence from 1 to about 65. Having learned and practiced the language of addition in Unit 1, *How Many of Each?,* English Language Learners must now become familiar with the language of subtraction. They must be able to recognize and use subtraction-related words such as *less than, minus, subtract,* and *take away.*

As they work with the concept of subtraction, English Language Learners need to comprehend and use the words *fewer* and *less.* You can demonstrate these ideas with objects or number cards. Javier has six cubes and Marta has three. Marta has *fewer* cubes than Diego. Isabel's card says three and Tuan's card says eight. Isabel's number is *less than* Tuan's. You can assess students' understanding with simple questions. Who has *fewer* cubes—Leah or Rajan? Whose number is *less*—Aiko's or Felipe's? To develop students' English speaking skills, have them create their own sets of objects or number cards and ask each other questions about them.

As story problems become increasingly important, English Language Learners must also learn English words and expressions that are often used in addition and subtraction situations. Students will need to understand the verbs used in these problems (e.g., *give/gave, get/got, have/had* and *give away/gave away, go away/went away, take away/took away*). As these words come up, use gestures, drawings, or objects to demonstrate the actions they represent. Make a list of these words with illustrations to show their meanings and keep it posted where students can refer to it as needed.

Working with the Range of Learners: Classroom Cases is a set of episodes written by teachers that focuses on meeting the needs of the range of learners in the classroom. In the first section, *Setting up the Mathematical Community,* teachers write about how they create a supportive and productive learning environment in their classrooms. In the next section, *Accommodations for Learning,* teachers focus on specific modifications they make to meet the needs of some of their learners. In the last section, *Language and Representation,* teachers share how they help students use representations and develop language to investigate and express mathematical ideas. The questions at the end of each case provide a starting point for your own reflection or for discussion with colleagues. See *Implementing Investigations in Grade 1* for this set of episodes.

22 UNIT 3 | Solving Story Problems

Differentiation suggestions are embedded in the curriculum units.

Curriculum Unit 3, p. 145

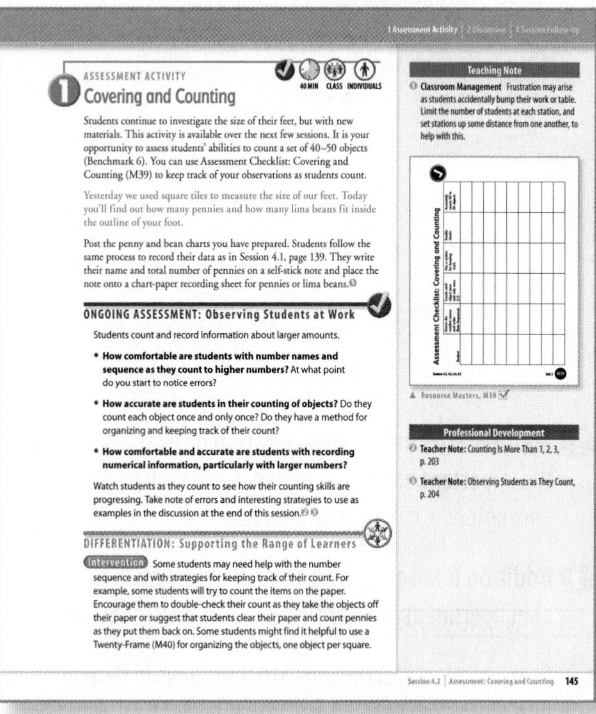

1 Assessment Activity | 2 Discussion | 3 Session Follow-Up

ASSESSMENT ACTIVITY

1 Covering and Counting

40 MIN CLASS INDIVIDUALS

Students continue to investigate the size of their feet, but with new materials. This activity is available over the next few sessions. It is your opportunity to assess students' abilities to count a set of 40–50 objects (Benchmark 6). You can use Assessment Checklist: Covering and Counting (M39) to keep track of your observations as students count.

Yesterday we used square tiles to measure the size of our feet. Today you'll find out how many pennies and how many lima beans fit inside the outline of your foot.

Post the penny and bean charts you have prepared. Students follow the same process to record their data as in Session 4.1, page 139. They write their name and total number of pennies on a self-stick note and place the note onto a chart-paper recording sheet for pennies or lima beans.

ONGOING ASSESSMENT: Observing Students at Work

Students count and record information about larger amounts.

- **How comfortable are students with number names and sequence as they count to higher numbers?** At what point do you start to notice errors?
- **How accurate are students in their counting of objects?** Do they count each object once and only once? Do they have a method for organizing and keeping track of their count?
- **How comfortable and accurate are students with recording numerical information, particularly with larger numbers?**

Watch students as they count to see how their counting skills are progressing. Take note of errors and interesting strategies to use as examples in the discussion at the end of this session.

DIFFERENTIATION: Supporting the Range of Learners

Intervention Some students may need help with the number sequence and with strategies for keeping track of their count. For example, some students will try to count the items on the paper. Encourage them to double-check their count as they take the objects off their paper or suggest that students clear their paper and count pennies as they put them back on. Some students might find it helpful to use a Twenty-Frame (M40) for organizing the objects, one object per square.

Teaching Note

Classroom Management Frustration may arise as students accidentally bump their work or table. Limit the number of students at each station, and set stations up some distance from one another, to help with this.

Assessment Checklist: Covering and Counting

Resource Masters, M39

Professional Development

Teacher Note: Counting Is More Than 1, 2, 3, p. 203

Teacher Note: Observing Students as They Count, p. 204

Session 4.2 | Assessment: Covering and Counting 145

The Differentiation and Intervention Guide *enhances the existing differentiation suggestions in the curriculum units.*

Understanding This Guide

The *Differentiation and Intervention Guide* contains support pages for every Investigation in the curriculum units. The first page provides teachers with an overview of the key mathematics in the Investigation and descriptions of student performance. The remaining three pages provide easy-to-use activities based on the Math Focus Points in the Investigation. Each activity features built-in ELL support and resource masters for students.

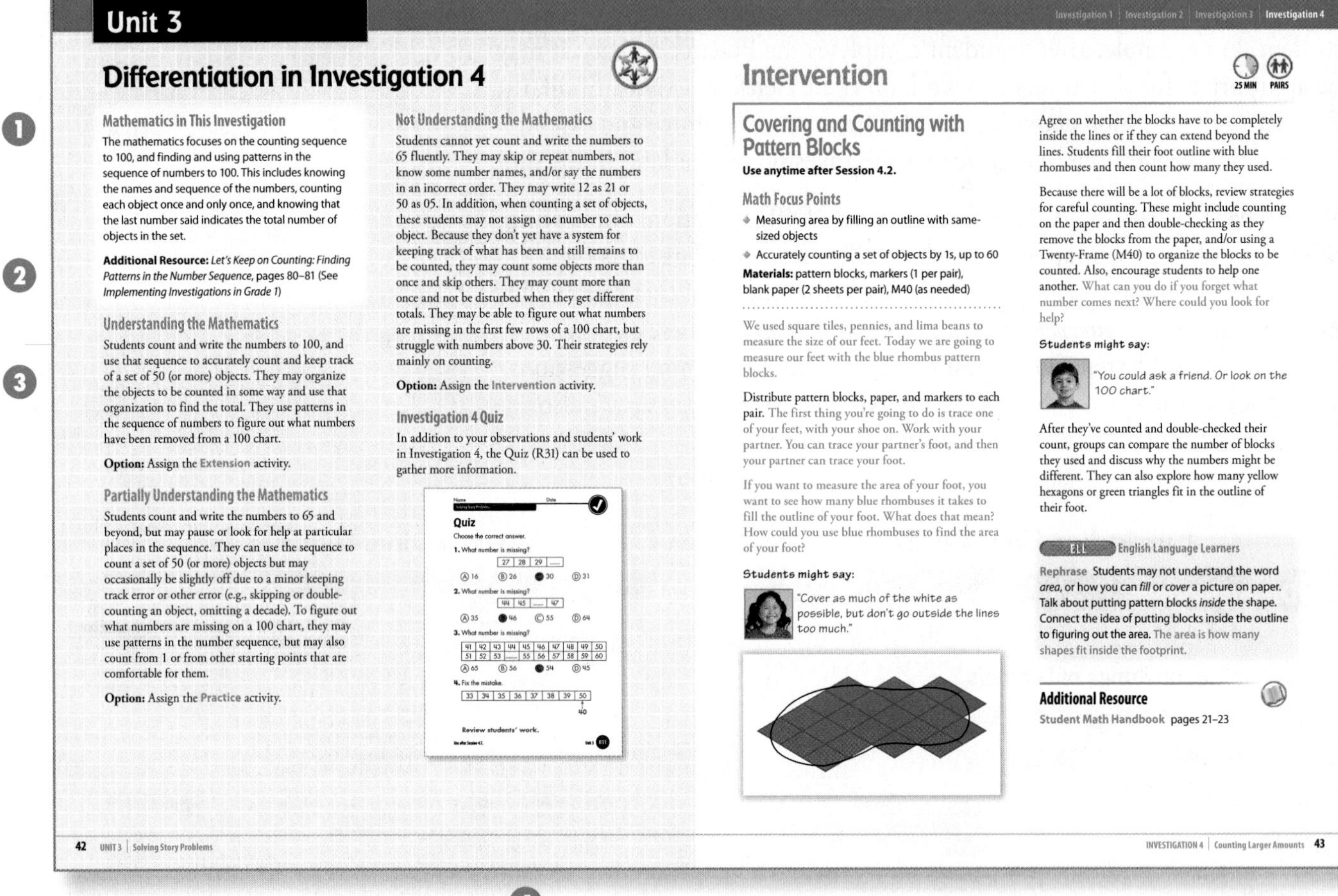

Unit 3

Investigation 1 | Investigation 2 | Investigation 3 | Investigation 4

Differentiation in Investigation 4

Mathematics in This Investigation

The mathematics focuses on the counting sequence to 100, and finding and using patterns in the sequence of numbers to 100. This includes knowing the names and sequence of the numbers, counting each object once and only once, and knowing that the last number said indicates the total number of objects in the set.

Additional Resource: *Let's Keep on Counting: Finding Patterns in the Number Sequence*, pages 80–81 (See *Implementing Investigations in Grade 1*)

Understanding the Mathematics

Students count and write the numbers to 100, and use that sequence to accurately count and keep track of a set of 50 (or more) objects. They may organize the objects to be counted in some way and use that organization to find the total. They use patterns in the sequence of numbers to figure out what numbers have been removed from a 100 chart.

Option: Assign the Extension activity.

Partially Understanding the Mathematics

Students count and write the numbers to 65 and beyond, but may pause or look for help at particular places in the sequence. They can use the sequence to count a set of 50 (or more) objects but may occasionally be slightly off due to a minor keeping track error or other error (e.g., skipping or double-counting an object, omitting a decade). To figure out what numbers are missing on a 100 chart, they may use patterns in the number sequence, but may also count from 1 or from other starting points that are comfortable for them.

Option: Assign the Practice activity.

Not Understanding the Mathematics

Students cannot yet count and write the numbers to 65 fluently. They may skip or repeat numbers, not know some number names, and/or say the numbers in an incorrect order. They may write 12 as 21 or 50 as 05. In addition, when counting a set of objects, these students may not assign one number to each object. Because they don't yet have a system for keeping track of what has been and still remains to be counted, they may count some objects more than once and skip others. They may count more than once and not be disturbed when they get different totals. They may be able to figure out what numbers are missing in the first few rows of a 100 chart, but struggle with numbers above 30. Their strategies rely mainly on counting.

Option: Assign the Intervention activity.

Investigation 4 Quiz

In addition to your observations and students' work in Investigation 4, the Quiz (R31) can be used to gather more information.

Quiz

Intervention

25 MIN PAIRS

Covering and Counting with Pattern Blocks

Use anytime after Session 4.2.

Math Focus Points

- Measuring area by filling an outline with same-sized objects
- Accurately counting a set of objects by 1s, up to 60

Materials: pattern blocks, markers (1 per pair), blank paper (2 sheets per pair), M40 (as needed)

We used square tiles, pennies, and lima beans to measure the size of our feet. Today we are going to measure our feet with the blue rhombus pattern blocks.

Distribute pattern blocks, paper, and markers to each pair. The first thing you're going to do is trace one of your feet, with your shoe on. Work with your partner. You can trace your partner's foot, and then your partner can trace your foot.

If you want to measure the area of your foot, you want to see how many blue rhombuses it takes to fill the outline of your foot. What does that mean? How could you use blue rhombuses to find the area of your foot?

Students might say:

"Cover as much of the white as possible, but don't go outside the lines too much."

Agree on whether the blocks have to be completely inside the lines or if they can extend beyond the lines. Students fill their foot outline with blue rhombuses and then count how many they used.

Because there will be a lot of blocks, review strategies for careful counting. These might include counting on the paper and then double-checking as they remove the blocks from the paper, and/or using a Twenty-Frame (M40) to organize the blocks to be counted. Also, encourage students to help one another. What can you do if you forget what number comes next? Where could you look for help?

Students might say:

"You could ask a friend. Or look on the 100 chart."

After they've counted and double-checked their count, groups can compare the number of blocks they used and discuss why the numbers might be different. They can also explore how many yellow hexagons or green triangles fit in the outline of their foot.

ELL English Language Learners

Rephrase Students may not understand the word *area*, or how you can *fill* or *cover* a picture on paper. Talk about putting pattern blocks *inside* the shape. Connect the idea of putting blocks inside the outline to figuring out the area. The area is how many shapes fit inside the footprint.

Additional Resource

Student Math Handbook pages 21–23

42 UNIT 3 | Solving Story Problems

INVESTIGATION 4 | Counting Larger Amounts 43

1 **Mathematics in This Investigation** gives an overview of the important mathematical ideas and skills students encounter during the Investigation.

2 **Additional Resources** provide teachers with information about pertinent Teacher Notes and/or Classroom Cases.

3 **Performance descriptions** assist teachers in determining differentiation activities based on observations of students throughout the Investigation and analyzing students' work.

4 The **Quiz** consists of 3 multiple-choice questions and 1 performance-based question. It can be used as an additional tool to help teachers identify students' levels of understanding of the mathematics in each Investigation.

5 Each differentiation activity is designed to be covered in 15 to 30 minutes in small groups, pairs, or as individuals.

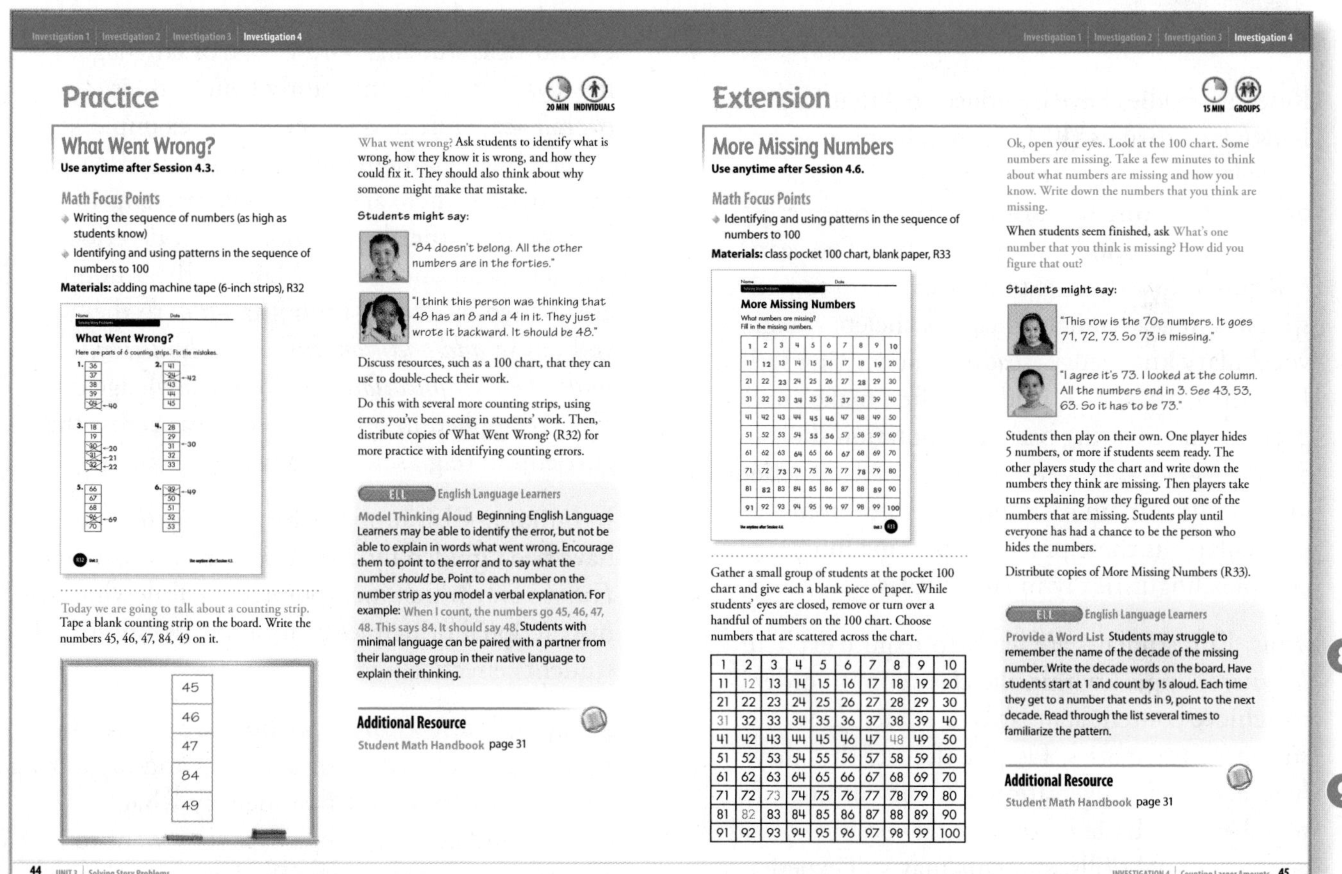

Investigation 1 | Investigation 2 | Investigation 3 | Investigation 4

Practice

20 MIN INDIVIDUALS

6 **What Went Wrong?**

Use anytime after Session 4.3.

Math Focus Points

- Writing the sequence of numbers (as high as students know)
- Identifying and using patterns in the sequence of numbers to 100

Materials: adding machine tape (6-inch strips), R32

7

Name Date

Solving Story Problems

What Went Wrong?

Here are parts of 6 counting strips. Fix the mistakes.

1. 36, 37, 38, 39, 04 ← 40
2. 41, 24 ← 42, 43, 44, 45
3. 18, 19, 30 ← 20, 31 ← 21, 32 ← 22
4. 28, 29, 31 ← 30, 32, 33
5. 66, 67, 68, 96 ← 69, 70
6. 39 ← 49, 50, 51, 52, 53

Today we are going to talk about a counting strip. Tape a blank counting strip on the board. Write the numbers 45, 46, 47, 84, 49 on it.

45
46
47
84
49

What went wrong? Ask students to identify what is wrong, how they know it is wrong, and how they could fix it. They should also think about why someone might make that mistake.

Students might say:

"84 doesn't belong. All the other numbers are in the forties."

"I think this person was thinking that 48 has an 8 and a 4 in it. They just wrote it backward. It should be 48."

Discuss resources, such as a 100 chart, that they can use to double-check their work.

Do this with several more counting strips, using errors you've been seeing in students' work. Then, distribute copies of What Went Wrong? (R32) for more practice with identifying counting errors.

ELL English Language Learners

Model Thinking Aloud Beginning English Language Learners may be able to identify the error, but not be able to explain in words what went wrong. Encourage them to point to the error and to say what the number *should* be. Point to each number on the number strip as you model a verbal explanation. For example: When I count, the numbers go 45, 46, 47, 48. This says 84. It should say 48. Students with minimal language can be paired with a partner from their language group in their native language to explain their thinking.

Additional Resource

Student Math Handbook page 31

44 UNIT 3 | Solving Story Problems

Investigation 1 | Investigation 2 | Investigation 3 | Investigation 4

Extension

15 MIN GROUPS

More Missing Numbers

Use anytime after Session 4.6.

Math Focus Points

- Identifying and using patterns in the sequence of numbers to 100

Materials: class pocket 100 chart, blank paper, R33

Name Date

Solving Story Problems

More Missing Numbers

What numbers are missing?
Fill in the missing numbers.

1	2	3	4	5	6	7	8	9	10
11	12	13	14	15	16	17	18	19	20
21	22	23	24	25	26	27	28	29	30
31	32	33	34	35	36	37	38	39	40
41	42	43	44	45	46	47	48	49	50
51	52	53	54	55	56	57	58	59	60
61	62	63	64	65	66	67	68	69	70
71	72	73	74	75	76	77	78	79	80
81	82	83	84	85	86	87	88	89	90
91	92	93	94	95	96	97	98	99	100

Gather a small group of students at the pocket 100 chart and give each a blank piece of paper. While students' eyes are closed, remove or turn over a handful of numbers on the 100 chart. Choose numbers that are scattered across the chart.

1	2	3	4	5	6	7	8	9	10
11	12	13	14	15	16	17	18	19	20
21	22	23	24	25	26	27	28	29	30
31	32	33	34	35	36	37	38	39	40
41	42	43	44	45	46	47	48	49	50
51	52	53	54	55	56	57	58	59	60
61	62	63	64	65	66	67	68	69	70
71	72	73	74	75	76	77	78	79	80
81	82	83	84	85	86	87	88	89	90
91	92	93	94	95	96	97	98	99	100

Ok, open your eyes. Look at the 100 chart. Some numbers are missing. Take a few minutes to think about what numbers are missing and how you know. Write down the numbers that you think are missing.

When students seem finished, ask What's one number that you think is missing? How did you figure that out?

Students might say:

"This row is the 70s numbers. It goes 71, 72, 73. So 73 is missing."

"I agree it's 73. I looked at the column. All the numbers end in 3. See 43, 53, 63. So it has to be 73."

Students then play on their own. One player hides 5 numbers, or more if students seem ready. The other players study the chart and write down the numbers they think are missing. Then players take turns explaining how they figured out one of the numbers that are missing. Students play until everyone has had a chance to be the person who hides the numbers.

Distribute copies of More Missing Numbers (R33).

ELL English Language Learners

Provide a Word List Students may struggle to remember the name of the decade of the missing number. Write the decade words on the board. Have students start at 1 and count by 1s aloud. Each time they get to a number that ends in 9, point to the next decade. Read through the list several times to familiarize the pattern. 8

Additional Resource 9

Student Math Handbook page 31

INVESTIGATION 4 | Counting Larger Amounts 45

6 Activities can be used anytime after the session content is covered giving increased flexibility to teachers.

7 **Resource Masters** provide additional practice or are used as a recording sheet.

8 **ELL notes** provide teachers with suggestions to support students with language and vocabulary.

9 **Additional Resources** for students provide useful Student Math Handbook references or games to play for extra practice.

English Language Learners in the Math Classroom

Dr. Jim Cummins
University of Toronto

Research studies have demonstrated that English Language Learners (ELLs) generally pick up everyday conversational fluency within a year or two of starting to learn English. However, a much longer period (generally at least five years) is required for students to fully catch up to native speakers in academic language proficiency (e.g., vocabulary knowledge, reading and writing skills). In mathematics, ELL students often make good progress in acquiring basic computation skills in the early grades; however, they typically experience greater difficulty in carrying out word problems particularly as these problems become more complex linguistically in later grades.

Thus, ELL students are likely to require explicit *language* support within the classroom in order to achieve content standards in subject areas such as mathematics. Despite the fact that they have acquired conversational fluency in English together with basic mathematical vocabulary and computational skills, students may still experience gaps in their knowledge of more sophisticated vocabulary, syntax, and discourse features of mathematical language.

The linguistic challenges faced by ELL students in learning math reflect the fact that language is central to the teaching of virtually every school subject. The concepts embedded in the curriculum are inseparable from the language we use to teach these concepts to our students. For example, most mathematical problems require students to understand prepositions and logical relations that are expressed through language.

This fusion of language and content across the curriculum presents both challenges and opportunities in teaching ELL students. The challenges are to provide the instructional supports to enable ELL students to understand math content and carry out math tasks and operations. However, math instruction also provides teachers with the opportunity to extend ELL students' knowledge of language in ways that will significantly benefit their overall academic development. For example, as they learn mathematics, students are also learning that there are predictable patterns in how we form the abstract nouns that describe mathematical operations. Many of these nouns are formed by adding the suffix *–tion* to the verb, as in *add/addition, subtract/subtraction, multiply/multiplication,* etc. This knowledge can then be applied in other subject areas across the curriculum (e.g., science, language arts).

In building ELL supports for *Investigations*, we have been guided by *The Pearson ELL Curriculum Framework*, which incorporates the following five instructional principles central to teaching ELL students effectively.

1. Identify and Communicate Content and Language Objectives In planning and organizing a lesson, teachers must first identify what content and language objectives they want to communicate to students. The language objectives might include providing definitions, descriptions, examples, and visual supports for explaining vocabulary.

2. Frontload the Lesson Frontloading refers to the use of prereading or preinstructional strategies that prepare ELL students to understand new academic content. Frontloading strategies include activating prior knowledge, building background, previewing text, preteaching vocabulary, and making connections.

3. Provide Comprehensible Input Language and content that students can understand is referred to as comprehensible input. Teachers make use of nonlinguistic supports to enable students to understand language and content that would otherwise have been beyond their comprehension. Typical supports include visuals, models, and manipulatives.

4. Enable Language Production Language production complements comprehensible input and is an essential element in developing expertise in academic language. Use of both oral and written language enables students to solve problems, generate insights, express their ideas, and obtain feedback from teachers and peers.

5. Assess for Content and Language Understanding Finally, the instructional cycle flows into assessing what students have learned and then spirals upward into further development of students' content knowledge and language expertise.

These principles come to life in the *Differentiation and Intervention Guide* in the form of seven specific instructional strategies.

- ***Model Thinking Aloud*** When ELL students articulate their thinking processes through language, they are enabled to complete activities, identify gaps in their knowledge, and receive feedback from teachers. Teachers, however, must model this process in order for students to learn how to use it effectively. When modeling thinking aloud, it is important for teachers to use visuals and gestures.
- ***Partner Talk*** When it comes to working on a math activity of any kind, two heads are often better than one. Partner talk provides an audience for students' thinking aloud and an opportunity for the teacher to direct students to listen for particular vocabulary and linguistic structures as they engage in a task with their partner.
- ***Provide a Word List*** When students make a list of relevant vocabulary in a lesson with examples of how these words are used, it reinforces their knowledge of this vocabulary and provides an opportunity for teachers to monitor their understanding and provide additional explanation as needed. Paying special attention to homophones, such as *sum* and *some*, is particularly helpful for ELL students.
- ***Provide Sentence Stems*** Sentence stems provide support for ELL students to gain access to the sequence of steps in an activity, and they expand students' knowledge of how to communicate their thinking processes to the teacher and their peers.
- ***Rephrase*** Students struggling with vocabulary and language acquisition are often confused by extra details in word problems or overly wordy statements. Rephrasing statements in a different way that utilizes simpler language, shorter sentences, and eliminates unnecessary information helps students focus on and understand the important information needed to work through an activity.
- ***Suggest a Sequence*** Sequencing of steps is crucial to solving many math problems, and ELL students may need additional help in this process. Providing struggling ELL students with a sequence of steps to follow provides them with a guide for how to complete an activity or report their findings. When suggesting a sequence, be sure to use concise language.
- ***Use Repetition*** Repetition of instructions or explanations may also be required to enable ELL students to fully understand instruction. Because students are still in the process of learning English, they may need repetition, paraphrasing, or elaboration to understand teacher talk containing new vocabulary or structures.

Differentiation in Investigation 1

Mathematics in This Investigation

The mathematics focuses on developing accurate strategies for counting a set of up to 20 objects by ones. This includes knowing the names and sequence of the numbers, counting each object once and only once, and knowing that the last number said indicates the total number of objects in the set.

Additional Resource: *Building the Math Community: Setting Norms for Discussions,* pages 75–76 (See *Implementing Investigations in Grade 1*)

Understanding the Mathematics

Students count fluently to 20 (and beyond) and use that sequence to accurately count and keep track of a set of 20 (or more) objects. They may organize the objects to be counted in some way (e.g., groups of 5) and use that organization to find the total.

Option: Assign the **Extension** activity.

Partially Understanding the Mathematics

Students count to 20 but may pause or look for help at particular places in the sequence (e.g., the early teens). They can use the sequence to count a set of 20 objects but may occasionally be slightly off due to a minor tracking error or other error (e.g., skipping or double-counting an object, omitting a number).

Option: Assign the **Practice** activity.

Not Understanding the Mathematics

Students cannot yet count to 20 fluently. They may skip numbers (or not know some number names) and/or say the numbers in an incorrect order. In addition, when counting a set of objects, these students may not assign one number to each object. Because they don't yet have a system for keeping track of what has been and still remains to be counted, they may count some objects more than once and skip others. They may not know that the last number they say represents the total.

Option: Assign the **Intervention** activity.

Investigation 1 Quiz

In addition to your observations and students' work in Investigation 1, the Quiz (R1) can be used to gather more information.

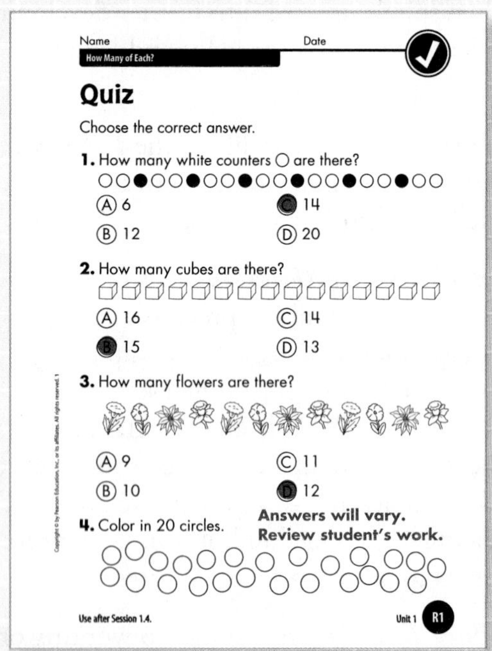

Name Date

How Many of Each?

Quiz

Choose the correct answer.

1. How many white counters ○ are there?

Ⓐ 6 ● 14
Ⓑ 12 Ⓓ 20

2. How many cubes are there?

Ⓐ 16 Ⓒ 14
● 15 Ⓓ 13

3. How many flowers are there?

Ⓐ 9 Ⓒ 11
Ⓑ 10 ● 12

4. Color in 20 circles. **Answers will vary. Review student's work.**

Use after Session 1.4. Unit 1 R1

Intervention

20 MIN

PAIRS

Using a Twenty-Frame to Count

Use anytime after Session 1.4.

Math Focus Points

- Counting a set of objects up to 20 by 1s

Materials: counters (20 per student), M5

Today we will be using a twenty-frame to count.

Distribute a Twenty-Frame (M5) and 20 counters to each student. We're going to practice counting. Put the first counter here. Show students where to start by placing the first counter in the top left square on the frame.

How many counters are on the twenty-frame? Students point to the counter and count aloud: 1. Let's add another counter and count: 1, 2. Continue adding counters and counting aloud with students until the twenty-frame is full.

Next, show a twenty-frame with 5 counters on it. How many counters are on the twenty-frame?

Count them together and highlight the fact that there are 5 squares in each row. I'm going to show another number on this twenty-frame.

●	●	●	●	●
●	●			

How many counters are there? How do you know?

Students might say:

"I counted them—1, 2, 3, 4, 5, 6, 7."

"We just said the first row is 5, so I kept counting 6, 7 for the extra counters."

Model students' strategies, being sure to point to each counter as it is counted.

Now it is your turn. Partners take turns placing different amounts of counters in the twenty-frame and counting the counters. Player 1 shows a number on the twenty-frame. Player 2 counts the counters, but players should agree on the total number. Listen for students who disagree on the number of counters. Let's count them together. Count with students as you point to each counter.

If necessary, suggest a range of numbers for students to play with (e.g., up to 10, less than 15).

ELL **English Language Learners**

Provide a Word List Some English Language Learners may need more practice with number names, especially those greater than 10. List the number words for *one* through *twenty* next to their corresponding numerals on chart paper. Read through the list with students. Then, point to various numbers and have them practice saying the name aloud. Post this list in the classroom for reference.

Additional Resource

Student Math Handbook pages 21–23

Practice

20 MIN

PAIRS

Counting to 20

Use anytime after Session 1.4.

Math Focus Points

- Counting a set of objects up to 20 by 1s

Materials: counters (20 per student), bags (1 per student), R2

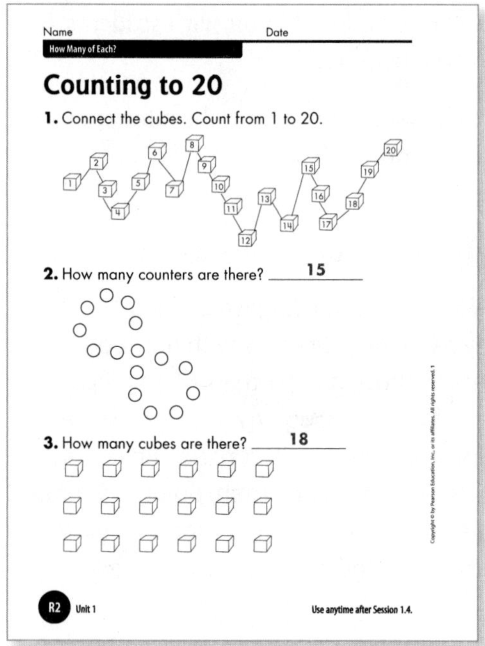

Name Date

How Many of Each?

Counting to 20

1. Connect the cubes. Count from 1 to 20.

2. How many counters are there? 15

3. How many cubes are there? 18

R2 Unit 1 Use anytime after Session 1.4.

Materials to Prepare: Place 20 counters in each bag. Prepare and distribute 1 bag to each student.

Reach into the bag and pull out a handful of counters. How many counters do you have?

Encourage partners to check each other's work and to recount if they disagree. Ask students to model their strategies for determining the correct number of counters. Students may use a variety of strategies for counting. They may arrange the counters in rows, or they may move the counters from an uncounted pile to a counted pile as they count.

Once you agree on how many counters each of you has, your job is to find out how many you have together. Model and discuss this as necessary and then give students time to work.

Put the counters back in the bag, then do the same thing. Take a handful of counters and count them. Check each other's work. Then count how many you have altogether.

End by discussing a few strategies you have seen students using to count.

Students might say:

"I put the counters in a line. Then I move each counter when I count it."

Distribute copies of Counting to 20 (R2).

ELL **English Language Learners**

Partner Talk Have pairs explain their counting strategies to each other. Listen for strategies such as organizing the counters and touching or moving each counter as it is counted. Beginning English Language Learners may only be able to use short phrases or work with a partner who speaks their native language. Encourage students to try different strategies.

Additional Resource

Student Math Handbook

Game: *Collect 20 Together* SMH G1

Materials: dot cubes, counters

Extension

15 MIN PAIRS

Counting Quantities to 20

Use anytime after Session 1.4.

Math Focus Points

- Counting a set of objects up to 20 by 1s

Materials: Primary Number Cards (only the 0, 1, 2, and 3 cards; 1 deck per pair), counters (20 per pair), R3

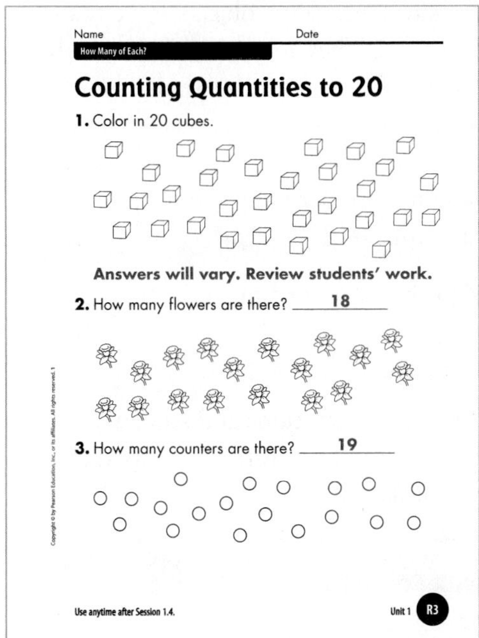

Name Date

How Many of Each?

Counting Quantities to 20

1. Color in 20 cubes.

Answers will vary. Review students' work.

2. How many flowers are there? 18

3. How many counters are there? 19

Use anytime after Session 1.4. Unit 1 R3

Introduce students to a variation of *Collect 20 Together*. You will take turns turning over 2 Number Cards and taking the number of counters that they show. Keep taking cards until you and your partner have collected 20 counters. The two of you win when you can show that you have collected at least 20 counters *together*.

Let's play a practice game. Choose a volunteer to be your partner. Turn over 2 number cards. I got [1] and [3]. How many counters should I take? Now it's [Diego's] turn. He turned over [2] and [2]. How many counters should [Diego] take? How many counters do we have together? How do you know?

Students might say:

"You have [4], then count [Diego's 4]: [5, 6, 7, 8]."

"I'd line all the counters up and count them."

Model the different strategies that are suggested. Demonstrate additional turns, as needed. Continue to ask students how they determined how many counters in all.

The game is over as soon as you and your partner have at least 20 counters. Depending on the numbers rolled, they may get exactly 20 or they may end up with a few more than 20.

Distribute a deck of Primary Number Cards (with only the 0, 1, 2, and 3 cards) and counters to each pair. Have them play a round or two of *Collect 20 Together* with Number Cards.

Distribute copies of Counting Quantities to 20 (R3).

ELL English Language Learners

Model Thinking Aloud Model your thinking for finding the number of counters for 2 number cards. Show students a card showing a 3 and another showing a 2. I got a 3 and a 2. I started with 3 counters. Then I counted 2 more: 4, 5. There are 5 counters in all. Have each student verbalize the thought process for finding his or her total before adding them to the growing set of counters.

Additional Resource

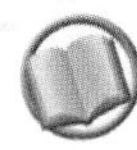

Student Math Handbook

Game: *Collect 20 Together* SMH G1

Materials: dot cubes, counters

Variation: Try to collect exactly 20 counters.

Differentiation in Investigation 2

Mathematics in This Investigation

The mathematics focuses on the counting sequence to 30, and on using it to count and represent, and to compare and order, quantities to 20.

Understanding the Mathematics

Students count fluently to 30 (and beyond) and use that sequence to accurately count and keep track of a set of 20 (or more) objects. They may organize the objects to be counted in some way (e.g., groups of 5) and use that organization to find the total. They compare and order numbers to 20 without a visual representation of the amounts (e.g., using just the numerals).

Option: Assign the **Extension** activity.

Partially Understanding the Mathematics

Students count to 30 but may pause or look for help at particular places in the sequence (e.g., the early teens). They can use the sequence to count a set of 20 objects but may occasionally be slightly off due to a minor keeping track error or other error (e.g., skipping or double-counting an object, omitting a number). They use visual representations (e.g., pictures on playing cards or cube towers) to accurately compare and order amounts to 20.

Option: Assign the **Practice** activity.

Not Understanding the Mathematics

Students cannot yet count to 20 fluently. They may skip numbers, or not know some number names, and/or say the numbers in an incorrect order. In addition, when counting a set of objects, these students may not assign one number to each object. Because they don't yet have a system for keeping track of what has been and still remains to be counted, they may count some objects more than once and skip others. They may not know that the last number they say represents the total. These students may need to build cube towers to compare and order numbers, and may not yet understand the equivalence among number names, numerals, and quantities (e.g., three = 3 = ***).

Option: Assign the **Intervention** activity.

Investigation 2 Quiz

In addition to your observations and students' work in Investigation 2, the Quiz (R4) can be used to gather more information.

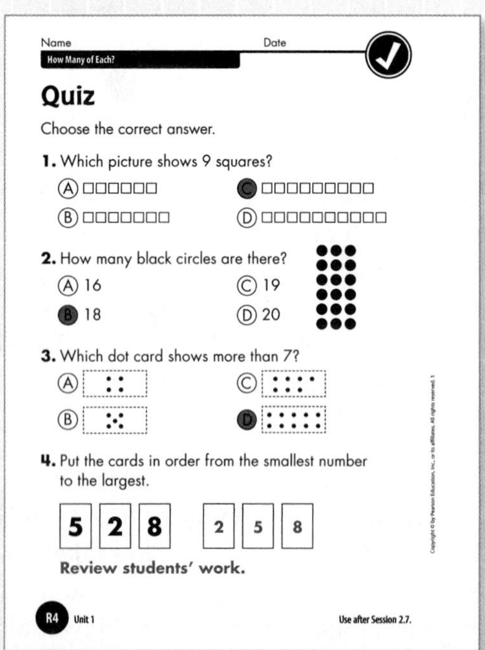

Name Date

How Many of Each?

Quiz

Choose the correct answer.

1. Which picture shows 9 squares?
   (A) (B) (C) (D)

2. How many black circles are there?
   (A) 16 (B) 18 (C) 19 (D) 20

3. Which dot card shows more than 7?
   (A) (B) (C) (D)

4. Put the cards in order from the smallest number to the largest.
   5 2 8 → 2 5 8
   Review students' work.

R4 Unit 1 Use after Session 2.7.

Intervention

20 MIN

PAIRS

What's in the Mystery Box?

Use anytime after Session 2.3.

Math Focus Points

- Counting a set of up to 20 objects by 1s
- Connecting number names and written numbers to the quantities they represent
- Recording a solution to a problem

Materials: Mystery Boxes with 10–15 items (1 per pair), M8, R5

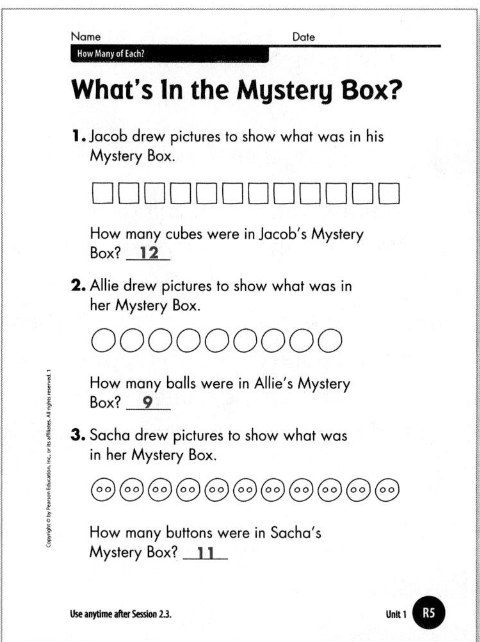
Name Date

How Many of Each?

What's In the Mystery Box?

1. Jacob drew pictures to show what was in his Mystery Box.

How many cubes were in Jacob's Mystery Box? 12

2. Allie drew pictures to show what was in her Mystery Box.

How many balls were in Allie's Mystery Box? 9

3. Sacha drew pictures to show what was in her Mystery Box.

How many buttons were in Sacha's Mystery Box? 11

Use anytime after Session 2.3. Unit 1 R5

Distribute a Mystery Box to each pair. Your job is to show *what* is inside the Mystery Box and *how many* there are. First, open the box and count the items together. What did you find out?

Students might say:

"We have 7 chips in our box."

What could you draw or write to tell someone about your Mystery Box? Encourage students to share their ideas which might include writing words and/or numbers and drawing pictures.

[Paul] said he would draw a picture of [7 chips] and write the numbers.

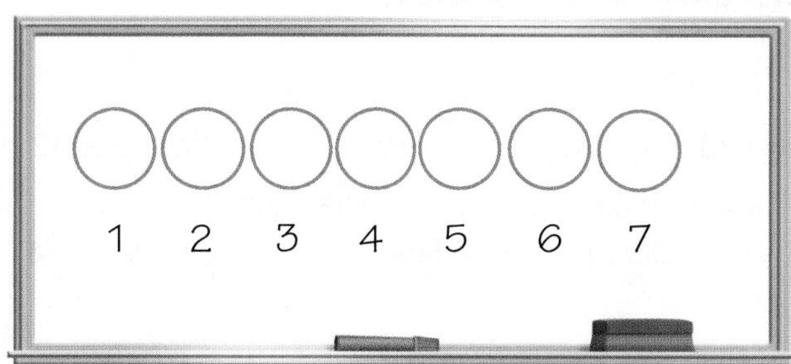

[Jacinta] said she would write ["11 bears"] on her paper. What if you didn't know how to write the number [11], what could you do?

Students might say:

"Count up to 11 on the number line."

Now, students work to represent the contents of their Mystery Box on Mystery Boxes (M8). Support students as needed, taking dictation or pointing them to resources such as the class number line to figure out how to write a number.

Distribute copies of What's In the Mystery Box (R5).

ELL English Language Learners

Suggest a Sequence If students have difficulty verbalizing the process they used to count and record the items, suggest the following sequence.

First, count the items. *Next,* make a picture or mark for each item. *Then,* write the number.

Additional Resource

Student Math Handbook

Game: *Collect 20 Together* SMH G1

Materials: dot cubes, counters

Variation: Play to 15 instead of 20.

Practice

Missing Steps

Use anytime after Session 2.3.

Math Focus Points

- Ordering a set of numbers and quantities up to 12

Materials: complete set of labeled cube towers for the numbers 1–12 (from Session 2.3; 1 set per pair), R6

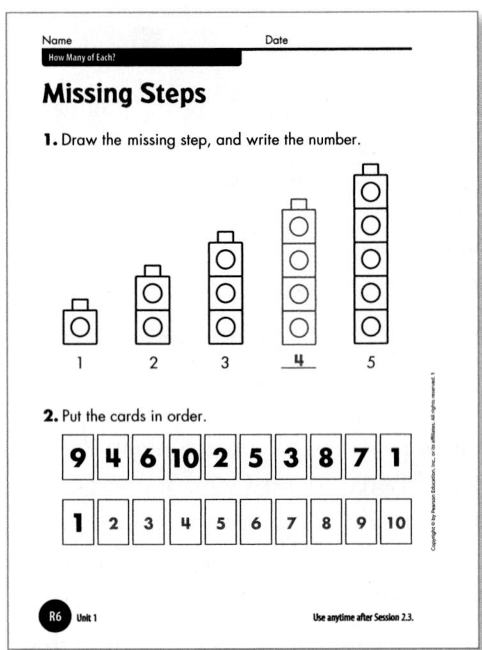
Name Date

How Many of Each?

Missing Steps

1. Draw the missing step, and write the number.

1 2 3 4 5

2. Put the cards in order.

9	4	6	10	2	5	3	8	7	1
1	2	3	4	5	6	7	8	9	10

R6 Unit 1 Use anytime after Session 2.3.

We're going to do some more work with the staircases. You will try to find a missing step.

First, put your towers in order. Next, Player 1 closes his or her eyes. Player 2 secretly takes one of the steps away. Then Player 1 figures out which step is missing.

Model one round with the 1–6 towers. Which step is missing? How do you know?

Students might say:

"I counted the towers. The numbers go 1, 2, 3, 4. There's no step for the number 3."

"When they are lined up you can see where there's a step that's too big. That's where the missing tower goes."

Students now play in pairs, using towers 1–12. If students seem ready, they can remove more than 1 tower on a turn.

Distribute copies of Missing Steps (R6).

ELL English Language Learners

Use Repetition Demonstrate the meanings of *in order, small/smaller/smallest* and *big/bigger/biggest*. Show students three cube towers of different sizes and have them identify the smallest and largest. Then have them compare two cube towers using the terms *smaller* and *larger*. You can also use related language such as short/tall and more/fewer as you compare the different towers.

Additional Resource

Student Math Handbook

Game: *Collect 20 Together* SMH G1

Materials: dot cubes, counters

Extension

20 MIN PAIRS

Mystery Boxes with Larger Numbers

Use anytime after Session 2.3.

Math Focus Points

- Counting a set of up to 20 objects by 1s
- Ordering a set of numbers and quantities up to 12

Materials: Mystery Boxes (from Session 2.2 with 20–30 items; 1 per pair), M8

Distribute a copy of Mystery Boxes (M8) to each student. You will each use the Mystery Boxes sheet to show *what* is inside the box and *how many* there are. These boxes have a lot of things in them so keeping track of your count can be challenging. You might want to try counting two different ways to double-check your work.

Pairs work together to count the number of items in their Mystery Box. Encourage students to check each other's work, and to share strategies for keeping track of so many objects.

Once pairs agree on the number of objects, each student makes a representation of what and how many items are in their box.

Once students are finished, discuss some of the strategies you have seen for counting larger sets of objects and for recording their work.

Students might say:

"We put the bears in groups by color. We added the [3 red] and the [3 blue] and then counted the rest."

"We put the cubes in groups of 5 and then counted them by 5s."

If time permits, record the total number in each box on the board.

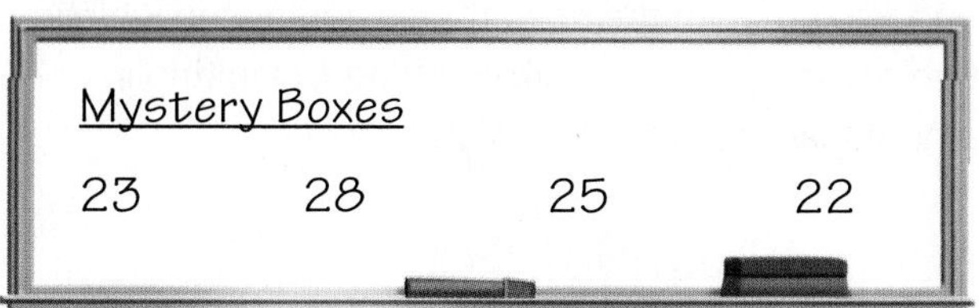

Pairs work together to order the Mystery Boxes from the smallest to the largest number. If I had another Mystery Box with 26 items in it, where would it belong? Why?

ELL English Language Learners

Provide Sentence Stems Some students may have difficulty comparing and ordering the number of items in the Mystery Boxes. Help them by providing sentence stems. For example: Box [A] had ____ items. Box [B] had ____ items. Box ____ had [more/fewer] than Box ____.

Additional Resource

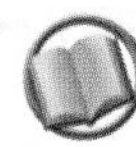

Student Math Handbook

Game: *Collect 20 Together* SMH G1

Materials: dot cubes, counters

Variation: Play to 30 instead of 20.

Differentiation in Investigation 3

Mathematics in This Investigation

The mathematics focuses on developing an understanding of the operation of addition in which two or more quantities are combined, resulting in an amount larger than either of the parts.

Understanding the Mathematics

Students efficiently add single-digit numbers. They may count on from one number, use known number combinations, or reason about a sum they do know (e.g., 5 + 5) to solve a problem they don't know (e.g., 5 + 6). They explain their strategy for solving the problem and show it on paper.

Option: Assign the **Extension** activity.

Partially Understanding the Mathematics

Students add single-digit numbers, often using manipulatives or drawings to count all. They may occasionally make small counting or keeping track errors that result in the wrong answer. Articulating how they solved the problem, and showing that strategy on paper, may be challenging. They may record a strategy that is easy to show on paper, rather than the one actually used.

Option: Assign the **Practice** activity.

Not Understanding the Mathematics

Students may have trouble retelling or interpreting a story problem. They count all to solve addition problems, but because they are still developing fluency with counting, they may have trouble accurately representing the groups and recounting them all from one. They may get different answers each time they count. Articulating how they solved the problem, and accurately showing that strategy on paper, is challenging.

Option: Assign the **Intervention** activity.

Investigation 3 Quiz

In addition to your observations and students' work in Investigation 3, the Quiz (R7) can be used to gather more information.

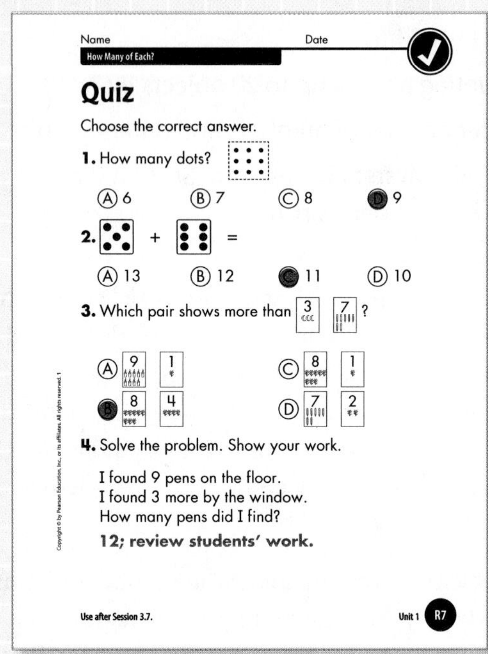

Name Date

How Many of Each?

Quiz

Choose the correct answer.

1. How many dots?

(A) 6 (B) 7 (C) 8 (D) 9

2. [dot card] + [dot card] =

(A) 13 (B) 12 (C) 11 (D) 10

3. Which pair shows more than 3 7 ?

(A) 9 1 (C) 8 1

(B) 8 4 (D) 7 2

4. Solve the problem. Show your work.

I found 9 pens on the floor.
I found 3 more by the window.
How many pens did I find?

12; review students' work.

Use after Session 3.7. Unit 1 R7

Intervention

20 MIN PAIRS

Solving Story Problems with Objects

Use anytime after Session 3.3.

Math Focus Points

- Visualizing and retelling the action in an addition situation
- Modeling the action of an addition problem with counters or drawings
- Finding the total of two or more quantities up to a total of 20 by counting all, counting on, or using number combinations

Materials: paper clips, counters, blank paper, markers

I am going to tell a story. Try to see it in your mind. I wanted to make a paper clip bracelet. I started with 6 paper clips. The bracelet was not big enough to fit on my wrist. I used 6 more paper clips. Then the bracelet was perfect.

Encourage students to think about what they saw in their minds as you told the story. Have them retell the story to their partners, without discussing the answer. Their summaries should focus on the action of the problem and on whether there will be more or fewer paper clips at the end of the story.

Now your job is to figure out how many paper clips I used to make the bracelet. Students can use paper clips, counters, or drawings to model and solve the problem. Discuss and model different strategies for solving the problem. How did you find out how many paper clips I used?

Students might say:

"I counted out 6 paper clips and then I counted out 6 more paper clips. Then I counted them all."

"I made two lines of paper clips and then I counted them."

Review and model strategies for accurately counting the paper clips, as needed, and then model ways to record students' strategies for solving the problem.

[Keena] said she made two lines of paper clips. How many were in one line? How many were in the other line? Then what did she do? She counted them. So, I'm going to write the numbers she said.

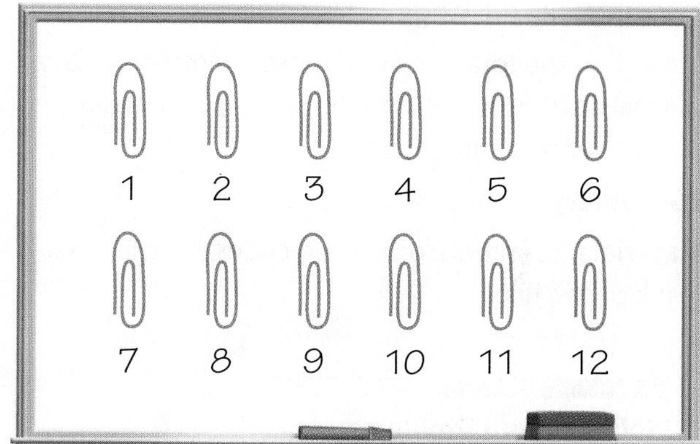

ELL English Language Learners

Rephrase Students may become overwhelmed by the amount of information in story problems. Shorten story problems by leaving out extra details that complicate the story. For example: I made a bracelet. I started with 6 paper clips. Then I used 6 more. How many paper clips did I use?

Additional Resource

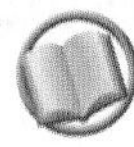

Student Math Handbook

Game: *Double Compare* SMH G6

Materials: Primary Number Cards (without Wild Cards)

Variation: Have students use only cards 1–6.

Practice

Solving Story Problems

Use anytime after Session 3.3.

Math Focus Points

- Visualizing and retelling the action in an addition situation
- Modeling the action of an addition problem with counters or drawings
- Finding the total of two or more quantities up to a total of 20 by counting all, counting on, or using number combinations

Vocabulary: more, fewer

Materials: counters (connecting cubes, pencils, etc.), blank paper, R8

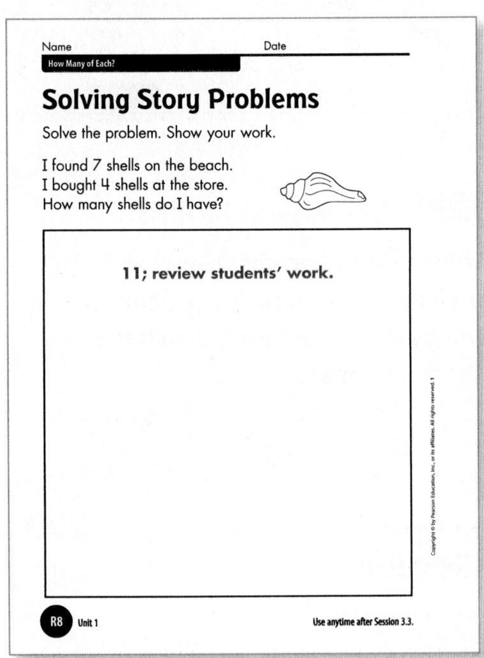
Name Date

How Many of Each?

Solving Story Problems

Solve the problem. Show your work.

I found 7 shells on the beach.
I bought 4 shells at the store.
How many shells do I have?

11; review students' work.

R8 Unit 1 Use anytime after Session 3.3.

I am going to tell a story. Try to see it in your mind. I found 5 pencils on my desk. I found 4 more pencils on the floor.

Pairs retell the story to each other, without discussing the answer.

At the end of the story, will I have more pencils than when I started or fewer pencils than when I started?

Encourage students to explain their answers. Then distribute paper to each student. Explain the tools that are available to solve the problem (pencils, counters) and then set them to work.

How many pencils did I find? Solve the problem and find a way to show your solution on paper. You want someone else to be able to look at your paper and tell how you solved the problem.

When students are finished, model and discuss the different strategies, as well as ways to show them on paper.

[Teo] said he used his fingers to count on. Counting on can be tricky to show on paper. [Teo], can you show us what you did? How could I show that on the board?

Students might say:

"First he said '5' so write 5."

"Then he put up 4 fingers for the 4 pencils. You could draw 4 fingers."

Distribute copies of Solving Story Problems (R8).

ELL English Language Learners

Model Thinking Aloud Model your thinking for solving the problem aloud. Show students 5 pencils on your desk. I found 5 pencils on my desk. Pick up 4 pencils from the floor. I found 4 pencils on the floor. Hold up the pencils as you count them. Now I will count them: 1, 2, 3, 4, 5, 6, 7, 8, 9. I found 9 pencils.

Additional Resource

Student Math Handbook

Game: *Double Compare* SMH G6

Materials: Primary Number Cards (without Wild Cards)

Extension

20 MIN PAIRS

Solving Story Problems with Larger Numbers

Use anytime after Session 3.3.

Math Focus Points

- Visualizing and retelling the action in an addition situation
- Modeling the action of an addition problem with counters or drawings
- Finding the total of two or more quantities up to a total of 20 by counting all, counting on, or using number combinations

Vocabulary: more, fewer

Materials: counters, blank paper, markers, R9

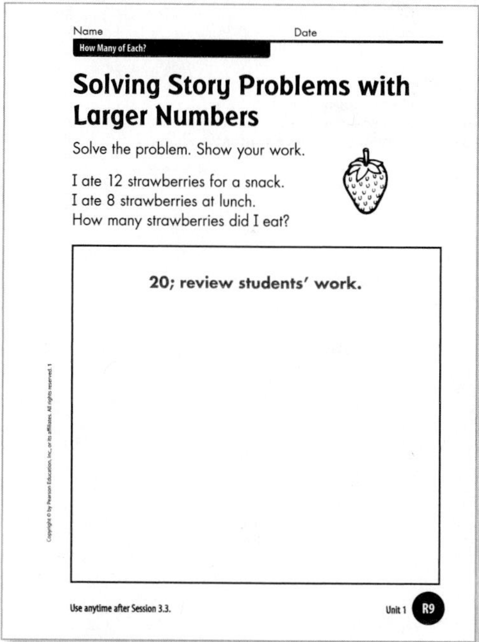
Name Date
How Many of Each?

Solving Story Problems with Larger Numbers

Solve the problem. Show your work.

I ate 12 strawberries for a snack.
I ate 8 strawberries at lunch.
How many strawberries did I eat?

20; review students' work.

Use anytime after Session 3.3. Unit 1 R9

I am going to tell a story. Try to see it in your mind. I have a beautiful flower garden. I picked 12 flowers to put in a vase. When I put them in the vase, it was not full. I went back to the garden and picked 7 more flowers. I put the new flowers in the vase too. The vase was now full!

Have students retell the story to their partners and think about the following question: Did I have fewer flowers or more flowers at the end of my story?

Students work with a partner to find the number of flowers in the vase and show their solution on paper.

Distribute paper and markers and point out that counters are also available. After students have recorded their solutions, ask a few volunteers to share. How many flowers were in the vase? How do you know?

Students might say:

"19 because I started with 12 and counted 7 more."

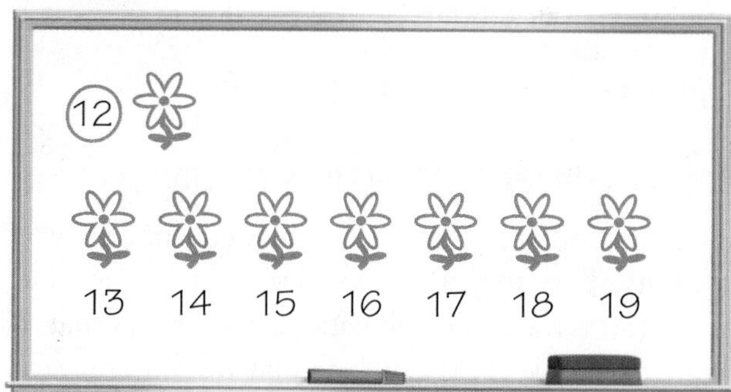

Distribute copies of Solving Story Problems with Larger Numbers (R9).

ELL English Language Learners

Provide Sentence Stems Provide sentence stems for students to use to summarize the story.

I picked ________ flowers.

Then I picked ________ more.

I picked ________ flowers in all.

Additional Resource

Student Math Handbook

Game: *Double Compare Dots* SMH G7

Materials: Dot Cards

Variation: Players each turn over 3 cards and compare the totals.

Differentiation in Investigation 4

Mathematics in This Investigation

The mathematics focuses on understanding that a quantity can be composed and decomposed in different ways, and finding a missing part when the total and one part are given.

Understanding the Mathematics

Students find several or all combinations of a given quantity. They have strategies for using one combination to generate others, and have a system for finding and showing all the possible combinations. To solve a missing part problem, these students count up, or use an addition combination or subtraction fact they know.

Option: Assign the **Extension** activity.

Partially Understanding the Mathematics

Students find one or more combinations for a given quantity. They may work more randomly, using trial and error to test out combinations of numbers that equal the whole. This approach may result in repeat solutions that the student is unaware of. When solving a missing part problem students may struggle to visualize the action. They may need to represent what the missing part of the problem *might* be, count all of the parts, and then adjust until they find the correct solution.

Option: Assign the **Practice** activity.

Not Understanding the Mathematics

Students have difficulty composing and decomposing a given quantity in different ways. When solving missing part problems, they may not understand what parts of the problem are known/unknown and/or what the relationship is between the parts. These students may guess how many are missing instead of using a strategy to figure it out.

Option: Assign the **Intervention** activity.

Investigation 4 Quiz

In addition to your observations and students' work in Investigation 4, the Quiz (R10) can be used to gather more information.

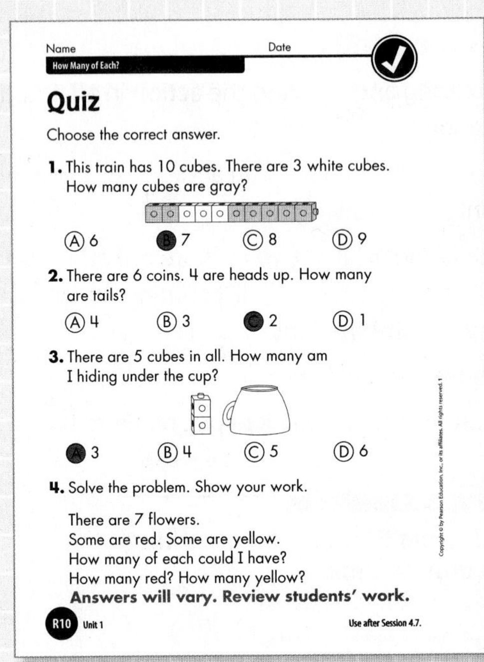

Name Date

How Many of Each?

Quiz

Choose the correct answer.

1. This train has 10 cubes. There are 3 white cubes. How many cubes are gray?

Ⓐ 6 Ⓑ 7 Ⓒ 8 Ⓓ 9

2. There are 6 coins. 4 are heads up. How many are tails?

Ⓐ 4 Ⓑ 3 Ⓒ 2 Ⓓ 1

3. There are 5 cubes in all. How many am I hiding under the cup?

Ⓐ 3 Ⓑ 4 Ⓒ 5 Ⓓ 6

4. Solve the problem. Show your work.

There are 7 flowers.
Some are red. Some are yellow.
How many of each could I have?
How many red? How many yellow?
Answers will vary. Review students' work.

R10 Unit 1 Use after Session 4.7.

Intervention

15 MIN PAIRS

Five Blueberries and Strawberries

Use anytime after Session 4.1.

Math Focus Points

- Finding combinations of numbers up to 10
- Solving a problem with multiple solutions
- Recording a solution to a problem

Materials: connecting cubes (5 red, 5 blue per pair), blank paper (1 sheet per pair), markers

Distribute cubes, paper, and markers to each pair.

Last night, I ate some blueberries and strawberries. Imagine that I put 5 pieces of fruit on my plate. Some of them were blueberries and some of them were strawberries. How many blueberries? How many strawberries?

Have students retell the story to their partners. Make sure students understand the situation, and then set them to work.

Encourage students to use cubes to represent the blueberries and strawberries.

Listen as students solve the problem. Help students who are struggling by suggesting an amount of one kind of fruit. What if I had 4 blueberries on my plate? What would that look like? How many strawberries would I need so that I would have 5 in all?

Another strategy is having students build towers of 5 cubes using the 2 colors and helping them determine how many strawberries and blueberries their towers show.

Once students have found one combination, they record their work.

What combinations of blueberries and strawberries did you find?

Students might say:

"I have 4 blueberries and 1 strawberry."

"I have 2 blueberries and 3 strawberries."

Gather all of the combinations that pairs found. Model each with cubes and record them on the board. Be sure to discuss the variety of solutions, and the fact that there is more than one answer to this problem, which may surprise some students.

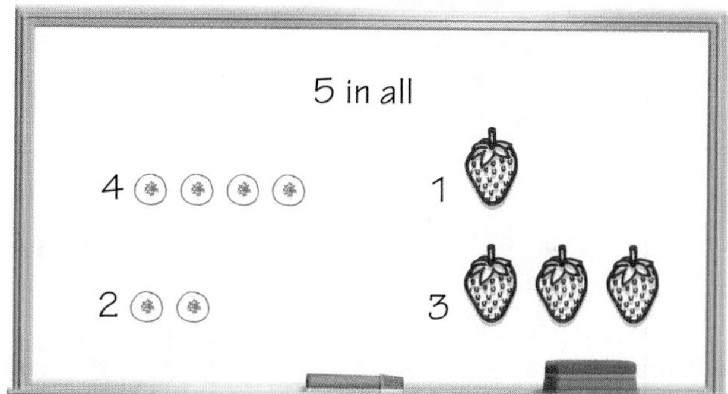

ELL English Language Learners

Rephrase The question How many of each? may confuse beginning English Language Learners. Throughout the activity, whenever this question is asked, follow it with two other questions that relate to the objects: How many [object 1]? and How many [object 2]?

Additional Resource

Student Math Handbook pages 46–47

Practice

Pencils and Crayons

Use anytime after Session 4.5.

Math Focus Points

- Finding and exploring relationships among combinations of numbers up to 10
- Solving a problem with multiple solutions
- Representing number combinations with numbers, pictures, and/or words

Materials: connecting cubes, blank paper (1 sheet per pair), markers, R11

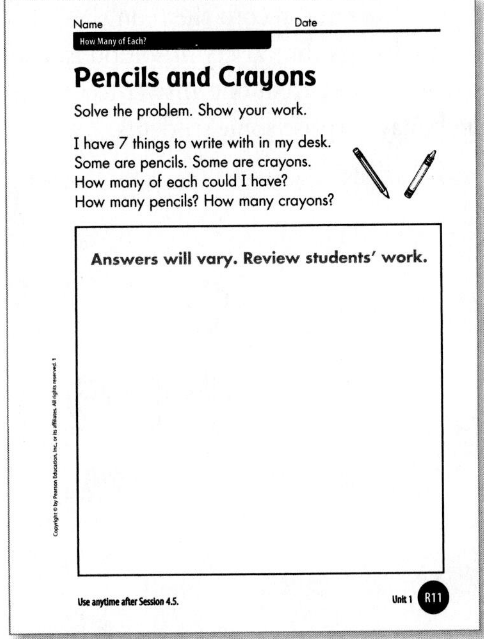
Name Date

How Many of Each?

Pencils and Crayons

Solve the problem. Show your work.

I have 7 things to write with in my desk.
Some are pencils. Some are crayons.
How many of each could I have?
How many pencils? How many crayons?

Answers will vary. Review students' work.

Use anytime after Session 4.5. Unit 1 R11

Distribute paper and markers to each pair.

In my desk, I have 8 things to write with. Some of them are pencils. Some of them are crayons. How many of each could I have?

Students work with their partners to find how many pencils and how many crayons you could have.

Have cubes available and suggest that students use pictures, numbers, and/or words to record their work.

Talk with students as they work, encouraging them to check that each solution they find is, in fact, a new solution.

Let's look at these 2 solutions—7 pencils and 1 crayon and 1 crayon and 7 pencils. Are they the same or different? Why do you think so?

Students might say:

"They are different because the first one is 7 and 1 and the other one is 1 and 7."

"I think they are the same because they both have 7 pencils and 1 crayon."

Model the two situations with cubes. If there is time, contrast this pair with another pair of solutions: 7 pencils and 1 crayon and 1 pencil and 7 crayons.

Distribute copies of Pencils and Crayons (R11).

ELL English Language Learners

Provide a Word List Write *how many, each,* and *in all* on chart paper. Make sure students understand what each word or phrase means and can use it when working toward a solution. They should understand that the answer to the question *How many?* is a number. *Each* refers to the type of object, while *in all* refers to the entire group.

Additional Resource

Student Math Handbook

Game: *How Many Am I Hiding?* SMH G14

Materials: connecting cubes, M37

Extension

20 MIN GROUPS

Dogs and Cats

Use anytime after Session 4.5.

Math Focus Points

- Finding and exploring relationships among combinations of numbers up to 10
- Solving a problem with multiple solutions
- Representing number combinations with numbers, pictures, and/or words

Materials: connecting cubes (as needed), blank paper (1 sheet per group), markers, R12

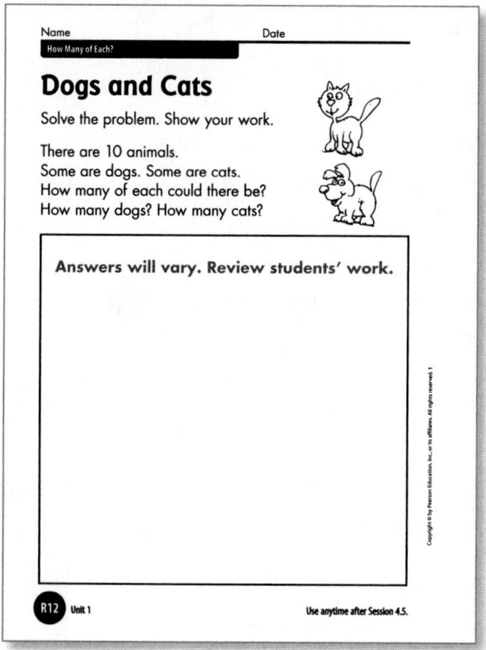
Name Date

How Many of Each?

Dogs and Cats

Solve the problem. Show your work.

There are 10 animals.
Some are dogs. Some are cats.
How many of each could there be?
How many dogs? How many cats?

Answers will vary. Review students' work.

R12 Unit 1 Use anytime after Session 4.5.

Today you are going to try to find as many solutions as you can for a How Many of Each? problem.

There are 8 animals. Some of the animals are dogs. Some of the animals are cats. How many of each could there be?

Distribute paper and markers to each group and make cubes available. Students work with their groups to find as many solutions as possible for this problem.

Remember, you are trying to find as many solutions as you can.

When the groups seem like they have slowed down, ask them to share their solutions. Record them on the board. How many of each?

4 dogs + 4 cats = 8

1 dog + 7 cats = 8

Look at how many solutions you found. Do you think you found them *all*? Do you think there could be more?

Students might say:

"I think there are more because I don't see a way that uses 2 cats."

"I think we found them all because I tried lots and lots of combinations and I couldn't find any more."

Encourage groups to look for more or to find a way to prove they've found them all.

Distribute copies of Dogs and Cats (R12).

ELL English Language Learners

Provide Sentence Stems To help students verbalize their findings, provide sentence stems. For example:
I think we found them all because _______.
I don't think we found them all because _______.

Additional Resource

Student Math Handbook pages 46–47, 49

Differentiation in Investigation 1

Mathematics in This Investigation

The mathematics focuses on describing and comparing familiar 2-D shapes and their attributes, and using different shapes to completely cover a region or fill an outline.

Additional Resource: *Modeling, Molding, and Maintaining the Classroom Community,* pages 76–78 (See *Implementing Investigations in Grade 1*)

Understanding the Mathematics

Students are familiar with the names and attributes of many 2-D shapes, and can connect real-world examples with these shapes. They use 2-D shapes to completely cover given regions with no gaps or overlaps, seeing how shapes fit together and possibly using equivalencies among shapes in their work. When asked to cover the same region with more or fewer shapes, they understand the relationship between the size of the blocks and the numbers used (e.g., the smaller the blocks the more you will use).

Option: Assign the **Extension** activity.

Partially Understanding the Mathematics

Students are familiar with the names of some 2-D shapes and describe the attributes of those shapes in a variety of ways, but they do not necessarily focus on mathematical terms. They can find and generate real-world examples of those shapes. When using 2-D shapes to cover given regions, these students occasionally leave gaps or have overlaps because they aren't yet fluent with the ways the shapes fit together and with the relationships between the shapes. Finding a way to use more or fewer shapes on the same outline may be challenging, as these students may have a hard time seeing more than one way to fill a given area.

Option: Assign the **Practice** activity.

Not Understanding the Mathematics

Students are familiar with the names of only a few 2-D shapes and cannot necessarily attach those names to the shapes they identify. They may need support and examples in order to describe attributes of 2-D shapes and to find real-world examples of those shapes. They use 2-D shapes to cover given regions, but often leave gaps or have overlaps because they aren't yet fluent with the ways the shapes fit together, and may not understand what it means to completely cover or fill an area. They do not yet see or use relationships between shapes in their work.

Option: Assign the **Intervention** activity.

Investigation 1 Quiz

In addition to your observations and students' work in Investigation 1, the Quiz (R13) can be used to gather more information.

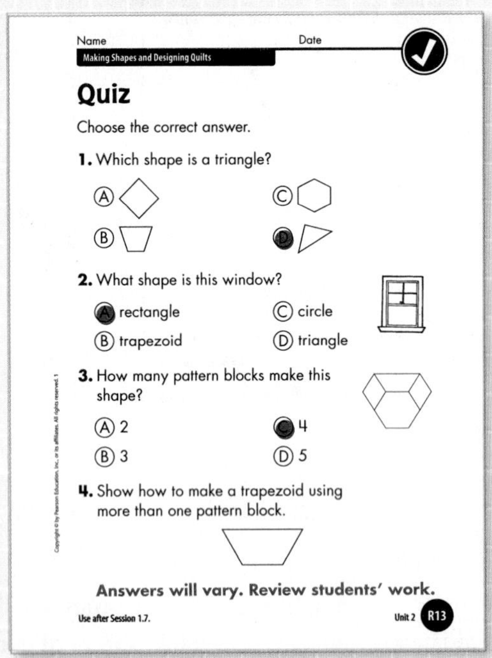

Name Date

Making Shapes and Designing Quilts

Quiz

Choose the correct answer.

1. Which shape is a triangle?
   - (A)
   - (B)
   - (C)
   - (D)

2. What shape is this window?
   - (A) rectangle
   - (B) trapezoid
   - (C) circle
   - (D) triangle

3. How many pattern blocks make this shape?
   - (A) 2
   - (B) 3
   - (C) 4
   - (D) 5

4. Show how to make a trapezoid using more than one pattern block.

Answers will vary. Review students' work.

Use after Session 1.7. Unit 2 R13

Intervention

15 MIN PAIRS

Describing 2-D Shapes

Use anytime after Session 1.1.

Math Focus Points

- Describing, comparing, and naming 2-D shapes

Vocabulary: rectangle, triangle, square, circle, hexagon, rhombus

Materials: M3–M5, M21–M23 (1 per student, stapled)

Materials to Prepare: Make one set of the following shapes from Paper Shape Cutouts (M3–M5).

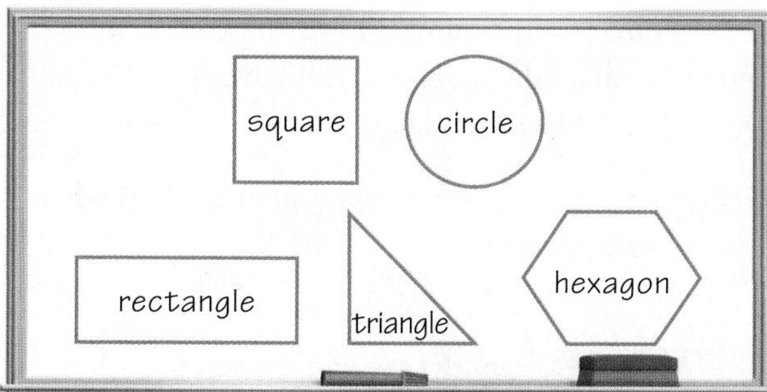

This activity previews the work students will do in Investigation 2.

I want you to name each shape that I show. Have students name each shape. As students identify the shapes, write the name of each shape inside or below the corresponding figure on the board. One way we can identify different shapes is by looking at the sides of the shape.

Direct students' attention to the square and circle.

What's different about the sides of these two shapes? Some shapes have straight sides and some shapes have curved sides.

Write "curved sides" next to the circle.

Distribute a set of Shape Cards (M21–M23) to each student. Look at the pages of shapes that you have. Find the shapes with curved sides. Once the group has identified D, F, H, and O, tell students to write "curved sides" on each of these shape cards.

Another way we can identify shapes is by looking at the number of sides. Using the shapes you have displayed, ask students to identify the number of sides on each shape. Record this information (e.g., 3 sides, 4 sides) under each shape.

Look at a shape card. Count the number of sides. Write this information on the card. Students should record "3 sides," "4 sides," etc. on each card.

If time permits, or on another day, discuss another aspect of shapes such as length of sides or number of corners (vertices). Students can also cut out the Shape Cards and sort them into groups.

ELL English Language Learners

Use Repetition Names of shapes may be completely new to beginning English Language Learners. Prior to the activity, show students drawings of the shapes, have them practice saying the name of each one, and then ask them to find similar shapes in the classroom. Emphasize the vocabulary terms in each question that is posed.

Additional Resource

Student Math Handbook pages 74–75

Practice

Identifying Shapes

Use anytime after Session 1.2.

Math Focus Points

- Describing, comparing, and naming 2-D shapes

Vocabulary: triangle, hexagon, rectangle, square, circle, rhombus

Materials: M3–M5, M21–M23, crayons, R14

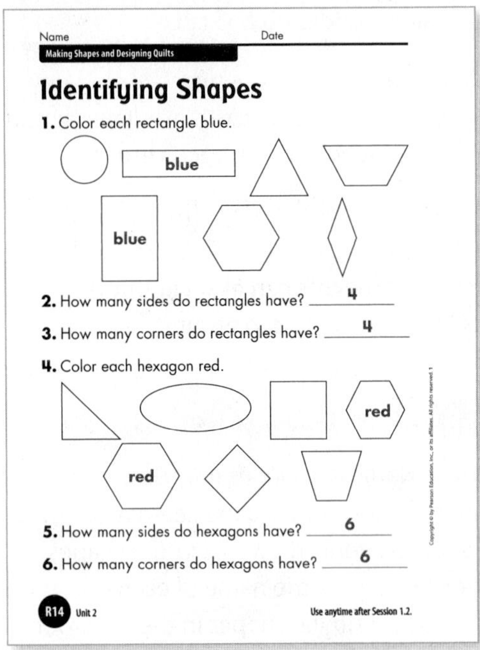
Name Date

Making Shapes and Designing Quilts

Identifying Shapes

1. Color each rectangle blue.

blue

blue

2. How many sides do rectangles have? 4

3. How many corners do rectangles have? 4

4. Color each hexagon red.

red

red

5. How many sides do hexagons have? 6

6. How many corners do hexagons have? 6

R14 Unit 2 Use anytime after Session 1.2.

Materials to Prepare: Make one set of Paper Shape Cutouts (M3–M5) and make each shape a different color. Also prepare a set of Shape Cards (M21–M23) for each student.

Hold up the triangle from the Paper Shape Cutouts. What shape is this? How do you know?

Students might say:

"It is a triangle. It has 3 corners."

"I know it's a triangle because it has 3 sides."

Are there any other ways to describe a triangle? After students respond, repeat that a triangle has 3 sides and 3 corners.

Help students understand that not all triangles look the same, but they do have something in common. What do all triangles have in common? Find all of the triangles in your Shape Cards. After you find all of the triangles, color them the same color as the Paper Shape Cutout triangle.

Repeat this activity with the hexagon, rectangle, square, circle, and rhombus. Are there any shapes that you did not use? When the hexagon, rectangle, square, circle, and rhombus have all been identified and colored, students should still have shape cards D, H, N, and O unused.

Distribute copies of Identifying Shapes (R14) when students are ready.

ELL English Language Learners

Provide Sentence Stems Students may not understand that the same name can be used to describe shapes that do not look exactly alike. Help students identify the most important attributes of each Paper Shape Cutout using sentence stems.

The triangle has ________.

The hexagon has ________.

Additional Resource

Student Math Handbook

Game: *Fill the Hexagons* SMH G8

Materials: pattern blocks, pattern block cubes, M19

Extension

20 MIN PAIRS

Shape Puzzles

Use anytime after Session 1.2.

Math Focus Points

- Noticing shapes in the environment
- Describing, comparing, and naming 2-D shapes

Vocabulary: square, hexagon, triangle, trapezoid, rhombus, side, corner

Materials: M21-M23, R15

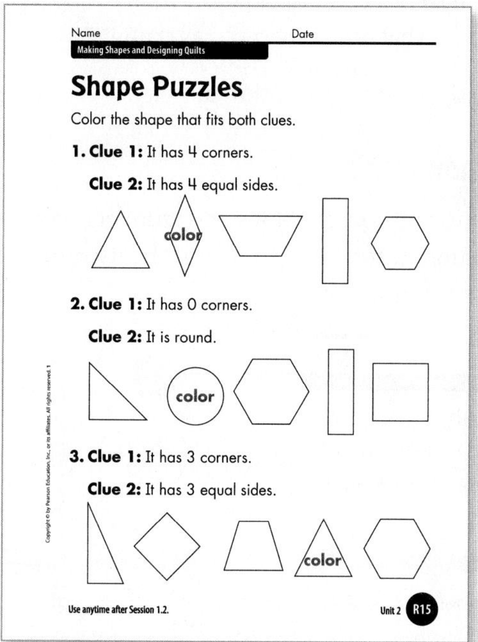
Name Date

Making Shapes and Designing Quilts

Shape Puzzles

Color the shape that fits both clues.

1. Clue 1: It has 4 corners.

Clue 2: It has 4 equal sides.

color

2. Clue 1: It has 0 corners.

Clue 2: It is round.

color

3. Clue 1: It has 3 corners.

Clue 2: It has 3 equal sides.

color

Use anytime after Session 1.2. Unit 2 R15

Materials to Prepare: Prepare a set of Shape Cards (M21–M23) for each student.

Write the following clues on the board, but cover Clues 2 and 3.

Clue 1: This shape has 4 sides.

Clue 2: All sides are the same length.

Clue 3: This shape has 4 square corners.

Distribute a set of shape cards to each student. Have the group read the first clue. Students find the Shape Cards that fit Clue 1 (A, C, G, I, K, N, R).

Read Clue 2. Students look at their subset of cards to find the shapes that fit (A, I, K, R).

Reveal Clue 3. You may need to explain the term "square corner" (90 degrees) by demonstrating how a square tile can fit into the corner.

Which Shape Cards fit all three rules? *(A, I, R)* What shape is this? Right, all of these cards are squares.

Write the following clues on the board.

Clue 1: This shape has 3 sides.

Clue 2: This shape has sides that are different lengths.

Clue 3: This shape has 1 square corner.

Which shape fits these clues? Students should identify the right triangles, shapes, E, J, and Q.

Now, partners give shape clues to each other. If appropriate, help students record their clues so that they can be presented to the group.

Distribute copies of Shape Puzzles (R15).

ELL English Language Learners

Model Thinking Aloud Support students by reviewing the second set of clues and highlighting the important words in each clue (3 sides, different lengths, square corner). Hold up a shape with 4 sides. This shape has 4 sides. Trace and count them. So this shape does not fit Clue 1. Model each shape and discuss whether or not the shape fits the clues.

Additional Resource

Student Math Handbook pages 71–75

Differentiation in Investigation 2

Mathematics in This Investigation

The mathematics focuses on attributes of 2-D shapes, particularly triangles and quadrilaterals, and using those attributes to sort and compare a group of shapes.

Understanding the Mathematics

Students describe mathematical attributes of shapes and use them to sort 2-D shapes into mutually exclusive groups. They identify and draw different kinds of triangles and explain *why* they are triangles by referring to mathematical attributes (e.g., number of sides, straight sides, number of vertices).

Option: Assign the **Extension** activity.

Partially Understanding the Mathematics

Students describe 2-D shapes using a variety of attributes. They sort shapes into categories that may not be consistent or that contain minor errors. Many of the triangles they create are equilateral triangles standing on their base. They identify most triangles, but may find it challenging to explain why they think some shapes are/are not triangles.

Option: Assign the **Practice** activity.

Not Understanding the Mathematics

Students describe 2-D shapes but with limited use of the correct geometric language. They may sort shapes in ways that are not recognizable, use labels that are not accurate for the shapes included, or incorrectly categorize the shapes. Identifying and creating shapes that are triangles, and explaining their reasoning, is likely a challenge. They may consider only equilateral triangles, standing on their base, to be triangles. Conversely, they may consider shapes that have 3 sides and curved edges, or 3 straight sides that are not closed, a triangle.

Option: Assign the **Intervention** activity.

Investigation 2 Quiz

In addition to your observations and students' work in Investigation 2, the Quiz (R16) can be used to gather more information.

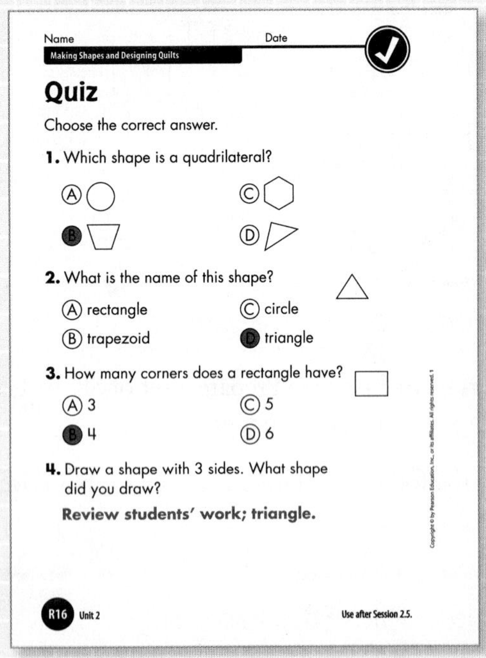

Name Date

Making Shapes and Designing Quilts

Quiz

Choose the correct answer.

1. Which shape is a quadrilateral?

(A) (C)

(B) (D)

2. What is the name of this shape?

(A) rectangle (C) circle

(B) trapezoid (D) triangle

3. How many corners does a rectangle have?

(A) 3 (C) 5

(B) 4 (D) 6

4. Draw a shape with 3 sides. What shape did you draw?

Review students' work; triangle.

R16 Unit 2 Use after Session 2.5.

Intervention

Geoboard Triangles

Use anytime after Session 2.2.

Math Focus Points

- Identifying characteristics of triangles and quadrilaterals
- Identifying and making triangles and quadrilaterals of different shapes and sizes

Vocabulary: triangle

Materials: rubber bands, Geoboards, R17 (several copies per student)

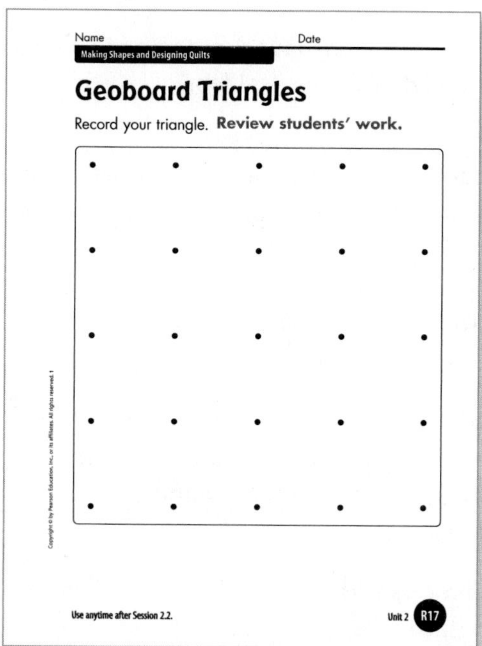
Name Date
Making Shapes and Designing Quilts

Geoboard Triangles

Record your triangle. **Review students' work.**

Use anytime after Session 2.2. Unit 2 R17

We're going to be thinking about triangles today. What do you know about triangles? Refer back to the triangle poster the class made in Session 1.1. Focus in particular on the fact that triangles have 3 sides.

You're going to make triangles on a Geoboard. You will use one rubber band for each side of the triangle. How many rubber bands will you use for each triangle?

Students might say:

"3, because a triangle has 3 sides."

Model using 3 rubber bands, one for each side, to make a triangle. Trace each side and count them together with students.

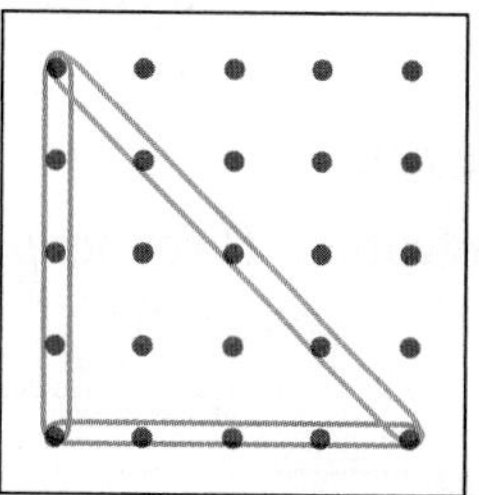

Now distribute rubber bands and a Geoboard to each student to use to make triangles. Encourage students to trace and count their rubber bands to make sure their triangle has 3 sides before recording it on a copy of Geoboard Triangles (R17). Students should create and record several different triangles.

Ask each child to choose a favorite triangle. Tape them on the board.

Look at the different shapes that you made. What do you notice? Are they all triangles? Why do you think so?

ELL English Language Learners

Use Repetition Repeat the words *triangle, sides,* and *corners* as you interact with students. Students should understand that the rubber bands are the *sides* of the triangles. They also should be associating the pegs on the Geoboard with the *corners (vertices)* of the triangles.

Additional Resource

Student Math Handbook page 75

Practice

15 MIN PAIRS

Find the Rule

Use anytime after Session 2.4.

Math Focus Points

- Identifying common attributes of a group of shapes
- Describing, comparing, and naming 2-D shapes
- Identifying characteristics of triangles and quadrilaterals

Vocabulary: quadrilateral

Materials: Power Polygons™ (1 set per pair), yarn (1 foot piece per pair), markers, R18

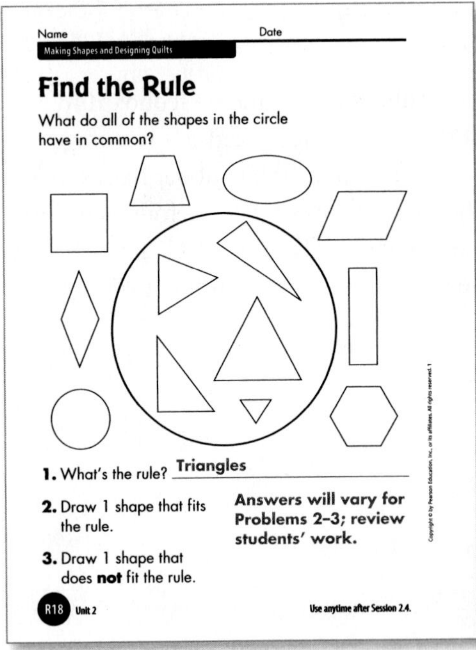
Name Date

Making Shapes and Designing Quilts

Find the Rule

What do all of the shapes in the circle have in common?

1. What's the rule? Triangles

2. Draw 1 shape that fits the rule.

3. Draw 1 shape that does **not** fit the rule.

Answers will vary for Problems 2–3; review students' work.

R18 Unit 2 Use anytime after Session 2.4.

Use yarn to make a circle. Place Power Polygon shapes B and M inside the circle. Put shape H outside the circle. I am thinking of a rule. The shapes in the circle fit my rule. The shape outside the circle does not.

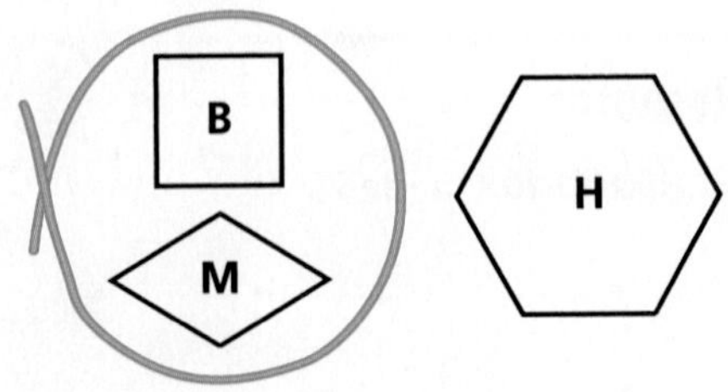

Ask students to think about how the shapes inside the circle are alike. Ask volunteers to place other shapes where they think the shapes belong. Give feedback, using shapes that have 4 sides as your rule, and moving shapes to the appropriate category as needed. When most students seem sure, ask What do you think my rule is?

Students might say:

"All the shapes inside the circle have 4 sides."

"Shapes that have 4 sides and shapes that don't have 4 sides."

Now distribute a piece of yarn and a small set of the Power Polygon shapes to each pair. Students sort them using this rule. Make a yarn circle. Put all of the quadrilaterals—the shapes that have 4 sides—inside the circle. Shapes that are not quadrilaterals should go outside the circle.

Observe students as they sort. Bring any shapes that cause confusion, such as shape K and O, to the group for discussion. Model tracing and counting the number of sides.

Repeat this process with a new rule. Shapes that are triangles go inside the circle. Shapes that are not triangles go outside the circle.

Distribute copies of Find the Rule (R18).

ELL English Language Learners

Rephrase Students may not understand how shapes can "follow rules." Rephrase this idea by talking about how the shapes are the same or different. Explain that a *rule* tells how the shapes are alike.

Additional Resource

Student Math Handbook pages 78–79

Extension

15 MIN PAIRS

Making Triangles

Use anytime after Session 2.2.

Math Focus Points

- Identifying characteristics of triangles and quadrilaterals
- Identifying and making triangles and quadrilaterals of different shapes and sizes

Materials: M30

You are going to practice drawing triangles. The goal is to draw many different triangles.

Model the activity with a volunteer.

Player 1 connects 2 dots to create one side of a triangle. Then player 2 draws the second side of the triangle. Finally, player 1 finishes the triangle.

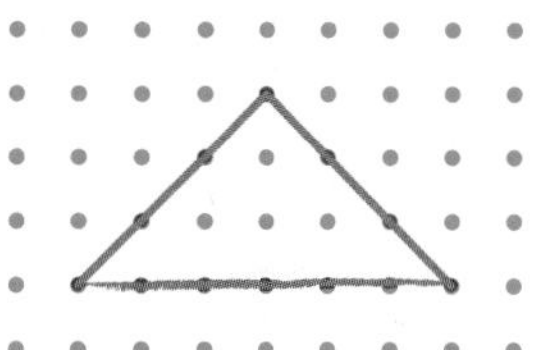

Distribute Dot Paper (M30) to each pair. Students draw triangles, taking turns being the starting player.

Once students have mostly filled their Dot Paper with triangles, call them back together.

Triangles come in a lot of different sizes and shapes. Did you make any triangles with only 2 sides that were the same length?

Students look for examples on their copy of M30. If they did not make such a triangle, challenge them to do so on a new copy of M30. Then compare a few examples of triangles with only 2 sides equal.

Let's look for examples of another special kind of triangle. Did you make any triangles where all 3 sides are different lengths?

Follow the same process with these triangles.

Note that students may want to investigate triangles with 3 equal sides, which cannot be drawn on this dot paper. If this comes up, be sure to point out that such triangles do exist using an equilateral triangle from the pattern block or Power Polygon sets.

If time remains, students might like to color the triangles with only 2 equal sides [red], and the triangles with 3 sides of different lengths [blue]. Then they can count and record how many triangles they made.

ELL English Language Learners

Provide Sentence Stems Students may have difficulty describing the triangles they made. Help them by providing sentence stems. For example: This triangle has ________ *(2 sides)* that are ________ *(the same length).* All of the sides on this triangle are ________ *(different lengths).*

Additional Resource

Student Math Handbook page 75

Differentiation in Investigation 3

Mathematics in This Investigation

The mathematics focuses on how shapes combine to form other shapes, and how a set of shapes, or a unit, can be iterated over an area to form a pattern. In particular, the focus is on the relationships between triangles and squares.

Understanding the Mathematics

Students design a unit in the form of a quilt square and iterate this unit to make a quilt pattern. They identify and name the shapes they use and the shapes that result when these shapes are combined. They are able to identify patterns that emerge as they iterate a single unit to make a quilt.

Option: Assign the **Extension** activity.

Partially Understanding the Mathematics

Students design a quilt square and repeat this unit. They identify and name the shapes they use, but may have a hard time seeing the shapes that result when units are combined. They may be inconsistent with the names and attributes of these new shapes.

Option: Assign the **Practice** activity.

Not Understanding the Mathematics

Students design a single quilt square, but translating that unit into a full and accurate quilt is challenging. They may be able to identify and name the shapes they use, but find it difficult to see how new shapes results when quilt squares are combined. The names and attributes of those shapes are likely unfamiliar. Overall, designing the quilt pattern may be challenging.

Option: Assign the **Intervention** activity.

Investigation 3 Quiz

In addition to your observations and students' work in Investigation 3, the Quiz (R19) can be used to gather more information.

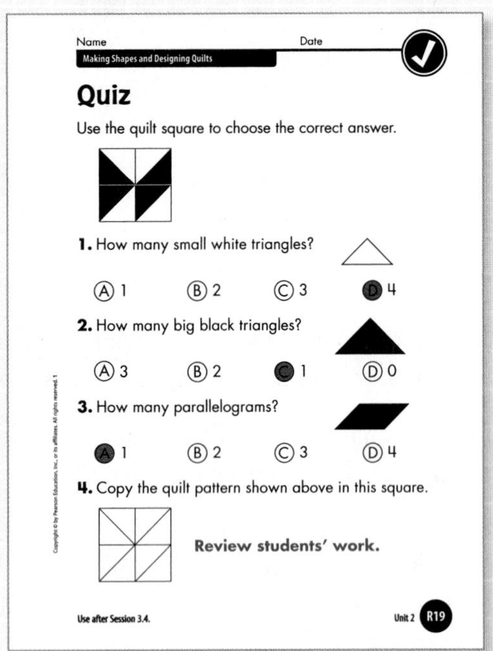

Name Date

Making Shapes and Designing Quilts

Quiz

Use the quilt square to choose the correct answer.

1. How many small white triangles?

Ⓐ 1 Ⓑ 2 Ⓒ 3 Ⓓ 4

2. How many big black triangles?

Ⓐ 3 Ⓑ 2 Ⓒ 1 Ⓓ 0

3. How many parallelograms?

Ⓐ 1 Ⓑ 2 Ⓒ 3 Ⓓ 4

4. Copy the quilt pattern shown above in this square.

Review students' work.

Use after Session 3.4.

Unit 2 R19

Intervention

30 MIN INDIVIDUALS

Making Paper Quilts

Use anytime after Session 3.2.

Math Focus Points

- Using a repeated unit to create a pattern
- Examining how shapes come together to make other shapes

Materials: quilt frames (optional), crayons or markers, scissors, M36, M41

Today you are going to create a new paper quilt. Distribute crayons or markers, scissors, and a copy of Quilt Squares (M36) to each student. Choose two colors and create a design on Quilt Square Pattern E. When you are finished coloring, cut out the square. Remind students that they can leave some spaces white when coloring their quilt square.

When students are finished, hold up a sample colored-in quilt square.

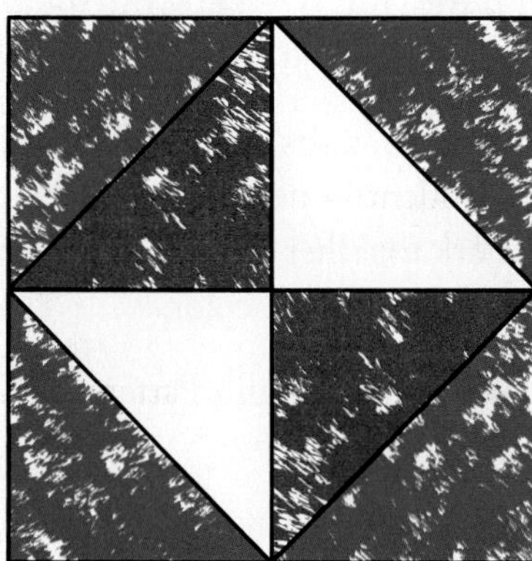

What shapes do you see?

Students might say:

"I see red triangles."

"I see a blue and white square."

Ask students to point to or trace the shapes that are mentioned. Discuss how shapes can come together to make a different shape (e.g., two triangles making a square or making another triangle).

Now you are going to make a quilt by copying your quilt square onto a paper quilt. Distribute a copy of Paper Quilt E (M41) to each student. Remind students of the strategies you've discussed in class for coloring in a paper quilt. You can hold the quilt square right next to the square you are coloring on the paper quilt. Or, you can use a quilt frame to help you focus on just one square at a time.

If time permits, spend a few minutes discussing students' quilts.

Look at your paper quilt. Do you see any new shapes? Turn to a partner and describe the shapes you see. Students might recognize new shapes that were formed when quilt squares were put next to each other. Encourage them to be specific about the shapes they see.

Students might like to count the number of triangles and squares of each color in their quilt.

ELL English Language Learners

Use Repetition As partners discuss the shapes in the quilts, have each student trace the shape that he or she names. Then encourage his or her partner to find that same shape in a different part of the quilt.

Additional Resource

Student Math Handbook page 82

Practice

20 MIN PAIRS

More Quilt Patterns

Use anytime after Session 3.3.

Math Focus Points

- Using a repeated unit to create a pattern
- Examining how shapes come together to make other shapes

Materials: crayons or markers, scissors, M36, M40, R20

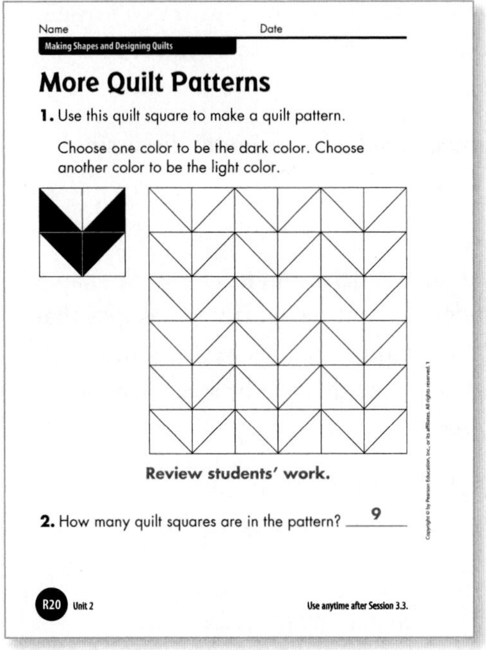

Name Date

Making Shapes and Designing Quilts

More Quilt Patterns

1. Use this quilt square to make a quilt pattern.

Choose one color to be the dark color. Choose another color to be the light color.

Review students' work.

2. How many quilt squares are in the pattern? 9

R20 Unit 2 Use anytime after Session 3.3.

Today you will design a quilt square that your partner will use to make a paper quilt. Distribute crayons or markers, scissors, and a copy of Quilt Squares (M36) to each student. Use two colors to create a design on Quilt Square Pattern D. Remember that you can leave some spaces white if you want. Have students cut out their squares.

Look at your quilt square. What shapes do you see? Encourage students to trace the shapes they see.

Students might say:

"I see lots of triangles. It makes me think of a pinwheel."

"I see 2 green triangles that come together and make a big green triangle."

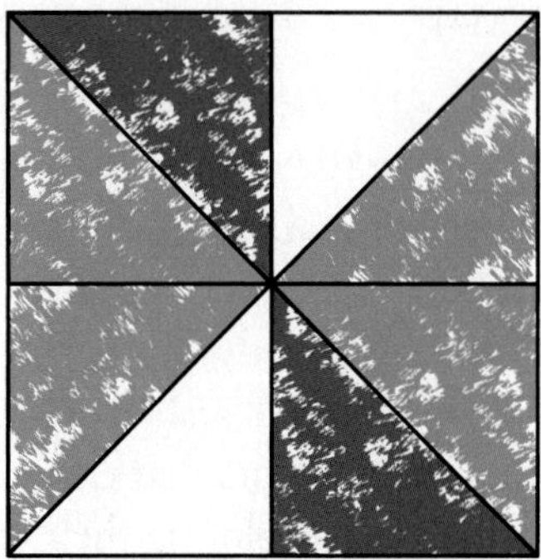

Distribute Paper Quilt D (M40). Have pairs trade quilt squares. Use your partner's quilt square to make a paper quilt. You will copy the square over and over onto the paper quilt.

When students finish, pairs share their work with each other. They identify new shapes that they see in the quilt and work together to count the number of triangles and squares of each color.

Distribute copies of More Quilt Patterns (R20).

ELL English Language Learners

Partner Talk Have pairs discuss the following question: What new shapes do you see? Beginning English Language Learners may only be able to point to the shapes and use simple phrases to describe the new shapes. Encourage more proficient speakers to use complete sentences and mathematical vocabulary as they explain what they see.

Additional Resource

Student Math Handbook page 82

Extension

20 MIN

PAIRS

Finding Shapes

Use anytime after Session 3.3.

Math Focus Points

- Using a repeated unit to create a pattern
- Examining how shapes come together to make other shapes

Materials: crayons or markers, scissors, M36, M42, R21

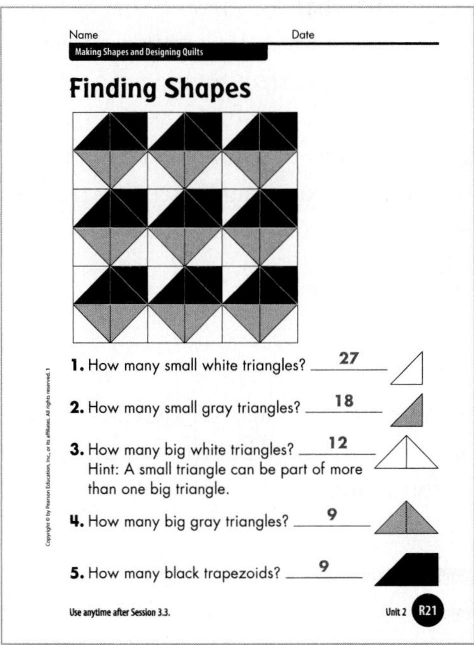

Name Date

Making Shapes and Designing Quilts

Finding Shapes

1. How many small white triangles? 27
2. How many small gray triangles? 18
3. How many big white triangles? 12
   Hint: A small triangle can be part of more than one big triangle.
4. How many big gray triangles? 9
5. How many black trapezoids? 9

Use anytime after Session 3.3. Unit 2 R21

Today you and your partner will design quilt squares that are almost the same. Then you will use the squares to make paper quilts.

Distribute crayons or markers, scissors, and a copy of Quilt Squares (M36) to each student. First, work together to design one Pattern F quilt square that uses two colors.

Now, decide with your partner how to change one part of your quilt square to make a new Pattern F quilt square on your other copy of M36. You might discuss a few ideas for making two quilt squares that are very similar.

Students might say:

"We switched the orange and the blue triangles; they traded places."

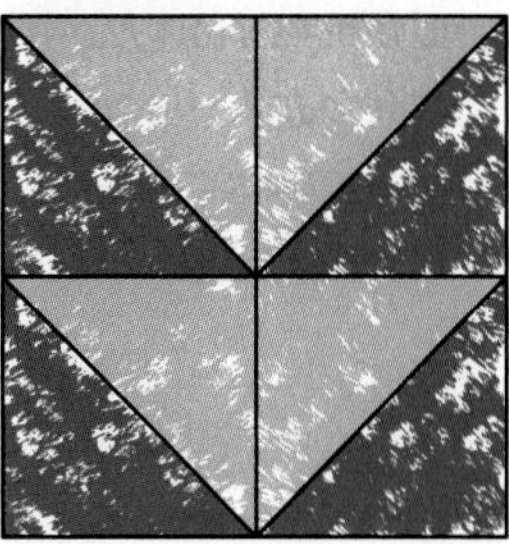
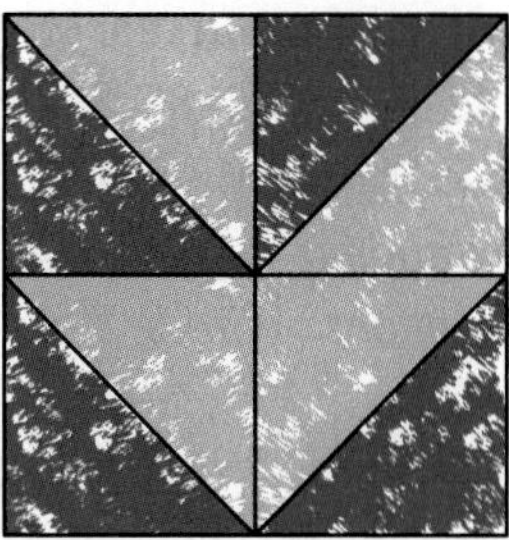

Distribute a copy of Paper Quilt F (M42) to each student. Pairs complete two paper quilts, one for each quilt square. When you finish, look at the quilts next to each other.

Discuss how changing something small on the quilt square made a big difference in the whole quilt. What are the different shapes that you see in the quilts? Students should identify and count triangles and squares as well as other shapes that are made when triangles and squares are put together. Then distribute copies of Finding Shapes (R 21) when students are ready.

ELL English Language Learners

Model Thinking Aloud Show students one of the paper quilts. Model your thinking for finding shapes aloud. I see a lot of triangles and squares. When I combine these two triangles, I see a bigger triangle. When I combine this triangle and this square, I see a trapezoid.

Additional Resource

Student Math Handbook page 82

Differentiation in Investigation 1

Mathematics in This Investigation

The mathematics focuses on developing strategies for solving addition problems, and understanding that a quantity can be composed and decomposed in different ways.

Additional Resources: *Marbles and Blocks: How Many of Each?*, pages 83–85 (See *Implementing Investigations in Grade 1*); *How Many of Each? Probing Student Understanding*, pages 91–92 (See *Implementing Investigations in Grade 1*)

Understanding the Mathematics

Students find all of the combinations of a given quantity with strategies that use one combination to generate others. They show that they have a system for finding all of the combinations. They count on or use a fact they know to solve missing part problems, and efficiently add single-digit numbers by counting on or reasoning about a sum they know.

Option: Assign the **Extension** activity.

Partially Understanding the Mathematics

Students find many or most of the combinations for a given quantity. They are beginning to work more systematically, using one combination to generate another, and considering whether a solution is a repeat before recording it. These students are beginning to count on or use known facts as they solve missing part problems, but may still rely on trial and error for some. To add single-digit numbers, many count all. Some may be beginning to count on, but cannot yet do so consistently because of confusion about where to start counting, where to stop counting, and how to determine the answer.

Option: Assign the **Practice** activity.

Not Understanding the Mathematics

Students may find several combinations of a number but with much effort. Some combinations may include repeat solutions that the student is unaware of. They work more randomly, using a trial-and -error approach rather than using relationships such as adding 1 to one addend and subtracting 1 from the other. When solving a missing part problem, students may struggle to visualize the action. They may need to represent what the missing part of the problem *might* be, count all of the parts, and then adjust until they find the correct solution. To add single-digit numbers, students often use manipulatives or drawings to count all. They may occasionally make small counting or keeping track errors that result in the wrong answer.

Option: Assign the **Intervention** activity.

Investigation 1 Quiz

In addition to your observations and students' work in Investigation 1, the Quiz (R22) can be used to gather more information.

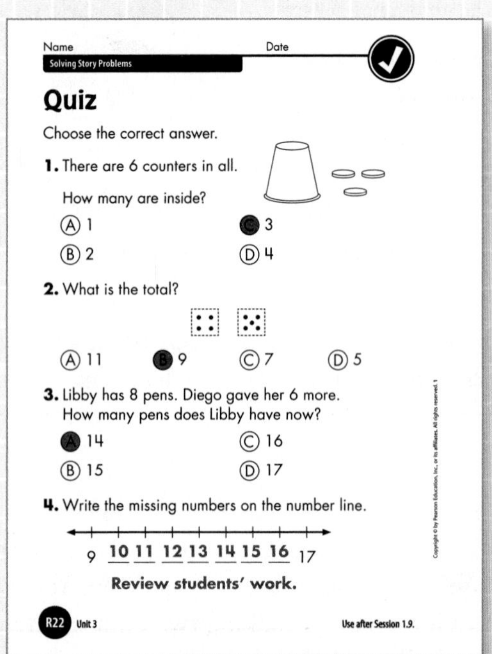

Name Date

Solving Story Problems

Quiz

Choose the correct answer.

1. There are 6 counters in all.

How many are inside?

Ⓐ 1 ● 3

Ⓑ 2 Ⓓ 4

2. What is the total?

Ⓐ 11 ● 9 Ⓒ 7 Ⓓ 5

3. Libby has 8 pens. Diego gave her 6 more.
How many pens does Libby have now?

● 14 Ⓒ 16

Ⓑ 15 Ⓓ 17

4. Write the missing numbers on the number line.

9 10 11 12 13 14 15 16 17

Review students' work.

R22 Unit 3 Use after Session 1.9.

Intervention

20 MIN PAIRS

Dot Addition with Smaller Numbers

Use anytime after Session 1.5.

Math Focus Points

- Finding and exploring relationships among combinations of numbers up to 12
- Connecting written numbers and standard notation (+, =) to the quantities and actions they represent

Vocabulary: combination, plus, add, equals

Materials: *Dot Addition* Cards (1 deck per pair), M11, M12 (as needed)

Materials to Prepare: Use one copy of *Dot Addition* Blank Gameboard (M11) to prepare a gameboard with the numbers 5, 6, 7, and 8 on the left side of each row. Make 3 copies per pair.

Today we are going to play *Dot Addition.* Imagine this is the first row on our gameboard.

Remind students how to deal out 4 rows of 5 *Dot Addition* Cards on the floor or on a table.

You need to find cards that make the number on the gameboard. I'm trying to make 4. What combinations could I use to make the total 4? How did you figure that out?

As students name combinations, record the corresponding dot patterns on your gameboard. Also use notation to represent the combinations.

How many dots were on the first card? The second card? So we combined 2 and 2 to make 4. We can write an equation to show that 2 plus 2 equals 4.

Are there other combinations you can think of that make 4? Students may suggest 1 + 3 or 3 + 1, or 4 + 0 or 0 + 4. Acknowledge that these combinations do equal 4, but remind students that there are no 0 or 1 *Dot Addition* Cards.

Now you're going to play *Dot Addition* with a partner. Distribute 3 copies of the prepared *Dot Addition* Gameboards and 1 deck of *Dot Addition* Cards to each pair. After dealing the cards, pairs take turns finding a combination of cards that make one of the numbers on the gameboard. Then, both players record the combination on their own gameboards.

Pairs play until the gameboard is complete. Compare your gameboard to another pair's. What do you notice?

Students might say:

"We both used 4 + 4 = 8. But we did something different for 6. We did 3 + 3 = 6. They did 2 + 2 + 2 = 6."

If time allows, encourage students to play the game again, making the same numbers using different combinations.

ELL English Language Learners

Partner Talk Students explain to their partners how they know a given combination makes the total. Beginning English Language Learners may only be able to use short phrases to express their thoughts. Listen for words such as *combination, plus, add,* and *equals*. Encourage students to use these words in their explanations.

Additional Resource

Student Math Handbook pages 33–35

Practice

How Many Rocks?

Use anytime after Session 1.8.

Math Focus Points

- Visualizing and retelling the action in addition situations
- Finding the total of two or more quantities up to a total of 20 by counting all, counting on, or using number combinations
- Connecting written numbers and standard notation (+, =) to the quantities and actions they represent

Vocabulary: more, fewer

Materials: counters (as needed), R23

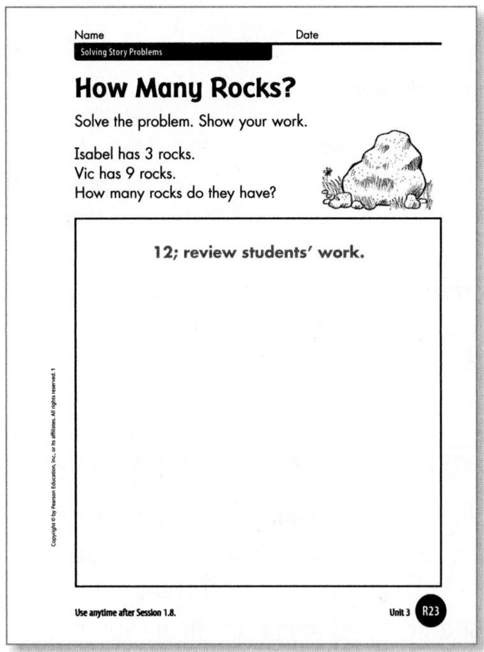

Name Date

Solving Story Problems

How Many Rocks?

Solve the problem. Show your work.

Isabel has 3 rocks.
Vic has 9 rocks.
How many rocks do they have?

12; review students' work.

Use anytime after Session 1.8. Unit 3 R23

Today we will be solving a story problem. Write the following problem on the board and read it aloud.

> Tamika has 5 rocks.
>
> Her brother has 4 rocks.
>
> How many rocks do they have?

Visualize the story in your mind. Have volunteers retell the story in their own words. Do you think there will be *more* or *fewer* rocks at the end of the story? Have students explain how they know.

What strategy will you use to solve this problem?

Students might say:

"I will use counters for rocks. Then I will count them all."

"I will start with 5. Then I will count on 4 more."

Students solve the problem and show their work so that someone else could look at their paper and tell how they solved it.

After students have finished, discuss their strategies for solving the problem and showing their work. If it doesn't come up, ask students to help you write an equation to represent the problem. Then, distribute copies of How Many Rocks? (R23).

ELL English Language Learners

Suggest a Sequence Some students may have difficulty remembering the steps they take to solve the story problem. Provide the following sequence of steps to guide them. *First,* visualize the action in the story. *Next,* retell the story using your own words. *Then,* decide if the answer will be *more* or *fewer.* *Finally,* solve the problem.

Additional Resources

Student Math Handbook

Game: *Five in-a-Row* SMH G9

Materials: dot cubes, counters, M15

Game: *Roll and Record* SMH G19

Materials: dot cubes, M13

Extension

Dot Addition D and E

Use anytime after Session 1.7.

Math Focus Points

- Finding and exploring relationships among combinations of numbers up to 12
- Connecting written numbers and standard notation (+, =) to the quantities and actions they represent

Materials: *Dot Addition* Cards (1 deck per pair), M23 (1 per pair), M24 (optional), R24

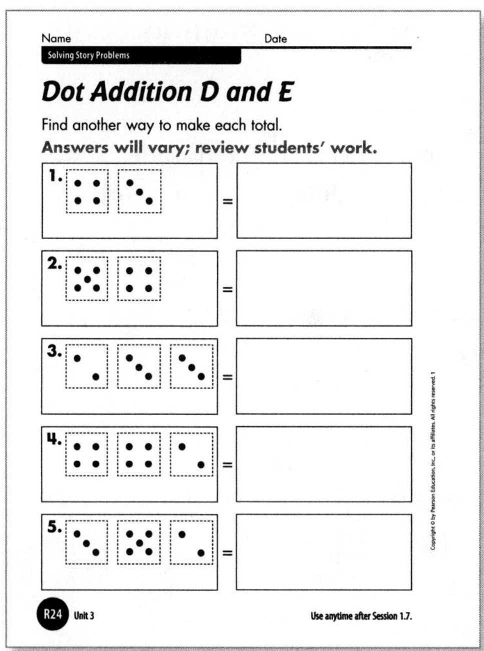
Name Date
Solving Story Problems

Dot Addition D and E

Find another way to make each total.

Answers will vary; review students' work.

1. [dot cards] =
2. [dot cards] =
3. [dot cards] =
4. [dot cards] =
5. [dot cards] =

R24 Unit 3 Use anytime after Session 1.7.

Today we are going to play *Dot Addition* on new gameboards. Distribute *Dot Addition* Gameboard D (M23) and *Dot Addition* Cards to each pair. What do you notice about the new gameboard? Students should notice that each row presents a combination rather than a number.

So, what do you think you are trying to do? Make sure students understand that they are to make a combination that equals the given combination. Then they play the game and record the combinations they find. When students finish playing, ask for a combination that was equivalent to 4 + 4.

How do you know that [5] + [3] equals 4 + 4? Students may count all, count on, or just know that [5] + [3] = 8. Draw the dots on the board and write the standard notation below it. So what this row on our gameboard says is that 4 + 4 = [5] + [3].

What do you think about that equation? Some students may think an equation can only be written with 3 numbers (e.g., A + B = C) or that only 1 number can follow the equal sign. Record more combinations that equal 8 on the board to give students experience with such notation.

Students might say:

"I made 8 with 2 and 2 and 2 and 2."

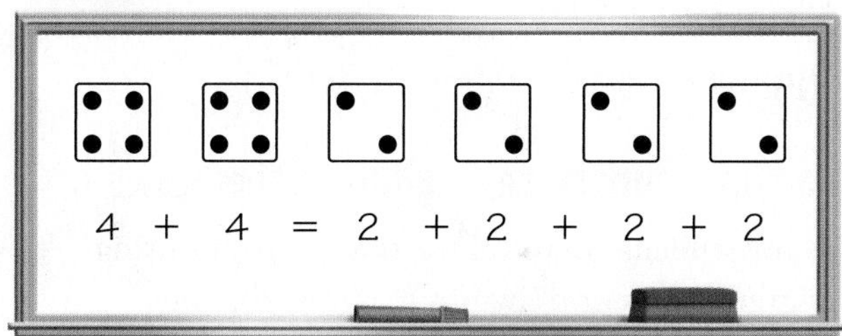

If time remains, distribute *Dot Addition* Gameboard E (M24) which asks students to find two different ways to make a number of their own choosing. Then, distribute copies of *Dot Addition D and E* (R24).

ELL English Language Learners

Model Thinking Aloud Show students a 3 + 3 dot card combination that totals 6. 3 plus 3 equals 6. I have to find *another* way to make 6. I will use a 4. I need 5, 6. I need 2 more. 4 + 2 = 6.

Additional Resource

Student Math Handbook

Game: *Five-in-a-Row* SMH G9

Materials: dot cubes, counters, M21–M22

Variation: Play with Gameboards B and C.

Differentiation in Investigation 2

Mathematics in This Investigation

The mathematics focuses on developing an understanding of the operation of subtraction, in which one quantity is removed from a whole, resulting in an amount smaller than that whole.

Additional Resources: *Supporting Students as They Solve Story Problems,* pages 190–191 (See Curriculum Unit 3), *Supporting Students as They Record Story Problem Work,* pages 192–193 (see Curriculum Unit 3)

Understanding the Mathematics

Students efficiently subtract single-digit numbers. They may count back from one number, use known number combinations, or reason about something they know to solve a problem they don't know. They explain their strategy for solving the problem and show it on paper.

Option: Assign the **Extension** activity.

Partially Understanding the Mathematics

Many students solve subtraction problems using manipulatives or drawings to count all. Some students count back, but cannot yet do so consistently because of confusion about where to start counting, where to stop counting, and where/how to find the answer. Because these subtraction problems are about an amount being removed, it is often challenging for students to show their solutions on paper.

Option: Assign the **Practice** activity.

Not Understanding the Mathematics

Students may have trouble retelling or interpreting a story problem about removing one amount from another. Some students add the numbers in the problem. Others count all, but may have trouble keeping track of the total, the amount to be removed, and the amount left. They are still developing fluency with counting, which may lead to difficulty representing and counting these sets. Articulating how they solved the problem, and accurately showing that strategy on paper, is challenging.

Option: Assign the **Intervention** activity.

Investigation 2 Quiz

In addition to your observations and students' work in Investigation 2, the Quiz (R25) can be used to gather more information.

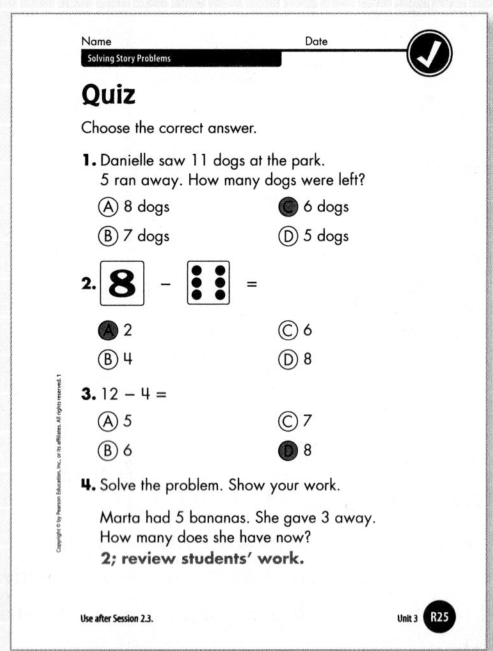

Name Date

Solving Story Problems

Quiz

Choose the correct answer.

1. Danielle saw 11 dogs at the park.
5 ran away. How many dogs were left?

Ⓐ 8 dogs ● 6 dogs
Ⓑ 7 dogs Ⓓ 5 dogs

2. 8 − [dot card: 6] =

● 2 Ⓒ 6
Ⓑ 4 Ⓓ 8

3. 12 − 4 =

Ⓐ 5 Ⓒ 7
Ⓑ 6 ● 8

4. Solve the problem. Show your work.

Marta had 5 bananas. She gave 3 away.
How many does she have now?
2; review students' work.

Use after Session 2.3. Unit 3 R25

Intervention

More Solving Subtraction Story Problems

Use anytime after Session 2.2.

Math Focus Points

- Visualizing and retelling the action in subtraction situations involving removal
- Developing strategies for solving subtraction (removal) problems
- Modeling the action of subtraction (removal) problems with counters or drawings

Vocabulary: more than, less than

Materials: counters (as needed)

I'm going to tell you a story. As you listen to the story, picture what is happening in your head. Leah is going to play tennis. She starts with 8 tennis balls. While she is playing, she loses 2 of the balls when she hits them over the fence.

Have students retell the story in their own words, putting the emphasis on what happened in the story, not on finding an answer.

After her game, is the number of tennis balls Leah has *more than* or *less than* when she started?

Students might say:

"Some went over the fence so she has less."

Now you are going to solve a problem about this story. Write the story on the board, adding a question to the end: How many balls does she have at the end of her game? Then, read it aloud and set students to work.

Ask students who are struggling to retell the story. Acting out the story or using counters to model it can support them in making sense of the action of the story.

Can you show how many balls Leah starts with? Can you show how many she hits over the fence? How could we figure out how many she ends up with?

Encourage students to record their work. Then, spend time discussing strategies for solving and recording.

Students might say:

"I took 8 chips and pretended they were tennis balls. She lost 2 of them so I crossed out 2. Then I counted how many were left."

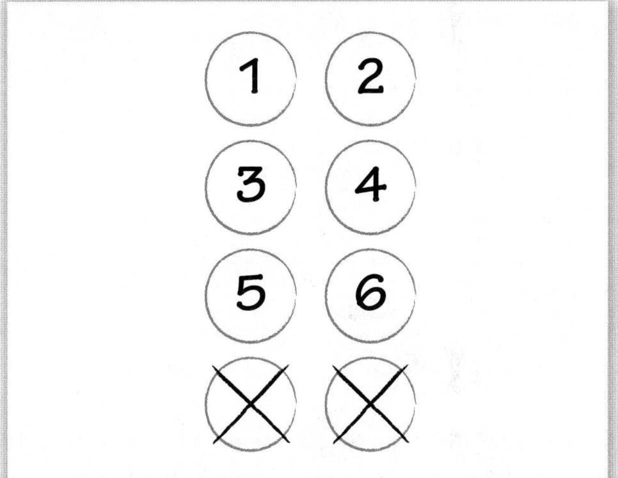

Ask students to help you write a subtraction equation for this problem, talking through the connections between the numbers and symbols with what happened in the story.

ELL English Language Learners

Rephrase Students may be overwhelmed when there are a lot of details in a story problem. Rephrase the story so that it only has the important details. For example: Leah starts with 8 tennis balls. She loses 2 balls. How many balls does she have left?

Additional Resource

Student Math Handbook pages 38–40

Practice

15 MIN

PAIRS

Subtracting Dots

Use anytime after Session 2.3.

Math Focus Points

- Subtracting one number from another, with initial totals up to 12
- Using numbers and standard notation (+, –, =) to record

Materials: counters (as needed), *Dot Addition* Cards (1 deck per pair), R26

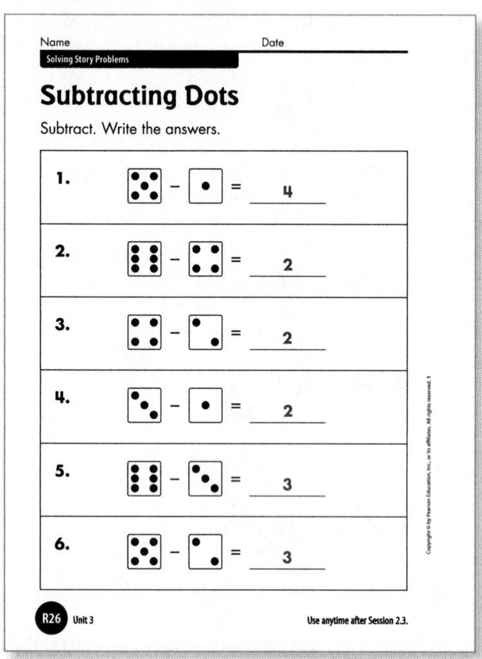

Name Date

Solving Story Problems

Subtracting Dots

Subtract. Write the answers.

1.	– =	4
2.	– =	2
3.	– =	2
4.	– =	2
5.	– =	3
6.	– =	3

R26 Unit 3 Use anytime after Session 2.3.

Today we are going to solve some problems that are just like the ones you solved in *Roll & Record: Subtraction* and *Five-in-a-Row: Subtraction.* Draw two dot cards on the board, a 5 and a 2, with a subtraction sign between them.

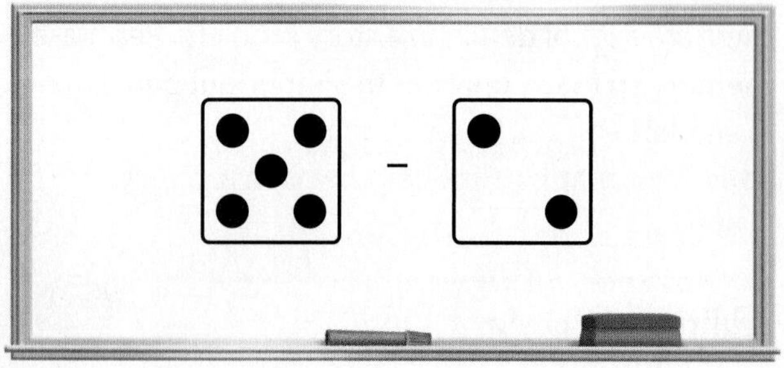

What is this problem asking? Be sure that students understand that this problem is asking how many are left if you subtract 2 from 5. How would you solve this problem?

Students might say:

"I would draw 5 dots on my paper and cross out 2 of them. Then I would count the dots that are left."

"I would count backward from 5."

Pairs solve the problem and generate an equation for it. Record the equation on the board.

Distribute a deck of *Dot Addition* Cards to each pair. Start with the cards facing down. Each partner draws one card. Decide which card has more dots. Then, subtract the other card from it. If you draw the same number, put the cards back and draw two different cards.

Students use subtraction equations to record their work. Then, distribute copies of Subtracting Dots (R26).

ELL English Language Learners

Provide Sentence Stems Help students verbalize the steps they used to solve the problem by providing sentence stems. For example:

First, I ____ *(drew 5 dots).* Then, I ____ *(crossed out 2 dots).* Finally, I ____ *(counted the dots that were left).*

Additional Resource

Student Math Handbook

Game: *Roll and Record: Subtraction* SMH G20

Materials: 7–12 number cubes, dot cubes, counters, M28

Extension

15 MIN

PAIRS

How Many Fish?

Use anytime after Session 2.2.

Math Focus Points

- Visualizing and retelling the action in subtraction situations involving removal
- Developing strategies for solving subtraction (removal) problems
- Developing methods for recording subtraction (removal) strategies

Vocabulary: counting backward, minus sign, subtraction sign

Materials: counters (as needed), R27

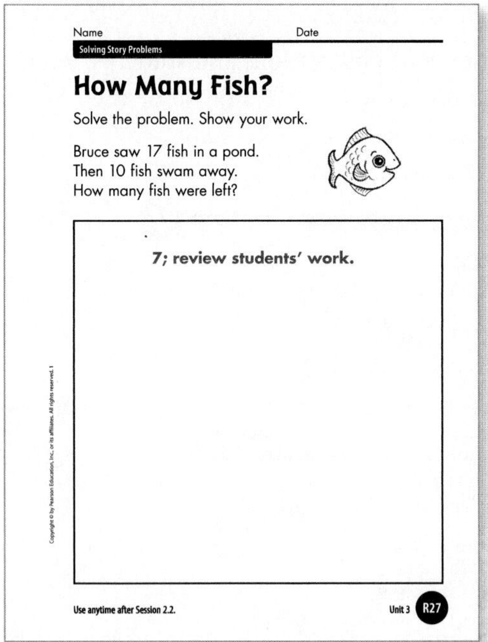
Name Date

Solving Story Problems

How Many Fish?

Solve the problem. Show your work.

Bruce saw 17 fish in a pond.
Then 10 fish swam away.
How many fish were left?

7; review students' work.

Use anytime after Session 2.2. Unit 3 R27

Read the following problem aloud. Chris sees 17 fish in a pond. They are very colorful. All of a sudden, 7 of the fish swim away and hide.

Have students retell the story to their partners. Is the number of fish Chris sees at the end more than or less than at the beginning?

Now introduce the question. How many fish can he still see? Write the problem on the board and give students time to solve it. Then, discuss and model a few strategies.

Students might say:

"I counted back 7 from 17 and got to 10."

"I know that 17 − 7 = 10."

Now pose a related problem. Encourage students to think about what they know, and about how other students solved the first problem, as they work on it.

Chris went back to the pond. He saw 17 fish. This time, 8 of the fish swam away while he watched. How many fish were still there?

If there is time and students seem ready you might ask students to compare the two situations.

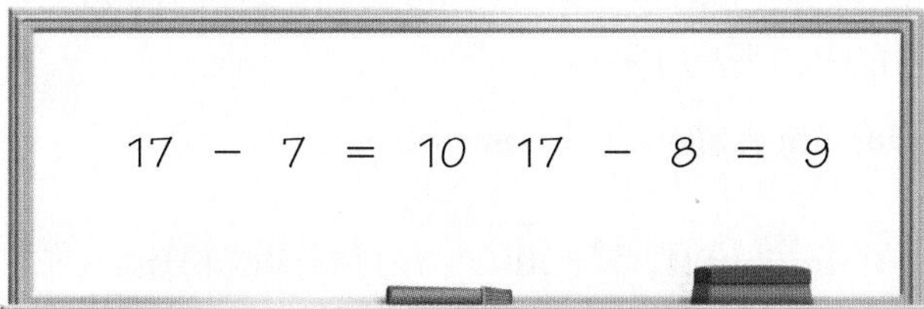

Distribute copies of How Many Fish? (R27).

ELL English Language Learners

Use Repetition Some students may have difficulty understanding that *minus sign* and *subtraction sign* are interchangeable. To help these students, use both terms when a question is posed. Once students become familiar with both terms, switch to using only one term at a time.

Additional Resource

Student Math Handbook pages 41–42

Differentiation in Investigation 3

Mathematics in This Investigation

The mathematics focuses on developing an understanding of the operations of addition and subtraction, and developing accurate strategies to solve addition and subtraction problems.

Additional Resources: *Supporting Students as They Solve Story Problems,* pages 190–191 (See Curriculum Unit 3), *Supporting Students as They Record Story Problem Work,* pages 192–193 (see Curriculum Unit 3)

Understanding the Mathematics

Students efficiently add and subtract single-digit numbers. To add, they count on, or reason about a sum they know. To subtract, they count back from one number, add up, use a known fact, and/or use what they know about the relationship between addition and subtraction. They can solve a problem in more than one way, explain their strategy, and represent it on paper.

Option: Assign the **Extension** activity.

Partially Understanding the Mathematics

Many students count all to add and subtract single-digit numbers. Some may be beginning to count on/count back, but cannot yet do so consistently because of confusion about where to start counting, where to stop counting, and how to determine the answer. These students may occasionally use a fact they know to solve a related problem. Their ability to represent their work is improving, but they may still occasionally record a strategy that is easy to show on paper rather than the one actually used, particularly as they begin to use the strategies of counting on/back or using a fact they know.

Option: Assign the **Practice** activity.

Not Understanding the Mathematics

Students may have trouble retelling story problems, or deciding whether a story is asking them to combine amounts or remove one amount from another. To add or subtract single-digit numbers, these students use manipulatives or drawings to count all. They may occasionally make small counting or keeping track errors that result in the wrong answer. Articulating how they solved the problem, and showing that strategy on paper, may be challenging. They may record a strategy that is easy to show on paper, rather than the one actually used.

Option: Assign the **Intervention** activity.

Investigation 3 Quiz

In addition to your observations and students' work in Investigation 3, the Quiz (R28) can be used to gather more information.

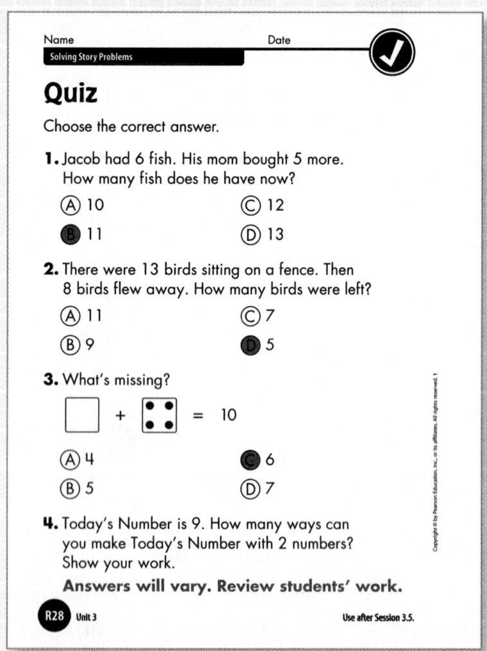

Name Date

Solving Story Problems

Quiz

Choose the correct answer.

1. Jacob had 6 fish. His mom bought 5 more. How many fish does he have now?
   - Ⓐ 10
   - Ⓑ 11 (filled)
   - Ⓒ 12
   - Ⓓ 13

2. There were 13 birds sitting on a fence. Then 8 birds flew away. How many birds were left?
   - Ⓐ 11
   - Ⓑ 9
   - Ⓒ 7
   - Ⓓ 5 (filled)

3. What's missing?

   ☐ + ⁙ = 10

   - Ⓐ 4
   - Ⓑ 5
   - Ⓒ 6 (filled)
   - Ⓓ 7

4. Today's Number is 9. How many ways can you make Today's Number with 2 numbers? Show your work.

   Answers will vary. Review students' work.

R28 Unit 3 Use after Session 3.5.

Intervention

Addition and Subtraction with Counters

Use anytime after Session 3.1.

Math Focus Points

- Visualizing and retelling the action in addition situations and subtraction situations involving removal
- Developing strategies for solving addition and subtraction (removal) problems

Materials: counters

I am going to read you a story. Picture the story in your mind.

Felipe loves apples. He had 5 red apples. Then he went to the store and bought 3 green apples.

Students take turns retelling the story in their own words. Let students who struggle with remembering story problems go after other students, so they will hear the story a few times before having to retell it.

Will Felipe have more or fewer apples after he buys the green ones? How do you know?

Write the story on the board. Distribute counters to each student. Let's use counters to help us figure out how many apples Felipe has now. Can you use counters to show how many red apples Felipe has? How many counters do you need to show the green apples? Have students help you model the process of counting out 5 counters, adding 3 counters, and counting the total. Model one way to record this strategy on the board and work together to write an equation to go with it.

I have another story. Felipe now has 8 apples. He decides to give 4 apples to Keena.

Students retell the story. Will Felipe have more or fewer apples at the end of the story? How could we use counters to find how many apples Felipe has left?

Students might say:

"Get 8 counters because he started with 8 apples."

"Then take away the 4 he gave to Keena and count how many are left."

Students use counters to model and solve the problem. Again, model one way to record and ask the students to help you write an equation for the problem on the board.

ELL English Language Learners

Provide Sentence Stems Help students make generalizations about the operations in these stories by providing sentence stems. For example: When you add, you end up with ________ *(more)*. When you subtract, you end up with ________ *(less)*.

Additional Resource

Student Math Handbook pages 38–39

Practice

20 MIN INDIVIDUALS

How Many?

Use anytime after Session 3.5.

Math Focus Points

- Developing strategies for solving addition and subtraction (removal) problems
- Recording solutions to a problem

Materials: counters, R29

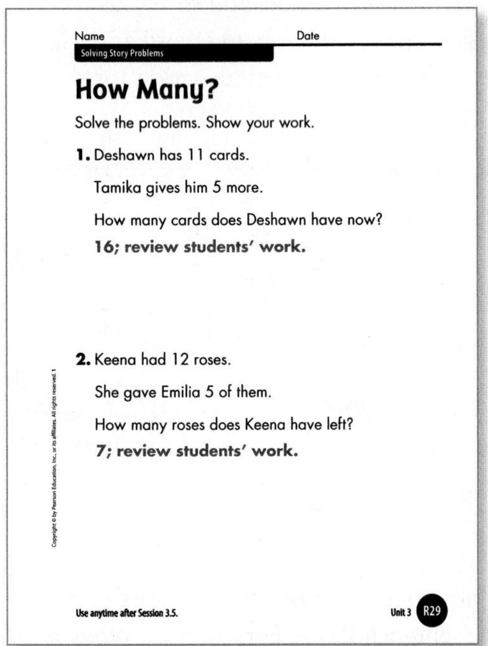

Name Date

Solving Story Problems

How Many?

Solve the problems. Show your work.

1. Deshawn has 11 cards.

   Tamika gives him 5 more.

   How many cards does Deshawn have now?

   16; review students' work.

2. Keena had 12 roses.

   She gave Emilia 5 of them.

   How many roses does Keena have left?

   7; review students' work.

Use anytime after Session 3.5. Unit 3 R29

Today we are going to talk about strategies for solving word problems. Write the following problems on the board.

1. Teo has 10 stamps. He gives 3 of them to Toshi. How many stamps does Teo have left?
2. Teo has 10 stamps. Toshi gives him 3 more. How many stamps does Teo have now?

Read the first problem aloud. Remind students to picture the story in their minds as they listen. Have students retell the story in their own words.

Students solve the first story and record their work. Discuss the different strategies used, such as counting all, counting backward, or using a known fact (e.g., $3 + 7 = 10$).

Follow the same process for the second story.

If there's time, ask students to compare the two stories. How were these stories the same? How were they different?

Students might say:

"They're about the same people and the same numbers. But they're different because in the first one Teo ends up with less and in the other one he ends up with more."

Record an equation for each story to illustrate this idea: $10 - 3 = 7$ and $10 + 3 = 13$.

Distribute copies of How Many? (R29).

ELL English Language Learners

Model Thinking Aloud Model the actions being described with counters to support the student with minimal language. Teo has 10 stamps, so I will show 10 counters. He gave 3 stamps to Toshi, so I will take away 3 counters. There are 1, 2, 3, ..., 7 counters left. So, $10 - 3 = 7$.

Additional Resource

Student Math Handbook

Game: *Five-in-a-Row: Subtraction* SMH G10

Materials: 7–12 number cubes, dot cubes, counters, M30

Extension

30 MIN PAIRS

Solving Challenging Story Problems

Use anytime after Session 3.3.

Math Focus Points

- Using numbers and standard notation (>, <, +, −, =) to record
- Developing strategies for solving addition and subtraction (removal) problems

Materials: chart paper, R30

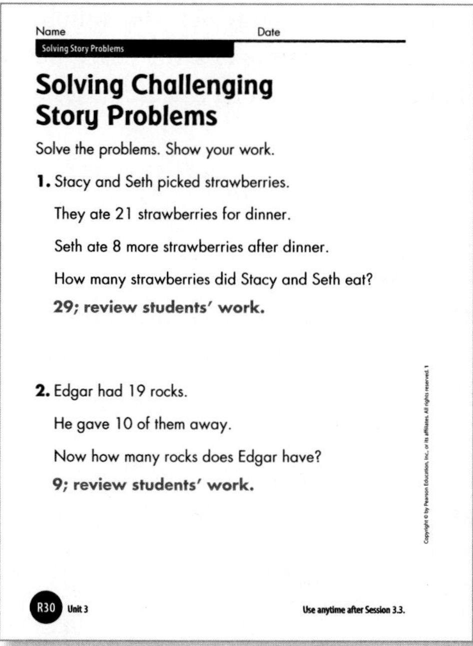
Name Date
Solving Story Problems

Solving Challenging Story Problems

Solve the problems. Show your work.

1. Stacy and Seth picked strawberries.
   They ate 21 strawberries for dinner.
   Seth ate 8 more strawberries after dinner.
   How many strawberries did Stacy and Seth eat?
   29; review students' work.

2. Edgar had 19 rocks.
   He gave 10 of them away.
   Now how many rocks does Edgar have?
   9; review students' work.

R30 Unit 3 Use anytime after Session 3.3.

Today you are going to solve some story problems. Read the following problem aloud, reminding students to picture it in their minds as you read it.

> Paula picked 16 flowers. She gave 9 to her teacher. How many flowers does Paula have?

Partners take turns retelling the story to each other and discussing strategies for solving the problem.

Give students time to solve the problem. How did you solve the problem?

Students might say:

"We knew that 16 − 6 = 10. But we had to subtract 9, so we had to subtract 3 more. 10 − 3 = 7."

"We used a number line. We started at 16 and counted back 9. We landed on 7."

Now I have a different story problem for you.

> There were 8 students in the classroom. When the bell rang, 10 more students came into the room. Then 2 more students came. How many students were in the room?

Follow the same procedure for this problem. Then distribute copies of Solving Challenging Story Problems (R30).

ELL English Language Learners

Model Thinking Aloud Discuss with students how they solved the problem. Then, help them verbalize their strategy. So, first you added 8 and 2 because that made 10. Then you did 10 + 10 = 20. Encourage students to repeat or rephrase your words to describe what they did to solve this problem.

Additional Resource

Student Math Handbook pages 33–42

Differentiation in Investigation 4

Mathematics in This Investigation

The mathematics focuses on the counting sequence to 100, and finding and using patterns in the sequence of numbers to 100. This includes knowing the names and sequence of the numbers, counting each object once and only once, and knowing that the last number said indicates the total number of objects in the set.

Additional Resource: *Let's Keep on Counting: Finding Patterns in the Number Sequence,* pages 80–81 (See *Implementing Investigations in Grade 1*)

Understanding the Mathematics

Students count and write the numbers to 100, and use that sequence to accurately count and keep track of a set of 50 (or more) objects. They may organize the objects to be counted in some way and use that organization to find the total. They use patterns in the sequence of numbers to figure out what numbers have been removed from a 100 chart.

Option: Assign the **Extension** activity.

Partially Understanding the Mathematics

Students count and write the numbers to 65 and beyond, but may pause or look for help at particular places in the sequence. They can use the sequence to count a set of 50 (or more) objects but may occasionally be slightly off due to a minor keeping track error or other error (e.g., skipping or double-counting an object, omitting a decade). To figure out what numbers are missing on a 100 chart, they may use patterns in the number sequence, but may also count from 1 or from other starting points that are comfortable for them.

Option: Assign the **Practice** activity.

Not Understanding the Mathematics

Students cannot yet count and write the numbers to 65 fluently. They may skip or repeat numbers, not know some number names, and/or say the numbers in an incorrect order. They may write 12 as 21 or 50 as 05. In addition, when counting a set of objects, these students may not assign one number to each object. Because they don't yet have a system for keeping track of what has been and still remains to be counted, they may count some objects more than once and skip others. They may count more than once and not be disturbed when they get different totals. They may be able to figure out what numbers are missing in the first few rows of a 100 chart, but struggle with numbers above 30. Their strategies rely mainly on counting.

Option: Assign the **Intervention** activity.

Investigation 4 Quiz

In addition to your observations and students' work in Investigation 4, the Quiz (R31) can be used to gather more information.

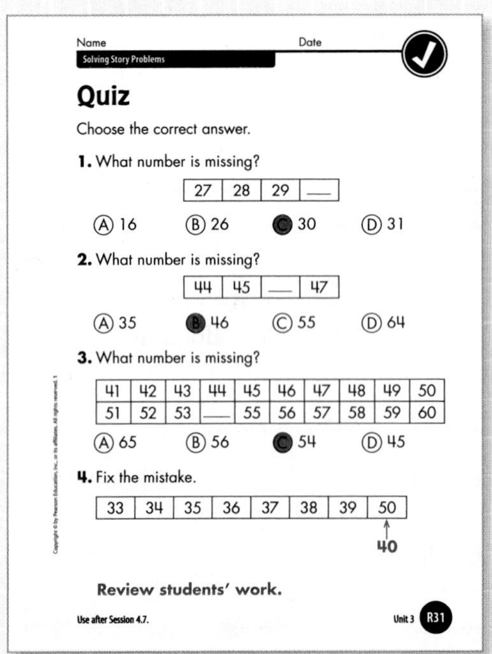

Name Date

Solving Story Problems

Quiz

Choose the correct answer.

1. What number is missing?

27	28	29	___

Ⓐ 16 Ⓑ 26 ● 30 Ⓓ 31

2. What number is missing?

44	45	___	47

Ⓐ 35 ● 46 Ⓒ 55 Ⓓ 64

3. What number is missing?

41	42	43	44	45	46	47	48	49	50
51	52	53	___	55	56	57	58	59	60

Ⓐ 65 Ⓑ 56 ● 54 Ⓓ 45

4. Fix the mistake.

33	34	35	36	37	38	39	50

40

Review students' work.

Use after Session 4.7. Unit 3 R31

Intervention

25 MIN PAIRS

Covering and Counting with Pattern Blocks

Use anytime after Session 4.2.

Math Focus Points

- Measuring area by filling an outline with same-sized objects
- Accurately counting a set of objects by 1s, up to 60

Materials: pattern blocks, markers (1 per pair), blank paper (2 sheets per pair), M40 (as needed)

We used square tiles, pennies, and lima beans to measure the size of our feet. Today we are going to measure our feet with the blue rhombus pattern blocks.

Distribute pattern blocks, paper, and markers to each pair. The first thing you're going to do is trace one of your feet, with your shoe on. Work with your partner. You can trace your partner's foot, and then your partner can trace your foot.

If you want to measure the area of your foot, you want to see how many blue rhombuses it takes to fill the outline of your foot. What does that mean? How could you use blue rhombuses to find the area of your foot?

Students might say:

"Cover as much of the white as possible, but don't go outside the lines too much."

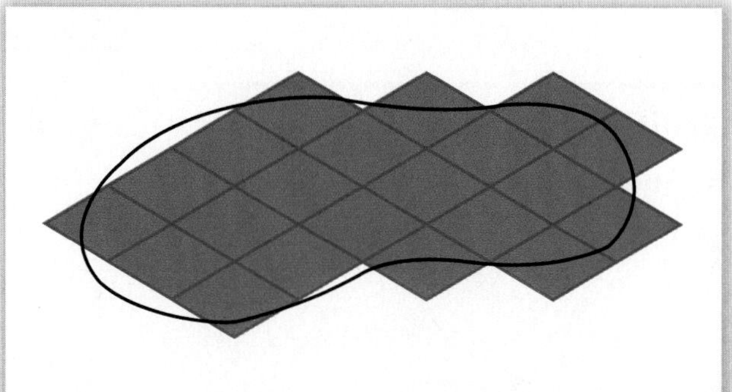

Agree on whether the blocks have to be completely inside the lines or if they can extend beyond the lines. Students fill their foot outline with blue rhombuses and then count how many they used.

Because there will be a lot of blocks, review strategies for careful counting. These might include counting on the paper and then double-checking as they remove the blocks from the paper, and/or using a Twenty-Frame (M40) to organize the blocks to be counted. Also, encourage students to help one another. What can you do if you forget what number comes next? Where could you look for help?

Students might say:

"You could ask a friend. Or look on the 100 chart."

After they've counted and double-checked their count, groups can compare the number of blocks they used and discuss why the numbers might be different. They can also explore how many yellow hexagons or green triangles fit in the outline of their foot.

ELL English Language Learners

Rephrase Students may not understand the word *area*, or how you can *fill* or *cover* a picture on paper. Talk about putting pattern blocks *inside* the shape. Connect the idea of putting blocks inside the outline to figuring out the area. The area is how many shapes fit inside the footprint.

Additional Resource

Student Math Handbook pages 21–23

Practice

What Went Wrong?

Use anytime after Session 4.3.

Math Focus Points

- Writing the sequence of numbers (as high as students know)
- Identifying and using patterns in the sequence of numbers to 100

Materials: adding machine tape (6-inch strips), R32

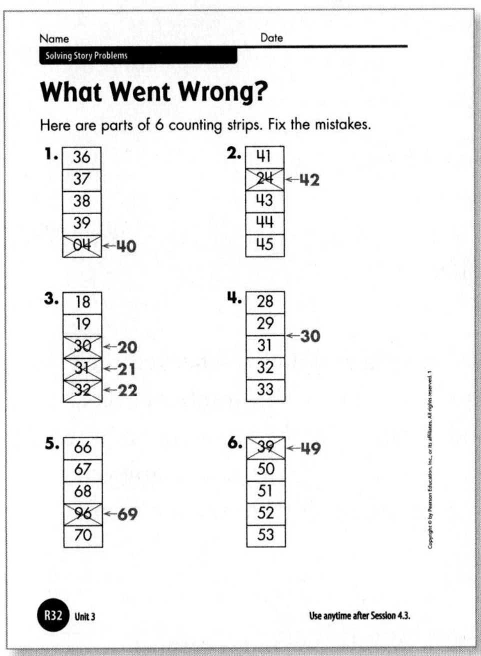

Name Date

Solving Story Problems

What Went Wrong?

Here are parts of 6 counting strips. Fix the mistakes.

1. 36, 37, 38, 39, ~~04~~ ←40
2. 41, ~~24~~ ←42, 43, 44, 45
3. 18, 19, ~~30~~ ←20, ~~31~~ ←21, ~~32~~ ←22
4. 28, 29, ←30, 31, 32, 33
5. 66, 67, 68, ~~96~~ ←69, 70
6. ~~39~~ ←49, 50, 51, 52, 53

R32 Unit 3 Use anytime after Session 4.3.

Today we are going to talk about a counting strip. Tape a blank counting strip on the board. Write the numbers 45, 46, 47, 84, 49 on it.

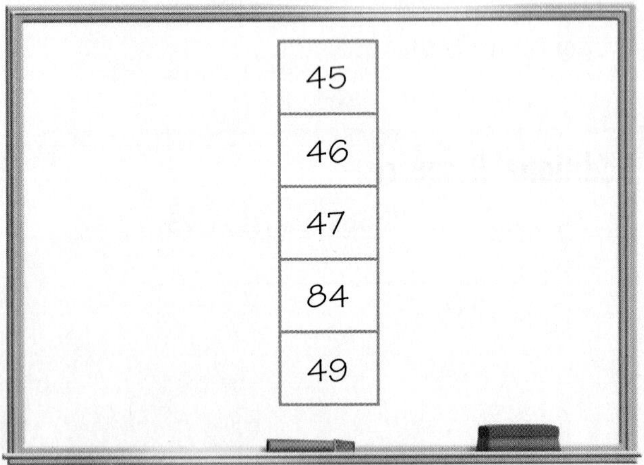

What went wrong? Ask students to identify what is wrong, how they know it is wrong, and how they could fix it. They should also think about why someone might make that mistake.

Students might say:

"84 doesn't belong. All the other numbers are in the forties."

"I think this person was thinking that 48 has an 8 and a 4 in it. They just wrote it backward. It should be 48."

Discuss resources, such as a 100 chart, that they can use to double-check their work.

Do this with several more counting strips, using errors you've been seeing in students' work. Then, distribute copies of What Went Wrong? (R32) for more practice with identifying counting errors.

ELL English Language Learners

Model Thinking Aloud Beginning English Language Learners may be able to identify the error, but not be able to explain in words what went wrong. Encourage them to point to the error and to say what the number *should* be. Point to each number on the number strip as you model a verbal explanation. For example: When I count, the numbers go 45, 46, 47, 48. This says 84. It should say 48. Students with minimal language can be paired with a partner from their language group in their native language to explain their thinking.

Additional Resource

Student Math Handbook page 31

Extension

15 MIN GROUPS

More Missing Numbers

Use anytime after Session 4.6.

Math Focus Points

- Identifying and using patterns in the sequence of numbers to 100

Materials: class pocket 100 chart, blank paper, R33

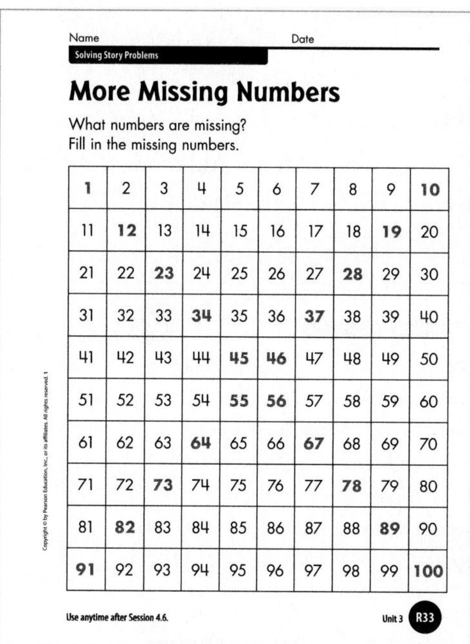

Name Date

Solving Story Problems

More Missing Numbers

What numbers are missing?
Fill in the missing numbers.

1	2	3	4	5	6	7	8	9	**10**
11	**12**	13	14	15	16	17	18	**19**	20
21	22	**23**	24	25	26	27	**28**	29	30
31	32	33	**34**	35	36	**37**	38	39	40
41	42	43	44	**45**	**46**	47	48	49	50
51	52	53	54	**55**	**56**	57	58	59	60
61	62	63	**64**	65	66	**67**	68	69	70
71	72	**73**	74	75	76	77	**78**	79	80
81	**82**	83	84	85	86	87	88	**89**	90
91	92	93	94	95	96	97	98	99	**100**

Use anytime after Session 4.6. Unit 3 R33

Gather a small group of students at the pocket 100 chart and give each a blank piece of paper. While students' eyes are closed, remove or turn over a handful of numbers on the 100 chart. Choose numbers that are scattered across the chart.

1	2	3	4	5	6	7	8	9	10
11	12	13	14	15	16	17	18	19	20
21	22	23	24	25	26	27	28	29	30
31	32	33	34	35	36	37	38	39	40
41	42	43	44	45	46	47	48	49	50
51	52	53	54	55	56	57	58	59	60
61	62	63	64	65	66	67	68	69	70
71	72	73	74	75	76	77	78	79	80
81	82	83	84	85	86	87	88	89	90
91	92	93	94	95	96	97	98	99	100

Ok, open your eyes. Look at the 100 chart. Some numbers are missing. Take a few minutes to think about what numbers are missing and how you know. Write down the numbers that you think are missing.

When students seem finished, ask What's one number that you think is missing? How did you figure that out?

Students might say:

"This row is the 70s numbers. It goes 71, 72, 73. So 73 is missing."

"I agree it's 73. I looked at the column. All the numbers end in 3. See 43, 53, 63. So it has to be 73."

Students then play on their own. One player hides 5 numbers, or more if students seem ready. The other players study the chart and write down the numbers they think are missing. Then players take turns explaining how they figured out one of the numbers that are missing. Students play until everyone has had a chance to be the person who hides the numbers.

Distribute copies of More Missing Numbers (R33).

ELL **English Language Learners**

Provide a Word List Students may struggle to remember the name of the decade of the missing number. Write the decade words on the board. Have students start at 1 and count by 1s aloud. Each time they get to a number that ends in 9, point to the next decade. Read through the list several times to familiarize the pattern.

Additional Resource

Student Math Handbook page 31

Differentiation in Investigation 1

Mathematics in This Investigation

The mathematics focuses on describing attributes of objects and using this information to sort and classify objects into groups.

Understanding the Mathematics

Students name and describe attributes and use them to accurately sort a set of objects according to one particular attribute. When playing *Guess My Rule,* students use both positive and negative information to refine their ideas and reason about the common characteristic of the set.

Option: Assign the **Extension** activity.

Partially Understanding the Mathematics

Students name and describe attributes. They use them to sort a set of objects though they may not correctly place *every* object. Identifying an attribute of a presorted set is more challenging than sorting by an attribute that they have identified.

Option: Assign the **Practice** activity.

Not Understanding the Mathematics

Students may have a hard time focusing on only one attribute, particularly given a set of widely varying objects like buttons of different colors, sizes, and shapes. They may group objects that are exactly the same together, creating many groups. They may struggle to identify and label a group of presorted objects according to a common attribute.

Option: Assign the **Intervention** activity.

Investigation 1 Quiz

In addition to your observations and students' work in Investigation 1, the Quiz (R34) can be used to gather more information.

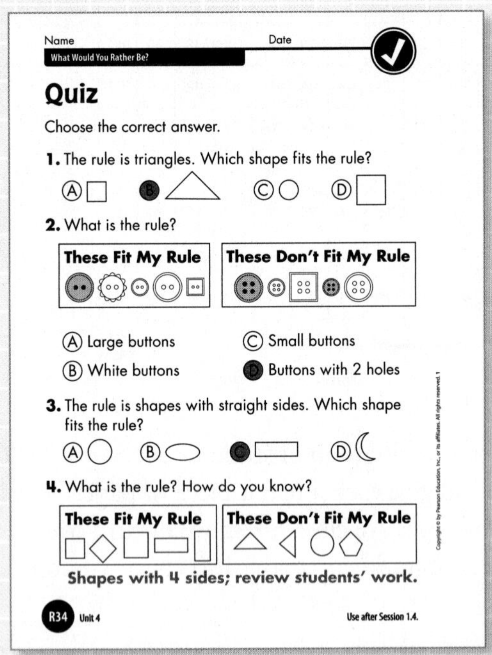

Name Date

What Would You Rather Be?

Quiz

Choose the correct answer.

1. The rule is triangles. Which shape fits the rule?

Ⓐ □ Ⓑ △ Ⓒ ○ Ⓓ □

2. What is the rule?

These Fit My Rule	These Don't Fit My Rule

Ⓐ Large buttons Ⓒ Small buttons
Ⓑ White buttons Ⓓ Buttons with 2 holes

3. The rule is shapes with straight sides. Which shape fits the rule?

Ⓐ Ⓑ Ⓒ Ⓓ

4. What is the rule? How do you know?

These Fit My Rule	These Don't Fit My Rule

Shapes with 4 sides; review students' work.

R34 Unit 4 Use after Session 1.4.

Intervention

Sorting Shapes

Use anytime after Session 1.3.

Math Focus Points

- Using attributes to sort a set of objects
- Looking carefully at a group of objects to determine how they have been sorted

Materials: Power Polygons (1 set per pair), M6 (1 per pair), M7 (1 per pair)

Take one of each of the Power Polygons shapes A–O and sort them into two groups using the These Fit My Rule (M6) and These Don't Fit My Rule (M7) mats. The first mat should have all large shapes; the second should have all small shapes. Ask students to look at the Power Polygons. What rule did I use to sort these shapes?

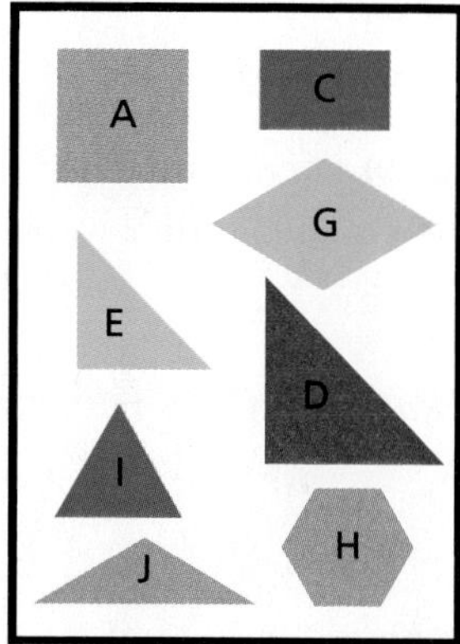

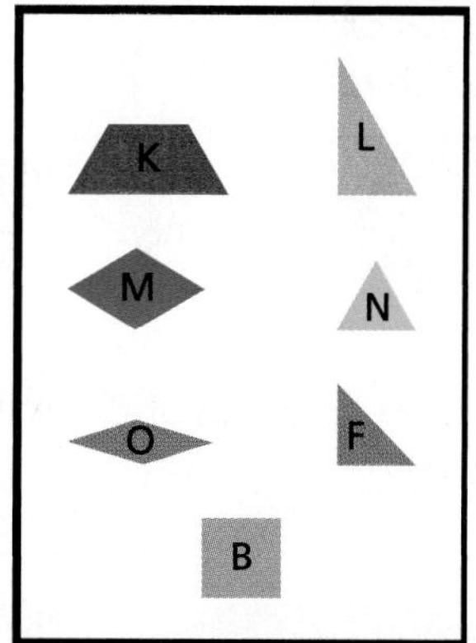

Students might say:

"The shapes in this group are all small."

"All of the large shapes are in the other group."

So I could say my rule is large shapes and small shapes. Or, big shapes, and shapes that *are not* big.

I used size to sort these shapes. Are there other ways they could be sorted? Can you see another way to sort these shapes?

Students may suggest sorting by shape, number of sides, or color. Work together to resort the shapes using one of the attributes students suggest. Limiting the sort to only two categories can be challenging.

[Vic] suggested sorting by color. So let's say blue shapes fit my rule. Who can place a shape on one of the mats?

Work together to sort the shapes by color and to name the categories—blue shapes and shapes that are *not* blue.

Now partners take a set of Power Polygons and decide on a way to sort them onto copies of M6 and M7. Decide on a rule. Then sort each of your shapes on to the correct mat—These Fit My Rule or These Don't Fit My Rule. Then try to name the two groups.

Observe students working together, providing assistance as needed. Pairs that seem ready can try playing *Guess My Rule* with the Power Polygons.

ELL English Language Learners

Provide Sentence Stems If students are having trouble sorting the shapes or naming the groups, provide sentence stems after asking the following questions.

What do all the shapes that fit the rule have in common?

These shapes are _____.
These shapes have _____.

What's true about the shapes that don't fit my rule?

These shapes are not _____.
These shapes do not have _____.
These shapes have _____.

Additional Resource

Student Math Handbook pages 78–79

Practice

20 MIN

GROUPS

Guess My Rule with Objects

Use anytime after Session 1.3.

Math Focus Points

- Using attributes to sort a set of objects
- Looking carefully at a group of objects to determine how they have been sorted

Materials: collections of objects (15 objects per group), M5–M7 (1 each per group), R35

Name Date

What Would You Rather Be?

Guess My Rule with Objects

1. The rule is buttons with 4 holes. Circle the buttons that fit the rule.

2. What rule was used to sort the shapes?

These Fit My Rule	These Don't Fit My Rule

Rule: Shapes with 4 sides
Review students' work.

3. Make your own rule. Then circle the shapes that fit your rule. **Answers will vary.**
Rule: **Review students' work.**

Use anytime after Session 1.3. Unit 4 R35

You're going to play *Guess My Rule* with a collection of objects. One player decides on a rule and places a few examples on each mat—These Fit My Rule (M6) or These Don't Fit My Rule (M7). Remind students to write their rule on a piece of scrap paper to help them remember it, turning it over so the other students can't see it. The other players then take turns placing one object on the mat where they think it belongs. You'll tell them whether it was correctly placed or not, and move it to the proper mat if necessary. Players keep placing objects until everyone thinks they know the rule you've chosen.

Remind students to use rules that can be identified by the other members of their group. If my rule was "Buttons I like," would you be able to tell what the rule was without me telling you?

Students might say:

"No, because I don't know which buttons you like."

Allow time for students to play several rounds of the game with their groups.

Did you find different ways to sort the same set of objects? Were there any rules that didn't work well with your collection?

Students might say:

"We sorted the shells by size and by color."

"I used the rule blue buttons, but there was only 1 blue one so that didn't work so well."

Distribute copies of *Guess My Rule* with Objects (R35).

ELL English Language Learners

Provide a Word List Make a list of words that students could refer to for *Guess My Rule*, such as the names of colors (red, yellow, green, blue), sizes (large, small), or number of holes (2 holes, 4 holes). Since students may be using different collections of objects, it may be helpful to personalize the list for each group.

Additional Resource

Student Math Handbook

Game: *Guess My Rule* SMH G12

Materials: buttons, M6–M7

Extension

20 MIN GROUPS

Guess My Rule with 2 Rules

Use anytime after Session 1.4.

Math Focus Points

- Using attributes to sort a set of objects
- Looking carefully at a group of objects to determine how they have been sorted

Materials: Power Polygons (1 set per group), M6–M7 (1 each per group), R36

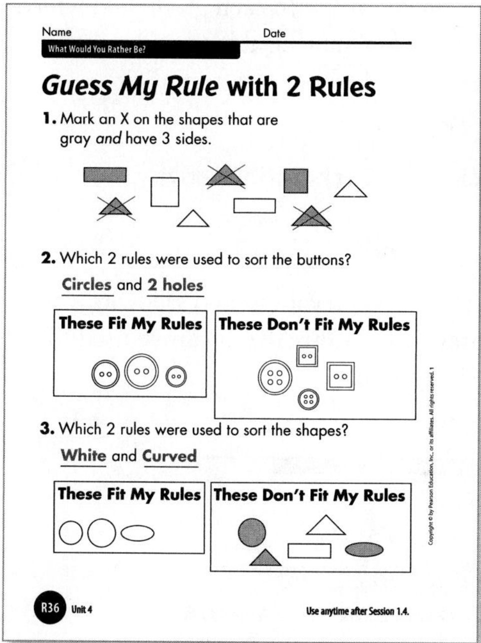
Name Date

What Would You Rather Be?

Guess My Rule with 2 Rules

1. Mark an X on the shapes that are gray *and* have 3 sides.

2. Which 2 rules were used to sort the buttons?
Circles and 2 holes

These Fit My Rules	These Don't Fit My Rules

3. Which 2 rules were used to sort the shapes?
White and Curved

These Fit My Rules	These Don't Fit My Rules

R36 Unit 4 Use anytime after Session 1.4.

Distribute Power Polygons to each group. We've been playing *Guess My Rule* with 1 rule. Now we're going to play using 2 rules. Only the things that match *both* rules go on the These Fit My Rule mat (M6). The things that *don't* match *both* rules go on the These Don't Fit My Rule mat (M7). Let's try a round. My rules are "Green" *and* "3 Sides." Look at your shapes. Hold up a shape that you think fits my rules.

Students might say:

"Shape N is green and it has 3 sides. So is shape E."

Try another rule, such as "Small" and "3 Sides." Make sure that students can sort correctly. This shape is small, and it has 4 sides. Does it fit both of my rules?

Students might say:

"No. It has to have 3 sides. So it goes on the other mat."

Now students take turns playing in groups. Review the different attributes they can use (color, size, shape, number of sides) as needed. Remind students to write their rules on a piece of scrap paper to help them remember, and to keep it hidden. Students continue until each has had a chance to make the rule.

Distribute copies of *Guess My Rule* with 2 Rules (R36).

ELL English Language Learners

Provide Sentence Stems Encourage students to use the following sentence stems to describe how the shapes fit or don't fit the 2 rules.

This shape fits both rules because ________.

This shape does **not** fit both rules because ________.

Additional Resource

Student Math Handbook

Game: *Guess My Rule* SMH G12

Materials: buttons, M6–M7

Variation: Have players choose 2 rules.

Differentiation in Investigation 2

Mathematics in This Investigation

The mathematics focuses on collecting and representing data, and interpreting different data representations.

Understanding the Mathematics

When planning a data investigation, students generate a survey question with only two possible answers. They have a plan for how to collect data from every person in the class, and can explain how they know they did this. They make representations that clearly show how many are in each group, which group has more, and can write an equation that represents this information. They can also use the representation to interpret the results of the survey.

Option: Assign the **Extension** activity.

Partially Understanding the Mathematics

Students generate a question with only two possible answers. They plan to collect data from every person in the class, but may have trouble accomplishing this, losing track of who has and hasn't been asked. Their representations may or may not show every piece of data they collected and which group has more may not be easy to discern. While their representation may not be totally accurate, they can describe the results of the survey.

Option: Assign the **Practice** activity.

Not Understanding the Mathematics

Students may have trouble with many of the steps of conducting a survey including generating a question with only two possible answers, collecting data from every person in the class, and keeping track of who has and hasn't been surveyed. They may not understand the connection between the number of students in the class, the number of responses, and the number of pieces of data represented. These students have difficulty making representations that clearly show how many are in each group and which group has more. They may be able to make a statement about the data but not from their representation.

Option: Assign the **Intervention** activity.

Investigation 1 Quiz

In addition to your observations and students' work in Investigation 1, the Quiz (R37) can be used to gather more information.

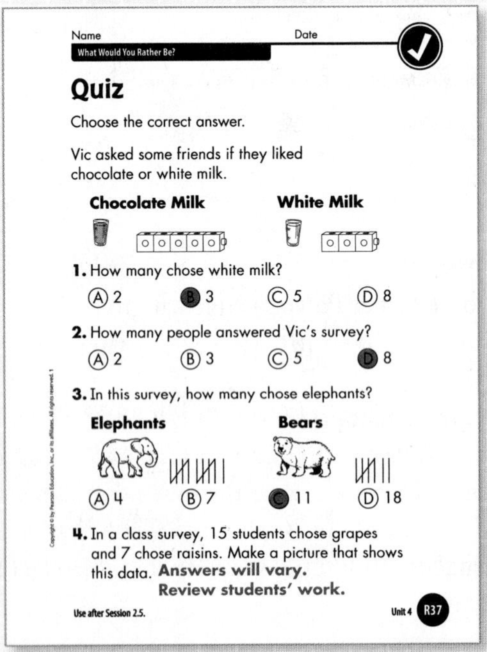
Name Date

What Would You Rather Be?

Quiz

Choose the correct answer.

Vic asked some friends if they liked chocolate or white milk.

Chocolate Milk **White Milk**

1. How many chose white milk?

Ⓐ 2 Ⓑ 3 Ⓒ 5 Ⓓ 8

2. How many people answered Vic's survey?

Ⓐ 2 Ⓑ 3 Ⓒ 5 Ⓓ 8

3. In this survey, how many chose elephants?

Elephants **Bears**

Ⓐ 4 Ⓑ 7 Ⓒ 11 Ⓓ 18

4. In a class survey, 15 students chose grapes and 7 chose raisins. Make a picture that shows this data. **Answers will vary. Review students' work.**

Use after Session 2.5. Unit 4 R37

Intervention

Representing Data

Use anytime after Session 2.4.

Math Focus Points

- Making a representation to communicate the results of a survey
- Interpreting the results of a data investigation

Vocabulary: survey, represent, representation

Materials: connecting cubes (12 per student), index cards or self-stick notes, blank paper

I did a survey with a small group of students. I asked them if they had a pet. Here are the data. One list shows people who said yes, they do have a pet. The other list shows people who said, no, they do not have a pet.

Yes: Carol, Diego, Lyle, Marta, Talisa, Emilia, Chris, and Neil

No: Seth, Jacob, Jacinta, Teo

Distribute 12 cubes to each student. Can you use the cubes to show the people who have a pet? How did you know how many cubes to take? Highlight the one-to-one correspondence between the names and the cubes. [Vic] said he took 1 cube for each name. [Allie] said she counted 8 names so she counted 8 cubes. Repeat this for the remaining data—people who do not have a pet.

If students did not snap each group of cubes together, have them do so now. Connect these towers back to the situation, labeling each tower with an index card or self-stick note. Everyone has two towers of cubes. What does the tower with 8 cubes represent? The tower with 4 cubes?

Students might say:

"The tower with 8 cubes is for the 8 kids who have a pet."

Let's look at these two towers. What do you notice? What do these tell us about our survey question?

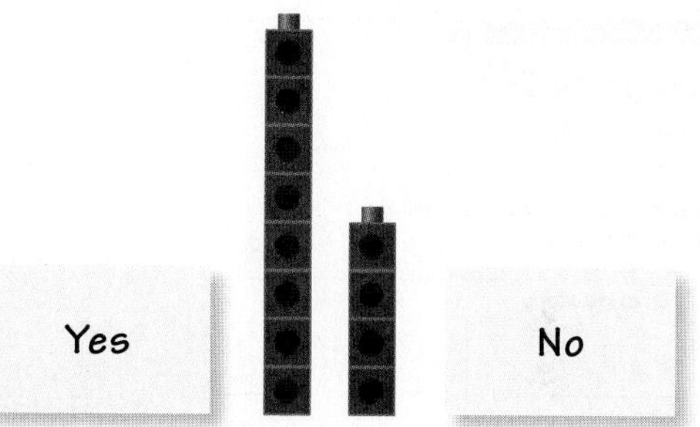

Students might say:

"More kids have pets."

"4 kids don't have a pet."

Now, your job is to find a way to represent the data—to show the data on paper so that someone else could tell what we found out in our survey. Distribute paper for students to use in making a representation. Some students may benefit from drawing what they did with the cubes. Help them record their findings beneath their representation.

ELL English Language Learners

Rephrase Use a variety of words and phrases for *data* and *representation*. For example: These are the *data*, or *information* about who has pets. How can we make a *representation* for our survey, something that shows what we found out?

Additional Resource

Student Math Handbook pages 65–68

Practice

30 MIN PAIRS

Analyzing Data

Use anytime after Session 2.4.

Math Focus Points

- Interpreting the results of a data investigation

Materials: R38

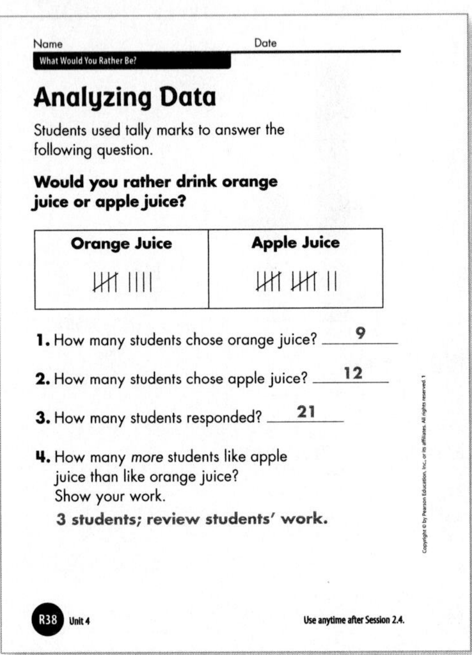
Name Date

What Would You Rather Be?

Analyzing Data

Students used tally marks to answer the following question.

Would you rather drink orange juice or apple juice?

Orange Juice	Apple Juice
𝍸 IIII	𝍸 𝍸 II

1. How many students chose orange juice? 9
2. How many students chose apple juice? 12
3. How many students responded? 21
4. How many *more* students like apple juice than like orange juice? Show your work.
 3 students; review students' work.

R38 Unit 4 Use anytime after Session 2.4.

Here is a quick survey from one class. The teacher asked her students if they would rather sing or dance. Here are their data.

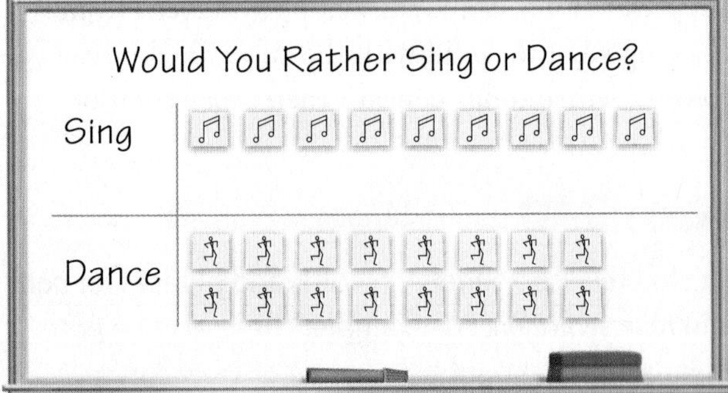

Take a minute and look at the data. Now talk to your partner about something you noticed. Give students time to share, and then discuss the data as a group. What did you notice? What can you tell us about this class?

Students might say:

"A lot of people like to sing, like me."

"More people like to dance."

As needed, ask questions that focus students' attention on the important information (e.g., which group has more or fewer, how many people are in each group, how many people participated). Students may want to come up to the board to count. Encourage students to connect the numbers to what they represent. [Felipe] counted 9 in this row. What does that mean? What does it tell us about this class?

Students might say:

"9 people like singing better."

End by asking partners to generate an equation about this survey. Discuss the equations, connecting the numbers and notation to the situation. What does the 9 in your equation represent? The 16? The 25? Then, distribute copies of Analyzing Data (R38).

ELL English Language Learners

Model Thinking Aloud Point to each part of the equation (e.g., $9 + 16 = 25$) and the table to support students with limited language. I count 1, 2, 3, ..., 9 students who like singing. I count 1, 2, 3, ..., 16 students who like dancing. 9 and 16 make 25 students in the class.

Additional Resource

Student Math Handbook pages 65–68

Extension

Different Ways of Showing Data

Use anytime after Session 2.4.

Math Focus Points

- Interpreting the results of a data investigation
- Making a representation to communicate the results of a survey

Materials: connecting cubes, self-stick notes, blank paper, R39

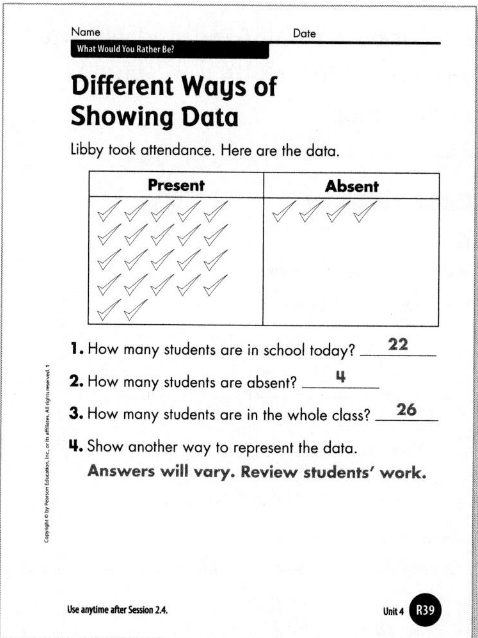
Name Date
What Would You Rather Be?

Different Ways of Showing Data

Libby took attendance. Here are the data.

Present	Absent
✓✓✓✓✓ ✓✓✓✓✓ ✓✓✓✓✓ ✓✓✓✓✓ ✓✓	✓✓✓✓

1. How many students are in school today? 22
2. How many students are absent? 4
3. How many students are in the whole class? 26
4. Show another way to represent the data.
Answers will vary. Review students' work.

Use anytime after Session 2.4. Unit 4 R39

Materials to Prepare: Make a class list for an imaginary class. List 20 names. Next to each write school or summer. Make about $\frac{3}{4}$ of the responses say school and $\frac{1}{4}$ say summer. Make one copy per pair.

I have a set of data here from a teacher who asked her students about their birthdays. She wanted to know whether their birthdays fell during the school year or over the summer. Hand out a class list to each student. How did the students decide to record their data?

Your job is to work with a partner and think about a couple of different ways you could represent the data. Explain the tools that are available—cubes, self-stick notes, paper, etc. Then, choose one way that you think shows something important about the data.

Pairs work together to think about ways of organizing the data, and then use one of those methods to represent the data. Then, spend some time sharing students' representations.

You might want to choose 1–2 in particular that you want students to consider. For each, focus the discussion on what the different representations highlight about the data. When you look at [Sacha] and [William's] representation, what do you notice? How does it compare to [Isabel] and [Edgar's]?

Students might say:

"It's really easy to see that there's more birthdays during school than during the summer."

"I agree. But you can't tell *how many* birthdays there are in each group, like we could on [Isabel] and [Edgar's]."

If there is time, encourage students to make another representation of the same set of data, trying out another pair's method. Try to represent the same data in a different way. Maybe you'd like to try using tally marks, or making two stacks of X's right next to each other, so it's almost like comparing cube towers.

Distribute copies of Different Ways of Showing Data (R39).

ELL English Language Learners

Provide a Word List Write the words *survey, data,* and *representation* on chart paper. Review the meaning of each. Encourage students to use these words as they discuss strategies for representing the data.

Additional Resource

Student Math Handbook pages 65–68

Differentiation in Investigation 3

Mathematics in This Investigation

The mathematics focuses on describing, representing, and interpreting numerical data—comparing the number of pieces of data in each category or at each value, and analyzing what that information says about the group.

Understanding the Mathematics

Students can describe and represent numerical data, and explain what the data say about the group surveyed. They are comfortable interpreting data that are not from their own class, and can compare two sets of data.

Option: Assign the **Extension** activity.

Partially Understanding the Mathematics

Students can describe and represent numerical data, though they may have difficulty with data that involve two quantities (e.g., 7 children that are 6 years old). It may also be a challenge to describe the similarities and/or differences in two very similar sets of data.

Option: Assign the **Practice** activity.

Not Understanding the Mathematics

Students have trouble describing and representing numerical data, in part because it is hard to keep track of the meaning of two different quantities. Because describing and representing one set of numerical data is difficult, comparing two sets is likely very challenging.

Option: Assign the **Intervention** activity.

Investigation 3 Quiz

In addition to your observations and students' work in Investigation 3, the Quiz (R40) can be used to gather more information.

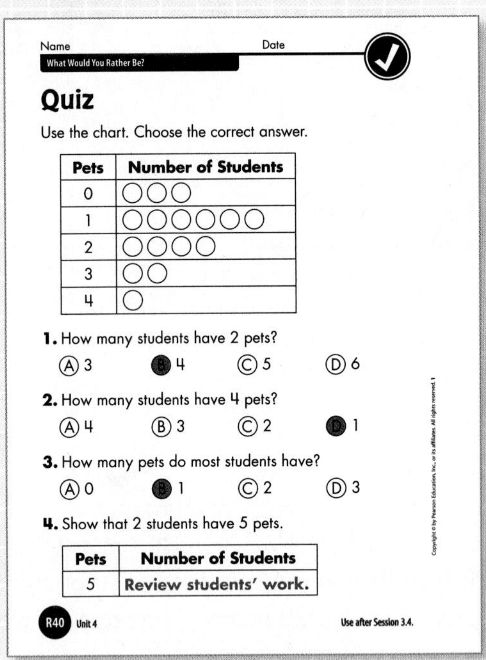

Name Date

What Would You Rather Be?

Quiz

Use the chart. Choose the correct answer.

Pets	Number of Students
0	○○○
1	○○○○○○
2	○○○○
3	○○
4	○

1. How many students have 2 pets?

Ⓐ 3 ● 4 Ⓒ 5 Ⓓ 6

2. How many students have 4 pets?

Ⓐ 4 Ⓑ 3 Ⓒ 2 ● 1

3. How many pets do most students have?

Ⓐ 0 ● 1 Ⓒ 2 Ⓓ 3

4. Show that 2 students have 5 pets.

Pets	Number of Students
5	Review students' work.

R40 Unit 4 Use after Session 3.4.

Intervention

30 MIN GROUPS

More Age Data

Use anytime after Session 3.2.

Math Focus Points

- Organizing data in numerical order
- Making a representation to communicate the results of a survey

Materials: connecting cubes

On the board, make a list of about 10 students and their ages.

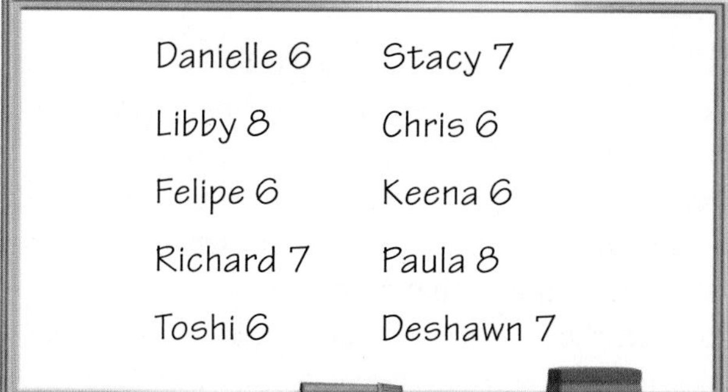

Danielle 6
Stacy 7
Libby 8
Chris 6
Felipe 6
Keena 6
Richard 7
Paula 8
Toshi 6
Deshawn 7

Ask questions that orient students to the data. How old is [Stacy]? What does this [7] tell us? Then, distribute cubes to students. What if I asked you to make a tower that shows how old [Toshi] is. How many cubes would you use? Why do you think so?

Students might say:

"I would use [6] cubes. Because [Toshi] is [6] years old."

Explain that now each group will make a set of cube towers for this data. Your job is to make one tower for each student. Your tower should show how old they are. So like [Lyle] said, if a student is [6] years old, that cube tower should have [6] cubes in it.

Once students have built an accurate set of cube towers, ask them to put them in order, if they haven't already done so.

Because it is often challenging for students to keep straight the two different quantities in a situation like this—the ages and the number of students who are that age—ask questions that get at these ideas. These cube towers represent the ages of a group of students. How many students in this group are 6 years old? Turn and talk to a partner about this. How many students are 6? How do you know?

Students might say:

"[5] kids are 6 years old. Because there are [5] towers with 6 cubes."

Repeat this for the remaining ages, highlighting how each tower represents one student and the number of cubes shows the age of that student. Then, each student makes a representation of the data. Explain that they can use words, numbers, and pictures. Support students as they work, asking questions and referring them back to their set of ordered cube towers.

ELL English Language Learners

Rephrase Students may have difficulty connecting the data, the cubes, and the representation. Ask short, simple questions to help them do this, such as: How old is [Danielle]? Make a tower with [6] cubes. [Libby] is [8] years old. How many cubes do you need for Libby's tower?

Additional Resource

Student Math Handbook pages 65–66

Practice

What Do You Know?

Use anytime after Session 3.2.

Math Focus Points

- Organizing data in numerical order
- Making a representation to communicate the results of a survey

Materials: connecting cubes, markers, chart paper, blank paper, R41

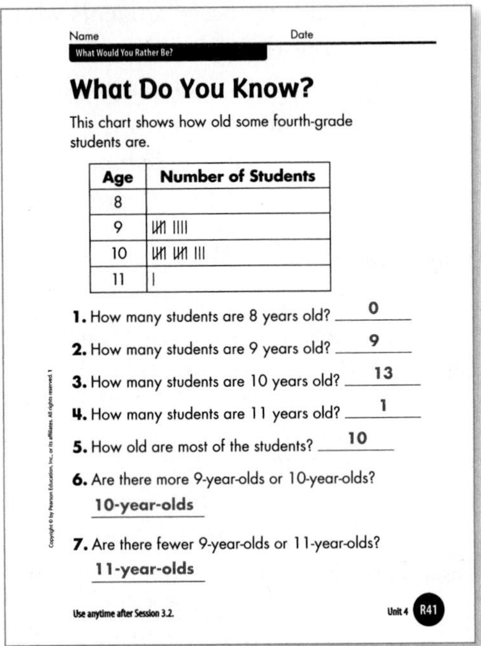

Name Date

What Would You Rather Be?

What Do You Know?

This chart shows how old some fourth-grade students are.

Age	Number of Students
8	
9	𝍸 IIII
10	𝍸 𝍸 III
11	I

1. How many students are 8 years old? 0
2. How many students are 9 years old? 9
3. How many students are 10 years old? 13
4. How many students are 11 years old? 1
5. How old are most of the students? 10
6. Are there more 9-year-olds or 10-year-olds? 10-year-olds
7. Are there fewer 9-year-olds or 11-year-olds? 11-year-olds

Use anytime after Session 3.2. Unit 4 R41

Materials to Prepare: Write the names and ages of 17 students from another class on chart paper.

Here are the ages of students in another class. You are going to make a representation of the ages of these students. You can choose how to represent the ages. Pairs work together to make a representation of the data. You may want to use connecting cubes. How could you use cubes to show the ages of the students?

Students might say:

"I would build a tower for each person. The number of cubes in the tower is their age."

Allow time for pairs to finish, then look at the representations students created. Then, have students help you make one more representation of the data. I am going to use tally marks to represent the data. Look at your representation. Ask how many students are each age. Record the results on the board using tally marks.

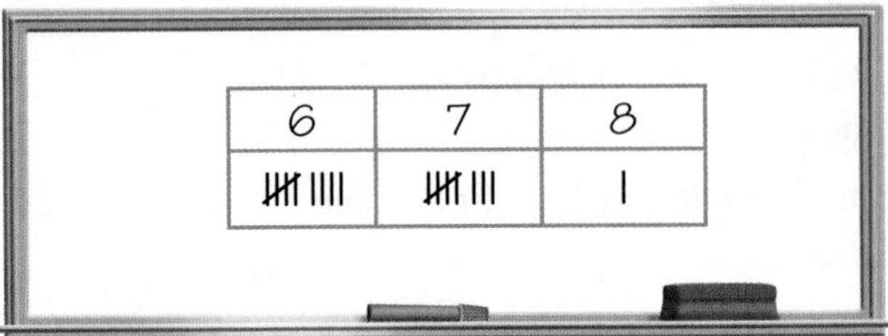

6	7	8
𝍸 IIII	𝍸 III	I

When you look at the data, what do you see? What do we know about this class? How many students are 6 years old? Ask students to point out the column for 6 years old and count the tally marks with them. Repeat this process for each age. Finally, ask some questions that encourage students to compare the number of students that are different ages. Are there more students who are 6 years old or 7 years old? Are there fewer students who are 7 years old or 8 years old?

Distribute copies of What Do You Know? (R41).

ELL English Language Learners

Rephrase Students may have difficulty understanding the questions being asked. Use shorter, simpler questions, such as: How many are 6? Are more students 6 or 7?

Additional Resource

Student Math Handbook pages 67–68

Extension

15 MIN

INDIVIDUALS

What Pencil Color?

Use anytime after Session 3.4.

Math Focus Points

- Describing and comparing the number of pieces of data in each category or at each value, and interpreting what the data tell you about the group

Materials: R42

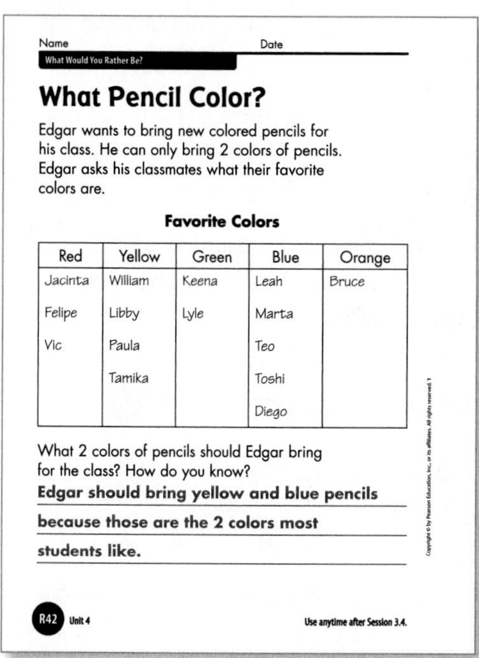

Name Date

What Would You Rather Be?

What Pencil Color?

Edgar wants to bring new colored pencils for his class. He can only bring 2 colors of pencils. Edgar asks his classmates what their favorite colors are.

Favorite Colors

Red	Yellow	Green	Blue	Orange
Jacinta	William	Keena	Leah	Bruce
Felipe	Libby	Lyle	Marta	
Vic	Paula		Teo	
	Tamika		Toshi	
			Diego	

What 2 colors of pencils should Edgar bring for the class? How do you know?

Edgar should bring yellow and blue pencils because those are the 2 colors most students like.

R42 Unit 4 Use anytime after Session 3.4.

Pencils come in many colors. If I were to bring new pencils for the class, how could I decide what colors to bring?

Students might say:

"You could ask what colors everyone likes and bring those colors."

Imagine that I did a survey to help me decide which 2 colors of pencils I should buy. Here are the data.

Red	Yellow	Green	Blue	Orange
Bruce	Marta	Seth	Allie	Talisa
Nicky		Teo	Chris	Felipe
Carol		Vic	Jacob	
Tamika			Richard	
			Emilia	

I can only buy 2 colors of pencils. Which 2 colors should I buy? Why are they the best choice? Use the data to explain why you think I should buy pencils in those two colors.

The discussion should focus on how blue and red were the most popular colors chosen by the students surveyed.

Distribute copies of What Pencil Color? (R42).

ELL English Language Learners

Partner Talk Have pairs explain how they made their decision about what color of pencils to bring. Listen for terms like *data* and *most*. They should identify the 2 best colors, and use the data to justify their choices. Beginning English Language Learners can be paired with a student who speaks the same native language to explain their answer choices.

Additional Resource

Student Math Handbook page 68

Unit 5

Differentiation in Investigation 1

Mathematics in This Investigation

The mathematics focuses on understanding length as an attribute of objects that can be measured, and developing strategies for measuring accurately. This includes knowing which dimension to measure, where to start and stop measuring, how to line up units/measuring tools, and understanding that many measurements are not reported in whole numbers.

Understanding the Mathematics

Students use different-sized units to accurately measure the longest dimension of an object. They analyze measurement techniques, and understand that if the same unit is used to measure the same object, the measurement should be the same. They may be exploring the idea that the bigger the unit used to measure, the smaller the total number of units will be (and vice versa). They have a fairly accurate sense of the size of an inch, use correct language to describe measurements, and are comfortable with measurements that fall between whole numbers.

Option: Assign the **Extension** activity.

Partially Understanding the Mathematics

Students use different-sized units to accurately measure the longest dimension of an object with a fair degree of accuracy. They may be able to analyze measurement techniques, but occasionally make minor measuring errors. They are beginning to understand the idea that if the same unit is used to measure the same object, the measurement should be the same. Measurements that fall between whole numbers may be challenging.

Option: Assign the **Practice** activity.

Not Understanding the Mathematics

Students are learning to determine the longest dimension of an object, and to use different-sized units to measure. Their measurement techniques are not consistent in that they may not start/stop measuring at the exact beginning/end of the object, and often leave gaps or overlaps as they line up units to measure. They may not understand that measurements of the same lengths should be the same when using the same unit. They report measurements that fall between whole numbers as whole numbers.

Option: Assign the **Intervention** activity.

Investigation 1 Quiz

In addition to your observations and students' work in Investigation 1, the Quiz (R43) can be used to gather more information.

Name Date

Fish Lengths and Animal Jumps

Quiz

Choose the correct answer.

1. How long?

Ⓐ 3 clips Ⓑ 4 clips ● 5 clips Ⓓ 6 clips

2. How tall?

● 9 cubes Ⓑ 8 cubes Ⓒ 7 cubes Ⓓ 6 cubes

3. How long?

Ⓐ 6 tiles Ⓑ 5 tiles Ⓒ 4 tiles ● 3 tiles

4. Use paper clips. Measure the pencil.

5 clips **Review students' work.**

Use after Session 1.6. Unit 5 R43

Intervention

Measuring Markers, Pencils, and Crayons

Use anytime after Session 1.2.

Math Focus Points

- Understanding what length is and how it can be measured
- Developing accurate measurement techniques

Vocabulary: measure, length, measurement, unit

Materials: markers (1 per pair), unsharpened pencil (1 per pair), crayon with tip broken off or worn down (1 per pair), color tiles and cubes (20 per pair).

Students measure the lengths of the items in a Measurement Collection—a marker, a pencil, and a crayon.

Explain to students that they will be measuring the objects using tiles. When we measure length using color tiles, we put them in a straight line along the edge of the object.

How do I measure this marker with tiles? Where should I start? Hold up a tile and a marker for students to see. As you put the tile next to the marker, point out that you start measuring at one end of the marker. Where should I put the second tile? Show students how to line the tiles up next to each other as close as possible.

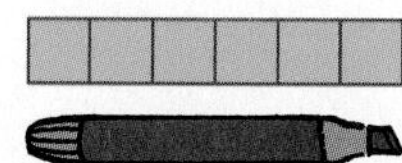

Agree on a measurement and then discuss how you would record it. Why do we have to write the word *tiles* after our measurements?

Students might say:

"To show that we used tiles to measure."

"So people know that the marker is 6 tiles long, not 6 cubes or 6 paper clips."

Partners now work together to measure a pencil and a crayon.

If students have trouble lining the tiles up without leaving gaps, suggest that they try measuring each item with cubes. Because these snap together, they can be easier for students to manage. Then you can discuss the difference with students.

How was it different, using cubes instead of tiles? What if you were going to go back to using tiles? What did you learn from using the cubes?

Students might say:

"It's easy to make a straight line because they link together."

"The tiles all have to touch at the sides. I have to be careful not to knock them because they slide apart."

ELL English Language Learners

Suggest a Sequence Help students by verbalizing the sequence of steps for measuring with tiles. *First,* line tiles up with one end of the object. *Next,* make sure tiles are close together. *Last,* count the tiles and write *tiles* as the unit.

Additional Resource

Student Math Handbook pages 97–98

Practice

15 MIN GROUPS

Measuring with Tiles

Use anytime after Session 1.2.

Math Focus Points

- Understanding what length is and how it can be measured
- Developing accurate measurement techniques
- Understanding that measurements of the same lengths should be the same when they are measured twice or by different people using the same unit

Vocabulary: unit

Materials: color tiles (20 per pair), identical rectangular tissue boxes (1 per group), R44

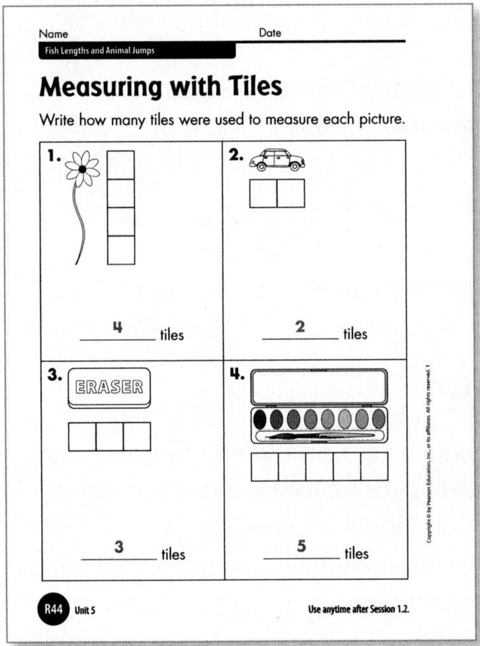

Name Date

Fish Lengths and Animal Jumps

Measuring with Tiles

Write how many tiles were used to measure each picture.

1. 4 tiles
2. 2 tiles
3. ERASER 3 tiles
4. 5 tiles

R44 Unit 5 Use anytime after Session 1.2.

Today you will measure the length of a tissue box. Distribute tiles and a tissue box to each group. What is the longest part of the box? Trace it with your finger. Point out that one side is longer than the other. The length of the box is its longest side.

How do we measure length with tiles?

Students might say:

"Put tiles along the side and count them."

"Line the tiles up, so they are straight and touching."

Remind students to think about where to start and stop measuring. Then, students measure their boxes.

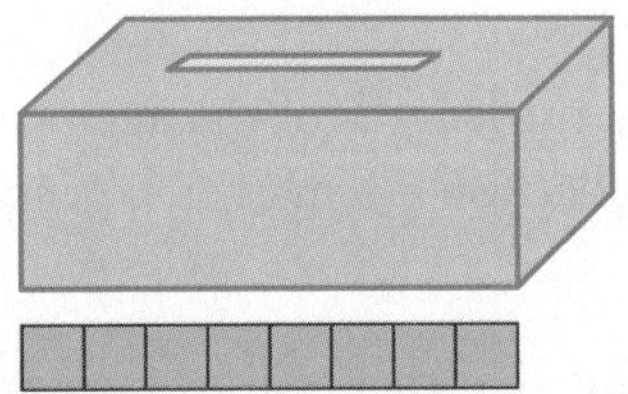

How long is your box? Record each group's measurement on the board. If different groups got different measurements, discuss this. [Diego] and [Paula] got [6] tiles. [Leah] and [Deshawn] got [7] tiles. What do you think about this? They both used tiles to measure the same box.

Have pairs model and compare how they measured to investigate why they got different measurements. Then, distribute copies of Measuring with Tiles (R44).

ELL English Language Learners

Provide a Word List Write the words *length, long,* and *longest* on chart paper. Review the meaning of each. Hold up the tissue box and slide your finger along the length to help them see what to measure.

Additional Resource

Student Math Handbook pages 97–98

Extension

20 MIN GROUPS

Measuring 3 Ways

Use anytime after Session 1.2.

Math Focus Points

- Measuring lengths using different-sized units
- Developing accurate measurement techniques
- Understanding that measuring an object using different-length units will result in different measurements

Vocabulary: unit

Materials: connecting cubes (20 per group), color tiles (20 per group), paper clips (20 per group), pencil box (1 per group), R45

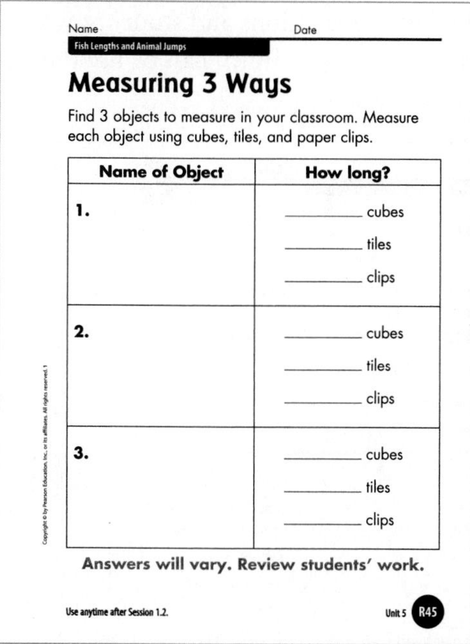

Name Date

Fish Lengths and Animal Jumps

Measuring 3 Ways

Find 3 objects to measure in your classroom. Measure each object using cubes, tiles, and paper clips.

Name of Object	How long?
1.	_____ cubes _____ tiles _____ clips
2.	_____ cubes _____ tiles _____ clips
3.	_____ cubes _____ tiles _____ clips

Answers will vary. Review students' work.

Use anytime after Session 1.2. Unit 5 R45

Show students a pencil box. Look at this pencil box. What part of it is the longest? Remind students that the length of the box is the longer side. When we measure length, we go in a straight line beside the long edge of the box. You are going to measure this box three ways, using three different units. You will use cubes, color tiles, and paper clips.

Have students measure the object using all 3 units, recording each measurement. As you observe each group, reinforce the importance of recording the unit of measurement.

Compare your measurements with another group. Do you have the same lengths? Why might your measurements be different from another group's measurements?

Students might say:

"We must have measured differently."

"The box was a little longer than 6 tiles, but we just wrote 6. Maybe they wrote 7 because it was a little longer than 6."

Have groups compare their measurement techniques to double-check any measurements that are different.

Distribute copies of Measuring 3 Ways (R45).

ELL English Language Learners

Provide a Word List Write the words *measurement, length,* and *unit* on chart paper. Review the meaning of each. Encourage students to use these words as they explain why their measurements are the same or different based on their units.

Additional Resource

Student Math Handbook pages 99–101

Differentiation in Investigation 2

Mathematics in This Investigation

The mathematics focuses on understanding length as a distance that can be measured, and developing strategies for accurately measuring distances.

Understanding the Mathematics

Students understand that using different-length units to measure the same distance will result in different measurements. They use craft sticks, basketball player steps, and baby steps to accurately measure distances. They understand the idea that the bigger the unit used to measure, the smaller the total number of units will be (and vice versa).

Option: Assign the **Extension** activity.

Partially Understanding the Mathematics

Students use craft sticks, basketball player steps, and baby steps to measure with a fair degree of accuracy, but occasionally leave gaps or overlaps as they line up units, or make other errors that result in inaccurate measurements. They are coming to understand that the unit being used to measure is important, and may be starting to explore the idea that the bigger the unit used to measure, the smaller the total number of units will be (and vice versa).

Option: Assign the **Practice** activity.

Not Understanding the Mathematics

Students use craft sticks, basketball player steps, and baby steps to measure but are still developing techniques for accurate measurement. They may not put units in a straight line, or start/stop measuring at the exact beginning/end of the object, or they may leave gaps or overlaps as they measure. They have difficulty with the concept that different-length measurements result in different measurements. They may not understand the importance of recording which unit they are using.

Option: Assign the **Intervention** activity.

Investigation 2 Quiz

In addition to your observations and students' work in Investigation 2, the Quiz (R46) can be used to gather more information.

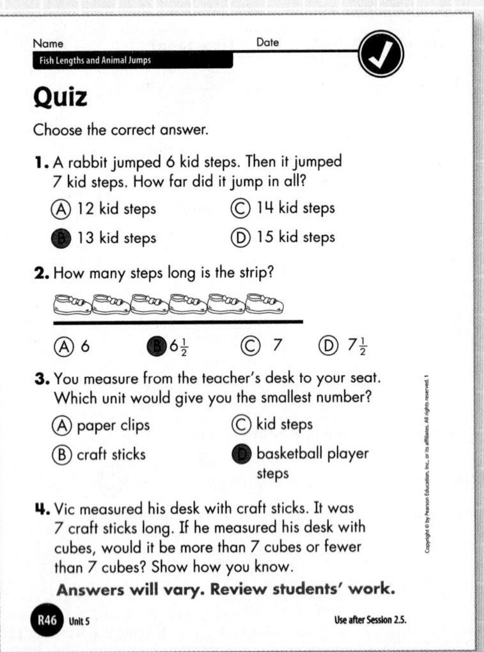

Name Date

Fish Lengths and Animal Jumps

Quiz

Choose the correct answer.

1. A rabbit jumped 6 kid steps. Then it jumped 7 kid steps. How far did it jump in all?

Ⓐ 12 kid steps Ⓒ 14 kid steps
● 13 kid steps Ⓓ 15 kid steps

2. How many steps long is the strip?

Ⓐ 6 ● $6\frac{1}{2}$ Ⓒ 7 Ⓓ $7\frac{1}{2}$

3. You measure from the teacher's desk to your seat. Which unit would give you the smallest number?

Ⓐ paper clips Ⓒ kid steps
Ⓑ craft sticks ● basketball player steps

4. Vic measured his desk with craft sticks. It was 7 craft sticks long. If he measured his desk with cubes, would it be more than 7 cubes or fewer than 7 cubes? Show how you know.

Answers will vary. Review students' work.

R46 Unit 5 Use after Session 2.5.

Intervention

20 MIN PAIRS

Measuring with Shoes

Use anytime after Session 2.1.

Math Focus Points

- Measuring length by iterating a single unit
- Comparing lengths to determine which is longer
- Describing measurements that are *in between* whole numbers of units

Vocabulary: distance

Materials: lengths of tape (from Session 2.1), yardstick (as needed)

Choose 2 of the tapes A–H that students did *not* compare on *Student Activity Book* page 16. Draw attention to Tape [E] and Tape [H] and explain what each represents. Tape [E] represents the distance between [Leah's] desk and [William's] desk. Tape [H] is the distance from the [rug] to the [door].

Students use kid steps to measure the tapes. Students who struggle to keep their balance while measuring can use a yardstick to steady themselves. Or, have one person from each pair take off his or her shoes to use to measure.

As you measure the tape, help each other keep track of how many kid steps have been taken by counting aloud. Ask students to leave the shoe on the tape in the next-to-final step. Use this concrete image of the remainder to help the students discuss how long the remaining tape is. So this shoe here was the 11th step. And a whole other shoe doesn't fit, but there's still some room on this tape. Place the other shoe above that space on the tape. How many steps should we say Tape [H] is?

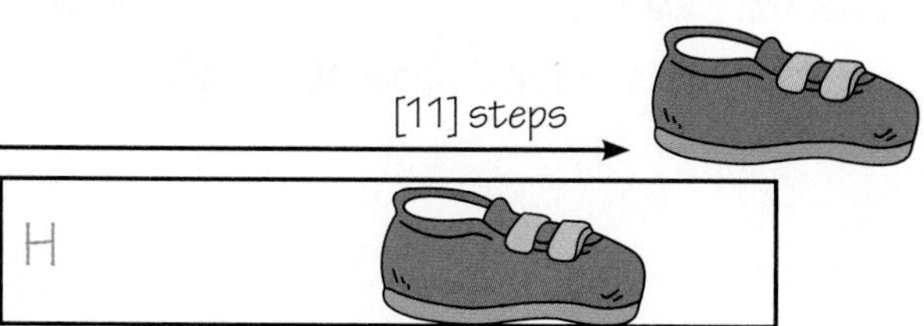

Students might say:

"It's a little more than [11]."

"It's less than [12], more like [$11\frac{1}{2}$]."

Students should record their measurements for Tape [E] and Tape [H]. Is it farther from [Leah's] desk to [William's] desk or from the [rug] to the [door]? Have students circle the farther distance. How do you know? Have pairs work together to verbalize how they know that one tape is farther than the other tape because it has a greater measurement.

If time allows, repeat the activity with 2 different lengths.

ELL English Language Learners

Partner Talk Have pairs discuss the following questions to practice their English. Which tape is longer? How did you decide? Beginning English Language Learners may complete the activity with a partner from their language group in their native language. More proficient speakers should explain how they know which tape measure is longer.

Additional Resource

Student Math Handbook pages 103–104

Practice

20 MIN PAIRS

Measuring with Kid Steps

Use anytime after Session 2.1.

Math Focus Points

- Measuring length by iterating a single unit
- Comparing lengths to determine which is longer

Vocabulary: distance

Materials: R47

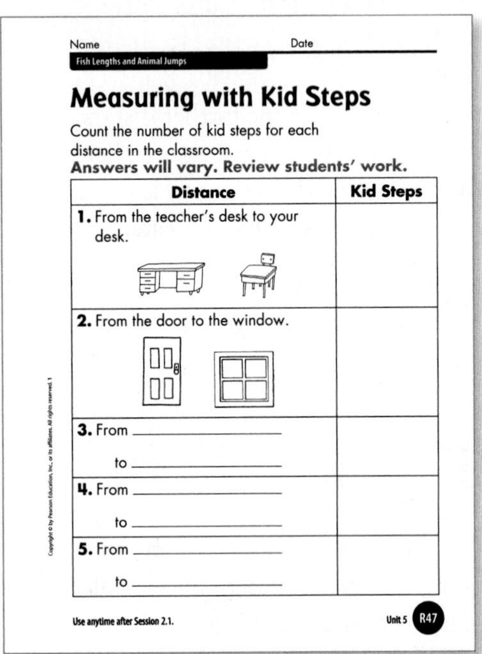

Name Date

Fish Lengths and Animal Jumps

Measuring with Kid Steps

Count the number of kid steps for each distance in the classroom.

Answers will vary. Review students' work.

Distance	Kid Steps
1. From the teacher's desk to your desk.	
2. From the door to the window.	
3. From ______ to ______	
4. From ______ to ______	
5. From ______ to ______	

Use anytime after Session 2.1. Unit 5 R47

On the board, list 3–4 pairs of places in the classroom that represent distances students have not yet measured.

Sink to Door

Door to Window

Calendar to Cubbies

Today you are going to measure the distance between things in the classroom in kid steps. What have you been learning about how to measure accurately using kid steps?

Students might say:

"Make sure that for each step your heel touches your other toe."

"You have to keep track of the counting and the last step can be tricky if it's only part of a step."

Partners work together to measure the distances, but each student should take his or her own measurements and record them.

Have partners compare their results. Did you get the same answers as your partner? Why or why not? Students should recognize that the tape is the same length, but their shoes aren't the same size.

Look at the measurements you took with your kid steps. Which tape is longer? Which distance is farther? Students record the lengths in order, from the shortest to the longest measure. Check with your partner. Do you agree about the order?

Distribute copies of Measuring with Kid Steps (R47).

ELL English Language Learners

Provide a Word List Write the words *measure, length,* and *distance* on the board. Review their meanings with students. Encourage students to use these words as they discuss how they know one tape is longer than the other or one distance is farther than the other.

Additional Resource

Student Math Handbook pages 103–104

Extension

15 MIN INDIVIDUALS

How Much Longer?

Use anytime after Session 2.1.

Math Focus Points

- Measuring length by iterating a single unit
- Comparing lengths to determine which is longer

Materials: *Student Activity Book* pp. 16–17, connecting cubes (as needed), R48

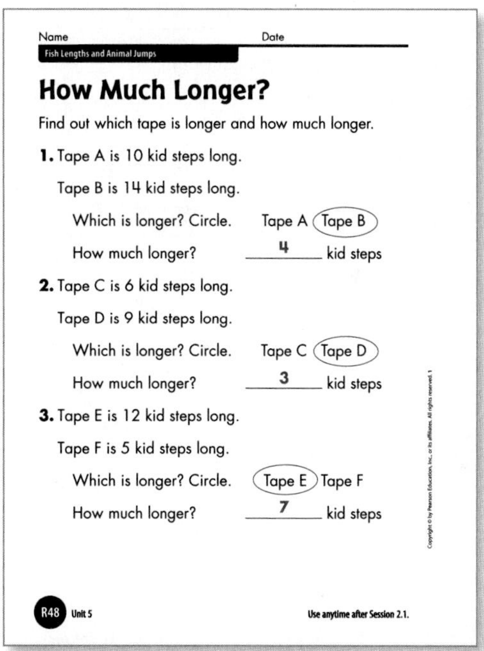

Name Date

Fish Lengths and Animal Jumps

How Much Longer?

Find out which tape is longer and how much longer.

1. Tape A is 10 kid steps long.
   Tape B is 14 kid steps long.
   Which is longer? Circle. Tape A (Tape B)
   How much longer? 4 kid steps
2. Tape C is 6 kid steps long.
   Tape D is 9 kid steps long.
   Which is longer? Circle. Tape C (Tape D)
   How much longer? 3 kid steps
3. Tape E is 12 kid steps long.
   Tape F is 5 kid steps long.
   Which is longer? Circle. (Tape E) Tape F
   How much longer? 7 kid steps

R48 Unit 5 Use anytime after Session 2.1.

Explain that students are going to look back at the work they did measuring in kid steps and comparing those lengths. Refer them to *Student Activity Book* page 16.

When you compared Tape A and Tape B, which one was longer?

Your job today is to figure out *how much longer* Tape A is compared to Tape B. How could you figure that out?

Students might say:

"Tape B is 6 kid steps. You need 3 more kid steps to get to 9. So Tape A is 3 kid steps longer than Tape B."

"Tape A is 9 kid steps. Tape B is 6 kid steps. I'll count up from 6: 7, 8, 9. It is 3 kid steps longer."

"Use cubes. Make a tower with 9 and a tower with 6 and compare them."

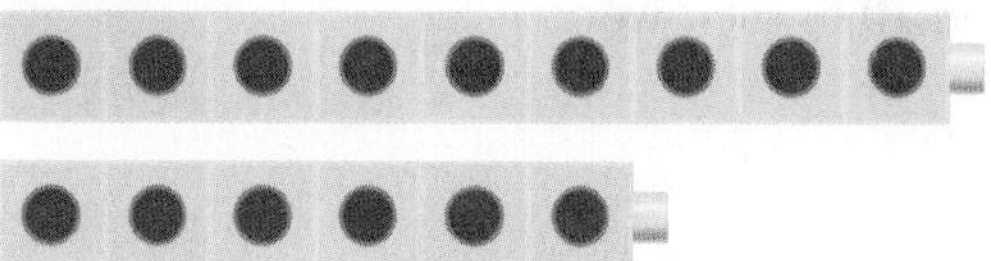

Students figure out how much longer the longer tape is for each of the problems on *Student Activity Book* pages 16–17.

Distribute copies of How Much Longer? (R48).

ELL English Language Learners

Model Thinking Aloud Some students may have difficulty verbalizing their process for finding how much longer Tape A is compared to Tape B. Help these students by modeling your thinking aloud for one method. For example: I know that Tape A is 9 kid steps. Tape B is 6 kid steps. To find out *how much longer* Tape A is, I can use cubes. Line up the two cube trains. Then point to the cube train with 9 cubes. I can see that there are 1, 2, 3 more cubes in this cube train.

Additional Resource

Student Math Handbook pages 104–105

Differentiation in Investigation 1

Mathematics in This Investigation

The mathematics focuses on beginning to develop fluency with combinations of 10. This is developed through many opportunities to work with those combinations through both addition and missing-part problems.

Understanding the Mathematics

Students are fluent with the combinations that make 10—they find combinations of 10 in a set of numbers and know what they need to add to a given number to make 10. They see and use relationships between combinations and rely on what they know about 5 and 10 in their work.

Option: Assign the **Extension** activity.

Partially Understanding the Mathematics

Students are fluent with some of the combinations that make 10, but count all, count on, or use a fact or relationship they know for others.

Option: Assign the **Practice** activity.

Not Understanding the Mathematics

Students are not yet fluent with many of the combinations that make 10. Many need to count all to find the sums or use manipulatives to directly model missing-part problems.

Option: Assign the **Intervention** activity.

Investigation 1 Quiz

In addition to your observations and students' work in Investigation 1, the Quiz (R49) can be used to gather more information.

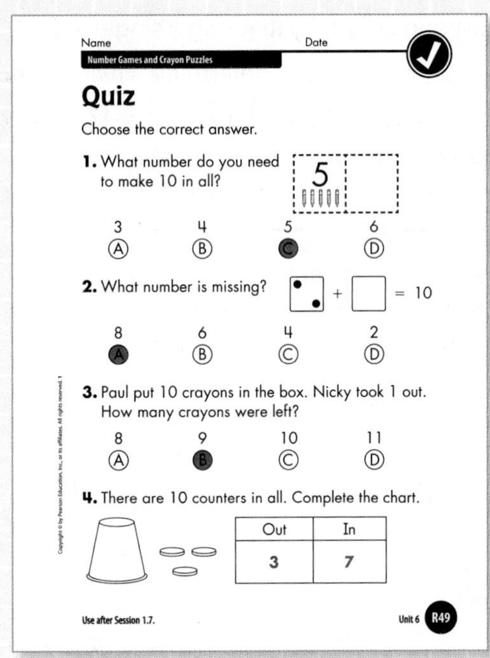

Name Date

Number Games and Crayon Puzzles

Quiz

Choose the correct answer.

1. What number do you need to make 10 in all? 5

3 Ⓐ 4 Ⓑ 5 Ⓒ 6 Ⓓ

2. What number is missing? [dice] + ☐ = 10

8 Ⓐ 6 Ⓑ 4 Ⓒ 2 Ⓓ

3. Paul put 10 crayons in the box. Nicky took 1 out. How many crayons were left?

8 Ⓐ 9 Ⓑ 10 Ⓒ 11 Ⓓ

4. There are 10 counters in all. Complete the chart.

Out	In
3	7

Use after Session 1.7. Unit 6 R49

Intervention

30 MIN PAIRS

Make 10 with Ten-Frame Cards

Use anytime after Session 1.4.

Math Focus Points

- Developing strategies for counting and combining groups of dots
- Developing fluency with the 2-addend combinations of 10
- Using numbers and standard notation (+, −, =) to record

Vocabulary: ten-frame, plus sign, combine

Materials: blank paper, M17 (as needed), M18

Materials to Prepare: Create a deck of Ten-Frame Cards by cutting out and combining 4 copies of Ten-Frame Cards (M18). Make one deck per pair.

Today we are going to play *Make 10* with Ten-Frame Cards. Review the cards with students and then model how to play. Deal 4 rows of 5 cards, with the ten-frames showing. Player 1 finds two cards that make 10.

Hold up one of the cards. I chose [7] for one of my cards. How can I use the ten-frame to help me figure out what number goes with 7 to make 10?

Students might say:

"You can count the number of empty spaces on the [7] card. There are [3], so you need the [3] card."

"The dots on the [3] card would fill up the spaces on the [7] card."

Model each strategy that students suggest.

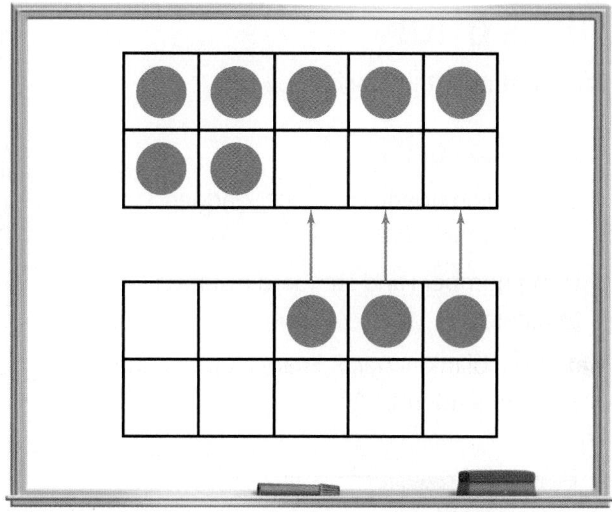

Ask students to help you record the combination on the board using an addition equation. Replace the two cards with new cards from the deck. Next, Player 2 finds two cards that make 10 and records the combination. Model another round if necessary. Players keep taking turns until there are no more cards or there are no more cards that make 10.

Distribute a deck of Ten-Frame Cards and paper to each pair. Have copies of *Make 10* (M17) available.

As pairs play *Make 10* with Ten-Frame Cards, listen to students' strategies and provide support as needed.

ELL English Language Learners

Model Thinking Aloud Model your thinking for how you choose cards for *Make 10*. Show students a card and count each dot. There are 6 dots on this card. Now I have to choose a card that goes with 6 to make 10. I'll count the empty squares. Point to each empty square as you count. There are 4 empty squares, so I need a card with 4 dots to make 10. 6 and 4 make 10.

Additional Resource

Student Math Handbook pages 48–49

Practice

15 MIN INDIVIDUALS

That's a 10!

Use anytime after Session 1.4.

Math Focus Points

- Developing fluency with the 2-addend combinations of 10
- Using numbers and standard notation (+, −, =) to record

Materials: blank paper, Primary Number Cards (1 deck per student), R50

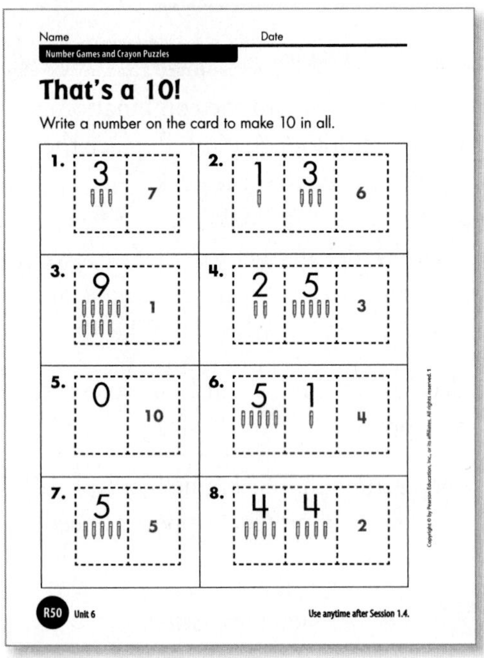

Name Date

Number Games and Crayon Puzzles

That's a 10!

Write a number on the card to make 10 in all.

1. 3 | 7
2. 1 | 3 | 6
3. 9 | 1
4. 2 | 5 | 3
5. 0 | 10
6. 5 | 1 | 4
7. 5 | 5
8. 4 | 4 | 2

R50 Unit 6 Use anytime after Session 1.4.

Today you are going to work on making 10. Distribute a deck of Primary Number Cards and a sheet of paper to each student. I am going to put a card up for you to see. Then you are going to find a card that makes 10 with it.

Using a deck of Primary Number Cards, display a 6. What card do you need to make 10? When you know how many more would make 10, hold up the card. Discuss students' strategies for figuring this out, which might include using the pictures on the bottom of the Primary Number Cards, counting up, just knowing the answer, or using cubes.

Model recording the combination on the board.

$$6 + 4 = 10$$

Let's play again. Display a 0 card. What card do I need to make 10? Give students time to find the card and hold it up. Discuss and record this combination.

Repeat this process with a variety of numbers or have students play in pairs, taking turns turning over a card and figuring out what's needed to make 10. End by looking at the list of combinations on their papers. What do you notice about the combinations?

Students might say:

"There are a lot of ways to make 10."

"For every number, there is just one other number that can be its partner to make 10."

Distribute copies of That's a 10! (R50).

ELL English Language Learners

Provide Sentence Stems Some students may need help verbalizing the combinations. Help them by providing sentence stems such as the following.

I have ______.

I need ______ more to make 10.

______ + ______ = 10

Additional Resource

Student Math Handbook

Game: *Three Towers of 10* SMH G25

Materials: dot cubes, connecting cubes (in 2 colors), crayons (in 2 colors), M4

Extension

15 MIN PAIRS

Make 10 with Wild Cards

Use anytime after Session 1.4.

Math Focus Points

- Developing fluency with the 2-addend combinations of 10
- Using numbers and standard notation (+, −, =) to record

Materials: blank paper, Primary Number Cards (1 deck per pair), M17 (1 per pair), R51

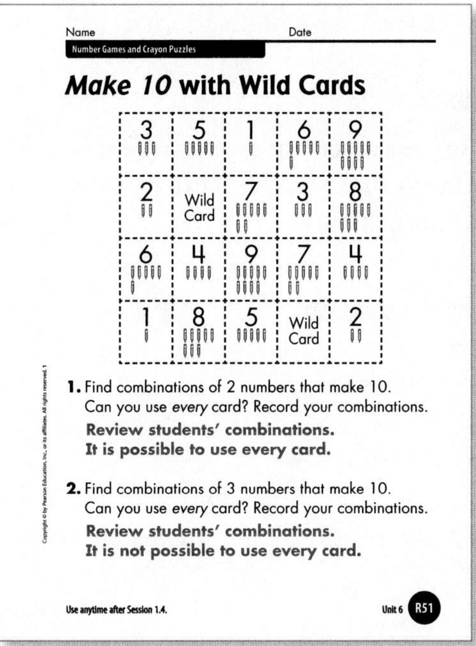

Name Date

Number Games and Crayon Puzzles

Make 10 with Wild Cards

3	5	1	6	9
2	Wild Card	7	3	8
6	4	9	7	4
1	8	5	Wild Card	2

1. Find combinations of 2 numbers that make 10. Can you use *every* card? Record your combinations.
   Review students' combinations.
   It is possible to use every card.

2. Find combinations of 3 numbers that make 10. Can you use *every* card? Record your combinations.
   Review students' combinations.
   It is not possible to use every card.

Use anytime after Session 1.4. Unit 6 R51

Distribute a deck of Primary Number Cards and a copy of *Make 10* (M17) to each pair. Today you are going to play *Make 10* with Wild Cards. Deal 4 rows of 5 cards, making sure one of the cards is a Wild Card. The goal is to find two cards that combine to make 10. What is a Wild Card? When should you use a Wild Card?

Students might say:

"A Wild Card can be any number."

"You can use a Wild Card if the number you need isn't there."

Choose a card that requires the use of a Wild Card to make 10. Is there a card I could put with the [8] to make 10? Discuss students' strategies for figuring this out and remind them that a Wild Card can be any number. Take the number card and the Wild Card and lay them aside. Write the combination on the board. When you use a Wild Card, write the number it stood for.

Replace the cards with two new cards. Continue taking turns with your partner. The game is over when no more combinations of 10 can be made.

Challenge students who seem ready to play with a new rule: do not replace the cards used until there are no more combinations of 10 left in the cards that are showing.

Distribute copies of *Make 10* with Wild Cards (R51).

ELL English Language Learners

Partner Talk As students play the game, encourage them to discuss how they are choosing which number to make the Wild Card. More proficient speakers can explain how the number was chosen while less proficient speakers can point to and name the number chosen. Both should agree that the value of the Wild Card helped them make 10.

Additional Resource

Student Math Handbook

Game: *Three Towers of 10* SMH G25

Materials: dot cubes, connecting cubes (in 2 colors), crayons (in 2 colors), M4

Variation: Have students play with 2 dot cubes.

Differentiation in Investigation 2

Mathematics in This Investigation

The mathematics focuses on composing and decomposing numbers up to 20.

Additional Resource: *Crayon Puzzles*, pages 87–90 (See *Implementing Investigations in Grade 1*)

Understanding the Mathematics

Students find all of the two-addend combinations of a given quantity, and can explain how they know they have found them all. They are flexible in finding two or more addends to make a number, and enjoy the challenge of using cards only once. They are not thrown off by the additional constraints of Crayon Puzzles and, in fact, are eager to solve a wide variety of them.

Option: Assign the **Extension** activity.

Partially Understanding the Mathematics

Students find most or all of the two-addend combinations of a given quantity, using strategies that use one combination to generate others. They may not yet have a way of convincing themselves that they have found them all. They can generate combinations of numbers using 2 or more addends, but may be challenged to do so without reusing any cards. Crayon Puzzles About More, with their additional constraints, are appropriately challenging.

Option: Assign the **Practice** activity.

Not Understanding the Mathematics

Students find many of the two-addend combinations of a given quantity. They are beginning to work more systematically, using one combination to generate another. They may now consider whether a solution is a repeat before recording it, but do not have a system for finding them all. They may find it difficult to find two or more addends to make a set of numbers without reusing some cards. Crayon Puzzles About More, with their additional constraints, are quite difficult.

Option: Assign the **Intervention** activity.

Investigation 2 Quiz

In addition to your observations and students' work in Investigation 2, the Quiz (R52) can be used to gather more information.

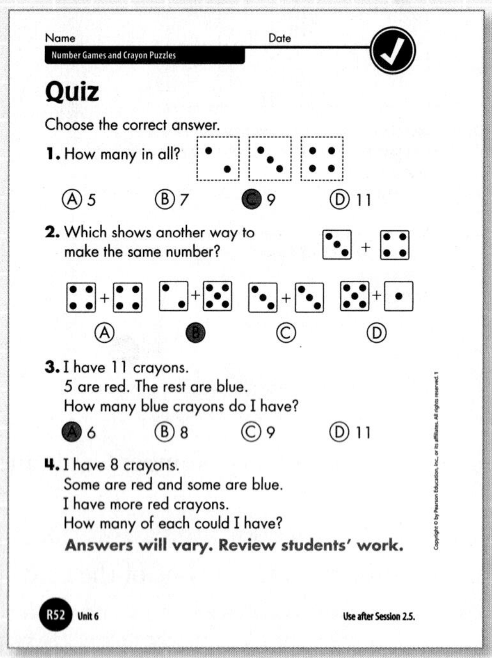

Name Date

Number Games and Crayon Puzzles

Quiz

Choose the correct answer.

1. How many in all?

Ⓐ 5 Ⓑ 7 Ⓒ 9 Ⓓ 11

2. Which shows another way to make the same number?

Ⓐ Ⓑ Ⓒ Ⓓ

3. I have 11 crayons.
5 are red. The rest are blue.
How many blue crayons do I have?

Ⓐ 6 Ⓑ 8 Ⓒ 9 Ⓓ 11

4. I have 8 crayons.
Some are red and some are blue.
I have more red crayons.
How many of each could I have?

Answers will vary. Review students' work.

R52 Unit 6 Use after Session 2.5.

Intervention

20 MIN PAIRS

Dot Addition with Smaller Numbers

Use anytime after Session 2.3.

Math Focus Points

- Adding 2 or more single-digit numbers
- Using numbers and standard notation (+, −, =) to record

Vocabulary: addition

Materials: connecting cubes (as needed), *Dot Addition* Cards (1 deck per pair), M30

Materials to Prepare: Use a copy of the *Dot Addition* Blank Gameboard (M30) to make a *Dot Addition* gameboard with 6, 7, 8, and 10. Make 3 copies for each pair.

Remind students of how to play *Dot Addition* by modeling the steps. Deal out 4 rows of 5 cards, with dots showing, next to the *Dot Addition* Gameboard you made. You will want to use *Dot Addition* Cards to make a combination for each number on the gameboard. What cards can I use to make a combination of 7?

Students might say:

"You can use a 5 and a 2."

"Use three cards: 2, 2, and 3."

Record student suggestions on the board.

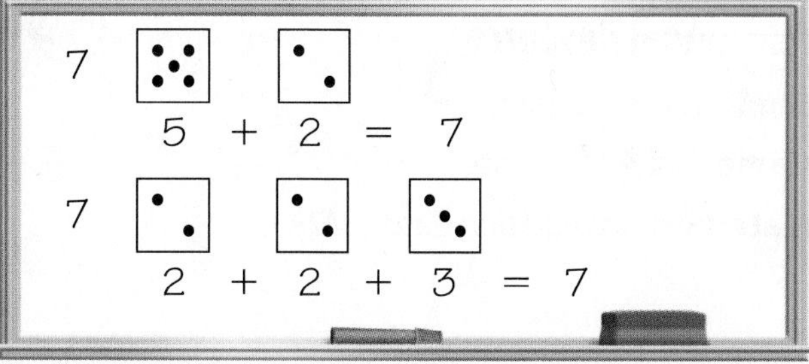

Tell students that even though more than one combination works, they'll have to agree on one to place on their gameboard.

Remind students that this time they are trying to fill their gameboard without reusing any cards. So they should try to make each number before recording it on their own copy of the gameboard.

Distribute a deck of *Dot Addition* Cards and 3 gameboards to each pair. Now you are going to play *Dot Addition* with your partner.

Circulate as pairs play *Dot Addition* with Smaller Numbers. If students have difficulty finding a combination, suggest cards to start with. You are trying to make 7. Suppose you start with 3 and 2. How many does that get you? How many more do you need to make 7? Students may need to use cubes to figure out how many more they need.

ELL English Language Learners

Provide Sentence Stems To help pairs communicate while they play *Dot Addition*, provide sentence stems, such as the following. The number I need to make is ______. I can use ______ cards. The cards I used are ______.

Additional Resource

Student Math Handbook pages 33–35

Practice

Dot and Number Totals

Use anytime after Session 2.3.

Math Focus Points

- Solving a problem in which the total and one part are known.
- Using numbers and standard notation (+, −, =) to record

Vocabulary: addition

Materials: dot cubes, number cubes, blank paper, R53

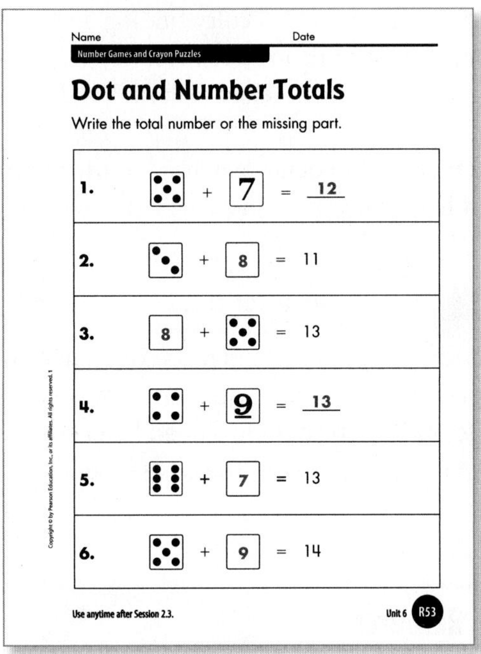

Name Date

Number Games and Crayon Puzzles

Dot and Number Totals

Write the total number or the missing part.

1.	[5 dots]	+	7	=	12
2.	[3 dots]	+	8	=	11
3.	8	+	[5 dots]	=	13
4.	[4 dots]	+	9	=	13
5.	[6 dots]	+	7	=	13
6.	[5 dots]	+	9	=	14

Use anytime after Session 2.3. Unit 6 R53

I am going to give you a number that will be your total number: 8. First you will roll the dot cube. Then you will figure out what number you would need to roll on the number cube to make 8.

Model the steps, recording the problem students are to solve on the board. Our total number is 8. Roll a dot cube. I rolled a [3]. Now we need to figure out what I need to roll on the number cube to make 8.

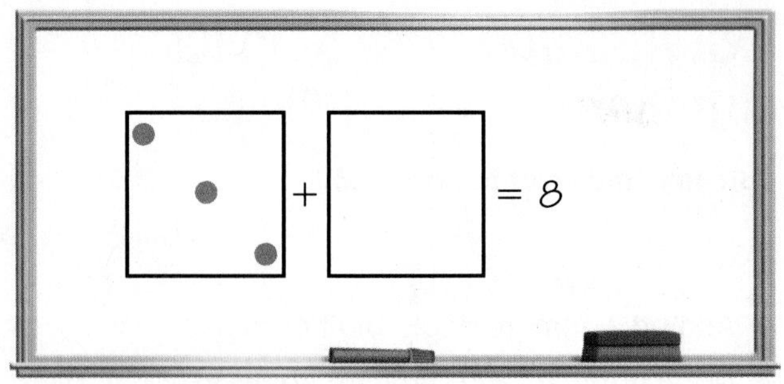

Students might say:

"You would need a [5] because [3] + [5] = 8."

"Start at [3], and count up to 8. You need [5]."

How should I record our answer? Model filling in the missing number on the board. Beneath it, write an addition equation.

Students play several rounds with the given total and record their results on their papers. Introduce a new total or two as time permits.

Distribute copies of Dot and Number Totals (R53).

ELL English Language Learners

Suggest a Sequence If students have difficulty, suggest a sequence of steps for them to follow.

1. Roll the dot cube.
2. Figure out how many more you need to make the total.
3. Record an addition equation.

Additional Resource

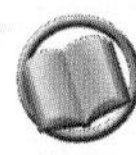

Student Math Handbook

Game: *Dot Addition* SMH G5

Materials: *Dot Addition* Cards, M28

Extension

15 MIN GROUPS

Crayon Puzzles About Fewer

Use anytime after Session 2.4.

Math Focus Points

- Reasoning about more, less, and equal amounts
- Finding a solution that fits several clues
- Adding 2 or more single-digit numbers

Vocabulary: fewer

Materials: blank paper, red and blue connecting cubes (as needed), R54

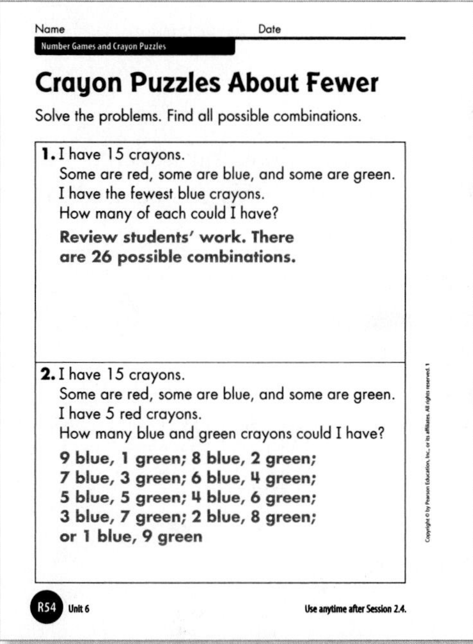

Name Date

Number Games and Crayon Puzzles

Crayon Puzzles About Fewer

Solve the problems. Find all possible combinations.

1. I have 15 crayons.
Some are red, some are blue, and some are green.
I have the fewest blue crayons.
How many of each could I have?
Review students' work. There are 26 possible combinations.

2. I have 15 crayons.
Some are red, some are blue, and some are green.
I have 5 red crayons.
How many blue and green crayons could I have?
9 blue, 1 green; 8 blue, 2 green; 7 blue, 3 green; 6 blue, 4 green; 5 blue, 5 green; 4 blue, 6 green; 3 blue, 7 green; 2 blue, 8 green; or 1 blue, 9 green

R54 Unit 6 Use anytime after Session 2.4.

Today you are going to solve another crayon puzzle. Read the following problem aloud. I have 15 red and blue crayons. There are *fewer* red crayons than blue crayons. How many of each could I have? Ask students to describe the puzzle in their own words.

We need combinations of 15 crayons with fewer red crayons than blue crayons. Students find a solution, using red and blue cubes if needed. What is one combination that works?

Students might say:

"We think 7 red crayons and 8 blue crayons works because there are 15 and there's less red."

Record all of your group's answers on one paper. See if, together, you can find all of the possible answers. Collect students' combinations.

red	blue
4	11
1	14
3	12
7	8
2	13
5	10
6	9

Do you think we have all the possible answers? I noticed there isn't a combination with 8 red crayons? Why is that?

Students might say:

"If you had 8 red there would be 7 blue and there would be more red, not fewer."

Distribute copies of Crayon Puzzles About Fewer (R54).

ELL English Language Learners

Model Thinking Aloud Help students understand the meaning of *fewer* by modeling your thinking aloud. I know that I need to have *fewer* red crayons. That means the number of red crayons has to be *smaller* than the number of blue crayons. Hold up a tower of 6 red cubes next to a tower of 11 blue cubes. There are *fewer* red cubes than blue cubes so this combination works.

Additional Resource

Student Math Handbook pages 46–47

Differentiation in Investigation 3

Mathematics in This Investigation

The mathematics focuses on developing an understanding of the operations of addition and subtraction, and on developing accurate strategies to solve addition and subtraction problems.

Understanding the Mathematics

Students efficiently add and subtract single-digit numbers. To add, they count on, or reason about a sum they know. To subtract, they count back from one number, add up, use known number combinations, or use something they know to solve a problem they don't know. They can solve a problem in more than one way, explain their strategy, and use notation to represent it on paper.

Option: Assign the **Extension** activity.

Partially Understanding the Mathematics

Students count on to solve addition problems, but inconsistently. They may make occasional mistakes that result in the wrong answer, or occasionally fall back on counting all. Many students count all to subtract single-digit numbers. They can record their work, though using the counting on or counting back strategy may still present a challenge. They can use addition and subtraction notation, though not always with accuracy.

Option: Assign the **Practice** activity.

Not Understanding the Mathematics

Students accurately add two numbers by counting all but are not yet counting on with understanding. They may stumble over where to start counting, where to stop, and how to find the answer once they have counted. Students use manipulatives or drawings to count all to subtract single-digit numbers. Their ability to represent their work is improving, but they may still record a strategy that is easy to show on paper, rather than the one actually used.

Option: Assign the **Intervention** activity.

Investigation 3 Quiz

In addition to your observations and students' work in Investigation 3, the Quiz (R55) can be used to gather more information.

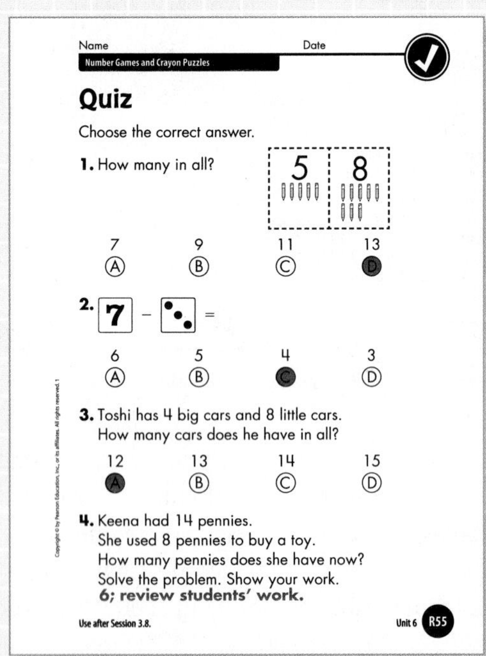

Name Date

Number Games and Crayon Puzzles

Quiz

Choose the correct answer.

1. How many in all?

5 | 8

7 (A) 9 (B) 11 (C) 13 (D)

2. 7 − [die showing 3] =

6 (A) 5 (B) 4 (C) 3 (D)

3. Toshi has 4 big cars and 8 little cars.
How many cars does he have in all?

12 (A) 13 (B) 14 (C) 15 (D)

4. Keena had 14 pennies.
She used 8 pennies to buy a toy.
How many pennies does she have now?
Solve the problem. Show your work.
6; review students' work.

Use after Session 3.8.

Unit 6 R55

Intervention

Story Problems

Use anytime after Session 3.4.

Math Focus Points

- Developing strategies for solving addition and subtraction story problems
- Developing strategies for recording solutions to story problems
- Using numbers and standard notation (+, −, =) to record

Materials: counters

Today we are going to solve story problems. Listen as I tell you this story.

Richard had 8 crayons. He gave 3 to Libby. How many crayons does Richard have now?

Encourage partners to retell the story to each other. How does the story start? What happens next? Ask a few students to describe in their own words what happens in the story. Does Richard have more or less at the end of the story than at the beginning?

Hand out counters to each pair. How could we solve this problem about Richard's crayons? Take students suggestions. Let's try using counters to model the problem. How many counters should I take?

Students might say:

"8 because Richard had 8 crayons."

Then what? What happened next in the story? Ask students to help you model the rest of the story—giving 3 away and counting how many are left.

Now, how could we record what we did? Students will likely suggest drawing a picture. Model one way to do this and encourage students to also help you write an equation.

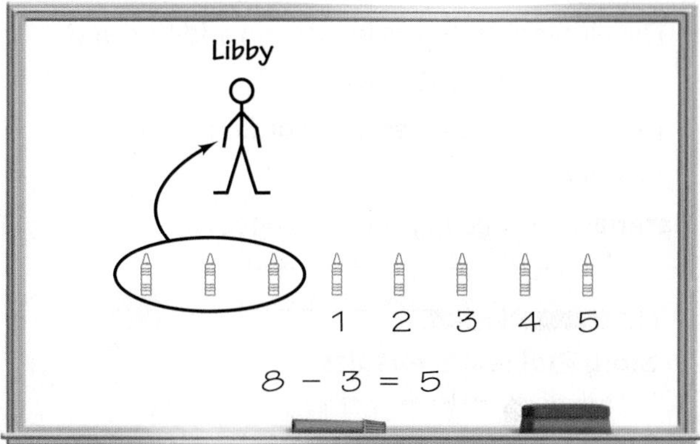

If time remains, present another story. This time, encourage students to try and solve it on their own and record their work.

ELL English Language Learners

Suggest a Sequence Suggest the following steps for solving problems. *First,* tell what happens in the story. *Then,* think about whether there are more or less at the end of the story. *Finally,* solve the problem and show your work.

Additional Resource

Student Math Handbook pages 33–37

Practice

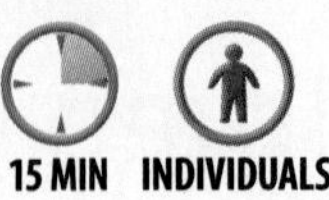

Story Problem Strategies

Use anytime after Session 3.5.

Math Focus Points

- Developing strategies for solving addition and subtraction story problems
- Developing strategies for recording solutions to story problems

Materials: connecting cubes (as needed), R56

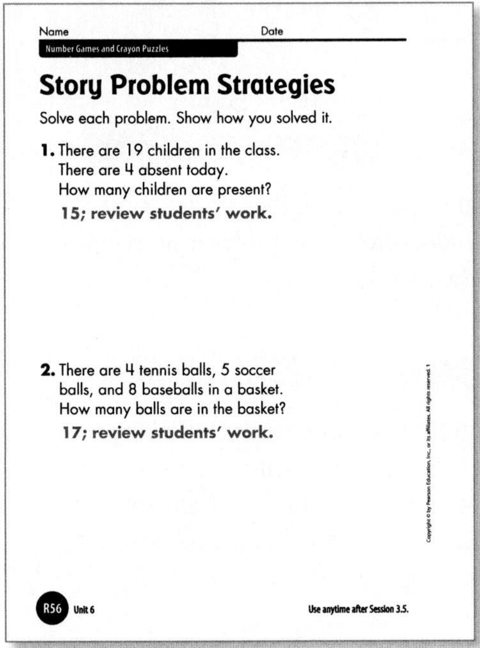

Name Date

Number Games and Crayon Puzzles

Story Problem Strategies

Solve each problem. Show how you solved it.

1. There are 19 children in the class.
   There are 4 absent today.
   How many children are present?
   15; review students' work.

2. There are 4 tennis balls, 5 soccer balls, and 8 baseballs in a basket.
   How many balls are in the basket?
   17; review students' work.

R56 Unit 6 Use anytime after Session 3.5.

Read this problem aloud: There were 17 children on the playground. 9 children went inside. How many children were still on the playground?

Give students time to work and then ask them to describe their strategies. How did you solve the problem? Many will count all. Acknowledge all of the strategies used, but focus on counting back, a strategy students may be ready to consider, particularly with support.

Students might say:

"I started at 17 and counted back 9."

Ask a volunteer to model how he or she counted back, focusing on how he or she knew where to start and stop counting and what his or her answer was.

Use a number line to talk through counting back. I'm going to use a number line to show [Stacy's] strategy. What number should it go to? How many children were there on the playground at the beginning? Then [Stacy] said she counted back, so I'm going to draw an arrow that shows 1 child leaving the playground. How many were there then? So after 1 child left, there were 16 children. Continue in this manner, connecting each jump to another child leaving the playground.

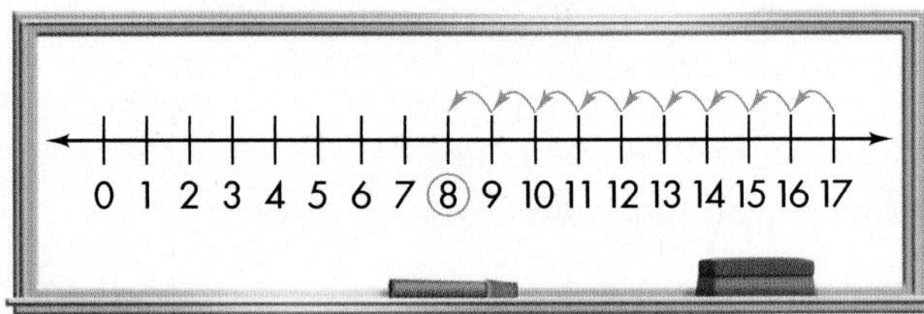

So what did we find out? After 9 children went inside, how many children were still on the playground?

Distribute copies of Story Problem Strategies (R56).

ELL English Language Learners

Provide Sentence Stems If students have difficulty verbalizing how they used the counting back strategy, provide sentence stems. For example: I started at ______. I counted back ______. I ended at ______. There are ______ children left.

Additional Resource

Student Math Handbook

Game: *Five-in-a-Row with Three Cards* SMH G11

Materials: Primary Number Cards (without Wild Cards), counters, M42

Extension

15 MIN PAIRS

Strategies for Solving Problems

Use anytime after Session 3.6.

Math Focus Points

- Developing strategies for solving addition and subtraction story problems
- Using numbers and standard notation (+, −, =) to record
- Developing strategies for recording solutions to story problems

Materials: R57

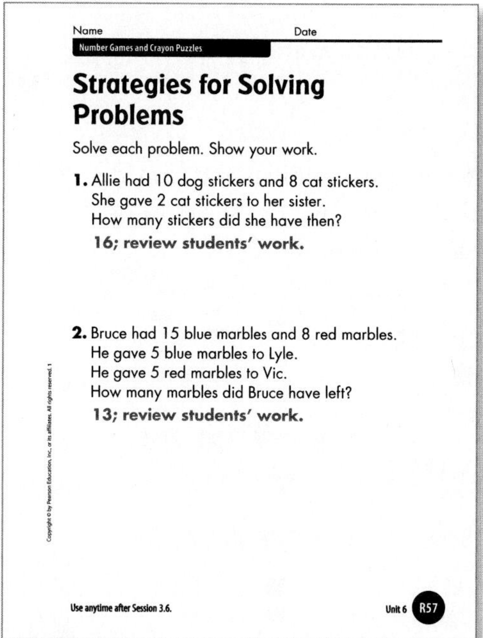
Name Date
Number Games and Crayon Puzzles

Strategies for Solving Problems

Solve each problem. Show your work.

1. Allie had 10 dog stickers and 8 cat stickers. She gave 2 cat stickers to her sister. How many stickers did she have then?
16; review students' work.

2. Bruce had 15 blue marbles and 8 red marbles. He gave 5 blue marbles to Lyle. He gave 5 red marbles to Vic. How many marbles did Bruce have left?
13; review students' work.

Use anytime after Session 3.6. Unit 6 R57

There are many strategies that can be used to solve story problems. I am going to read a story problem to you. Listen carefully and picture the story in your mind.

There are 17 bluebirds and 6 cardinals in the yard. Then 8 bluebirds flew away. How many birds are left in the yard? Allow pairs time to work on the problem. What strategies did you use to find the answer?

Students might say:

"We drew 17 blue squares and 6 red squares. Then we crossed off 8 blue squares. We counted the squares that were left."

"We did 17 + 6 to find out how many birds there were altogether. Then we subtracted 8 for the ones that flew away."

"We did 17 − 8 to figure out how many bluebirds there were. Then we added the cardinals and got 15."

Discuss students' strategies for solving the problem and for recording their work.

Distribute copies of Strategies for Solving Problems (R57).

ELL English Language Learners

Rephrase Some students may be unfamiliar with the bird names. To avoid confusion, retell the story using colors instead of bird names. There are 17 blue birds and 6 red birds in the yard. 8 of the blue birds flew away. How many birds are in the yard?

Additional Resource

Student Math Handbook pages 33–42

Differentiation in Investigation 1

Mathematics in This Investigation

The mathematics focuses on constructing, describing, extending, and identifying the unit of repeating patterns.

Understanding the Mathematics

Students make, describe, and extend repeating patterns, break patterns into units, and build them from units, even with fairly complicated units. To figure out future elements in a pattern, they may begin from the last known element, count by the number in the unit, or reason about that number. They recognize similarities in the structure of a pattern when comparing, for example, two ABC patterns composed of different elements (e.g., different colors).

Option: Assign the **Extension** activity.

Partially Understanding the Mathematics

Students make, describe, and extend repeating patterns, break patterns into units, and build them from units. To figure out future elements in a pattern, they begin from the first element in the pattern, or from the last known element and build from there. In all of this work, students may be quite comfortable with simple patterns, but less so with more complicated units. They may identify differences when comparing, for example, two ABC patterns constructed with different elements (e.g., colors) more clearly than the ways in which the two patterns are similar in structure.

Option: Assign the **Practice** activity.

Not Understanding the Mathematics

Students make and describe repeating patterns, and can generally figure out what comes next in a repeating pattern. What comes farther along in the pattern may be more challenging, particularly for patterns with units other than AB. Students generally read the pattern, beginning with the first element of the pattern, to figure this out. Similarly, breaking patterns into units, and building a pattern from given units, may be difficult for non-AB patterns. These students do not readily identify similarities or differences beyond color, in two differently colored ABC patterns.

Option: Assign the **Intervention** activity.

Investigation 1 Quiz

In addition to your observations and students' work in Investigation 1, the Quiz (R58) can be used to gather more information.

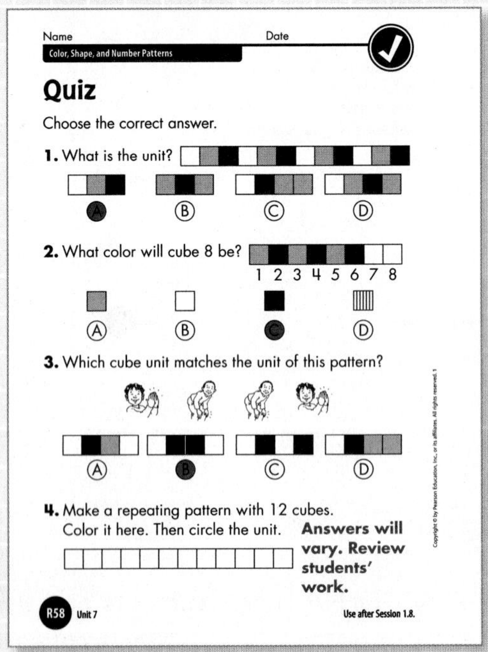

Name Date

Color, Shape, and Number Patterns

Quiz

Choose the correct answer.

1. What is the unit?

Ⓐ Ⓑ Ⓒ Ⓓ

2. What color will cube 8 be?

1 2 3 4 5 6 7 8

Ⓐ Ⓑ Ⓒ Ⓓ

3. Which cube unit matches the unit of this pattern?

Ⓐ Ⓑ Ⓒ Ⓓ

4. Make a repeating pattern with 12 cubes. Color it here. Then circle the unit. **Answers will vary. Review students' work.**

R58 Unit 7 Use after Session 1.8.

Intervention

Break a Train Match

Use anytime after Session 1.4.

Math Focus Points

- Describing a repeating pattern as a sequence built from a part that repeats over and over called the *unit*
- Identifying the unit of a repeating pattern

Vocabulary: repeating pattern, unit

Materials: connecting cubes, M6 (1 per student plus extras), colored pencils or crayons

Materials to Prepare: Using 5 red and 5 yellow connecting cubes, make a cube train with an AB pattern for each student.

Today we are going to work with more repeating patterns. Show students the red-yellow train and together "read" the pattern. What is the part that repeats? How do you know?

Students might say:

"The red and yellow repeat."

"The pattern starts over at the second red cube. So, the part that repeats is red-yellow."

Using one of the red-yellow cube trains, demonstrate for students how to record the cube train pattern and its unit using Break a Train (M6). The part that repeats is called the *unit.* Color only the first 2 squares of the unit on M6.

Distribute a cube train and a copy of M6 to each student. Students record the pattern and the unit. Remind students that they should only color 2 squares, red-yellow, since that is the unit that repeats in this pattern.

Now I want you to break your train into units. Demonstrate how to break apart a cube train into 5 units.

You can think of each unit as a train car. How many cars or units do you have? Mix them up and then try to put the train back together to match the pattern you colored on your sheet.

Monitor students as they break their trains into units. If students struggle to break the trains into units, have them describe the unit to you. If they can describe it, but cannot determine where to break the train, have them circle the units on their recording sheet and use this as a guide.

If students have difficulty reassembling their trains, have them match their trains to the pattern they colored. Have them put together 2 units and then try to add on to this without the aid of their paper.

Repeat the activity with an ABC pattern.

ELL English Language Learners

Provide Sentence Stems If students have difficulty verbalizing what the unit is or how to find it, provide the following sentence stems.

The pattern goes ______.

The part that repeats is ______.

The unit is ______.

Additional Resource

Student Math Handbook pages 54–57

Practice

20 MIN PAIRS

Matching Color Patterns

Use anytime after Session 1.4.

Math Focus Points

- Describing a repeating pattern as a sequence built from a part that repeats over and over called the *unit*
- Identifying the unit of a repeating pattern

Vocabulary: unit

Materials: connecting cubes (7 red, 7 yellow, and 7 blue per pair), R59

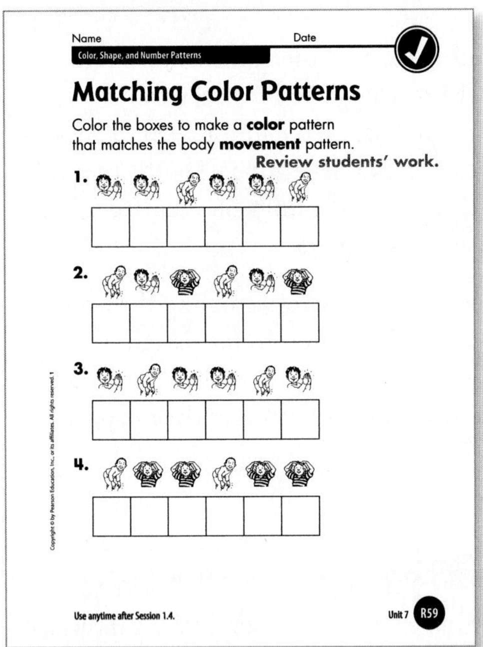

Name Date

Color, Shape, and Number Patterns

Matching Color Patterns

Color the boxes to make a **color** pattern that matches the body **movement** pattern.

Review students' work.

1.

2.

3.

4.

Use anytime after Session 1.4. Unit 7 R59

Today you will work with a partner to make 2 repeating patterns. First, you will work together to create a body-movement pattern. Then, you will use cubes to make a color pattern that matches the body-movement pattern.

Demonstrate for the group. Tap your head, shoulders, and toes. Repeat several times so students can see the pattern. Ask them to join in when they figure out the pattern. Have students say the pattern aloud as they do it. Record the pattern on the board. What was my unit? What part of this pattern is repeating? Circle Head-Shoulders-Toes on the board.

Build a red-yellow-blue train with cubes. It should be 12 cubes long. Show it to the students. This cube train represents my pattern. What color matches with touching your head? What matches with shoulders? What matches with toes?

Have students "read" the body pattern as you point to each cube. Label each body movement with a color, showing how the patterns match.

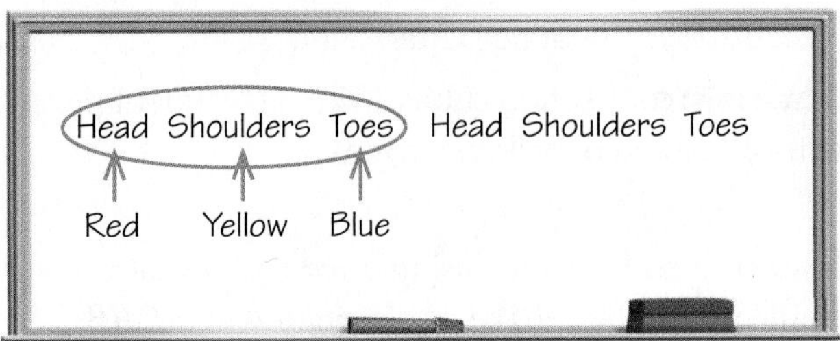

Explain to students that they will work with a partner to make up a pattern with body movements and then build a cube pattern to correspond to this pattern. Students should begin with an AB pattern and then make an ABB pattern.

Distribute copies of Matching Color Patterns (R59).

ELL English Language Learners

Model Thinking Aloud Use the correct colored cubes to model how you would find the color that matches each movement. Since *head* is first and *red* is first, they match up. *Yellow* and *shoulders* are next, so they match up. *Blue* and *toes* are last, so they match up. Have students verbalize their thinking as they match movements and colors.

Additional Resource

Student Math Handbook pages 53–57

Extension

Longer Patterns

Use anytime after Session 1.5.

Math Focus Points

- Identifying the unit of a repeating pattern
- Extending a repeating pattern by adding on units to the pattern

Materials: connecting cubes, R60

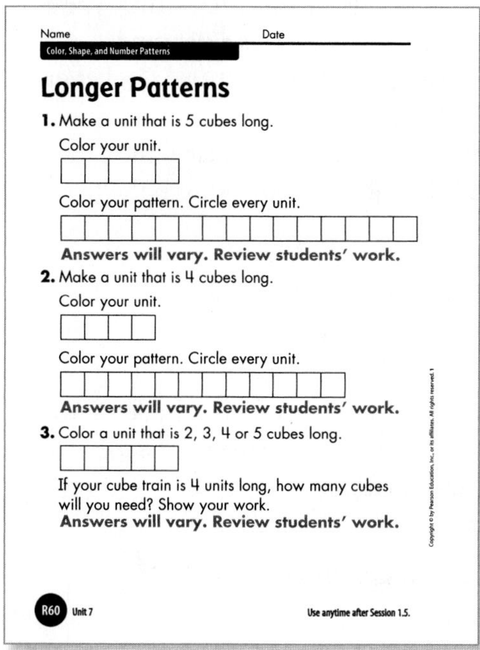
Name Date

Color, Shape, and Number Patterns

Longer Patterns

1. Make a unit that is 5 cubes long.
   Color your unit.
   Color your pattern. Circle every unit.
   Answers will vary. Review students' work.
2. Make a unit that is 4 cubes long.
   Color your unit.
   Color your pattern. Circle every unit.
   Answers will vary. Review students' work.
3. Color a unit that is 2, 3, 4 or 5 cubes long.
   If your cube train is 4 units long, how many cubes will you need? Show your work.
   Answers will vary. Review students' work.

R60 Unit 7 Use anytime after Session 1.5.

Materials to Prepare: Make a cube train that is 12 cubes long showing an ABCDB (red-blue-yellow-green-blue) repeating pattern.

Today you are going to work with repeating patterns with longer units. Hold up your train for the students to see. What is my pattern? What is the part of this train that repeats?

Students might say:

"The red-blue-yellow-green-blue repeats, but only one time."

"The first 5 cubes repeat."

Break the train into units. Show students how the last part of the train is only part of a unit.

Which colors would finish this unit? Complete the unit by adding the yellow-green-blue portion. Show students how to extend the pattern to show 3–4 repetitions. Help students realize that by making a longer train, they make the repeating pattern easier to see.

First you will build a unit using more than 4 cubes. Then build a train that shows the unit repeating 3–4 times. Explain to students that they will trade trains with a partner, break the train into units, mix up the units, and then put the train back together to match the original train.

Distribute copies of Longer Patterns (R60).

ELL English Language Learners

Partner Talk Have pairs discuss the following questions. How many times does your unit repeat? How do you know? Beginning English Language Learners may only be able to point out each repeating unit while more proficient speakers may be encouraged to use complete sentences to explain their thinking. Encourage students to use the words *unit*, *pattern*, and *repeat*.

Additional Resource

Student Math Handbook

Game: *Make a Train* SMH G16–G17

Materials: color cubes, connecting cubes, bag, blank paper, M13–M14

Variation: Replace 2 or 3 of the cards in Set A with cards from Set B.

Differentiation in Investigation 2

Mathematics in This Investigation

The mathematics focuses on constructing, describing, and extending number sequences generated by various contexts that have a constant rate of increase.

Additional Resource: *Seeing Connections: A First Grader Compares Representations of Number Sequences,* pages 95–97 (See *Implementing Investigations in Grade 1*)

Understanding the Mathematics

Students generate number sequences without having to model the given context. These students are familiar with the counting sequences and are comfortable counting by 2s or 3s from 1, 2, or 3. They recognize the same number patterns in different contexts (e.g., Penny Jar, Staircases, and Shape Patterns) and can see that some patterns result in the same number pattern. They figure out the number or shape associated with future outcomes by counting by groups or reasoning about the part of the pattern that has already been identified.

Option: Assign the **Extension** activity.

Partially Understanding the Mathematics

Students generate number sequences, often by modeling the given context and counting how many there are after each round. These students may be comfortable counting by 2s, but are less so if the count starts from 1, or with other sequences. They may recognize number patterns as they repeat in different contexts, but may not have ideas about why that might be so. They may figure out the number or shape associated with future outcomes by extending the pattern, and counting on by 1s from the part of the pattern that has already been identified.

Option: Assign the **Practice** activity.

Not Understanding the Mathematics

Students generate number sequences by modeling the given context and counting how many there are after each round, but have trouble keeping track of the growing group and what they represent. These students may be familiar with the counting by 2s sequence, but have trouble using it to count a set of objects. Counting by 2s from a number other than 0, or by 3s from any number, is quite challenging. They likely don't recognize number patterns that repeat in different contexts, seeing each as a new and unfamiliar situation. To figure out the number or shape associated with future outcomes, these students must work to extend and label the pattern, and then read the pattern, perhaps from the first element.

Option: Assign the **Intervention** activity.

Investigation 2 Quiz

In addition to your observations and students' work in Investigation 2, the Quiz (R61) can be used to gather more information.

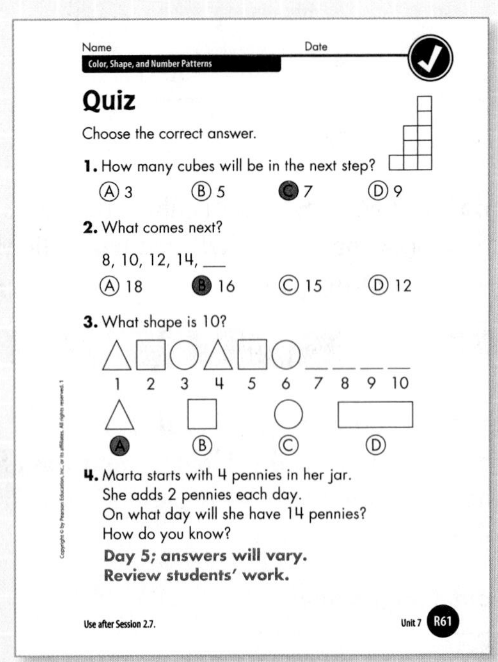

Name Date

Color, Shape, and Number Patterns

Quiz

Choose the correct answer.

1. How many cubes will be in the next step?
Ⓐ 3 Ⓑ 5 ● 7 Ⓓ 9

2. What comes next?
8, 10, 12, 14, ___
Ⓐ 18 ● 16 Ⓒ 15 Ⓓ 12

3. What shape is 10?
1 2 3 4 5 6 7 8 9 10
● Ⓑ Ⓒ Ⓓ

4. Marta starts with 4 pennies in her jar.
She adds 2 pennies each day.
On what day will she have 14 pennies?
How do you know?
Day 5; answers will vary.
Review students' work.

Use after Session 2.7. Unit 7 R61

Intervention

More Penny Jars

Use anytime after Session 2.3.

Math Focus Points

- Describing how a number sequence represents a situation with a constant rate of change
- Extending a number sequence associated with a situation with a constant rate of change

Materials: clear plastic jar, pennies, M18

Draw the following image on the board.

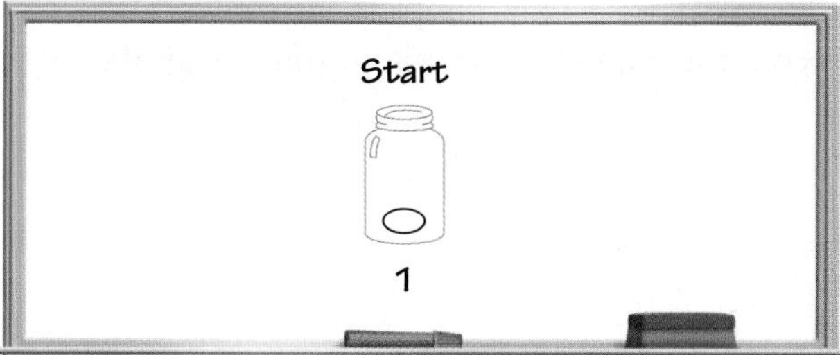

Distribute Penny Jar Problems (M18) to each student. Today we are going to look at patterns where something increases. We will use numbers to describe what happens. Place 1 penny in the jar. We are going to start with 1 penny in our jar. Students record 1 as their start number.

What would happen if we added 2 pennies to the jar each day?

Students might say:

"You count up 2 to see how many pennies there are the next day."

Add 2 pennies to the jar. Today is Day 1. How many pennies are in the jar now? How do you know? Record this information on the board and have students record it on M18.

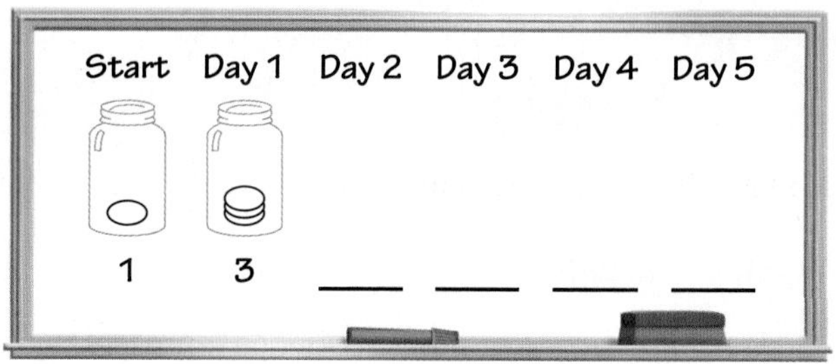

Each day we add 2 more pennies. Now it's Day 2. Put 2 more pennies in the jar. How many pennies are in the jar now? How do you know? Add 2 pennies for Days 3 and 4, asking students to say how many there are after each addition. Rather than drawing jars, record only the day and amount. Students record the sequence on M18. Can you predict how many pennies we will have on Day 5? How do you know?

Confirm that there are 11 pennies by counting them. Can you predict how many pennies will be in the jar on Day 7? Talk with a partner about what you think. Continue adding pennies up to Day 10. Confirm the total number of pennies and examine the number sequence.

Repeat the process, starting with 3 pennies in the jar and adding 2 each day and, if students are comfortable, starting with 3 pennies and adding 3 pennies each day.

ELL English Language Learners

Model Thinking Aloud Model ways to count and keep track of the pennies. We're starting with 3 pennies in the jar: 1, 2, 3. Now it's Day 1 and we're adding 2 pennies each day. I will count on from 3: 4, 5. There are 5 pennies in the jar. Continue adding pennies and modeling ways to find the total as needed.

Additional Resource

Student Math Handbook page 62

Practice

30 MIN PAIRS

Penny Jars with Different Start Numbers

Use anytime after Session 2.3.

Math Focus Points

- Describing how a number sequence represents a situation with a constant rate of change
- Extending a number sequence associated with a situation with a constant rate of change

Materials: cups (1 per pair), pennies (50 per pair), M18 (2 per pair), R62

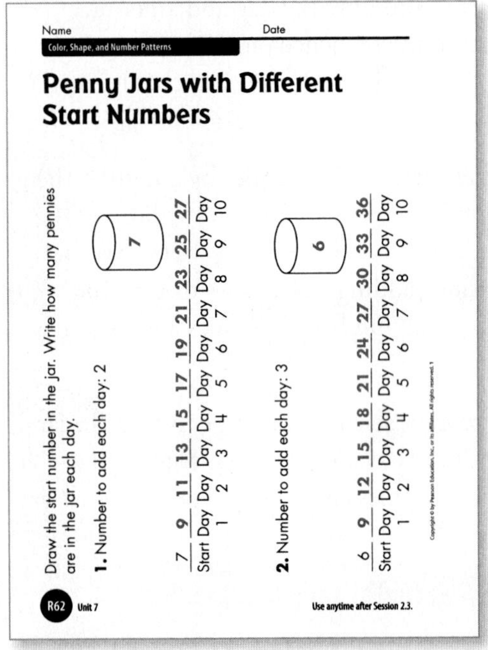
Name Date

Color, Shape, and Number Patterns

Penny Jars with Different Start Numbers

Draw the start number in the jar. Write how many pennies are in the jar each day.

1. Number to add each day: 2

Start	Day 1	Day 2	Day 3	Day 4	Day 5	Day 6	Day 7	Day 8	Day 9	Day 10
7	9	11	13	15	17	19	21	23	25	27

2. Number to add each day: 3

Start	Day 1	Day 2	Day 3	Day 4	Day 5	Day 6	Day 7	Day 8	Day 9	Day 10
6	9	12	15	18	21	24	27	30	33	36

R62 Unit 7 Use anytime after Session 2.3.

Distribute cups, pennies, and copies of Penny Jar Problems (M18) to each pair. Today you will work with a partner to create your own Penny Jar Problems. One of you needs to choose a start number of less than 10. Then, with your partner, decide how many pennies you will add each day.

Students record their numbers on their recording sheets. Demonstrate how they will use their cups to make their own penny jars. Choose a start number and put that number of pennies in the cup. My start number is 4. I will put 3 pennies in the jar each day. How many will be in the jar on Day 1? How do you know?

Students might say:

"Since you started at 4 and added 3, I know that there will be 7 on Day 1."

Observe pairs as they complete the activity and record the number of pennies through Day 10.

Now the other partner should choose a starting number. This time, add a different number each day. Work together to find the number of pennies through Day 10.

When students are finished, choose one or two pairs to share their number sequence with the class.

Distribute copies of Penny Jars with Different Start Numbers (R62).

ELL English Language Learners

Model Thinking Aloud Model your thinking using pennies and the jar to show how you would find the number of pennies for each day. We start with 8 pennies and add 2 each day. So, on Day 1 there are 8 pennies and 2 more: 9, 10. There are 10 pennies. 2 more for Day 2 makes 11, 12 pennies. Encourage students to verbalize their thinking as they find the number of pennies in the jar each day.

Additional Resource

Student Math Handbook pages 61–63

Extension

15 MIN

PAIRS

The Penny Jar with Larger Numbers

Use anytime after Session 2.3.

Math Focus Points

- Describing how a number sequence represents a situation with a constant rate of change
- Extending a number sequence associated with a situation with a constant rate of change

Materials: clear plastic jar, pennies, blank paper, M18, R63

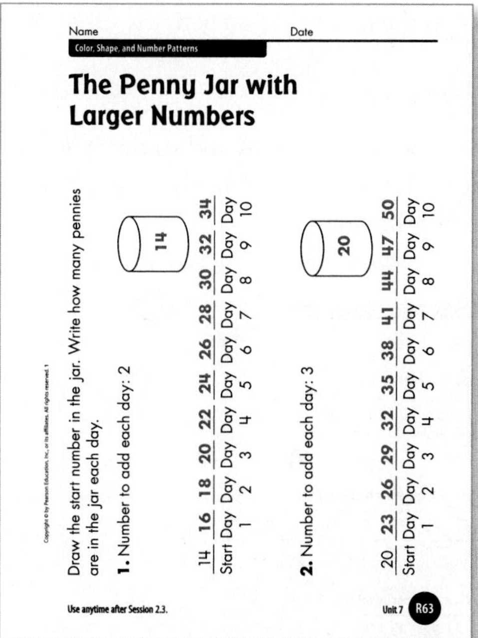
Name Date

Color, Shape, and Number Patterns

The Penny Jar with Larger Numbers

Draw the start number in the jar. Write how many pennies are in the jar each day.

1. Number to add each day: 2

Start	Day 1	Day 2	Day 3	Day 4	Day 5	Day 6	Day 7	Day 8	Day 9	Day 10
14	16	18	20	22	24	26	28	30	32	34

2. Number to add each day: 3

Start	Day 1	Day 2	Day 3	Day 4	Day 5	Day 6	Day 7	Day 8	Day 9	Day 10
20	23	26	29	32	35	38	41	44	47	50

Use anytime after Session 2.3. Unit 7 R63

Distribute a copy of Penny Jar Problems (M18) to each student. Today we are going to work with the penny jar. Have students count as you put 12 pennies in the jar. What is our starting number? We are going to add 3 each day. Have students write the numbers on their recording sheets.

Add 3 pennies to the jar. How many pennies are in the jar now? How do you know? Have students record the number above Day 1. Now it's Day 2. Put 3 more pennies in the jar. How many are in the jar now? How do you know? Continue adding 3 pennies, asking students how many there are after each addition until you have finished Day 10.

How many pennies would there be on Day 11?

Students might say:

"There would be 45 pennies, because it is 3 more than 42."

"I count 43, 44, 45. There would be 45 pennies."

Have students work with their partners to extend their patterns to Day 15, starting with Day 11, on a separate sheet of paper.

Day 11	Day 12	Day 13	Day 14	Day 15
45	48	51	54	57

How does this pattern remind you of other penny jars? Help students recognize that some of the numbers are the same as in other penny jar problems they have solved.

Distribute copies of The Penny Jar with Larger Numbers (R63).

ELL English Language Learners

Partner Talk Have pairs discuss the following question. How do you know what number comes next? Beginning English Language Learners may only be able to say phrases like "3 more" and "counting up." More proficient speakers should explain how they know the number chosen is the next number in the sequence.

Additional Resource

Student Math Handbook pages 61–63

Differentiation in Investigation 1

Mathematics in This Investigation

The mathematics focuses on the counting sequence to 100 and on finding and using patterns in that sequence of numbers to 100. It also focuses on developing strategies for counting a set of up to 60 objects by 1s. This includes knowing the names and sequence of the numbers, counting each object once, and knowing that the last number said indicates the total number of objects in the set.

Additional Resource: *What Comes after 49?*, pages 82–83 (See *Implementing Investigations in Grade 1*)

Understanding the Mathematics

Students count and write the numbers to 100 and beyond and use that sequence to accurately count and keep track of a set of up to 60 objects. They may organize the objects to be counted in some way and use that organization to keep from having to repeatedly count from 1, and to find the total. They use patterns in the sequence of numbers to figure out what numbers have been removed from a 100 chart.

Option: Assign the **Extension** activity.

Partially Understanding the Mathematics

Students count and write the numbers to 100 and beyond but may pause or look for help at particular places in the sequence. They can use the sequence to count a set of up to 60 objects but may count from one each time they add new objects to the set. To figure out what numbers are missing on a 100 chart, they may use patterns in the number sequence or count on from a number that is comfortable for them.

Option: Assign the **Practice** activity.

Not Understanding the Mathematics

Students cannot yet count and write the numbers to 100 fluently. They may get stuck at particular places in the sequence and still make occasional errors with the rote sequence. They may write 50 as 05 or 101 as 1001. When counting a set of objects, these students are occasionally off due to keeping track errors or other errors (e.g., skipping or double-counting an object, omitting a decade). They may be able to figure out what numbers are missing on the 100 chart up to 50, but struggle with numbers greater than 50. Their strategies rely mainly on counting.

Option: Assign the **Intervention** activity.

Investigation 1 Quiz

In addition to your observations and students' work in Investigation 1, the Quiz (R64) can be used to gather more information.

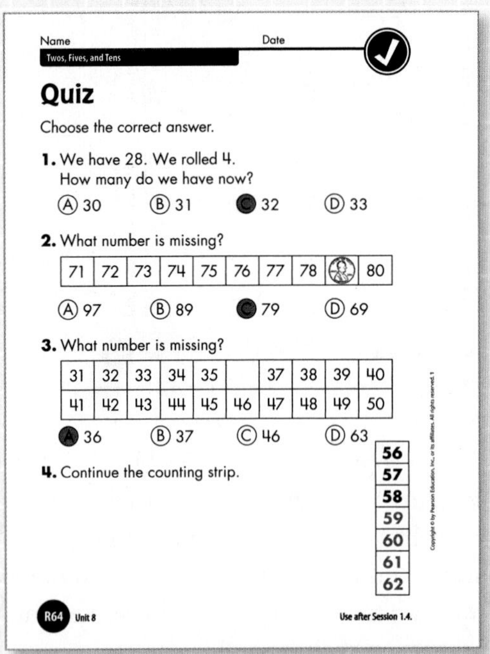

Name Date

Twos, Fives, and Tens

Quiz

Choose the correct answer.

1. We have 28. We rolled 4.
How many do we have now?

Ⓐ 30 Ⓑ 31 ● 32 Ⓓ 33

2. What number is missing?

71	72	73	74	75	76	77	78		80

Ⓐ 97 Ⓑ 89 ● 79 Ⓓ 69

3. What number is missing?

31	32	33	34	35		37	38	39	40
41	42	43	44	45	46	47	48	49	50

● 36 Ⓑ 37 Ⓒ 46 Ⓓ 63

4. Continue the counting strip.

56
57
58
59
60
61
62

R64 Unit 8 Use after Session 1.4.

Intervention

30 MIN PAIRS

Ten Turns with Ten-Frames

Use anytime after Session 1.1.

Math Focus Points

- Counting and keeping track of amounts up to 60
- Counting on from a known quantity
- Organizing objects to count them more efficiently

Vocabulary: counting on

Materials: counters (60 per pair), 1–3 number cubes (from Session 1.1; 1 per pair), M1 (1 per pair), M5 (1 per pair)

Today you are going to play *Ten Turns* with your partner. Remind students of the rules by playing a few rounds with a volunteer. Roll a number cube, take that many counters, and fill in the *Ten Turns* Recording Sheet (M1).

I rolled a [2], so I'll take that many counters. Then I fill in my recording sheet: "We rolled [2]" and "Now we have [2]." Now its [Teo's] turn to roll. He rolled a [3]. So we take that many counters and fill in the Turn 2 blank to show "We rolled [3]." What should I put next to "Now we have"?

Students might say:

"Put [5] because there are [1, 2, 3, 4, 5]."

"Write [5] because you had [2], and now you have [3] more: [3, 4, 5]."

Model students' strategies and record the results.

After a few rounds, I might have a lot of counters. Explain that students might want to use Ten-Frames for *Ten Turns* (M5) to help them count and keep track. Model placing [2] counters on it for your first roll and then adding [3] more. Then play a few more turns modeling how the ten-frame can keep you from having to count from 1 every time. Note that students will also benefit from double-checking the totals by counting by 1s. How could I use the ten-frames to help me count?

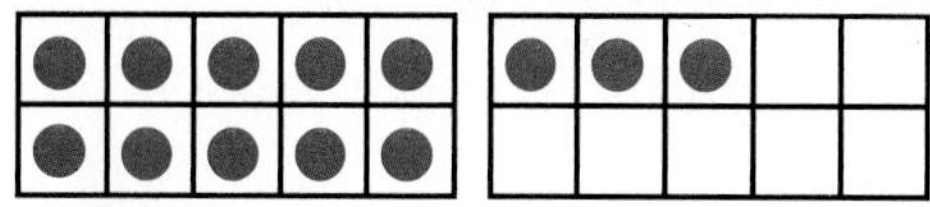

Students might say:

"We know that this frame is 10, so you could count these [3]: [11, 12, 13]."

Now distribute copies of M1 and M5, counters, and number cubes for pairs to use to play *Ten Turns* with Ten-Frames. Monitor to support students in using their ten-frames to organize and count their counters.

ELL English Language Learners

Partner Talk As students play, pose the following question. How are you keeping track of your counters? Listen for the word *count on* as students talk with their partners about how many counters they have on their ten-frames. Less proficient speakers may be encouraged to pair with a partner from their language group to explain their thinking.

Additional Resource

Student Math Handbook pages 21–23

Practice

Counting Strips

Use anytime after Session 1.4.

Math Focus Points

- Identifying, reading, writing, and sequencing numbers to 100 and beyond

Materials: adding machine tape (6-inch pieces), M15 (as needed), R65

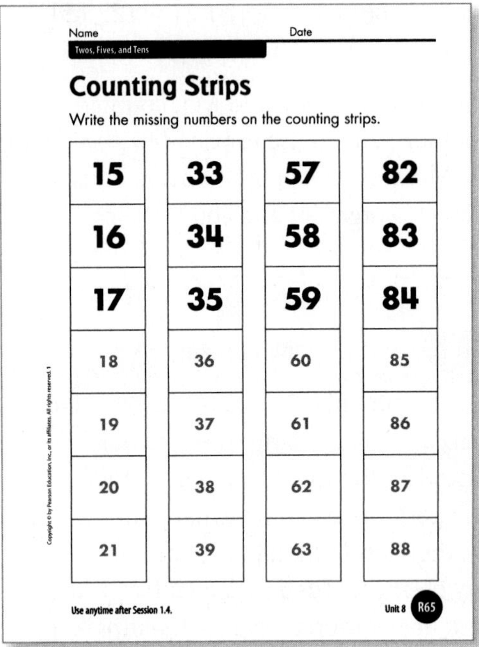

Name Date

Twos, Fives, and Tens

Counting Strips

Write the missing numbers on the counting strips.

15	**33**	**57**	**82**
16	**34**	**58**	**83**
17	**35**	**59**	**84**
18	36	60	85
19	37	61	86
20	38	62	87
21	39	63	88

Use anytime after Session 1.4. Unit 8 R65

Materials to Prepare: Use the adding machine tape pieces to prepare 7 counting strips that have common errors, such as skipping a number, skipping a decade, or reversing digits. Use numbers that are larger than 20. Tape two of the counting strips on the board.

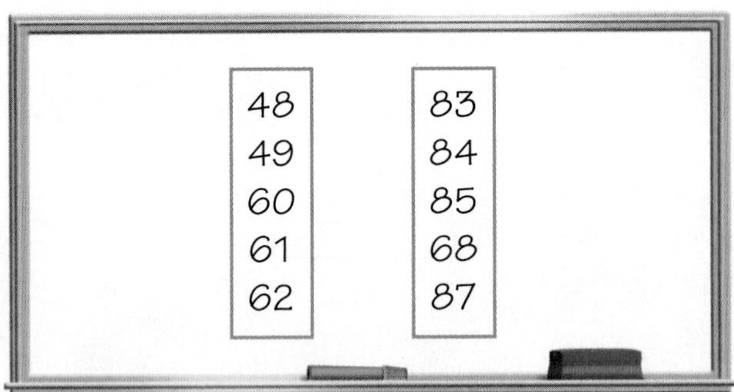

Can you find any mistakes on these counting strips?

Students might say:

"On the first strip, the numbers change after 49, but the 50s come next, not the 60s. They skipped the 50s."

"The 68 on the other strip isn't right. It should go 83, 84, 85, 86."

For each strip, have students discuss what is wrong, how they know that it is wrong, and what they could do to fix it. Why might someone make these mistakes? Encourage students to think of reasons why these mistakes might happen.

Tape the other 5 counting strips on the board. Distribute 5 blank counting strips to each group. Work together in your group to find the mistakes on these counting strips. Then someone should rewrite the counting strip correctly. Everyone should get to rewrite at least one strip. If needed, students may use the 100 Chart (M15). When groups are finished, have a similar discussion about those counting strips. Then distribute copies of Counting Strips (R65).

ELL English Language Learners

Rephrase As students explain their reasoning about counting errors, rephrase as needed so that all students understand the explanations. For example: [Libby] says that 68 isn't the way to write the number 86. To write the number 86, you write an 8 and then a 6. Write the number, then point to each digit as you read the number aloud. Eighty-six.

Additional Resource

Student Math Handbook

Game: *Missing Number* SMH G18

Materials: 100 chart, pennies, M16

Extension

15 MIN PAIRS

Missing Numbers Between 101 and 200

Use anytime after Session 1.3.

Math Focus Points

- Identifying, reading, writing, and sequencing numbers to 100 and beyond
- Identifying and using patterns in the number sequence and on the 100 chart

Materials: pennies (10 per pair), M16 (1 per pair), M19 (1 per pair), blank paper or M42 (from Unit 3; optional), R66

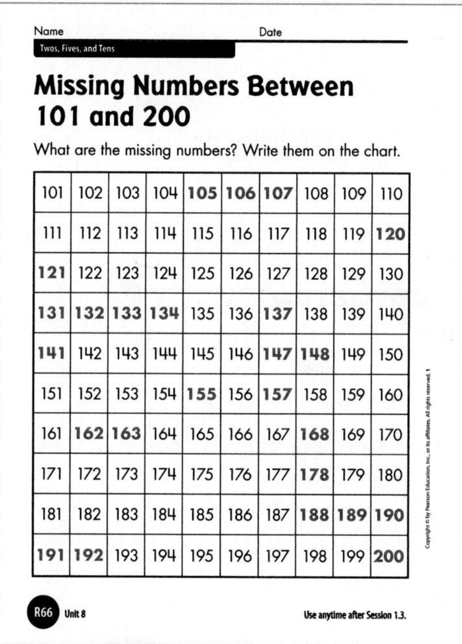

Name Date

Twos, Fives, and Tens

Missing Numbers Between 101 and 200

What are the missing numbers? Write them on the chart.

101	102	103	104	**105**	**106**	**107**	108	109	110
111	112	113	114	115	116	117	118	119	**120**
121	122	123	124	125	126	127	128	129	130
131	**132**	**133**	**134**	135	136	**137**	138	139	140
141	142	143	144	145	146	**147**	**148**	149	150
151	152	153	154	**155**	156	**157**	158	159	160
161	**162**	**163**	164	165	166	167	**168**	169	170
171	172	173	174	175	176	177	**178**	179	180
181	182	183	184	185	186	187	**188**	**189**	**190**
191	**192**	193	194	195	196	197	198	199	**200**

R66 Unit 8 Use anytime after Session 1.3.

Today you're going to play *Missing Numbers* on a 101 to 200 chart. How is this chart different from the 100 chart?

Give students a few minutes to share what they notice. Then ask students to locate a few numbers.

What number is 1 more than 138? 10 more? How do you know?

Students might say:

"I know it's 148 because each row is 10, and one row below 138 is 148."

Distribute the 101 to 200 Chart (M19), *Missing Numbers* Recording Sheet (M16), and pennies to each pair. Review the rules of the game as necessary. Then partners play *Missing Numbers* with 5 pennies. Challenge pairs who seem comfortable on the 101–200 chart to cover a cluster of 3 consecutive numbers with some of the pennies.

151	152	153	154		156	157	158	159	160
161	162	163				167	168	169	170
171	172	173	174		176	177	178	179	180

After a few rounds, challenge students to play with 10 pennies and to cover clusters of 4 or 5 numbers with some of their pennies. Students can record on blank paper or on the *Missing Numbers* Recording Sheet (M42) from Unit 3.

Distribute copies of Missing Numbers Between 101 and 200 (R66).

ELL English Language Learners

Model Thinking Aloud Model how to find a missing number on the 101 to 200 chart. I can count from the beginning of the row: 111, 112, 113. Then there's a penny, and the next number is 115. I think 114 is the missing number.

Additional Resource

Student Math Handbook pages 24–25

Differentiation in Investigation 2

Mathematics in This Investigation

The mathematics focuses on developing an understanding of what it means to count by groups. This involves knowing the counting sequence and understanding that each number said represents another equal group of things being added. It also focuses on beginning to develop strategies for counting a set of objects by groups.

Understanding the Mathematics

Students understand what it means to count by groups. They are fluent with the rote sequence for counting by 2s and 5s, and can use it to accurately count a set of objects by 2s or 5s. They count by groups to solve problems about things that come in groups, and use 2:1 and 5:1 relationships to figure out how many items a larger group would have. Given a mixed set of squares, students count efficiently, organizing the squares into equal groups, and accurately handle any leftovers.

Option: Assign the **Extension** activity.

Partially Understanding the Mathematics

Students understand what it means to count by groups, but may occasionally get carried away with the sequence, forgetting the relationship between the numbers they say and the objects they are counting. They may have issues once they hit a particular place in the sequence. To solve problems about things that come in groups, they model the problem, and then count mainly by 1s. Given a mixed set of squares, students may use some combination of counting by groups and by 1s.

Option: Assign the **Practice** activity.

Not Understanding the Mathematics

Students are just learning what it means to count by groups. They are less familiar with the rote counting sequence, and may need to say the numbers that other students skip (e.g., 1, **2**, 3, **4**). They may not see a connection between those numbers and a set of objects to be counted. To solve problems about things that come in groups, they model the problem with pictures or manipulatives and count by 1s. Given a mixed set of squares, students count by 1s, though they may try to organize them in some way. Because of the structure of the squares, keeping track of the count is challenging.

Option: Assign the **Intervention** activity.

Investigation 2 Quiz

In addition to your observations and students' work in Investigation 2, the Quiz (R67) can be used to gather more information.

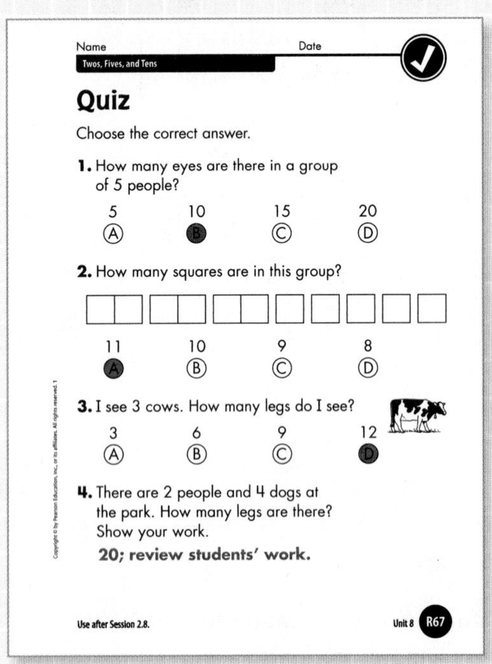

Name Date

Twos, Fives, and Tens

Quiz

Choose the correct answer.

1. How many eyes are there in a group of 5 people?

5 Ⓐ　10 Ⓑ　15 Ⓒ　20 Ⓓ

2. How many squares are in this group?

11 Ⓐ　10 Ⓑ　9 Ⓒ　8 Ⓓ

3. I see 3 cows. How many legs do I see?

3 Ⓐ　6 Ⓑ　9 Ⓒ　12 Ⓓ

4. There are 2 people and 4 dogs at the park. How many legs are there? Show your work.

20; review students' work.

Use after Session 2.8.

Unit 8 R67

Intervention

20 MIN INDIVIDUALS

How Many Hands?

Use anytime after Session 2.1.

Math Focus Points

- Counting and combining things that come in groups of 2
- Counting by 2s
- Recording strategies for counting and combining

Materials: counters (20 per student), blank paper, crayons

Distribute counters, paper, and crayons. Spend a few minutes having students share their ideas about body parts that come in groups of 2. Each person has 2 hands. So how can we find the number of hands there are in a group of people?

Students might say:

"Have the people stand in a line and then count their hands."

Model this context with 3 students. Count their hands by 2s and then by 1s, alternating a quiet voice with a louder voice (1, **2**, 3, **4**, 5, **6**).

Then, sketch 3 stick figures on the board. Label each person and model counting them by 2s and then by 1s.

Then ask students to help you use counters to model the problem. Since each person has 2 hands, we need 2 counters for each person. Model counting by 2s as you point to the groups of counters. Again, count by 1s to verify that the answer is correct.

Now, students solve a similar problem about a group of 5 people. They may draw pictures or use counters. Some may need to act out the problem with other students. Remind them to record their work so someone else could look at it and be able to tell how they solved the problem.

Once students are finished, discuss the different strategies students used to solve the problem. As you did for the sample problem, model counting by 2s with pictures, counters, or by acting it out with students. Also count by 1s to double check.

If time remains, ask students to solve another How Many Hands? problem. How many hands are there in a group of 6 people? Encourage them to think about the strategies you've been discussing as they solve it.

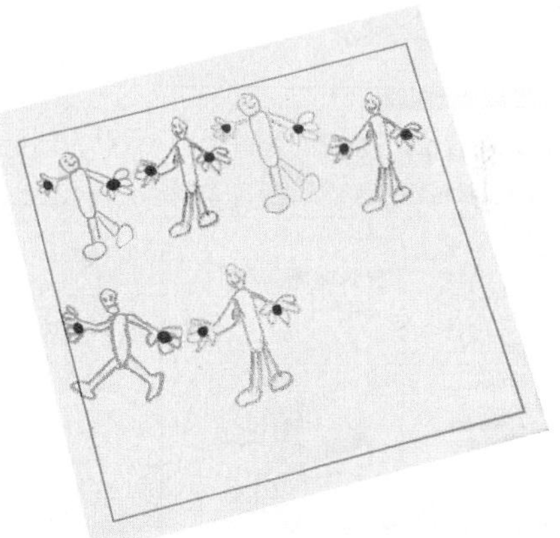

ELL English Language Learners

Model Thinking Aloud Model how you would solve a How Many Hands? problem. There are 5 people. Draw 5 circles. I know that each person has 2 hands. I'll use counters to show each hand. Place 2 counters in the first circle. That's 1 person with 1, 2 hands. Follow the same process with each circle. Then I'll count the hands: 1, 2, 3, 4, 5, 6, 7, 8, 9, 10. 5 people have 10 hands. Encourage students to verbalize their thinking as they find how many hands.

Additional Resource

Student Math Handbook pages 24–25

Practice

How Many Do I See?

Use anytime after Session 2.3.

Math Focus Points

- Counting by 2s
- Counting and combining things that come in groups of 2 and 4
- Recording strategies for counting and combining

Materials: counters (as needed), blank paper (as needed), crayons (as needed), R68

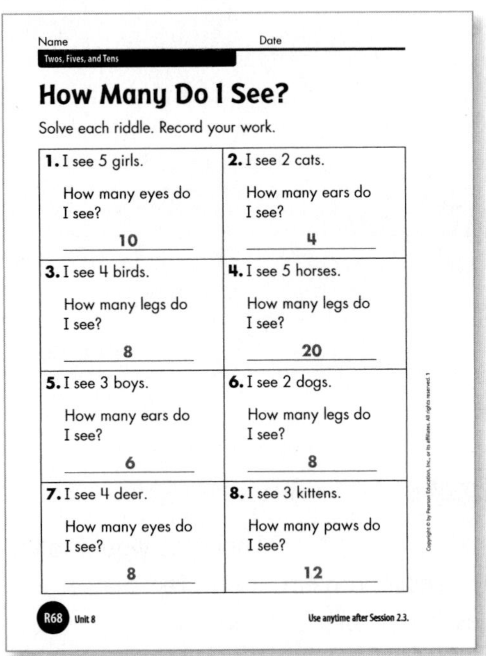
Name Date

Twos, Fives, and Tens

How Many Do I See?

Solve each riddle. Record your work.

1. I see 5 girls. How many eyes do I see? 10	**2.** I see 2 cats. How many ears do I see? 4
3. I see 4 birds. How many legs do I see? 8	**4.** I see 5 horses. How many legs do I see? 20
5. I see 3 boys. How many ears do I see? 6	**6.** I see 2 dogs. How many legs do I see? 8
7. I see 4 deer. How many eyes do I see? 8	**8.** I see 3 kittens. How many paws do I see? 12

R68 Unit 8 Use anytime after Session 2.3.

Today we are going to think about things that come in groups of 2 or 4. Brainstorm things that come in 2s. Once someone names a body part ask: How many [elbows] do you see in your group? Work together to count them.

Observe how groups approach the problem. Do they count by 1s or 2s? Do they use doubles? Other number combinations? Addition?

How many [ears] do you see in your group? Again, observe how students approach this problem.

Why are there the same number of [elbows] *and* [ears] in your group?

Students might say:

"Everybody in our group has 2 [elbows] and they also have 2 [ears]."

"You add the same number of 2s to get the number of [elbows] and [ears]."

Now let's talk about things that come in groups of 4. Take a few minutes to brainstorm with students. Then draw a sketch and pose the problem.

I see a group of 4 cars. How many wheels do I see? Ask students to compare this problem to the previous ones. Then, students work together to solve it.

Discuss and model students' strategies, which may include counting by 1s or 2s or adding. Then, pose the same problem in a different context. How many legs would I see on 4 horses? Let students predict how many, and then solve the problem.

Distribute copies of How Many Do I See? (R68).

ELL English Language Learners

Rephrase As students describe their solutions, rephrase as necessary so that all students understand the explanations. [Seth] says he used addition. He added 4, for the wheels on one car, plus 4, for the wheels on another car, plus two more 4s because there were 2 more cars. He wrote 4 + 4 + 4 + 4.

Additional Resource

Student Math Handbook pages 24–25

Extension

30 MIN PAIRS

How Many in All?

Use anytime after Session 2.4.

Math Focus Points

- Counting and combining things that come in groups of 2 and 4
- Counting by 2s

Materials: counters (as needed), blank paper (as needed), crayons (as needed), R69

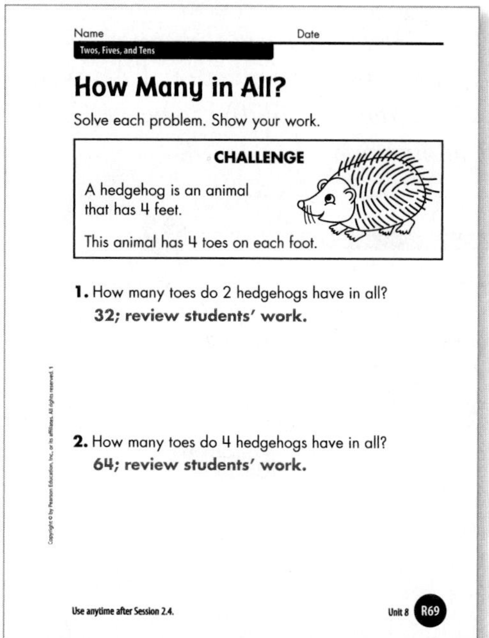
Name Date

Twos, Fives, and Tens

How Many in All?

Solve each problem. Show your work.

CHALLENGE

A hedgehog is an animal that has 4 feet.

This animal has 4 toes on each foot.

1. How many toes do 2 hedgehogs have in all?
32; review students' work.

2. How many toes do 4 hedgehogs have in all?
64; review students' work.

Use anytime after Session 2.4. Unit 8 R69

Draw a picture of a 4-toed hedgehog on the board.

This is a hedgehog and it has 4 feet. There are 4 toes on each foot. Take a minute to work with your partner. How many toes would there be on one hedgehog?

Give students time to solve the problem before discussing it. How many toes are on one hedgehog?

Students might say:

"Each foot has 4 toes so count by 4: 4, 8, 12, 16."

"I added 4 + 4 for 2 feet. That's 8. Then there's 2 more feet, so that's 8 more. 8 + 8 = 16."

Students now work together to figure out how many toes there are on 3 hedgehogs. Remind students that they can sketch pictures, use counters, or create a table like you've been doing in class to help them solve the problem. End by discussing and modeling students' strategies.

Distribute copies of How Many in All? (R69).

ELL English Language Learners

Rephrase Students may not clearly understand why you count by 4s to find the number of toes on a hedgehog. Show the picture of the hedgehog and ask the following questions to help. How many toes are on this foot? *(4)* How many toes are on this foot? *(4)* Continue asking this question for the remaining feet and then emphasize the pattern of 4s.

Additional Resource

Student Math Handbook pages 24–25

Differentiation in Investigation 3

Mathematics in This Investigation

The mathematics focuses on developing fluency with the combinations that make 10 and on developing strategies for counting a set of objects by 10s.

Understanding the Mathematics

Students are fluent with the combinations that make 10—they can find combinations of 10 in a set of numbers, know what they need to add to a given number to make 10, and use known number combinations of 10. They use this knowledge to figure out how many cubes they need to complete a row of 10, or how to complete equivalent expressions. They count cubes organized in rows of 10 by 10s, and accurately count what is left over by 1s. They are beginning to notice and understand some important place value ideas.

Option: Assign the **Extension** activity.

Partially Understanding the Mathematics

Students are fluent with most of the combinations that make 10, but count all, count on, or use a fact or relationship they know for a few. To complete equivalent expressions, they are likely to directly model the problem using manipulatives. They count cubes organized in rows of 10 by 10s, but may occasionally miscount what is left over by 10s as well.

Option: Assign the **Practice** activity.

Not Understanding the Mathematics

Students are not yet fluent with many of the combinations that make 10, and instead count all, count on, or use a fact or relationship they know to solve the problem. They have trouble understanding and completing equivalent expressions. Because they are just learning what it means to count by groups, they mostly count a set of cubes by 1s.

Option: Assign the **Intervention** activity.

Investigation 3 Quiz

In addition to your observations and students' work in Investigation 3, the Quiz (R70) can be used to gather more information.

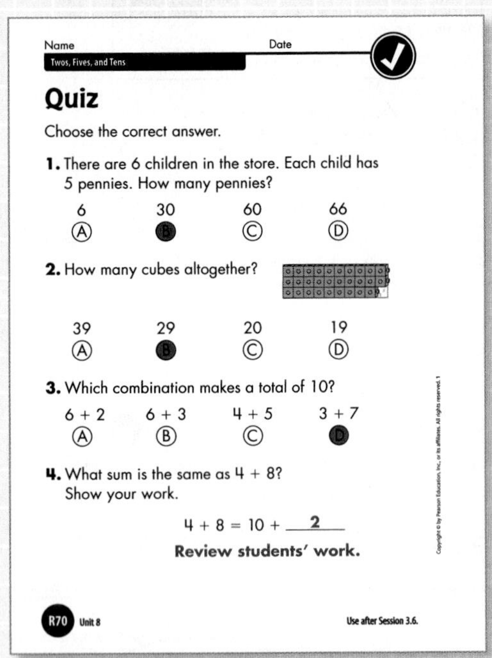

Name Date

Twos, Fives, and Tens

Quiz

Choose the correct answer.

1. There are 6 children in the store. Each child has 5 pennies. How many pennies?
   6 (A) 30 (B) 60 (C) 66 (D)

2. How many cubes altogether?
   39 (A) 29 (B) 20 (C) 19 (D)

3. Which combination makes a total of 10?
   6 + 2 (A) 6 + 3 (B) 4 + 5 (C) 3 + 7 (D)

4. What sum is the same as 4 + 8? Show your work.
   4 + 8 = 10 + 2
   Review students' work.

R70 Unit 8 Use after Session 3.6.

Intervention

20 MIN GROUPS

Roll Tens in a Small Group

Use anytime after Session 3.2.

Math Focus Points

- Adding single-digit numbers
- Organizing objects to count them more efficiently
- Counting by 10s

Materials: number cubes (1 per group), dot cubes (1 per group), connecting cubes (30 per group), M38 (1 per group)

Today we are going to play *Roll Tens* in small groups. Show students the *Roll Tens* 30 Mat (M38) covered with 3 rows of 10 cubes. When we are finished, the mat will look like this. How many cubes are there? Count with me by 10s: 10, 20, 30.

Clear the cubes from the board. Remind students how to play by modeling the game with 2 volunteers. Have a student roll the number cube and the dot cube. [Marta] rolled a [4] and a [3]. How many cubes should she take? What should she do with the cubes? Help the student collect the cubes, snap them together, and place them in a row along the top of the mat. How many more cubes do we need to complete a row of 10?

Have another student roll. [Vic] rolled a [1] and a [6]. How many cubes should he take? After he uses them to finish the first row, how many will be left to start the next row? How do you know? What's another way to figure that out?

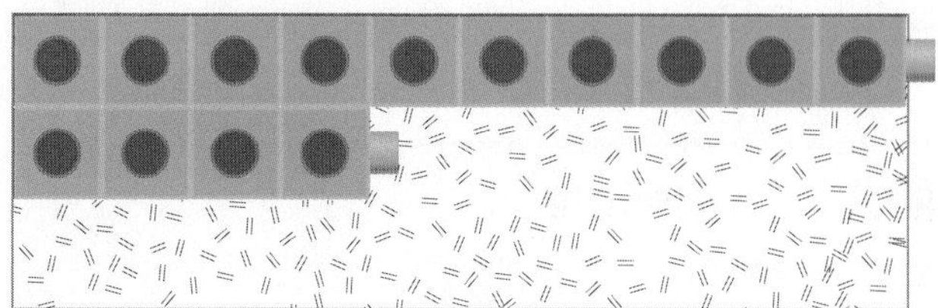

After each turn, have students count the cubes with you. Encourage them to count complete rows by 10s, and then transition to counting by 1s. How many cubes do we have now? How do you count them?

Students might say:

"First I counted 10. Then I added the [4] extras. 10 plus [4] is [14]."

"I counted 10, [11, 12, 13, 14]."

Distribute number cubes, dot cubes, connecting cubes, and copies of M38 to groups to use to play *Roll Tens* in a Small Group. Make sure students take turns rolling and using connecting cubes to make rows of 10. As you observe, ask questions like the ones above to support students in using groups of 10 as they count.

ELL English Language Learners

Suggest a Sequence Suggest the following concise steps to help students understand how to begin playing *Roll Tens*.

1. Roll 1 number and 1 dot cube.
2. Take that many connecting cubes.
3. Put the cubes on the mat.
4. Fill a row with 10 cubes. Use the extras to start a new row.
5. Count the rows of 10 and the extras to figure out how many cubes altogether.

Additional Resource

Student Math Handbook pages 24–25

Practice

20 MIN PAIRS

Solving *Ten Plus* Problems

Use anytime after Session 3.3.

Math Focus Points

- Adding single-digit numbers
- Thinking about numbers to 20 in terms of how they relate to 10 (e.g., 10 + ____ or < 10)
- Determining equivalent expressions for a given expression (e.g., 7 + 8 = 10 + ____)

Materials: connecting cubes (20 per pair), blank paper (1 per pair), R71

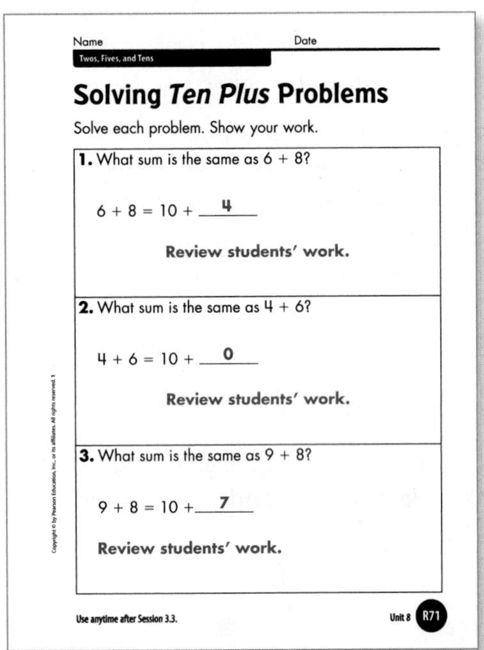

Name Date

Twos, Fives, and Tens

Solving *Ten Plus* Problems

Solve each problem. Show your work.

1. What sum is the same as 6 + 8?

6 + 8 = 10 + 4

Review students' work.

2. What sum is the same as 4 + 6?

4 + 6 = 10 + 0

Review students' work.

3. What sum is the same as 9 + 8?

9 + 8 = 10 + 7

Review students' work.

Use anytime after Session 3.3. Unit 8 R71

Distribute cubes and paper to each pair. Begin by writing 6 + 7 = ____ on the board. Let's add 6 plus 7. Help me write the sum. Complete the equation.

Now let's make an equivalent expression. Write 6 + 7 = 10 + ______ on the board. 6 + 7 is the same as 10 plus another number. What number can you add to 10 to make the same sum as 6 + 7? Work together to solve this problem.

6 + 7 = 13

6 + 7 = 10 + ____

Give students time to solve the problem. Then ask them to describe their strategies.

Students might say:

"I made a tower with 13 cubes. Then I broke off 10 and counted the cubes left over. 10 + 3 is 13."

"I know that 6 + 4 is 10. So I took 4 from the 7 and 3 are left. That's how I know that 10 + 3 = 13."

"We said 6 + 7 = 13, and 13 is the same as 10 + 3."

Write other problems on the board and have students solve each one. Remind them of the tools and strategies they can use. Observe students as they work. Do they use cubes? Work mentally? Use number combinations? Count all? Count on?

Distribute copies of Solving *Ten Plus* Problems (R71).

ELL English Language Learners

Rephrase As students describe their solutions, rephrase and demonstrate as needed so that all students understand the explanations. These cube towers show 6 + 7. [Stacy] said she knows that 6 + 4 is 10. So she took 4 from the 7 and gave it to the 6. Remove 4 cubes from the tower of 7 and add them to the tower of 6. Now these towers show 10 + 3.

Additional Resource

Student Math Handbook

Game: *Tens Go Fish* SMH G23

Materials: Primary Number Cards (without Wild Cards), blank paper

Extension

30 MIN PAIRS

Roll Tens with the 100 Mat

Use anytime after Session 3.2.

Math Focus Points

- Adding single-digit numbers
- Organizing objects to count them more efficiently
- Counting by 10s

Materials: number cubes (1 per pair), dot cubes (1 per pair), connecting cubes (100 per pair), M39 (as needed), M40–M41 (1 of each per pair), R72

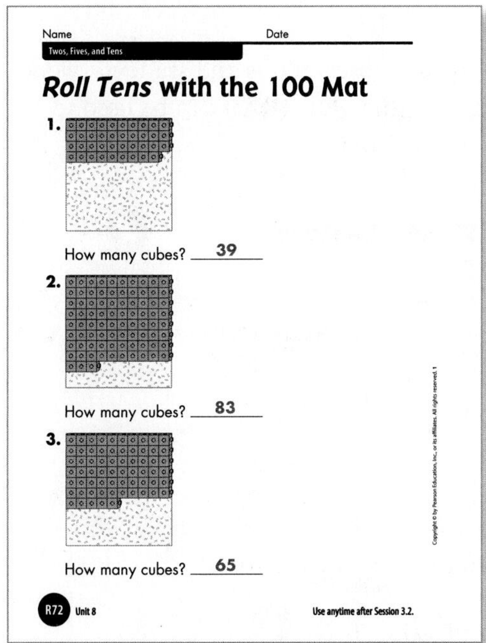

Name Date

Twos, Fives, and Tens

***Roll Tens* with the 100 Mat**

1. How many cubes? 39

2. How many cubes? 83

3. How many cubes? 65

R72 Unit 8 Use anytime after Session 3.2.

Materials to Prepare: Create a *Roll Tens* 100 Mat (M40–M41) for each pair.

Play a game of *Roll Tens* with students to introduce the 100 mat. Place 50-something cubes on your mat and explain that you're joining a game that's already in progress—the players have already taken several turns. How many cubes are on the mat so far? How did you figure this out?

Continue the game by taking a turn. I rolled [1] and [5]. How many cubes should I take? After I place them, how many will be left to start the next row? Continue playing, asking students to count the cubes with you after each turn.

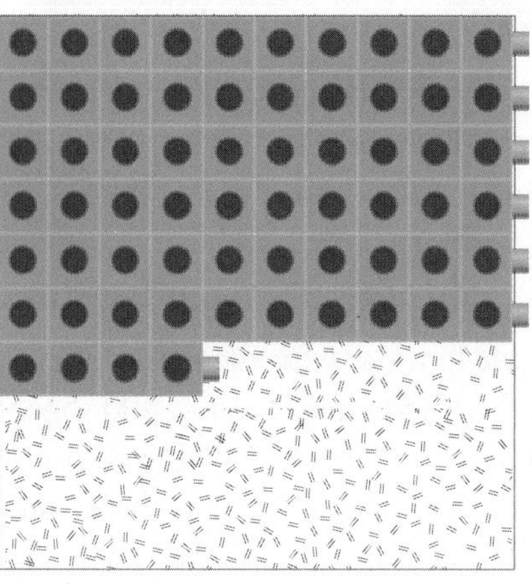

Students might say:

"There are [64]. I counted the rows by 10s and then I counted on the singles: [60, 61, 62, 63, 64]."

Establish the total number of cubes that will fit on this mat by asking students how many more cubes you need to fill it. How many cubes do we need to fill the row of [4]? How many rows of 10? Let's count all the cubes by 10s. Distribute a mat, number cube, dot cube, and connecting cubes to each pair to use to play on their own. When ready, distribute copies of *Roll Tens* with the 100 Mat (R72).

ELL English Language Learners

Model Thinking Aloud Model your thinking as you play. I'm going to count to figure out how many cubes I have in all: [10, 20 , 30, 40, 50, 60]. Trace each row of 10 with your finger as you count it. Now I'll count the singles: [61, 62, 63, 64]. Touch each cube as you count it. There are [64] cubes.

Additional Resource

Student Math Handbook pages 24–25

Differentiation in Investigation 1

Mathematics in This Investigation

The mathematics focuses on describing and comparing 3-D shapes, and on exploring the relationship between 2-D and 3-D shapes.

Understanding the Mathematics

Students are familiar with the names and mathematical attributes of many 3-D shapes. They are adept at moving between 2-D and 3-D shapes, for example, identifying the 2-D shapes on the faces of 3-D shapes and relating them to drawings of those 2-D shapes. They can determine the number of faces on a given block, and use 2-D rectangles to build 3-D boxes.

Option: Assign the **Extension** activity.

Partially Understanding the Mathematics

Students are familiar with the names of some 3-D shapes and describe the attributes of those shapes in a variety of ways. They are beginning to explore the relationship between 2-D and 3-D shapes. For example, they can "see" a rectangle on the face of a rectangular prism, but may use trial and error to figure out which rectangle on a page matches it exactly. Visualizing how 2-D pieces come together to form a 3-D box may be challenging.

Option: Assign the **Practice** activity.

Not Understanding the Mathematics

Students are familiar with the names of only a few 3-D shapes and cannot necessarily attach those names to the shapes they identify. They may need support to describe attributes of 3-D shapes. Students are working to connect 2-D and 3-D shapes. Visualizing how 2-D pieces come together to form a 3-D box may be quite difficult, and result in 3-D creations that are not rectangular prisms.

Option: Assign the **Intervention** activity.

Investigation 1 Quiz

In addition to your observations and students' work in Investigation 1, the Quiz (R73) can be used to gather more information.

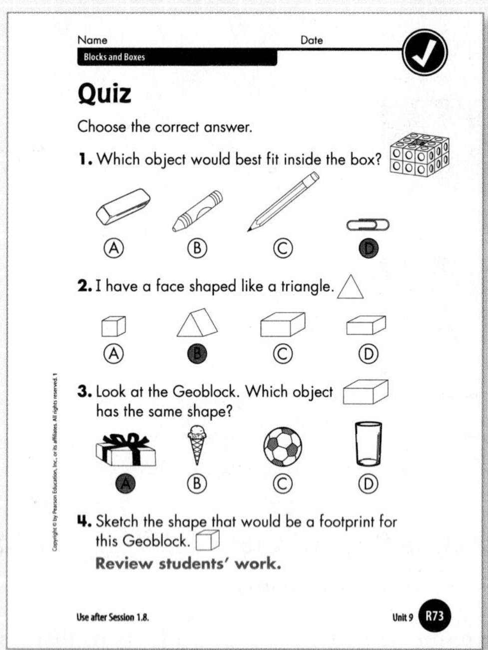

Name Date

Blocks and Boxes

Quiz

Choose the correct answer.

1. Which object would best fit inside the box?

Ⓐ Ⓑ Ⓒ Ⓓ

2. I have a face shaped like a triangle.

Ⓐ Ⓑ Ⓒ Ⓓ

3. Look at the Geoblock. Which object has the same shape?

Ⓐ Ⓑ Ⓒ Ⓓ

4. Sketch the shape that would be a footprint for this Geoblock.

Review students' work.

Use after Session 1.8. Unit 9 R73

Intervention

Geoblock Footprints

Use anytime after Session 1.1.

Math Focus Points

- Developing vocabulary to describe 3-D shapes and their attributes
- Comparing size, shape, and orientation of objects
- Matching a 3-D object to a 2-D outline of one of its faces

Vocabulary: footprint

Materials: Geoblocks, M1–M2

Distribute a copy of Geoblock Footprints: Set A (M1) to each student. Today we are going to find Geoblocks that fit on each footprint *exactly*.

Demonstrate by putting one of the Geoblocks on a footprint. You should find *one* block that fills the *whole* footprint, not combinations of blocks that fill the outline. Acknowledge that there may be more than one block that matches each outline.

Students work to find blocks that match the outlines on M1. As students match blocks and outlines, they should leave the block on the sheet until every outline has a block on it.

Monitor students as they match blocks to footprints. Watch for students who use two or more blocks to fill a given outline. Those blocks *do* fill the outline, but remember that we are trying to find *one* block that fills the footprint by itself. Try again. See if you can find *one* block that fits the footprint.

Also watch for students who only look for rectangles on blocks that have all rectangular faces. Here's a hint. Sometimes rectangles can be "hiding" within triangular-looking shapes. If students cannot find all of the shapes on a sheet and become frustrated, encourage them to put that sheet with the blocks that they have found so far aside and work on Geoblock Footprints: Set B (M2).

Introduce Set B by talking about one of the outlines together.

Point to one of the triangle footprints. How would you find a Geoblock that has this footprint?

Students might say:

"It won't be shaped like a box."

"It will be one of the blocks that is pointy. I can try different blocks to see what fits."

Have students find a matching Geoblock for that footprint. Model how the shape fits *exactly* in the footprint without any gaps or overlap.

ELL English Language Learners

Model Thinking Aloud Use mathematical vocabulary in context as you model how to find a block that fits a footprint. I want to find a block that fits this footprint. The footprint is a square. Trace the outline with your finger. So, I'm going to look for blocks that have square faces. Maybe this cube will work—it has a square face. Trace the edge of the face with your finger. No, it is too small. I need a bigger square. Encourage students to verbalize their thoughts as well.

Additional Resource

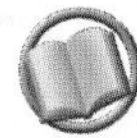

Student Math Handbook pages 89–90

Practice

20 MIN PAIRS

Is It a Match?

Use anytime after Session 1.2.

Math Focus Points

- Developing vocabulary to describe 3-D shapes and their attributes
- Matching a 3-D object to a 2-D outline of one of its faces

Vocabulary: face

Materials: Geoblocks, blank paper, R74

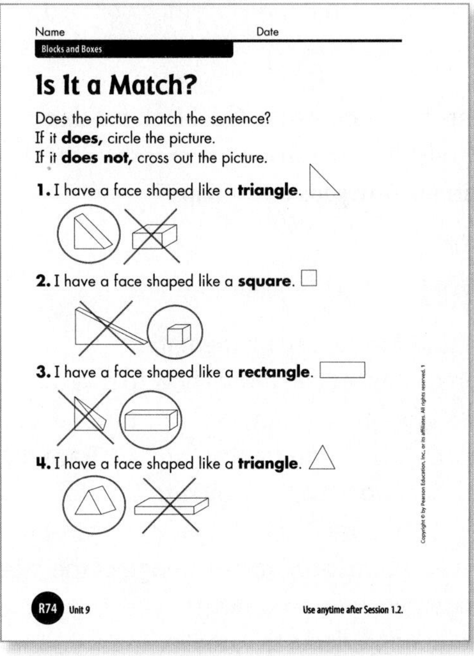
Name Date

Blocks and Boxes

Is It a Match?

Does the picture match the sentence?
If it **does,** circle the picture.
If it **does not,** cross out the picture.

1. I have a face shaped like a **triangle**.
2. I have a face shaped like a **square**.
3. I have a face shaped like a **rectangle**.
4. I have a face shaped like a **triangle**.

R74 Unit 9 Use anytime after Session 1.2.

Hold up a Geoblock and ask students to describe it.

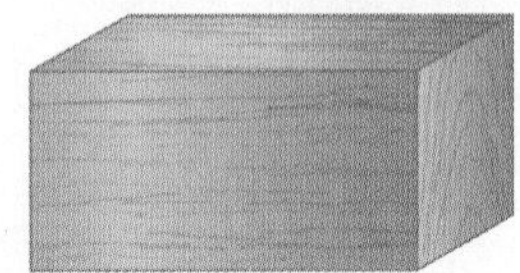

Students might say:

"I see 4 sides that are rectangles."

"And there is a square on both ends."

Put the block on a sheet of paper, with one of the rectangular faces down. Trace around it and remove the block. What shape is the face? Can you find the matching face on the block?

Now you are going to play a game with your partner. Player 1 chooses 2 Geoblocks and, while Player 2 is not looking, traces one face on a piece of paper. Then you show your partner the 2 blocks and the tracing. They have to figure out which block is a match. Once the correct block has been identified, partners switch roles. Depending on the blocks chosen, it is possible for both blocks to have a face that matches.

Distribute copies of Is It a Match? (R74). Students may use the Geoblocks to help.

ELL English Language Learners

Provide a Word List Write the words *face, vertex,* and *edge* on chart paper. Give each student a Geoblock. Have students point to or trace faces, vertices, and edges as you read through the list together. Be sure to discuss the fact that some words can have different meanings in everyday life and in mathematics (e.g., face, edge). Post the word list for students to reference.

Additional Resource

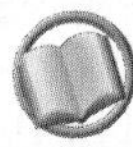

Student Math Handbook pages 86, 90

Extension

20 MIN PAIRS

Matching Footprints

Use anytime after Session 1.2.

Math Focus Points

- Developing vocabulary to describe 3-D shapes and their attributes
- Comparing size, shape, and orientation of objects
- Matching a 3-D object to a 2-D outline of one of its faces

Materials: Geoblocks, M5 (1 per pair), R75

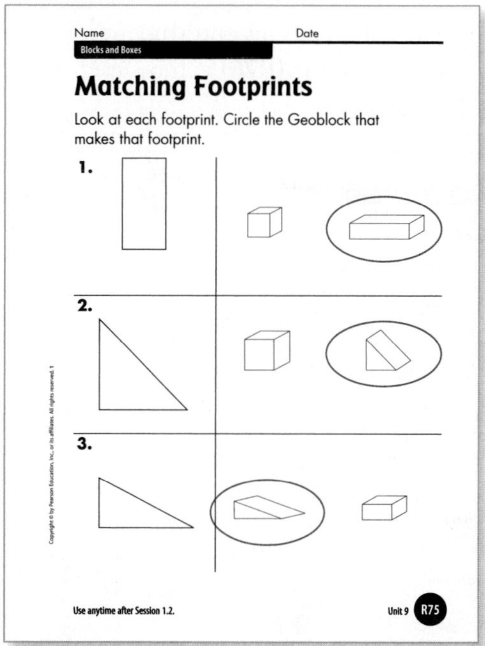

Name Date

Blocks and Boxes

Matching Footprints

Look at each footprint. Circle the Geoblock that makes that footprint.

1.

2.

3.

Use anytime after Session 1.2. Unit 9 R75

Remind students of their work with Geoblock Footprints in Session 1.1. Distribute a copy of Geoblock Footprints: Set C (M5) to each pair. Today we are going to find blocks that fill each footprint perfectly. What do you notice about these footprints?

Point to one of the footprints. How would you find a Geoblock that has this footprint?

Students might say:

"I would look for a Geoblock that has a [skinny triangle face]."

"I would pull out all of the blocks that have a [triangle] face. Then I'd look for that [triangle]."

Demonstrate putting a Geoblock on a footprint. Remember, you want to find *one* block that fills the *whole* footprint. Students may use the same type of block more than once. As students match blocks and outlines, they should leave the block on the sheet until every outline has a block on it.

Challenge students who complete the activity to use 8 different Geoblocks to fill the footprints.

Distribute copies of Matching Footprints (R75).

ELL English Language Learners

Partner Talk As pairs work, have them discuss the following questions. Are there any blocks that you know won't work without trying them? How do you know? Encourage more proficient speakers to use the words *face, vertex,* and *edge* in their discussion and explanations. Beginning English Language Learners can point to the blocks that do not work.

Additional Resource

Student Math Handbook pages 89–90

Differentiation in Investigation 2

Mathematics in This Investigation

The mathematics focuses on understanding the relationship between 2-D and 3-D shapes, and using that relationship to build a replica of a 3-D town.

Understanding the Mathematics

Students are comfortable drawing 2-D pictures of 3-D shapes. They draw one block at a time, often drawing more than one face for each block, and can connect the different parts of their drawing to the actual building. They end with a picture that others can use to build an accurate replica. Students can use their picture and visualize paths and distances between a start and end point.

Option: Assign the **Extension** activity.

Partially Understanding the Mathematics

Students work hard to draw 2-D pictures of 3-D shapes. They may draw one block at a time, or focus on the shape of the building as a whole. While they may need clarification in order to use their picture to build a building, these students can describe how their picture connects to different parts of their building. Students can identify different paths using a picture, but may not correctly describe directions between a start and end point.

Option: Assign the **Practice** activity.

Not Understanding the Mathematics

Drawing 2-D pictures of 3-D shapes is quite challenging. These students may focus on the overall shape of the building or draw individual blocks, but it is difficult for others to see the connection between the pictures and the actual blocks. Giving and following a set of directions for following a path may be challenging.

Option: Assign the **Intervention** activity.

Investigation 2 Quiz

In addition to your observations and students' work in Investigation 2, the Quiz (R76) can be used to gather more information.

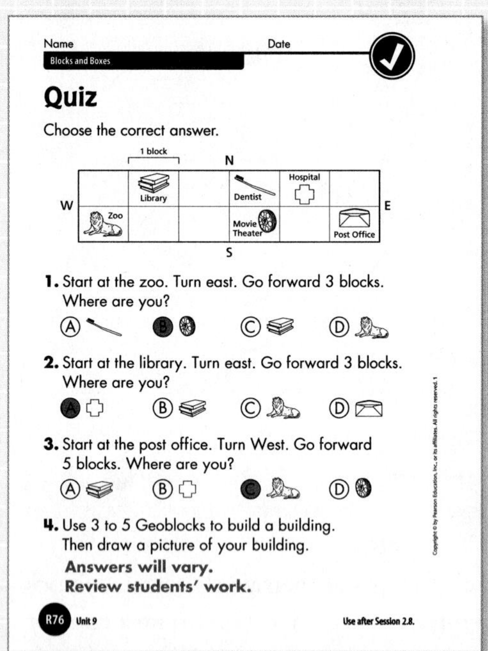

Name Date

Blocks and Boxes

Quiz

Choose the correct answer.

1. Start at the zoo. Turn east. Go forward 3 blocks. Where are you?

Ⓐ Ⓑ Ⓒ Ⓓ

2. Start at the library. Turn east. Go forward 3 blocks. Where are you?

Ⓐ Ⓑ Ⓒ Ⓓ

3. Start at the post office. Turn West. Go forward 5 blocks. Where are you?

Ⓐ Ⓑ Ⓒ Ⓓ

4. Use 3 to 5 Geoblocks to build a building. Then draw a picture of your building.

Answers will vary.
Review students' work.

R76 Unit 9 Use after Session 2.8.

Intervention

30 MIN INDVIDUALS

Building and Drawing

Use anytime after Session 2.2.

Math Focus Points

- Observing and describing characteristics of 3-D shapes
- Making a 2-D representation of a 3-D object or structure
- Building a 3-D construction from a 2-D representation

Materials: Geoblocks (1 set per pair), blank paper, crayons, M20 (1 per pair)

Distribute Geoblocks and Ways to Draw Blocks (M20) to each pair. Make a building using 3 or 4 blocks. When they have finished building, students work to draw a picture of it on blank paper. Try to draw the picture so that someone could easily recognize your building.

Encourage students who are overwhelmed by the task of drawing a building to focus on drawing one block at a time. Which block will you draw first? What shapes do you see when you look at that block? OK, you see a [square] and [rectangle]. Are they next to each other? On top of one another? How are they connected? Where do they connect? How could you show that in your drawing?

Encourage students to explain to you and to each other how the shapes in their drawings connect to each other and to their building. How were you looking at the building when you drew this? Which part of the building does this part of your drawing show?

Then students exchange drawings. Use the plan to build the building. Encourage students to do the best they can based on the plan. After making an attempt, students can meet to compare building plans and to discuss what was challenging.

Students might say:

"There was one spot I couldn't tell whether to pick a square shape or a triangle."

"The plan I had showed the outline-like a footprint. But I couldn't tell what to use inside."

Some students may want to revise their plan based on their partner's feedback.

ELL English Language Learners

Provide a Word List Write *next to, on top,* and *under* on chart paper. Using classroom objects, act out the meaning of each. For example, place a tissue box *next to* a book. Then, place the tissue box on the book to show *on top* and *under.*

Additional Resource

Student Math Handbook pages 84, 91

Practice

30 MIN GROUPS

Find the Blocks

Use anytime after Session 2.1.

Math Focus Points

- Observing and describing characteristics of 3-D shapes
- Making a 2-D representation of a 3-D object or structure

Vocabulary: two-dimensional (2-D), three-dimensional (3-D)

Materials: Geoblocks (1 set per group), blank paper, M20 (1 per group), R77

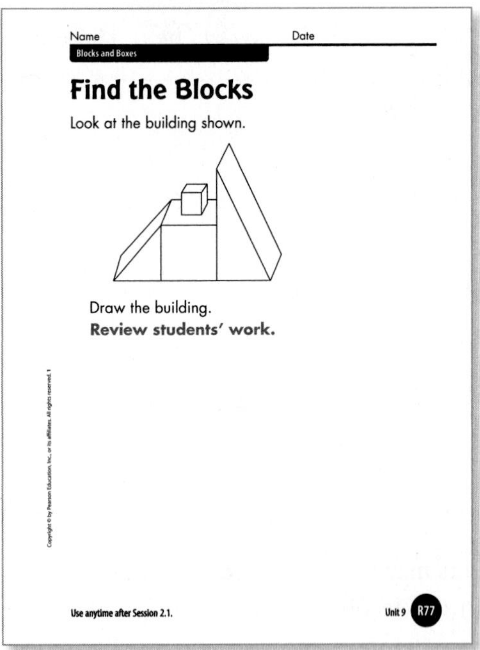
Name Date
Blocks and Boxes

Find the Blocks

Look at the building shown.

Draw the building.
Review students' work.

Use anytime after Session 2.1. Unit 9 R77

Build a building using Geoblocks H, C, and L.

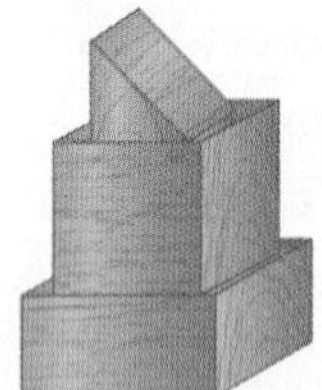

Distribute paper, copies of Ways to Draw Blocks (M20), and Geoblocks.

Direct students' attention to the building. What blocks were used to make this building? Groups work together to find the corresponding blocks from their set of Geoblocks and recreate the building.

Look at the building. What 2-D shapes do you see on the blocks that make this building?

Students might say:

"Rectangles and triangles."

"There are also some squares. The middle block is all squares and some of the bottom blocks are squares."

Now, each student draws the building on one sheet of paper, using M20 to help them. Try to make your drawings look 3-D.

Distribute copies of Find the Blocks (R77).

ELL English Language Learners

Rephrase Some students may have difficulty understanding the difference between 2-D and 3-D. Use words and expressions such as *flat* and *on paper* when referring to 2-D, and *solid* and *the real object* when referring to 3-D. Have students show you examples of 2-D and 3-D shapes in the classroom.

Additional Resource

Student Math Handbook pages 84, 91

Extension

20 MIN INDIVIDUALS

Drawing My Building

Use anytime after Session 2.1.

Math Focus Points

- Observing and describing characteristics of 3-D shapes
- Making a 2-D representation of a 3-D object or structure

Vocabulary: three-dimensional (3-D)

Materials: Geoblocks, blank paper, crayons, M20 (as needed), R78

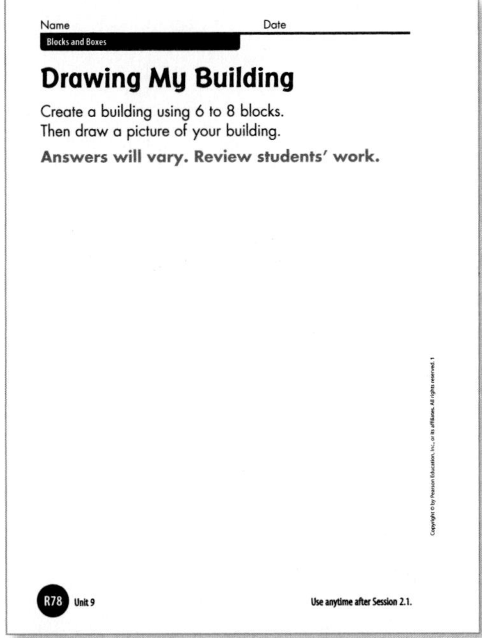

Name Date

Blocks and Boxes

Drawing My Building

Create a building using 6 to 8 blocks.
Then draw a picture of your building.

Answers will vary. Review students' work.

R78 Unit 9 Use anytime after Session 2.1.

Distribute Geoblocks and a sheet of paper to each student. Today you are going to draw a building so that it looks three-dimensional. What do I mean when I say three-dimensional?

Students might say:

"It looks like you could hold it. It looks real."

"It doesn't look flat even though it's drawn on flat paper."

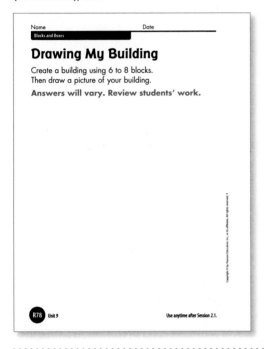

First, you will create a building using 6 to 8 blocks. Then, you will draw it on your paper. Remind students of the strategies you've discussed for making things look 3-D and point them to Ways to Draw Blocks (M20).

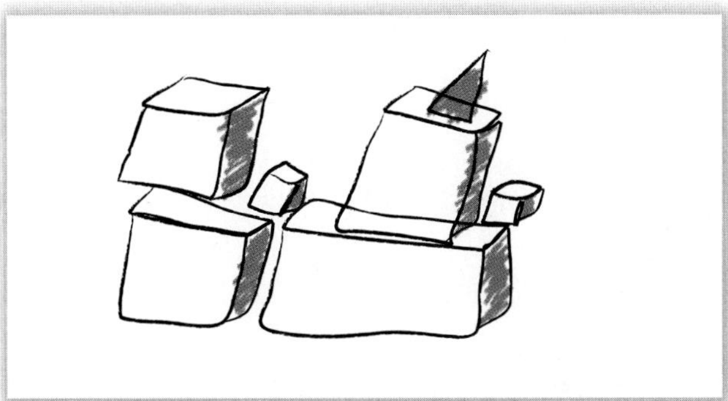

After students have finished, they trade drawings and try to build their partner's building. Encourage them to describe their drawing to their partners and to show how the building relates to the drawing.

Distribute copies of Drawing My Building (R78).

ELL English Language Learners

Provide a Word List Write the following words on the board and review the meaning of each: *face, rectangle, square, triangle, next to, under, on top.* Encourage students to use as many of these words as they can to describe the buildings they created and to describe how the blocks are related.

Additional Resource

Student Math Handbook pages 84, 91

Resource Masters

UNIT 1

INVESTIGATION 1

INVESTIGATION 2

INVESTIGATION 3

INVESTIGATION 4

UNIT 2

INVESTIGATION 1

INVESTIGATION 2

INVESTIGATION 3

UNIT 3

INVESTIGATION 1

INVESTIGATION 2

INVESTIGATION 3

INVESTIGATION 4

UNIT 4

INVESTIGATION 1

INVESTIGATION 2

INVESTIGATION 3

Name Date

Quiz

Choose the correct answer.

1. How many white counters ○ are there?

Ⓐ 6 Ⓒ 14

Ⓑ 12 Ⓓ 20

2. How many cubes are there?

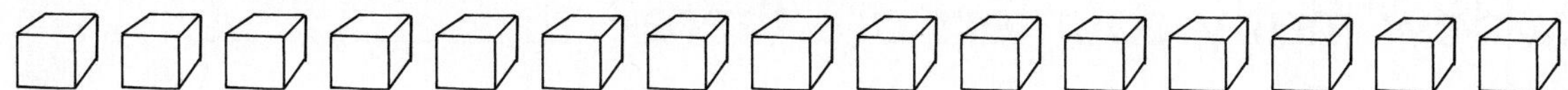

Ⓐ 16 Ⓒ 14

Ⓑ 15 Ⓓ 13

3. How many flowers are there?

Ⓐ 9 Ⓒ 11

Ⓑ 10 Ⓓ 12

4. Color in 20 circles.

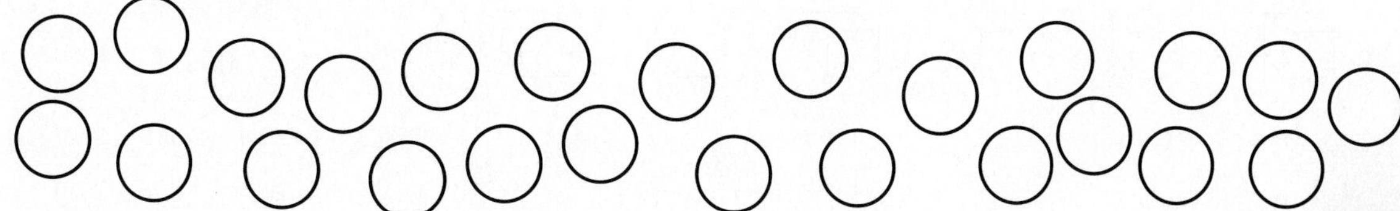

Name Date

How Many of Each?

Counting to 20

1. Connect the cubes. Count from 1 to 20.

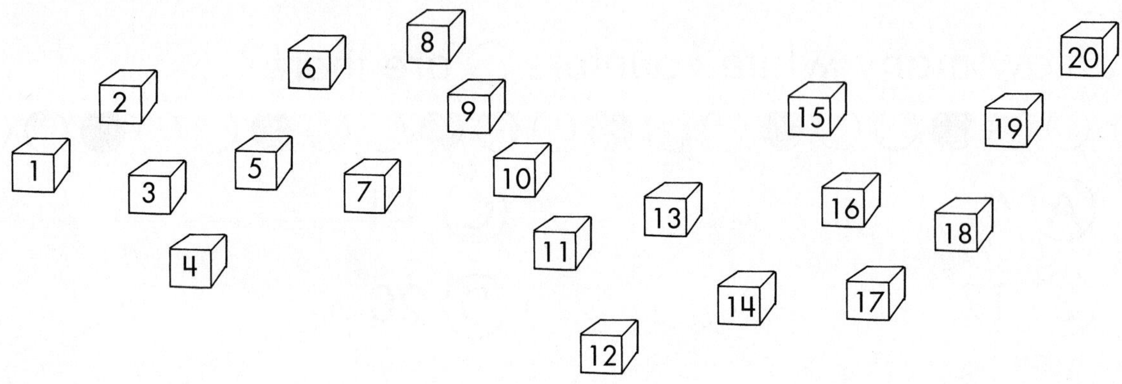

2. How many counters are there? ______________

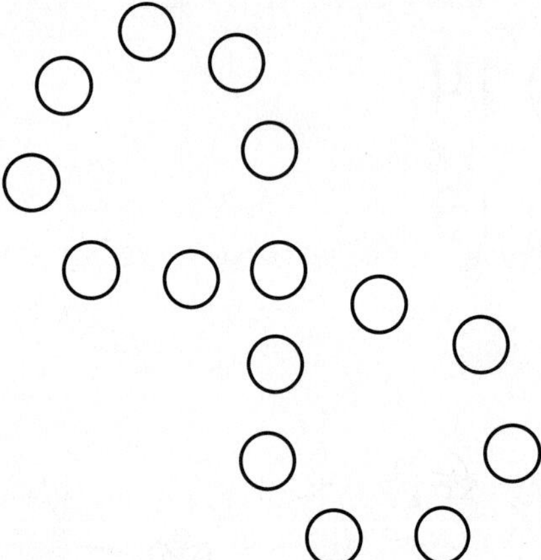

3. How many cubes are there? ______________

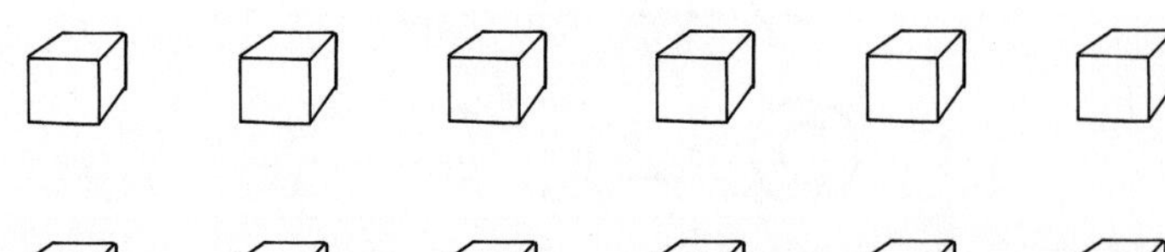

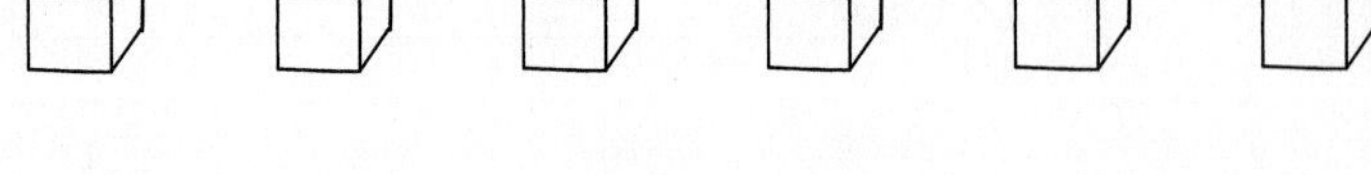

Use anytime after Session 1.4.

Name Date

Counting Quantities to 20

1. Color in 20 cubes.

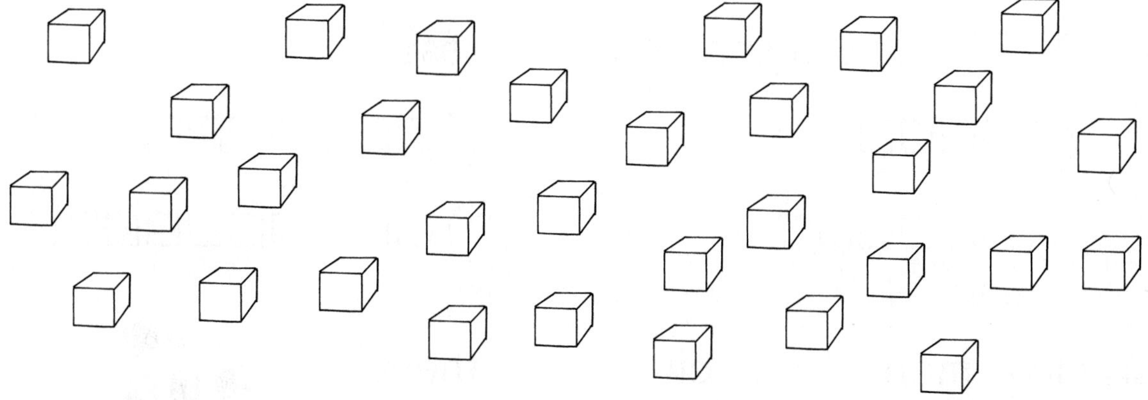

2. How many flowers are there? ____________

3. How many counters are there? ____________

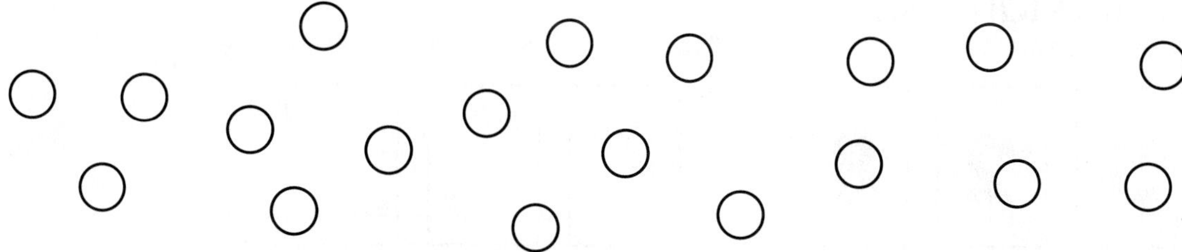

Name Date

Quiz

Choose the correct answer.

1. Which picture shows 9 squares?

Ⓐ □□□□□□ Ⓒ □□□□□□□□□

Ⓑ □□□□□□□ Ⓓ □□□□□□□□□□

2. How many black circles are there?

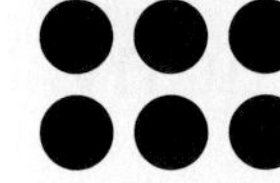

Ⓐ 16 Ⓒ 19

Ⓑ 18 Ⓓ 20

3. Which dot card shows more than 7?

Ⓐ Ⓒ

Ⓑ Ⓓ

4. Put the cards in order from the smallest number to the largest.

5	2	8

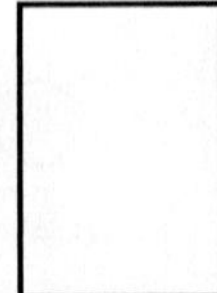

Name Date

What's In the Mystery Box?

1. Jacob drew pictures to show what was in his Mystery Box.

How many cubes were in Jacob's Mystery Box? ______

2. Allie drew pictures to show what was in her Mystery Box.

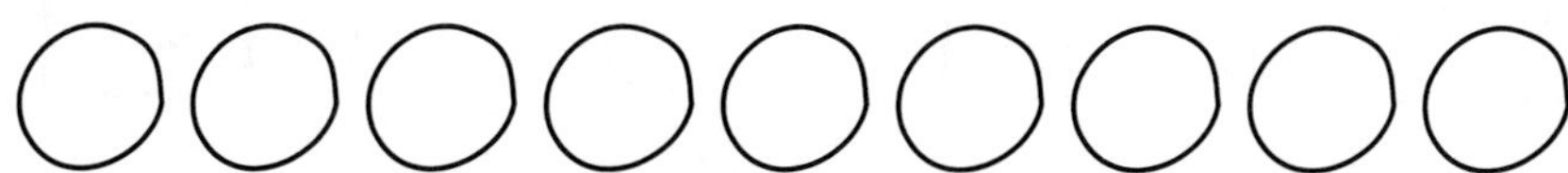

How many balls were in Allie's Mystery Box? ______

3. Sacha drew pictures to show what was in her Mystery Box.

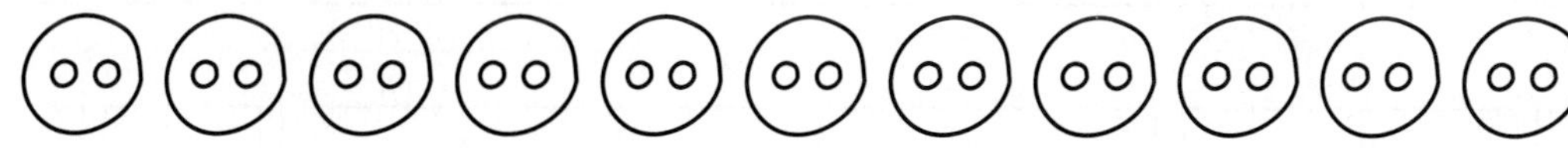

How many buttons were in Sacha's Mystery Box? ______

Name Date

Missing Steps

1. Draw the missing step, and write the number.

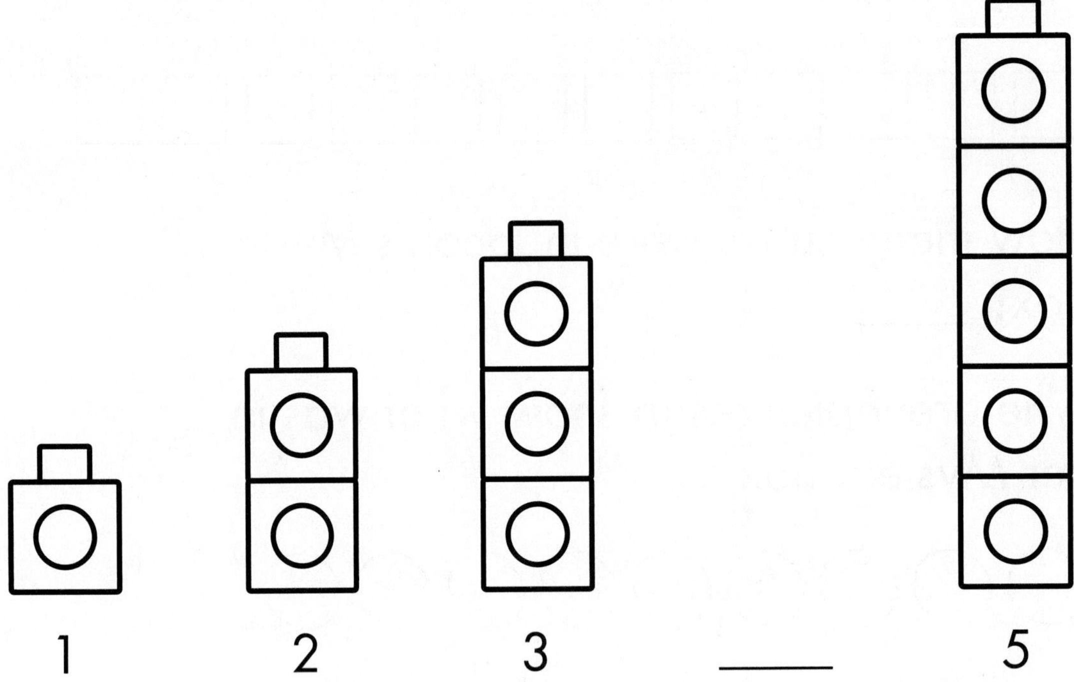

2. Put the cards in order.

9	4	6	10	2	5	3	8	7	1
1									

Use anytime after Session 2.3.

Name Date

How Many of Each?

Quiz

Choose the correct answer.

1. How many dots? 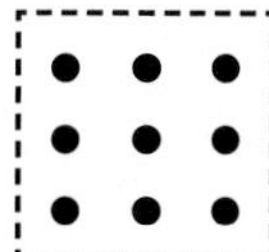

Ⓐ 6 Ⓑ 7 Ⓒ 8 Ⓓ 9

2. +  =

Ⓐ 13 Ⓑ 12 Ⓒ 11 Ⓓ 10

3. Which pair shows more than  7 ?

Ⓑ 8 

Ⓓ 7 

4. Solve the problem. Show your work.

I found 9 pens on the floor.
I found 3 more by the window.
How many pens did I find?

Name Date

How Many of Each?

Solving Story Problems

Solve the problem. Show your work.

I found 7 shells on the beach.
I bought 4 shells at the store.
How many shells do I have?

Name Date

Solving Story Problems with Larger Numbers

Solve the problem. Show your work.

I ate 12 strawberries for a snack.
I ate 8 strawberries at lunch.
How many strawberries did I eat?

Name Date

Quiz

Choose the correct answer.

1. This train has 10 cubes. There are 3 white cubes. How many cubes are gray?

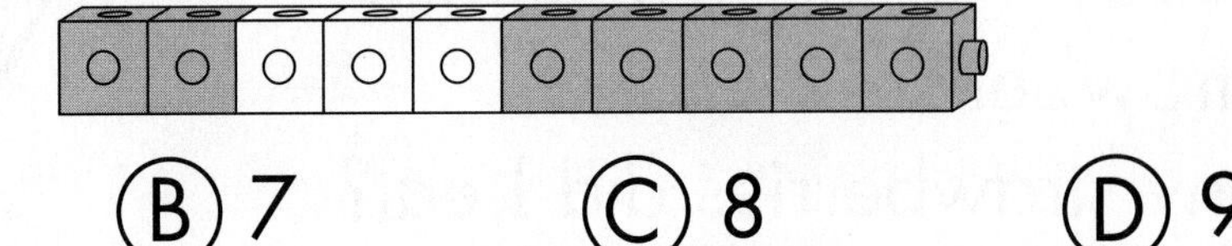

Ⓐ 6 Ⓑ 7 Ⓒ 8 Ⓓ 9

2. There are 6 coins. 4 are heads up. How many are tails?

Ⓐ 4 Ⓑ 3 Ⓒ 2 Ⓓ 1

3. There are 5 cubes in all. How many am I hiding under the cup?

Ⓐ 3 Ⓑ 4 Ⓒ 5 Ⓓ 6

4. Solve the problem. Show your work.

There are 7 flowers.
Some are red. Some are yellow.
How many of each could I have?
How many red? How many yellow?

Use after Session 4.7.

Name Date

How Many of Each?

Pencils and Crayons

Solve the problem. Show your work.

I have 7 things to write with in my desk.
Some are pencils. Some are crayons.
How many of each could I have?
How many pencils? How many crayons?

Name Date

Dogs and Cats

Solve the problem. Show your work.

There are 10 animals.
Some are dogs. Some are cats.
How many of each could there be?
How many dogs? How many cats?

Name Date

Quiz

Choose the correct answer.

1. Which shape is a triangle?

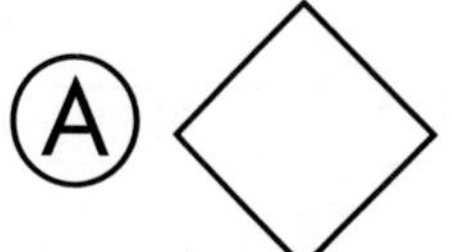

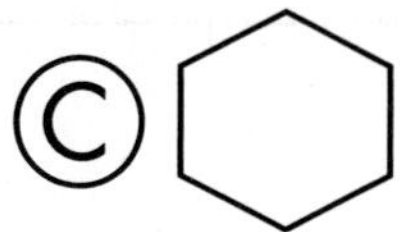

2. What shape is this window?

Ⓐ rectangle Ⓒ circle

Ⓑ trapezoid Ⓓ triangle

3. How many pattern blocks make this shape?

Ⓐ 2 Ⓒ 4

Ⓑ 3 Ⓓ 5

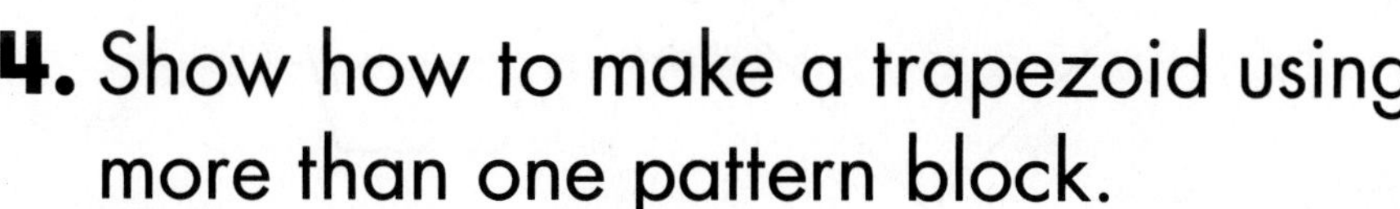

4. Show how to make a trapezoid using more than one pattern block.

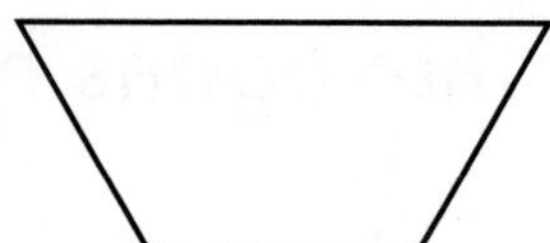

Name Date

Identifying Shapes

1. Color each rectangle blue.

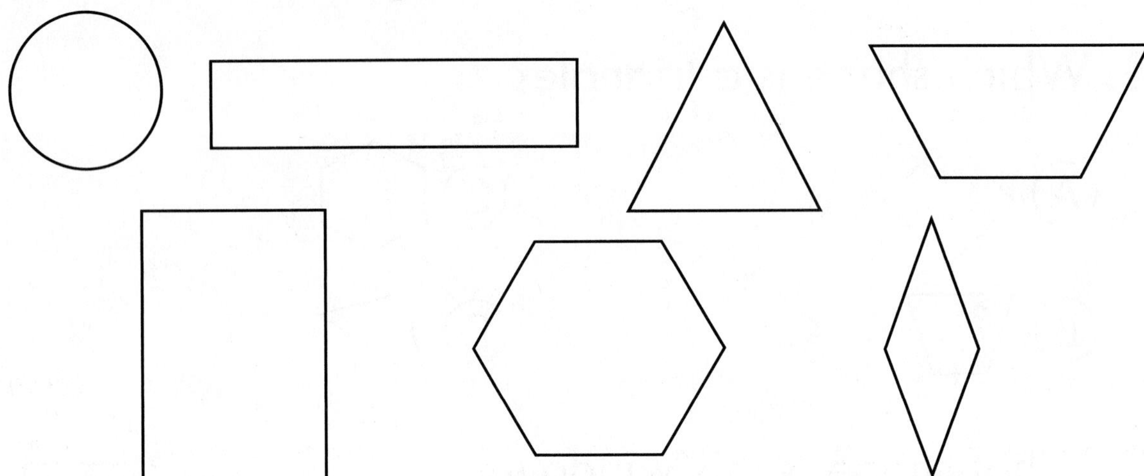

2. How many sides do rectangles have? ____________

3. How many corners do rectangles have? ____________

4. Color each hexagon red.

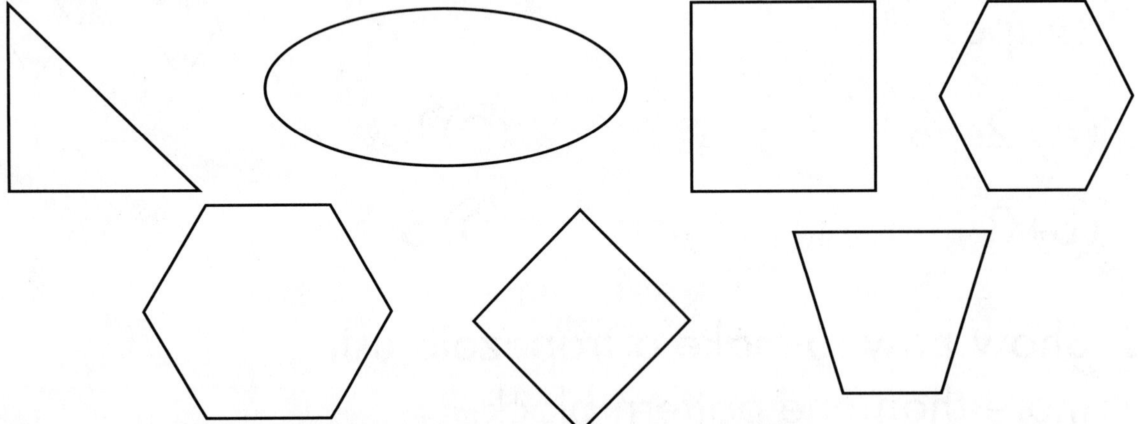

5. How many sides do hexagons have? ____________

6. How many corners do hexagons have? ____________

Use anytime after Session 1.2.

Name Date

Shape Puzzles

Color the shape that fits both clues.

1. Clue 1: It has 4 corners.

Clue 2: It has 4 equal sides.

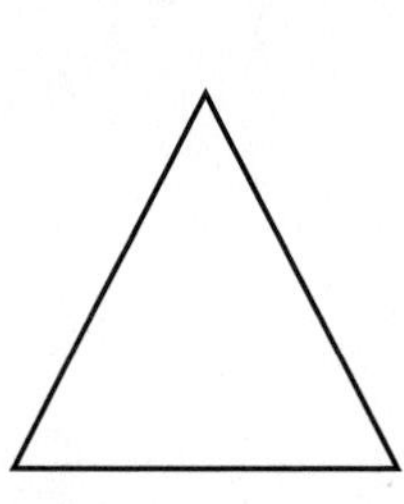

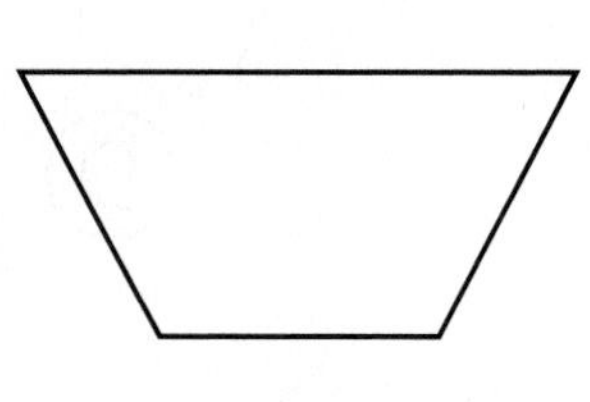
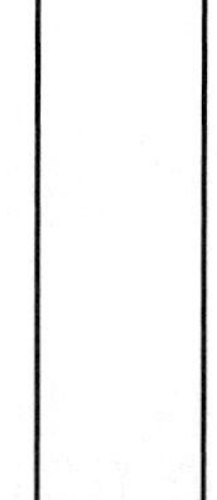
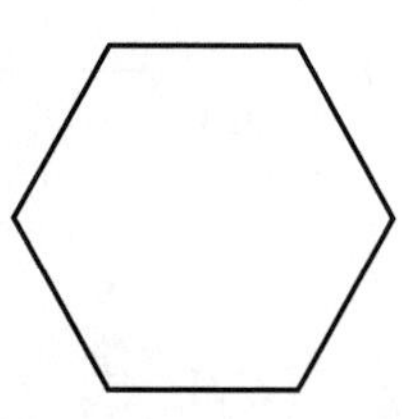

2. Clue 1: It has 0 corners.

Clue 2: It is round.

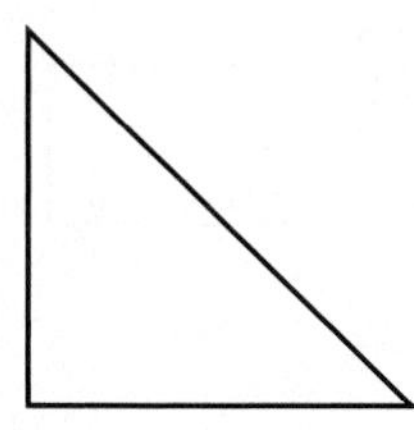
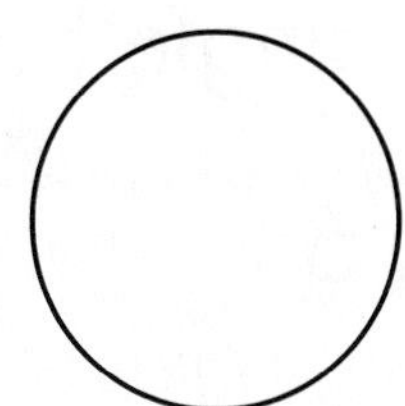
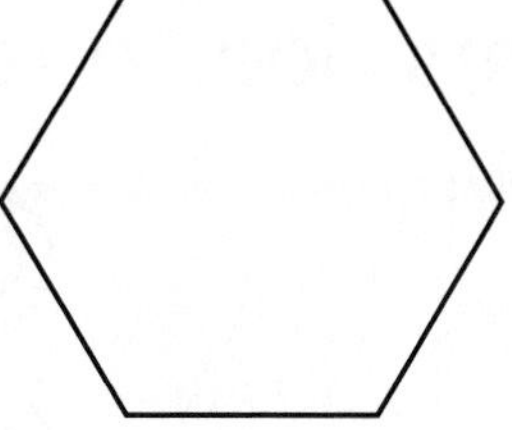
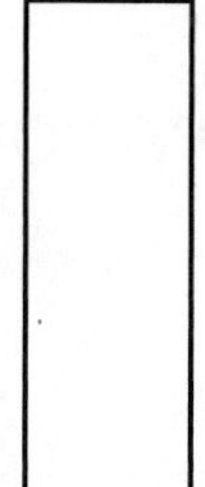
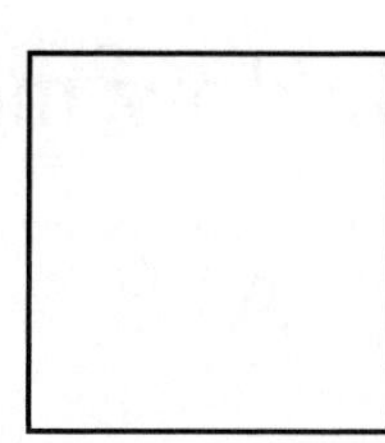

3. Clue 1: It has 3 corners.

Clue 2: It has 3 equal sides.

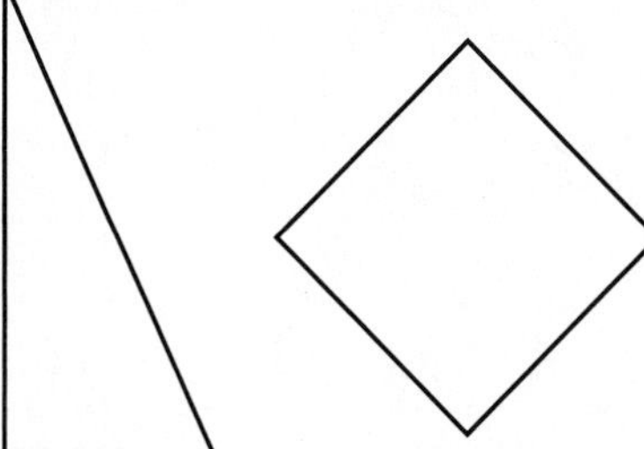
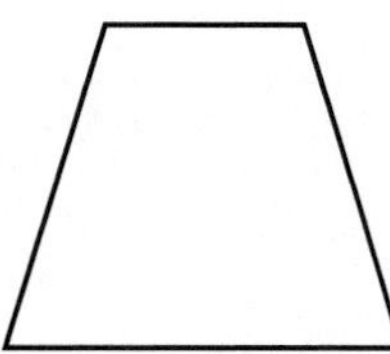
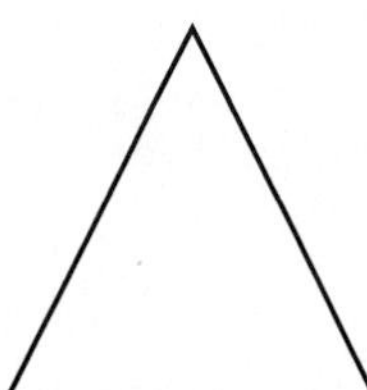
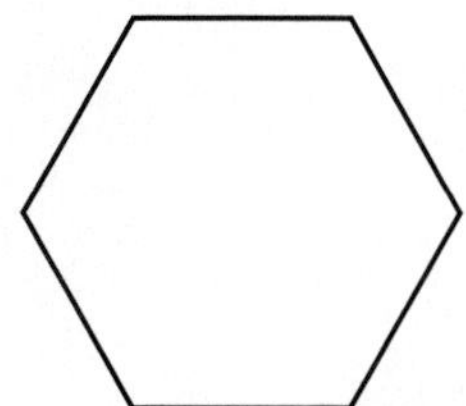

Name Date

Quiz

Choose the correct answer.

1. Which shape is a quadrilateral?

Ⓐ 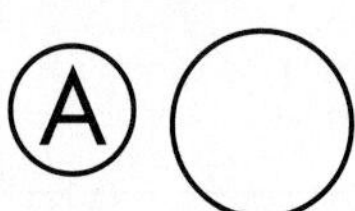

Ⓒ 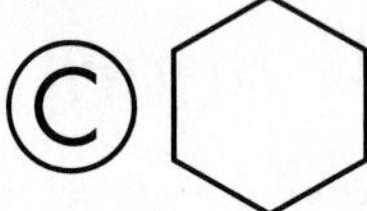

Ⓑ 

Ⓓ 

2. What is the name of this shape?

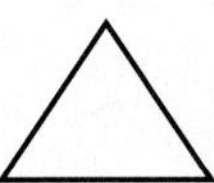

Ⓐ rectangle

Ⓒ circle

Ⓑ trapezoid

Ⓓ triangle

3. How many corners does a rectangle have?

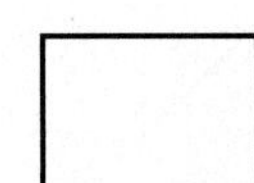

Ⓐ 3

Ⓒ 5

Ⓑ 4

Ⓓ 6

4. Draw a shape with 3 sides. What shape did you draw?

Name Date

Geoboard Triangles

Record your triangle.

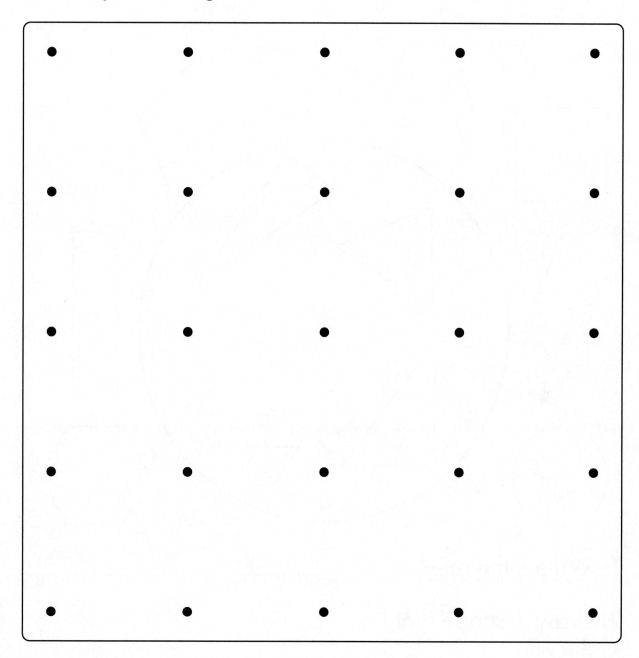

Name Date

Find the Rule

What do all of the shapes in the circle have in common?

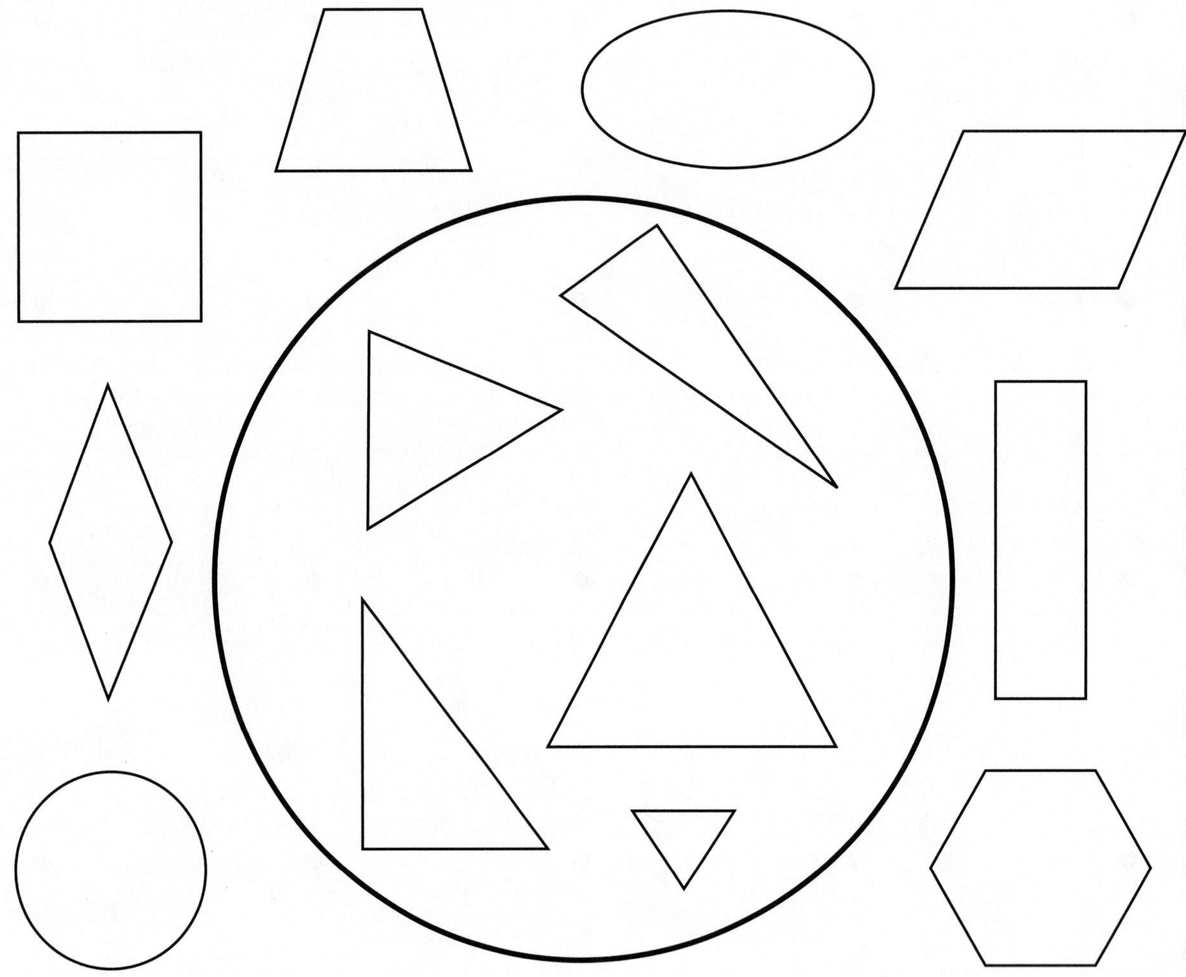

1. What's the rule? ______________________

2. Draw 1 shape that fits the rule.

3. Draw 1 shape that does **not** fit the rule.

Use anytime after Session 2.4.

Name Date

Quiz

Use the quilt square to choose the correct answer.

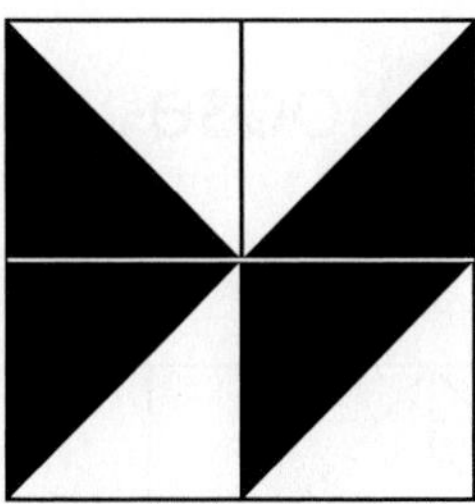

1. How many small white triangles?

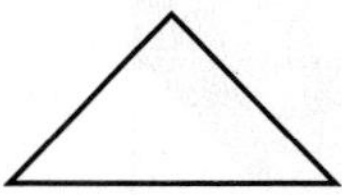

(A) 1 (B) 2 (C) 3 (D) 4

2. How many big black triangles?

(A) 3 (B) 2 (C) 1 (D) 0

3. How many parallelograms?

(A) 1 (B) 2 (C) 3 (D) 4

4. Copy the quilt pattern shown above in this square.

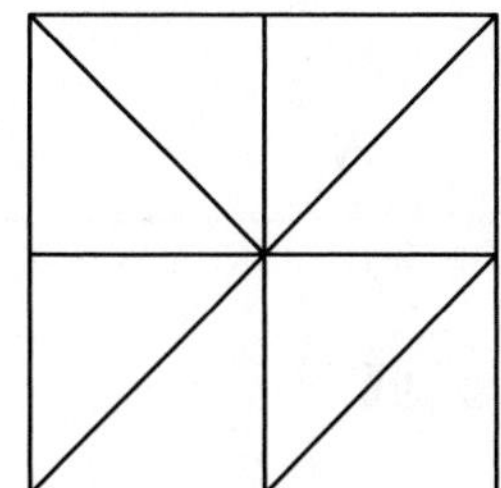

Name Date

More Quilt Patterns

1. Use this quilt square to make a quilt pattern.

Choose one color to be the dark color. Choose another color to be the light color.

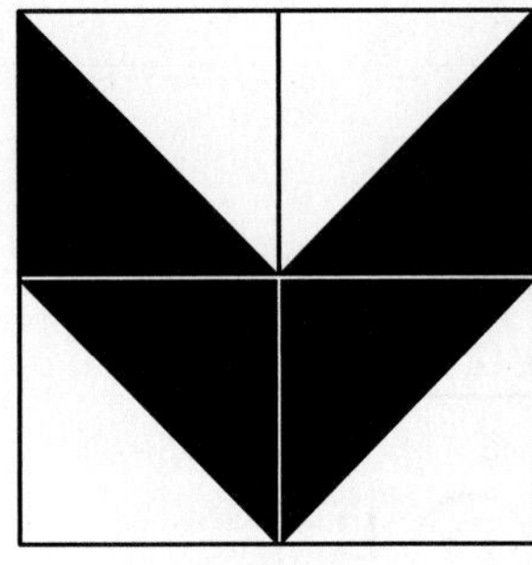

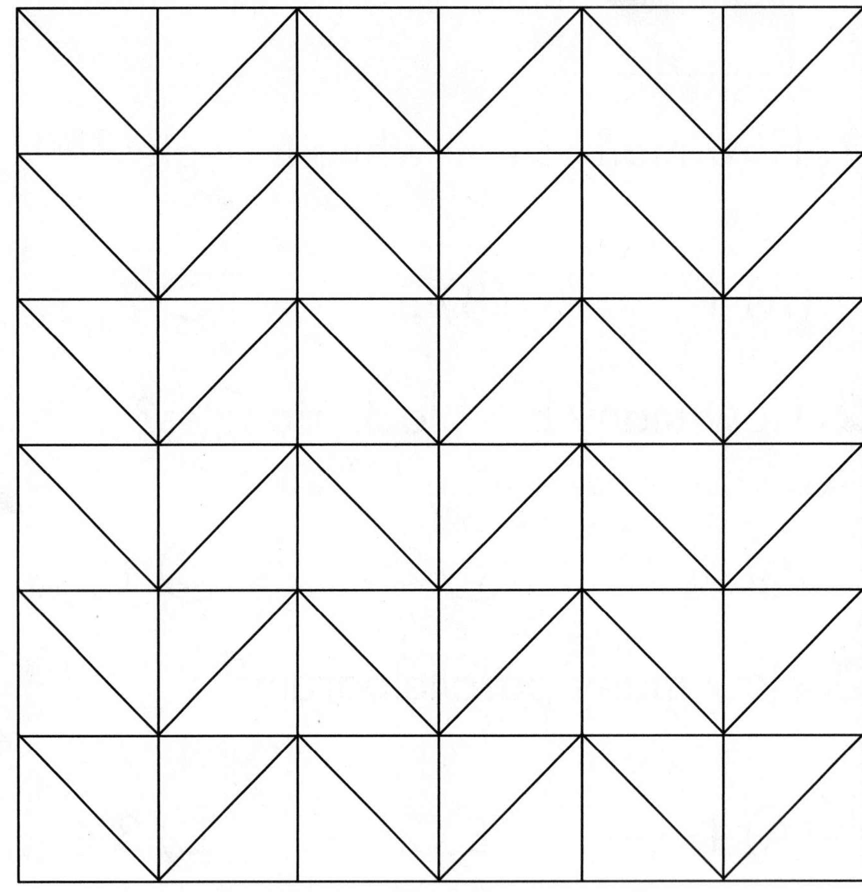

2. How many quilt squares are in the pattern? ________

Use anytime after Session 3.3.

Name Date

Finding Shapes

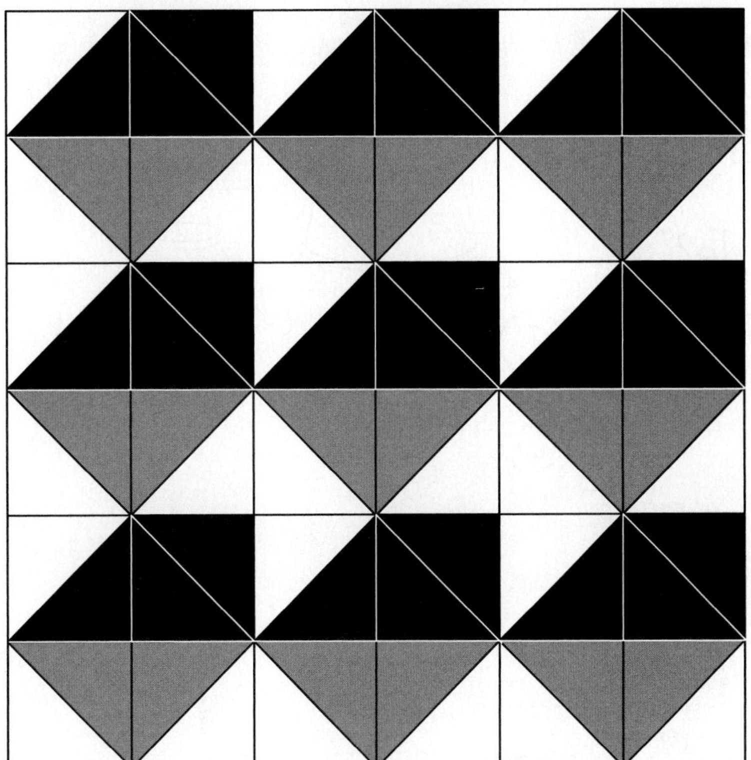

1. How many small white triangles? ____________

2. How many small gray triangles? ____________

3. How many big white triangles? ____________
Hint: A small triangle can be part of more than one big triangle.

4. How many big gray triangles? ____________

5. How many black trapezoids? ____________

Name Date

Quiz

Choose the correct answer.

1. There are 6 counters in all.

How many are inside?

Ⓐ 1 Ⓒ 3

Ⓑ 2 Ⓓ 4

2. What is the total?

Ⓐ 11 Ⓑ 9 Ⓒ 7 Ⓓ 5

3. Libby has 8 pens. Diego gave her 6 more. How many pens does Libby have now?

Ⓐ 14 Ⓒ 16

Ⓑ 15 Ⓓ 17

4. Write the missing numbers on the number line.

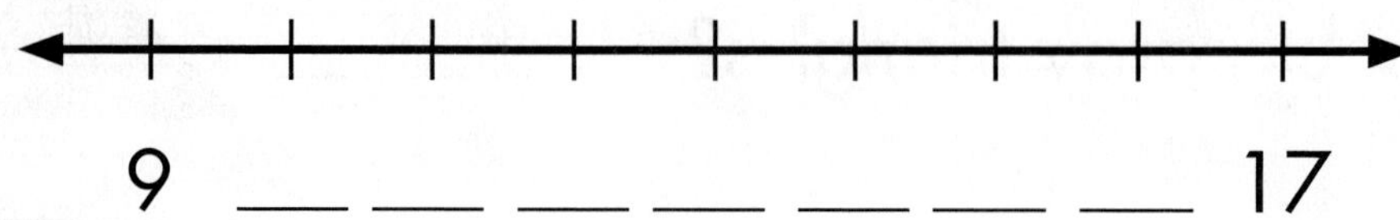

9 ___ ___ ___ ___ ___ ___ ___ 17

Name Date

How Many Rocks?

Solve the problem. Show your work.

Isabel has 3 rocks.
Vic has 9 rocks.
How many rocks do they have?

Name Date

Solving Story Problems

Dot Addition D and E

Find another way to make each total.

1. 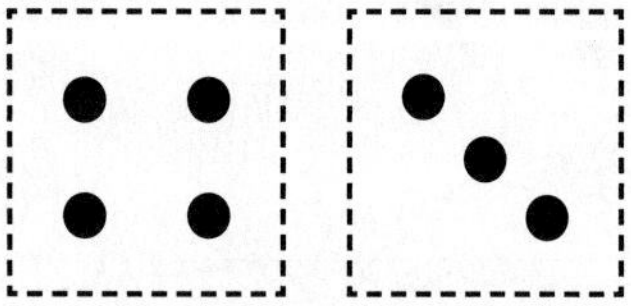 (dice: 4, 3) =

2. (dice: 5, 4) =

3. (dice: 2, 3, 3) =

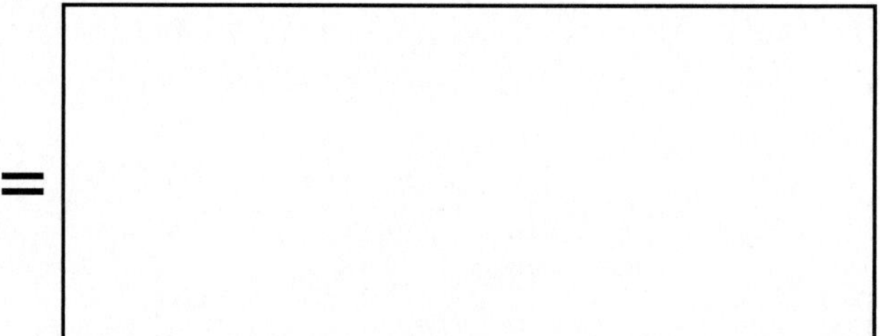

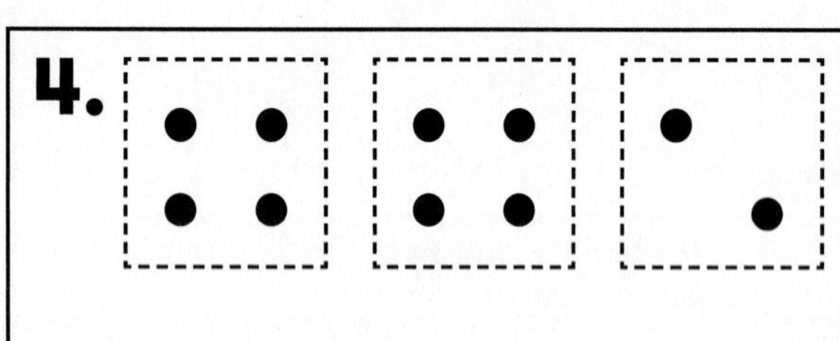

4. (dice: 4, 4, 2) =

5.  (dice: 3, 5, 2) =

Name Date

Quiz

Choose the correct answer.

1. Danielle saw 11 dogs at the park.
5 ran away. How many dogs were left?

Ⓐ 8 dogs Ⓒ 6 dogs

Ⓑ 7 dogs Ⓓ 5 dogs

2. 8 − ⁝⁝ =

Ⓐ 2 Ⓒ 6

Ⓑ 4 Ⓓ 8

3. 12 − 4 =

Ⓐ 5 Ⓒ 7

Ⓑ 6 Ⓓ 8

4. Solve the problem. Show your work.

Marta had 5 bananas. She gave 3 away.
How many does she have now?

Name Date

Subtracting Dots

Subtract. Write the answers.

1.  – [die: 1] = ______

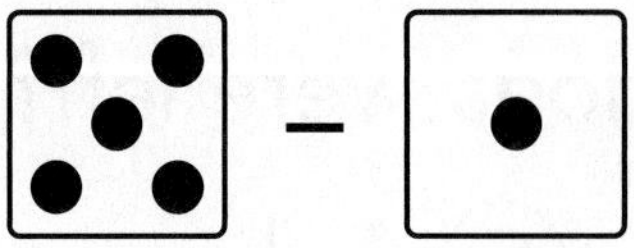

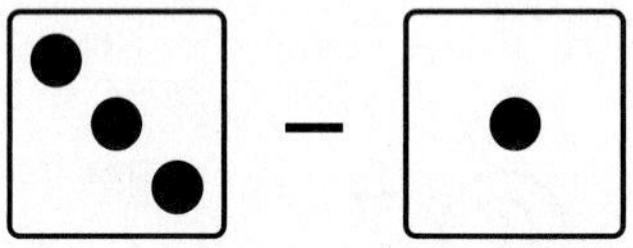

2. [die: 6] – [die: 4] = ______

3.  – [die: 2] = ______

4.  – [die: 1] = ______

5. [die: 6] – [die: 3] = ______

6. [die: 5] – [die: 2] = ______

Use anytime after Session 2.3.

Name Date

Solving Story Problems

How Many Fish?

Solve the problem. Show your work.

Bruce saw 17 fish in a pond.
Then 10 fish swam away.
How many fish were left?

Name Date

Solving Story Problems

Quiz

Choose the correct answer.

1. Jacob had 6 fish. His mom bought 5 more. How many fish does he have now?

Ⓐ 10 Ⓒ 12

Ⓑ 11 Ⓓ 13

2. There were 13 birds sitting on a fence. Then 8 birds flew away. How many birds were left?

Ⓐ 11 Ⓒ 7

Ⓑ 9 Ⓓ 5

3. What's missing?

☐ + ⁘ = 10

Ⓐ 4 Ⓒ 6

Ⓑ 5 Ⓓ 7

4. Today's Number is 9. How many ways can you make Today's Number with 2 numbers? Show your work.

Name Date

How Many?

Solve the problems. Show your work.

1. Deshawn has 11 cards.

Tamika gives him 5 more.

How many cards does Deshawn have now?

2. Keena had 12 roses.

She gave Emilia 5 of them.

How many roses does Keena have left?

Solving Challenging Story Problems

Solve the problems. Show your work.

1. Stacy and Seth picked strawberries.

They ate 21 strawberries for dinner.

Seth ate 8 more strawberries after dinner.

How many strawberries did Stacy and Seth eat?

2. Edgar had 19 rocks.

He gave 10 of them away.

Now how many rocks does Edgar have?

Name Date

Quiz

Choose the correct answer.

1. What number is missing?

27	28	29	___

Ⓐ 16 Ⓑ 26 Ⓒ 30 Ⓓ 31

2. What number is missing?

44	45	___	47

Ⓐ 35 Ⓑ 46 Ⓒ 55 Ⓓ 64

3. What number is missing?

41	42	43	44	45	46	47	48	49	50
51	52	53	___	55	56	57	58	59	60

Ⓐ 65 Ⓑ 56 Ⓒ 54 Ⓓ 45

4. Fix the mistake.

33	34	35	36	37	38	39	50

Name Date

Solving Story Problems

What Went Wrong?

Here are parts of 6 counting strips. Fix the mistakes.

1.

36
37
38
39
04

2.

41
24
43
44
45

3.

18
19
30
31
32

4.

28
29
31
32
33

5.

66
67
68
96
70

6.

39
50
51
52
53

Name Date

More Missing Numbers

What numbers are missing?
Fill in the missing numbers.

	2	3	4	5	6	7	8	9	
11		13	14	15	16	17	18		20
21	22		24	25	26	27		29	30
31	32	33		35	36		38	39	40
41	42	43	44			47	48	49	50
51	52	53	54			57	58	59	60
61	62	63		65	66		68	69	70
71	72		74	75	76	77		79	80
81		83	84	85	86	87	88		90
	92	93	94	95	96	97	98	99	

Name Date

Quiz

Choose the correct answer.

1. The rule is triangles. Which shape fits the rule?

Ⓐ 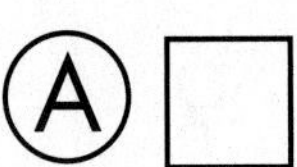 Ⓑ 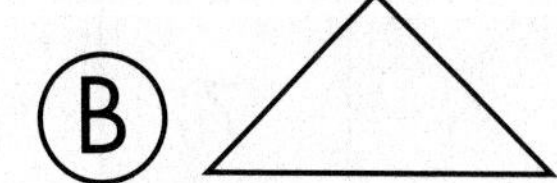 Ⓒ 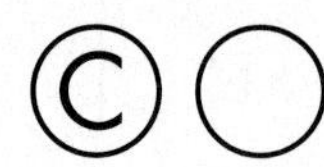 Ⓓ 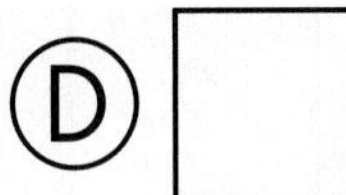

2. What is the rule?

These Fit My Rule

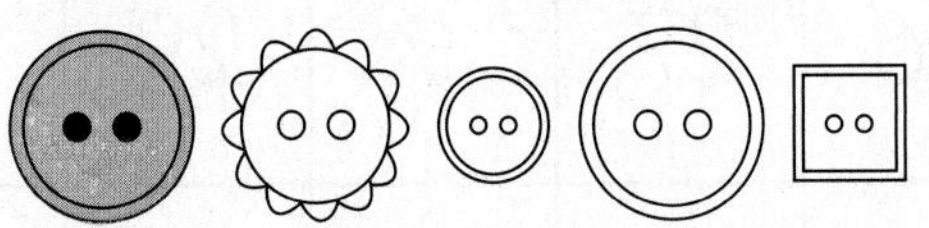

These Don't Fit My Rule

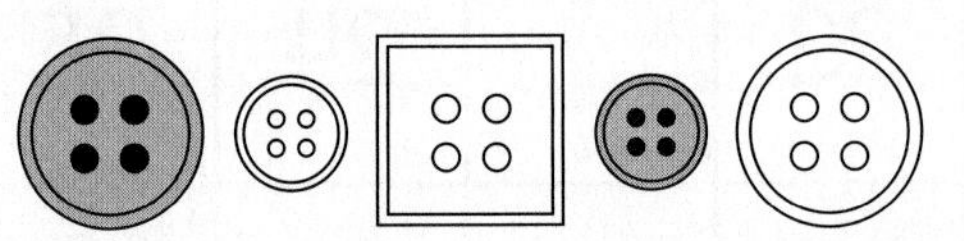

Ⓐ Large buttons

Ⓑ White buttons

Ⓒ Small buttons

Ⓓ Buttons with 2 holes

3. The rule is shapes with straight sides. Which shape fits the rule?

Ⓐ  Ⓑ 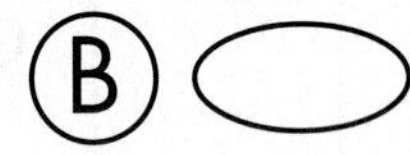 Ⓒ 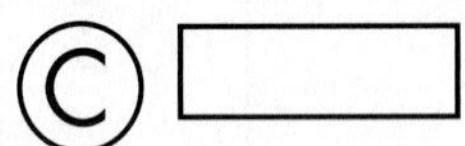 Ⓓ 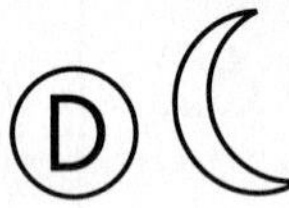

4. What is the rule? How do you know?

These Fit My Rule

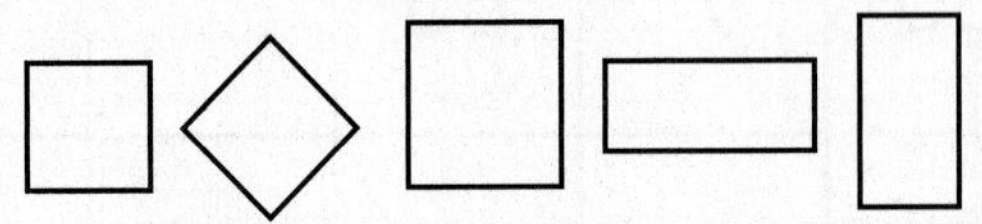

These Don't Fit My Rule

Name Date

Guess My Rule with Objects

1. The rule is buttons with 4 holes. Circle the buttons that fit the rule.

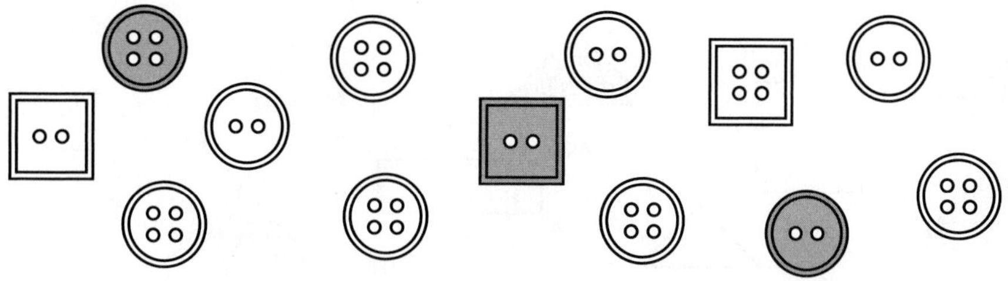

2. What rule was used to sort the shapes?

These Fit My Rule

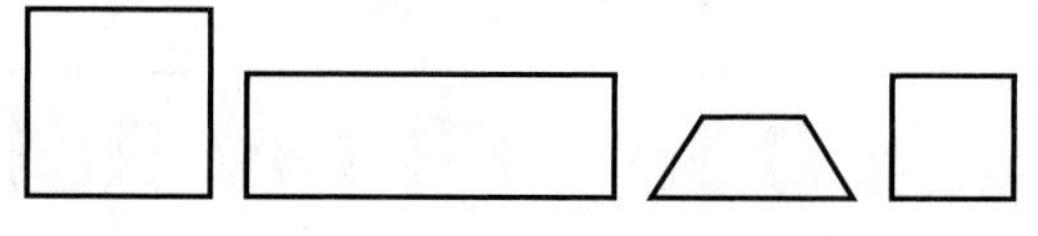

These Don't Fit My Rule

Rule: ______________________________

3. Make your own rule. Then circle the shapes that fit your rule.

Rule: ______________________________

Name Date

Guess My Rule with 2 Rules

1. Mark an X on the shapes that are gray *and* have 3 sides.

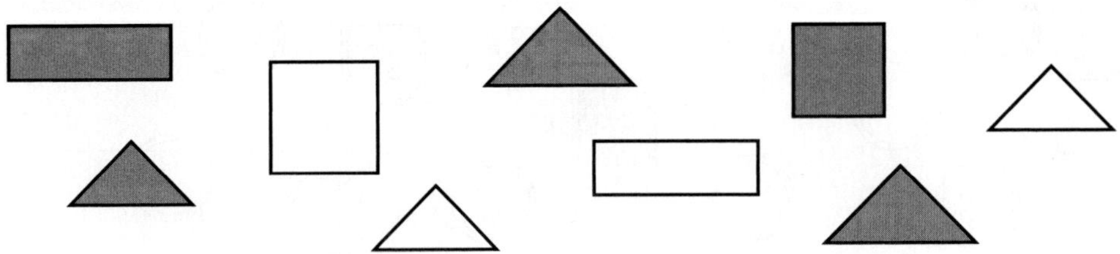

2. Which 2 rules were used to sort the buttons?

________ and ________

These Fit My Rules	These Don't Fit My Rules
	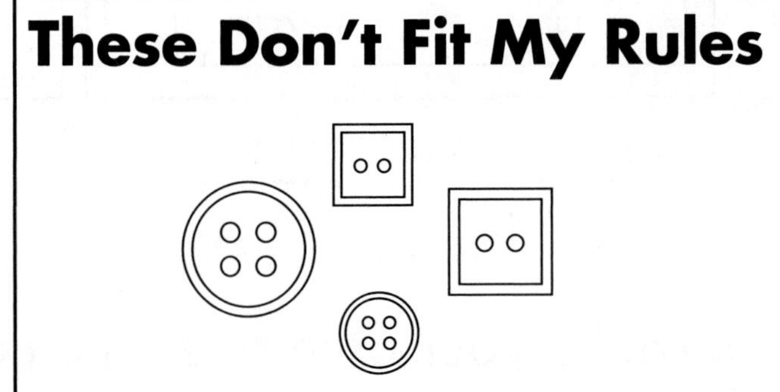

3. Which 2 rules were used to sort the shapes?

________ and ________

These Fit My Rules	These Don't Fit My Rules

Use anytime after Session 1.4.

Name Date

Quiz

Choose the correct answer.

Vic asked some friends if they liked chocolate or white milk.

Chocolate Milk

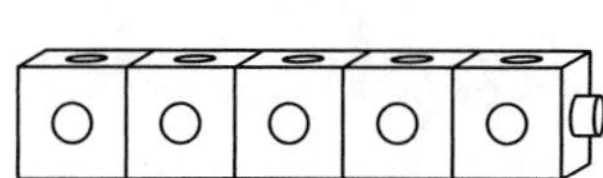

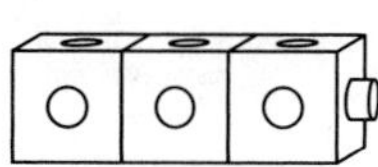

1. How many chose white milk?

Ⓐ 2 Ⓑ 3 Ⓒ 5 Ⓓ 8

2. How many people answered Vic's survey?

Ⓐ 2 Ⓑ 3 Ⓒ 5 Ⓓ 8

3. In this survey, how many chose elephants?

Elephants

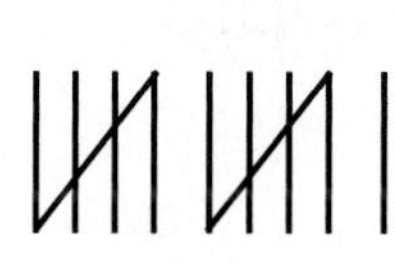

Ⓐ 4 Ⓑ 7 Ⓒ 11 Ⓓ 18

4. In a class survey, 15 students chose grapes and 7 chose raisins. Make a picture that shows this data.

Name Date

Analyzing Data

Students used tally marks to answer the following question.

Would you rather drink orange juice or apple juice?

Orange Juice	Apple Juice

1. How many students chose orange juice? ____________

2. How many students chose apple juice? ____________

3. How many students responded? ____________

4. How many *more* students like apple juice than like orange juice? Show your work.

Name Date

Different Ways of Showing Data

Libby took attendance. Here are the data.

Present	Absent
✓ ✓	✓ ✓ ✓ ✓

1. How many students are in school today? ____________

2. How many students are absent? ____________

3. How many students are in the whole class? ____________

4. Show another way to represent the data.

Name Date

Quiz

Use the chart. Choose the correct answer.

Pets	Number of Students
0	◯◯◯
1	◯◯◯◯◯◯
2	◯◯◯◯
3	◯◯
4	◯

1. How many students have 2 pets?

Ⓐ 3 Ⓑ 4 Ⓒ 5 Ⓓ 6

2. How many students have 4 pets?

Ⓐ 4 Ⓑ 3 Ⓒ 2 Ⓓ 1

3. How many pets do most students have?

Ⓐ 0 Ⓑ 1 Ⓒ 2 Ⓓ 3

4. Show that 2 students have 5 pets.

Pets	Number of Students
5	

Name Date

What Do You Know?

This chart shows how old some fourth-grade students are.

Age	Number of Students
8	
9	𝍸 IIII
10	𝍸 𝍸 III
11	I

1. How many students are 8 years old? ________

2. How many students are 9 years old? ________

3. How many students are 10 years old? ________

4. How many students are 11 years old? ________

5. How old are most of the students? ________

6. Are there more 9-year-olds or 10-year-olds?

____

7. Are there fewer 9-year-olds or 11-year-olds?

____

Name Date

What Pencil Color?

Edgar wants to bring new colored pencils for his class. He can only bring 2 colors of pencils. Edgar asks his classmates what their favorite colors are.

Favorite Colors

Red	Yellow	Green	Blue	Orange
Jacinta	William	Keena	Leah	Bruce
Felipe	Libby	Lyle	Marta	
Vic	Paula		Teo	
	Tamika		Toshi	
			Diego	

What 2 colors of pencils should Edgar bring for the class? How do you know?

____

____

____

Use anytime after Session 3.4.

Name Date

Quiz

Choose the correct answer.

1. How long?

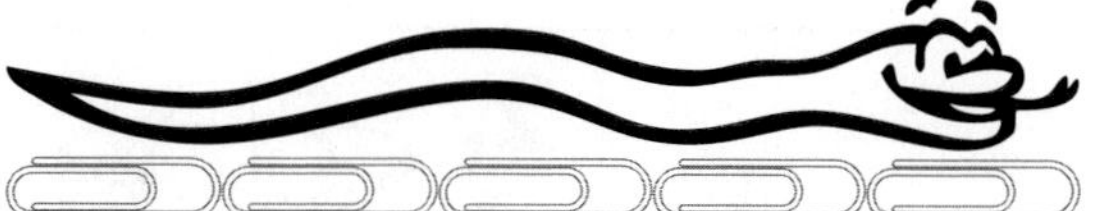

Ⓐ 3 clips Ⓑ 4 clips Ⓒ 5 clips Ⓓ 6 clips

2. How tall?

Ⓐ 9 cubes Ⓑ 8 cubes Ⓒ 7 cubes Ⓓ 6 cubes

3. How long?

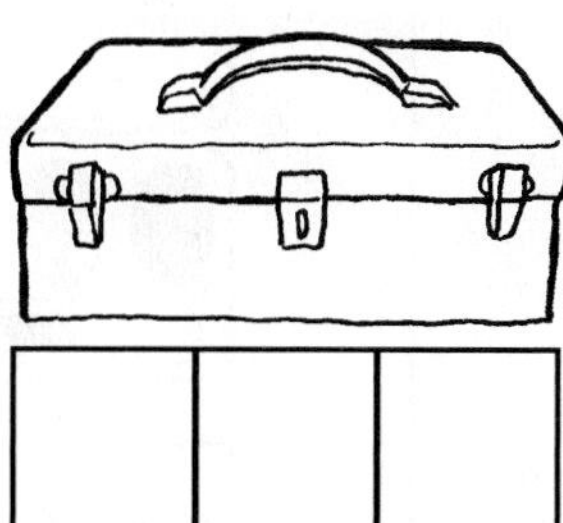

Ⓐ 6 tiles Ⓑ 5 tiles Ⓒ 4 tiles Ⓓ 3 tiles

4. Use paper clips. Measure the pencil.

_______________ clips

Name Date

Measuring with Tiles

Write how many tiles were used to measure each picture.

1. 

__________ tiles

2. 

__________ tiles

3. 

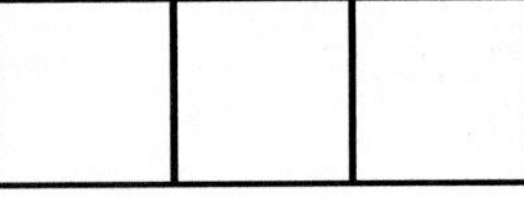

__________ tiles

4. 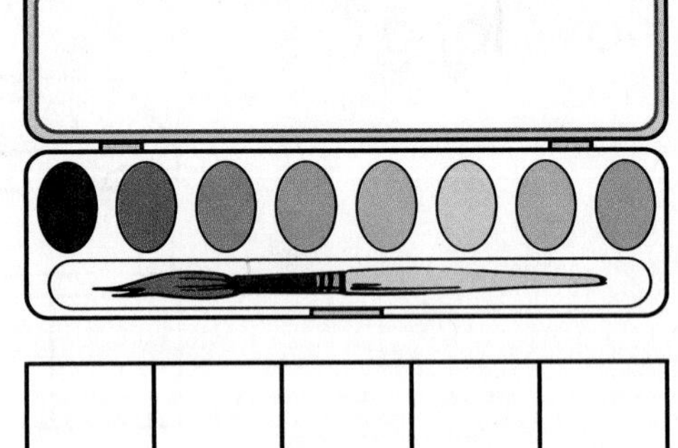

__________ tiles

Use anytime after Session 1.2.

Name Date

Measuring 3 Ways

Find 3 objects to measure in your classroom. Measure each object using cubes, tiles, and paper clips.

Name of Object	How long?
1.	______ cubes ______ tiles ______ clips
2.	______ cubes ______ tiles ______ clips
3.	______ cubes ______ tiles ______ clips

Name Date

Quiz

Choose the correct answer.

1. A rabbit jumped 6 kid steps. Then it jumped 7 kid steps. How far did it jump in all?

Ⓐ 12 kid steps Ⓒ 14 kid steps

Ⓑ 13 kid steps Ⓓ 15 kid steps

2. How many steps long is the strip?

Ⓐ 6 Ⓑ $6\frac{1}{2}$ Ⓒ 7 Ⓓ $7\frac{1}{2}$

3. You measure from the teacher's desk to your seat. Which unit would give you the smallest number?

Ⓐ paper clips Ⓒ kid steps

Ⓑ craft sticks Ⓓ basketball player steps

4. Vic measured his desk with craft sticks. It was 7 craft sticks long. If he measured his desk with cubes, would it be more than 7 cubes or fewer than 7 cubes? Show how you know.

Name Date

Measuring with Kid Steps

Count the number of kid steps for each distance in the classroom.

Distance	Kid Steps
1. From the teacher's desk to your desk.	
2. From the door to the window.	
3. From ______ to ______	
4. From ______ to ______	
5. From ______ to ______	

Name Date

How Much Longer?

Find out which tape is longer and how much longer.

1. Tape A is 10 kid steps long.

Tape B is 14 kid steps long.

Which is longer? Circle. Tape A Tape B

How much longer? ________ kid steps

2. Tape C is 6 kid steps long.

Tape D is 9 kid steps long.

Which is longer? Circle. Tape C Tape D

How much longer? ________ kid steps

3. Tape E is 12 kid steps long.

Tape F is 5 kid steps long.

Which is longer? Circle. Tape E Tape F

How much longer? ________ kid steps

Use anytime after Session 2.1.

Name Date

Quiz

Choose the correct answer.

1. What number do you need to make 10 in all?

3	4	5	6
Ⓐ	Ⓑ	Ⓒ	Ⓓ

2. What number is missing?

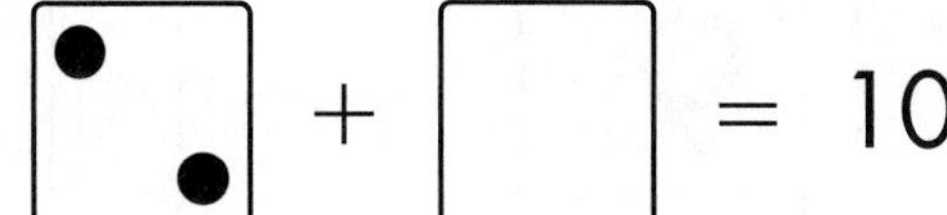

8	6	4	2
Ⓐ	Ⓑ	Ⓒ	Ⓓ

3. Paul put 10 crayons in the box. Nicky took 1 out. How many crayons were left?

8	9	10	11
Ⓐ	Ⓑ	Ⓒ	Ⓓ

4. There are 10 counters in all. Complete the chart.

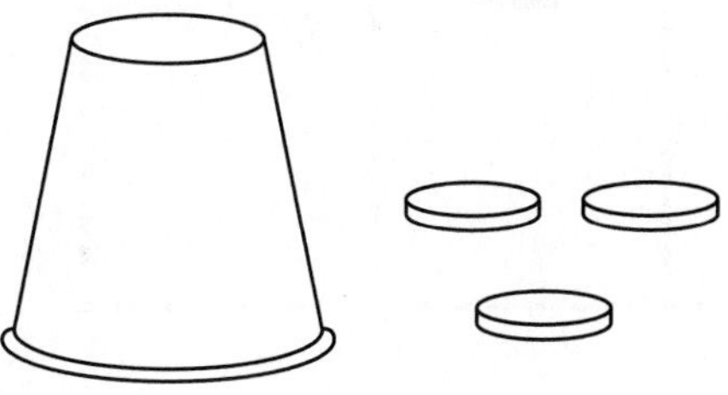

Out	In

Name Date

Number Games and Crayon Puzzles

That's a 10!

Write a number on the card to make 10 in all.

1. 3 |	2. 1 | 3 |
3. 9 |	4. 2 | 5 |
5. 0 |	6. 5 | 1 |
7. 5 |	8. 4 | 4 |

Name Date

Number Games and Crayon Puzzles

Make 10 with Wild Cards

3	5	1	6	9
2	Wild Card	7	3	8
6	4	9	7	4
1	8	5	Wild Card	2

1. Find combinations of 2 numbers that make 10.
Can you use *every* card? Record your combinations.

2. Find combinations of 3 numbers that make 10.
Can you use *every* card? Record your combinations.

Name Date

Quiz

Choose the correct answer.

1. How many in all?

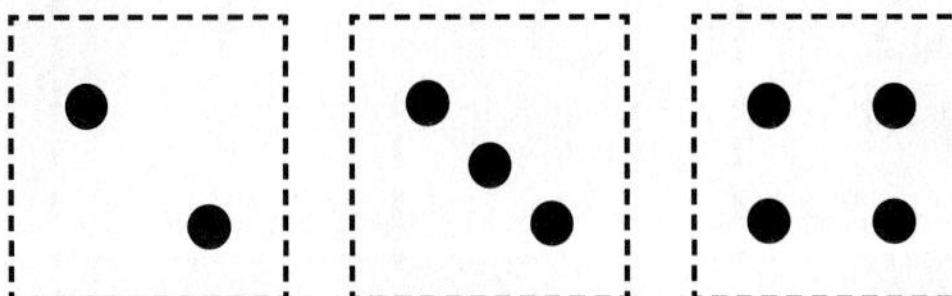

Ⓐ 5 Ⓑ 7 Ⓒ 9 Ⓓ 11

2. Which shows another way to make the same number?

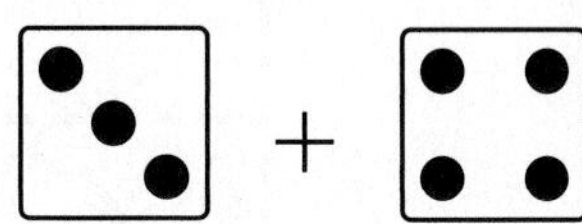

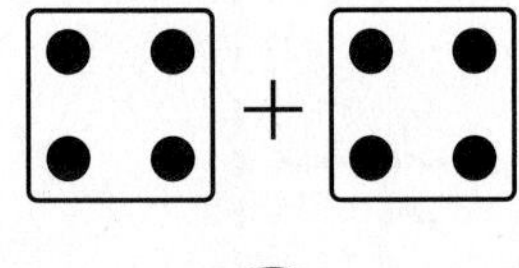

Ⓐ

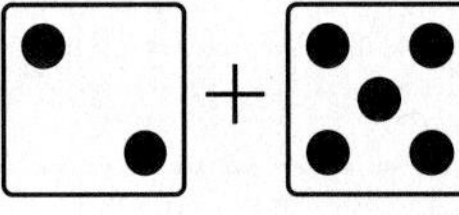

Ⓑ

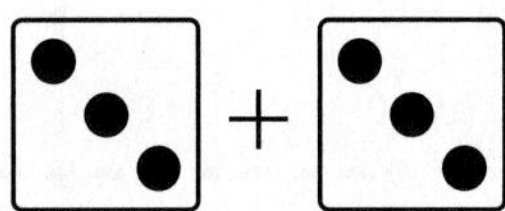

Ⓒ

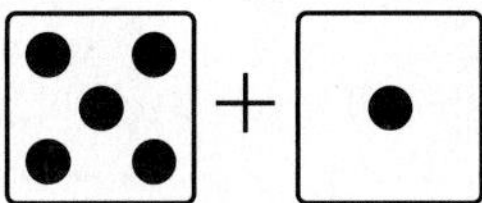

Ⓓ

3. I have 11 crayons.
5 are red. The rest are blue.
How many blue crayons do I have?

Ⓐ 6 Ⓑ 8 Ⓒ 9 Ⓓ 11

4. I have 8 crayons.
Some are red and some are blue.
I have more red crayons.
How many of each could I have?

Name Date

Dot and Number Totals

Write the total number or the missing part.

1.	⁙ (5)	+	7	=	____
2.	⋱ (3)	+	☐	=	11
3.	☐	+	⁙ (5)	=	13
4.	∷ (4)	+	9	=	____
5.	⠿ (6)	+	☐	=	13
6.	⁙ (5)	+	☐	=	14

Name Date

Crayon Puzzles About Fewer

Solve the problems. Find all possible combinations.

1. I have 15 crayons.
Some are red, some are blue, and some are green.
I have the fewest blue crayons.
How many of each could I have?

2. I have 15 crayons.
Some are red, some are blue, and some are green.
I have 5 red crayons.
How many blue and green crayons could I have?

Quiz

Choose the correct answer.

1. How many in all?

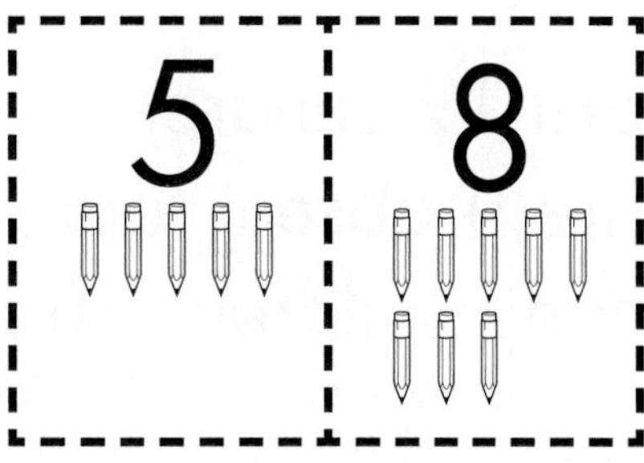

7	9	11	13
	Ⓑ	Ⓒ	

2. **7** – ⚂ =

6	5	4	3
	Ⓑ		

3. Toshi has 4 big cars and 8 little cars.
How many cars does he have in all?

12	13	14	15
Ⓐ	Ⓑ	Ⓒ	Ⓓ

4. Keena had 14 pennies.
She used 8 pennies to buy a toy.
How many pennies does she have now?
Solve the problem. Show your work.

Name Date

Story Problem Strategies

Solve each problem. Show how you solved it.

1. There are 19 children in the class. There are 4 absent today. How many children are present?

2. There are 4 tennis balls, 5 soccer balls, and 8 baseballs in a basket. How many balls are in the basket?

Use anytime after Session 3.5.

Strategies for Solving Problems

Solve each problem. Show your work.

1. Allie had 10 dog stickers and 8 cat stickers.
   She gave 2 cat stickers to her sister.
   How many stickers did she have then?

2. Bruce had 15 blue marbles and 8 red marbles.
   He gave 5 blue marbles to Lyle.
   He gave 5 red marbles to Vic.
   How many marbles did Bruce have left?

Quiz

Choose the correct answer.

1. What is the unit?

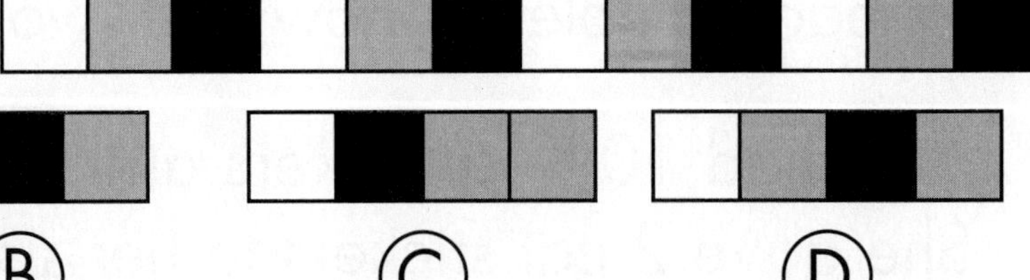

Ⓐ Ⓑ Ⓒ Ⓓ

2. What color will cube 8 be?

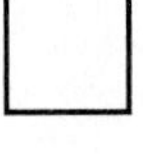

 Ⓐ
 Ⓑ
 Ⓒ
Ⓓ

3. Which cube unit matches the unit of this pattern?

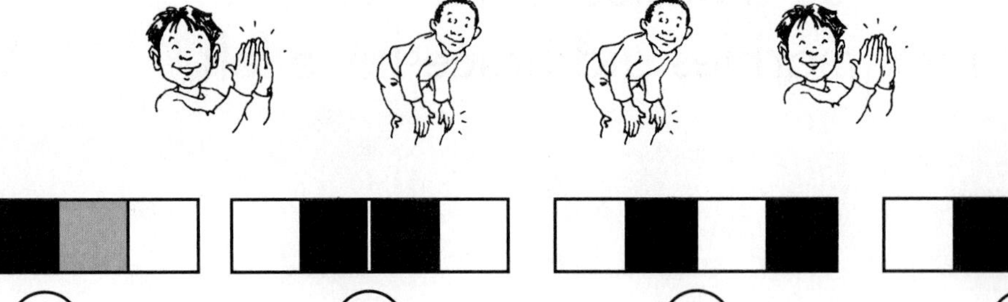

Ⓐ Ⓑ Ⓒ Ⓓ

4. Make a repeating pattern with 12 cubes.
Color it here. Then circle the unit.

Name Date

Matching Color Patterns

Color the boxes to make a **color** pattern that matches the body **movement** pattern.

1.

2.

3.

4.

Name Date

Longer Patterns

1. Make a unit that is 5 cubes long.

Color your unit.

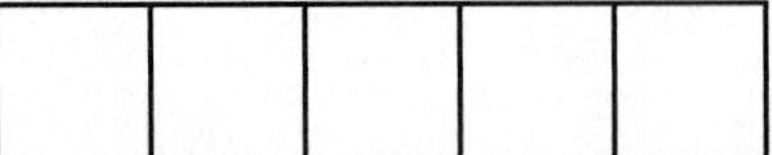

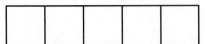

Color your pattern. Circle every unit.

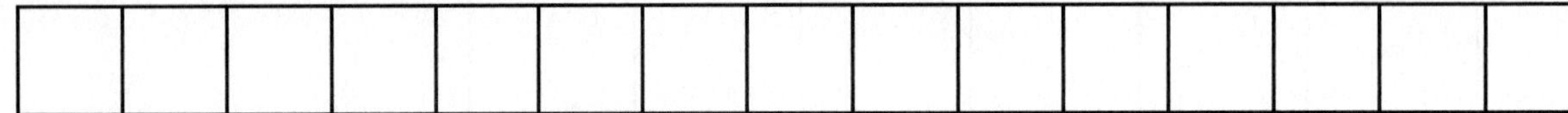

2. Make a unit that is 4 cubes long.

Color your unit.

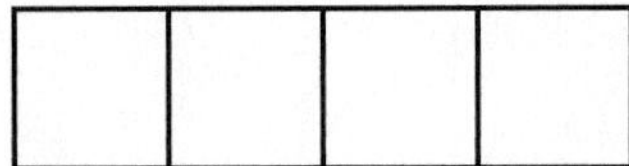

Color your pattern. Circle every unit.

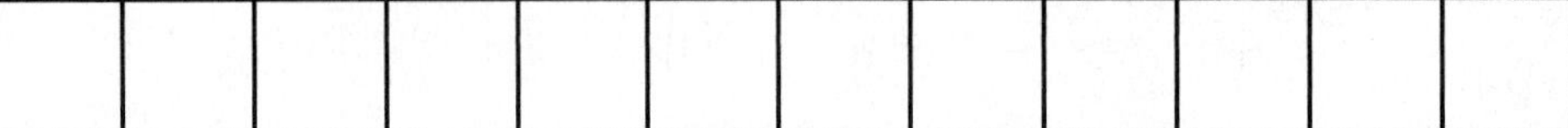

3. Color a unit that is 2, 3, 4 or 5 cubes long.

If your cube train is 4 units long, how many cubes will you need? Show your work.

Name Date

Quiz

Choose the correct answer.

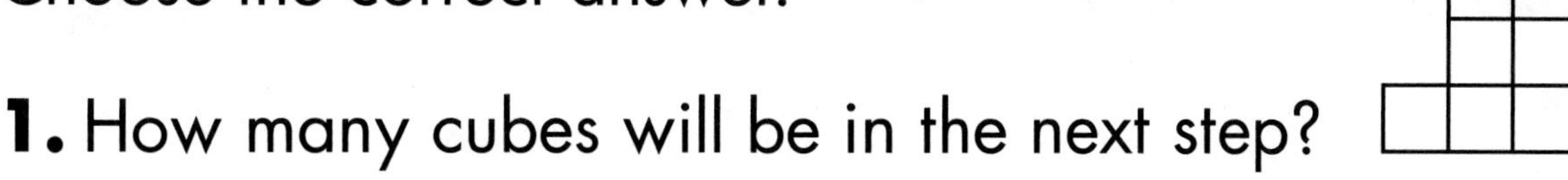

1. How many cubes will be in the next step?

Ⓐ 3 Ⓑ 5 Ⓒ 7 Ⓓ 9

2. What comes next?

8, 10, 12, 14, ___

Ⓐ 18 Ⓑ 16 Ⓒ 15 Ⓓ 12

3. What shape is 10?

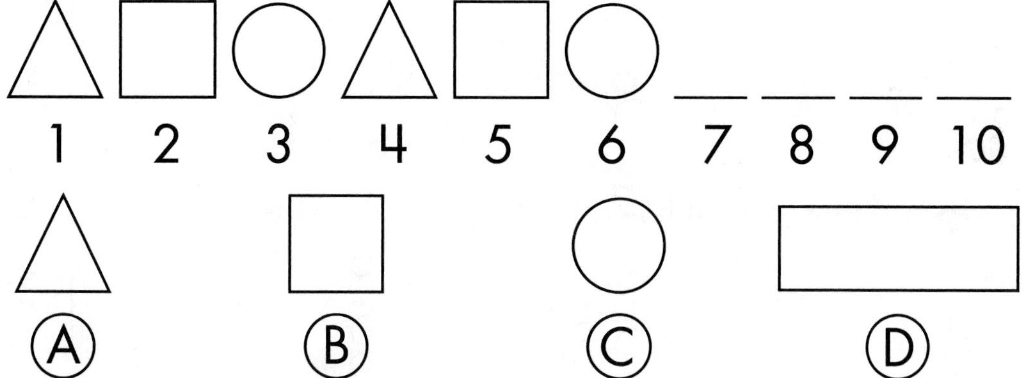

4. Marta starts with 4 pennies in her jar.
She adds 2 pennies each day.
On what day will she have 14 pennies?
How do you know?

Name Date

Penny Jars with Different Start Numbers

Draw the start number in the jar. Write how many pennies are in the jar each day.

1. Number to add each day: 2

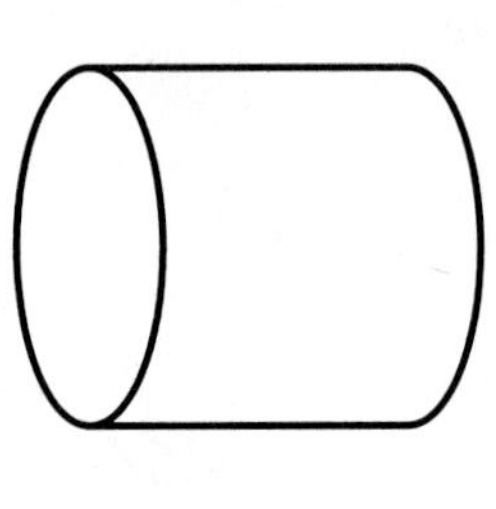
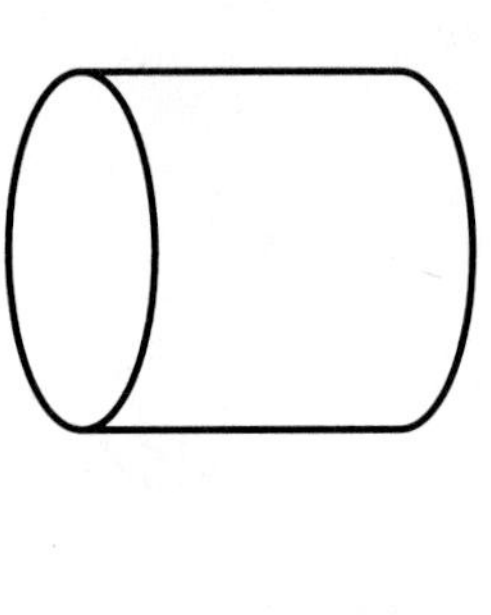
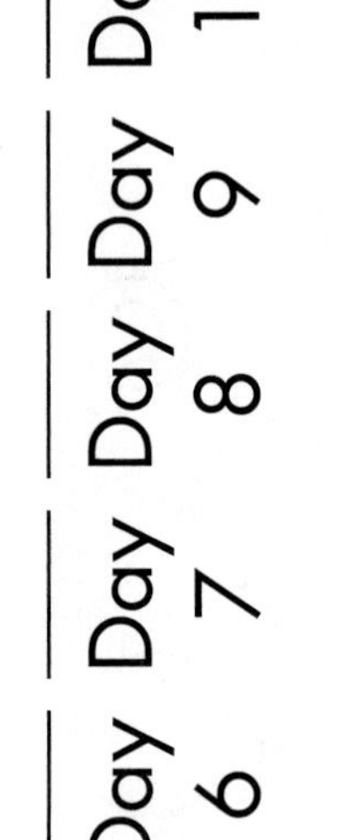

7										
Start	Day 1	Day 2	Day 3	Day 4	Day 5	Day 6	Day 7	Day 8	Day 9	Day 10

2. Number to add each day: 3

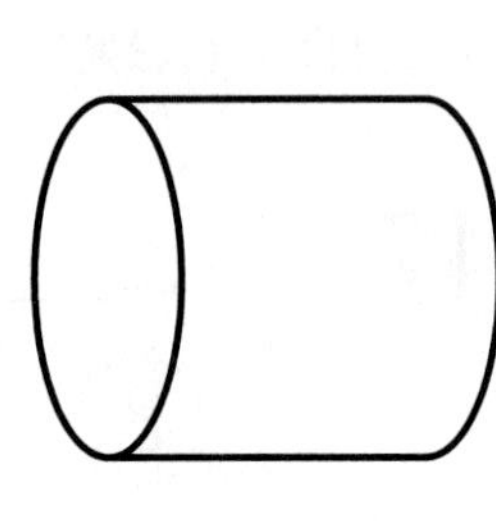

6										
Start	Day 1	Day 2	Day 3	Day 4	Day 5	Day 6	Day 7	Day 8	Day 9	Day 10

Use anytime after Session 2.3.

Name Date

Color, Shape, and Number Patterns

The Penny Jar with Larger Numbers

Draw the start number in the jar. Write how many pennies are in the jar each day.

1. Number to add each day: 2

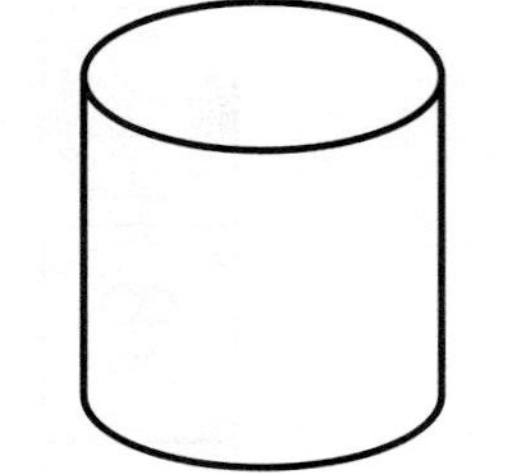

14	___	___	___	___	___	___	___	___	___	___
Start	Day 1	Day 2	Day 3	Day 4	Day 5	Day 6	Day 7	Day 8	Day 9	Day 10

2. Number to add each day: 3

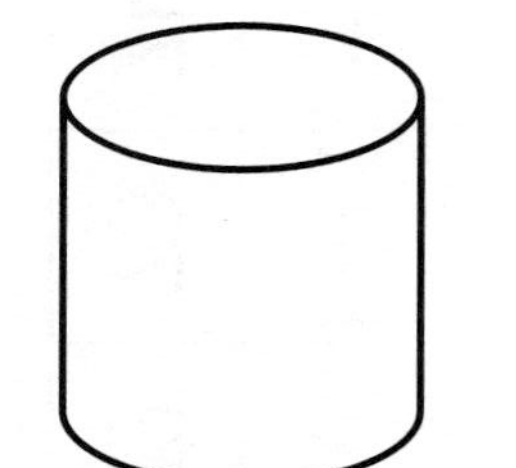

20	___	___	___	___	___	___	___	___	___	___
Start	Day 1	Day 2	Day 3	Day 4	Day 5	Day 6	Day 7	Day 8	Day 9	Day 10

Name Date

Quiz

Choose the correct answer.

1. We have 28. We rolled 4.
How many do we have now?

Ⓐ 30 Ⓑ 31 Ⓒ 32 Ⓓ 33

2. What number is missing?

71	72	73	74	75	76	77	78		80

Ⓐ 97 Ⓑ 89 Ⓒ 79 Ⓓ 69

3. What number is missing?

31	32	33	34	35		37	38	39	40
41	42	43	44	45	46	47	48	49	50

Ⓐ 36 Ⓑ 37 Ⓒ 46 Ⓓ 63

4. Continue the counting strip.

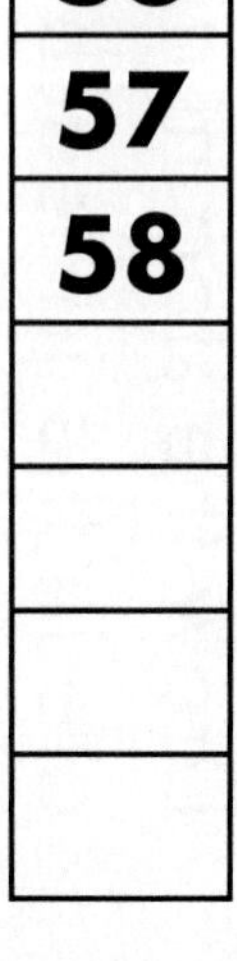

Name Date

Counting Strips

Write the missing numbers on the counting strips.

15	33	57	82
16	34	58	83
17	35	59	84

Name Date

Missing Numbers Between 101 and 200

What are the missing numbers? Write them on the chart.

101	102	103	104				108	109	110
111	112	113	114	115	116	117	118	119	
	122	123	124	125	126	127	128	129	130
				135	136		138	139	140
	142	143	144	145	146			149	150
151	152	153	154		156		158	159	160
161			164	165	166	167		169	170
171	172	173	174	175	176	177		179	180
181	182	183	184	185	186	187			
		193	194	195	196	197	198	199	

Use anytime after Session 1.3.

Name Date

Quiz

Choose the correct answer.

1. How many eyes are there in a group of 5 people?

5	10	15	20
Ⓐ	Ⓑ	Ⓒ	Ⓓ

2. How many squares are in this group?

□□ □□ □□ □ □ □ □ □

11	10	9	8
Ⓐ	Ⓑ	Ⓒ	Ⓓ

3. I see 3 cows. How many legs do I see?

3	6	9	12
Ⓐ	Ⓑ	Ⓒ	Ⓓ

4. There are 2 people and 4 dogs at the park. How many legs are there? Show your work.

Name Date

How Many Do I See?

Solve each riddle. Record your work.

1. I see 5 girls. How many eyes do I see? ____________	**2.** I see 2 cats. How many ears do I see? ____________
3. I see 4 birds. How many legs do I see? ____________	**4.** I see 5 horses. How many legs do I see? ____________
5. I see 3 boys. How many ears do I see? ____________	**6.** I see 2 dogs. How many legs do I see? ____________
7. I see 4 deer. How many eyes do I see? ____________	**8.** I see 3 kittens. How many paws do I see? ____________

Use anytime after Session 2.3.

Name Date

How Many in All?

Solve each problem. Show your work.

CHALLENGE

A hedgehog is an animal that has 4 feet.

This animal has 4 toes on each foot.

1. How many toes do 2 hedgehogs have in all?

2. How many toes do 4 hedgehogs have in all?

Name Date

Quiz

Choose the correct answer.

1. There are 6 children in the store. Each child has 5 pennies. How many pennies?

6	30	60	66
Ⓐ	Ⓑ	Ⓒ	Ⓓ

2. How many cubes altogether?

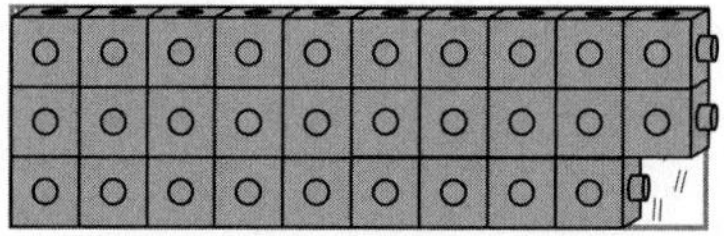

39	29	20	19
Ⓐ	Ⓑ	Ⓒ	Ⓓ

3. Which combination makes a total of 10?

6 + 2	6 + 3	4 + 5	3 + 7
Ⓐ	Ⓑ	Ⓒ	Ⓓ

4. What sum is the same as 4 + 8?
Show your work.

4 + 8 = 10 + ______

Use after Session 3.6.

Name Date

Solving *Ten Plus* Problems

Solve each problem. Show your work.

1. What sum is the same as 6 + 8?

6 + 8 = 10 + ______

2. What sum is the same as 4 + 6?

4 + 6 = 10 + ______

3. What sum is the same as 9 + 8?

9 + 8 = 10 + ______

Name Date

Roll Tens with the 100 Mat

1. 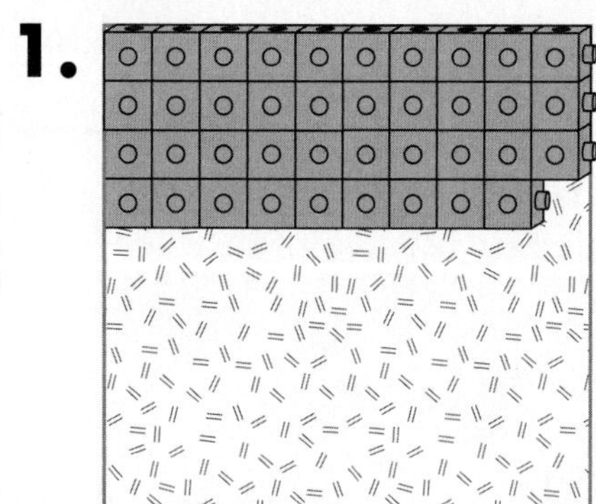

How many cubes? ________

2.

How many cubes? ________

3.

How many cubes? ________

Use anytime after Session 3.2.

Name Date

Quiz

Choose the correct answer.

1. Which object would best fit inside the box? 

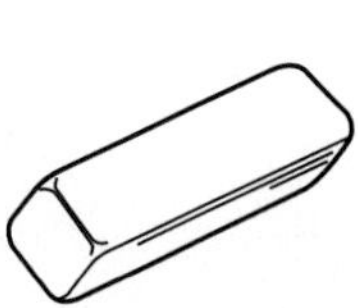 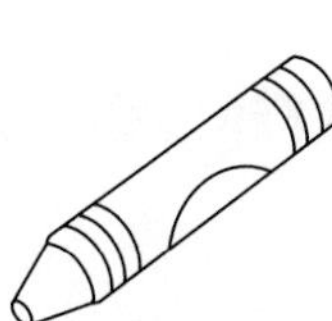  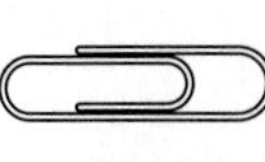

2. I have a face shaped like a triangle. 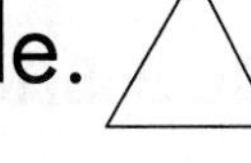

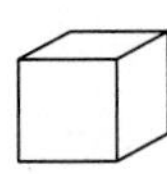 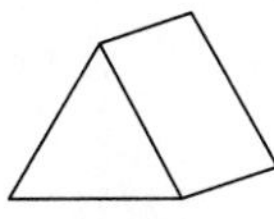 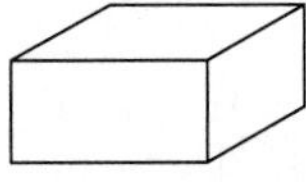 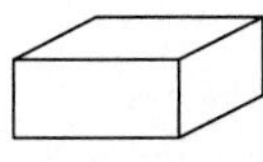

3. Look at the Geoblock. Which object has the same shape? 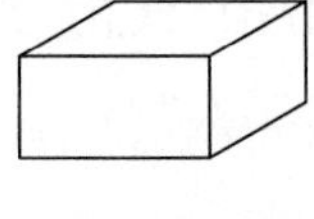

 Ⓑ  Ⓓ

4. Sketch the shape that would be a footprint for this Geoblock.

Name Date

Is It a Match?

Does the picture match the sentence?
If it **does,** circle the picture.
If it **does not,** cross out the picture.

1. I have a face shaped like a **triangle**.

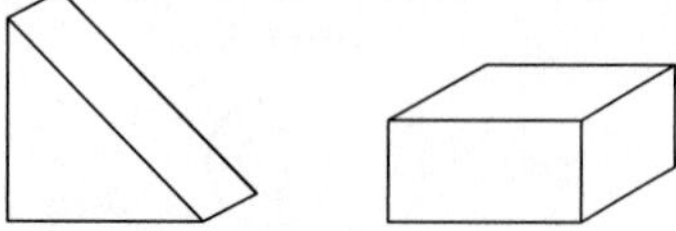

2. I have a face shaped like a **square**.

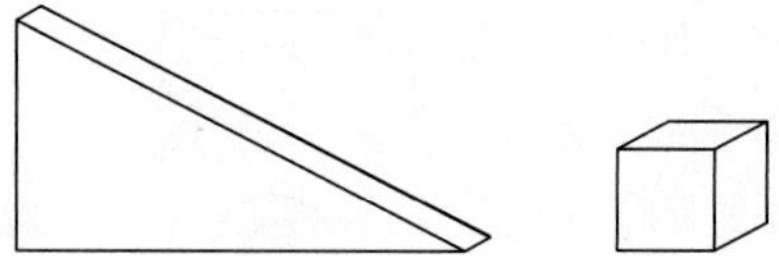

3. I have a face shaped like a **rectangle**.

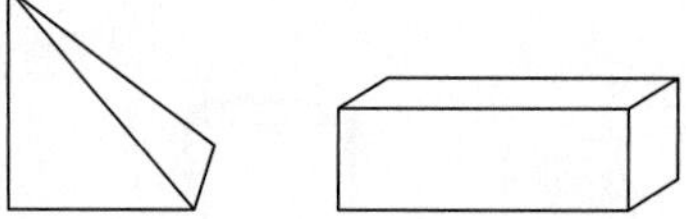

4. I have a face shaped like a **triangle**.

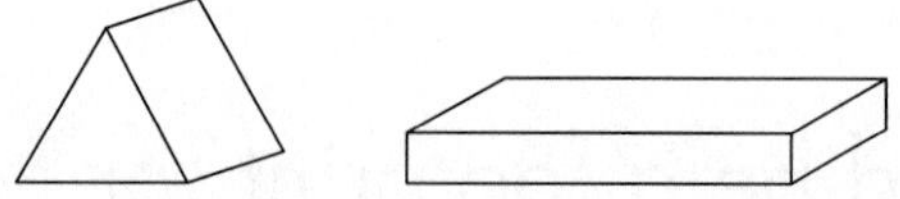

Use anytime after Session 1.2.

Name Date

Matching Footprints

Look at each footprint. Circle the Geoblock that makes that footprint.

1.

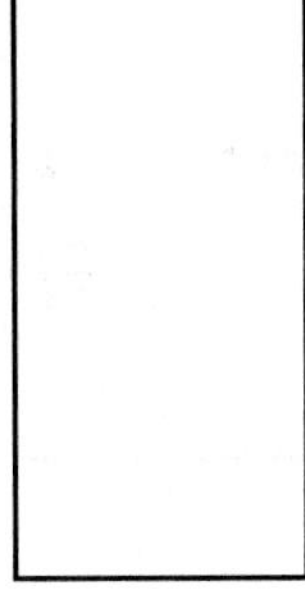

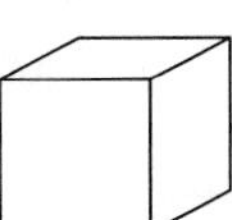

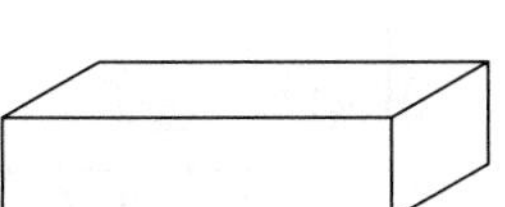

2.

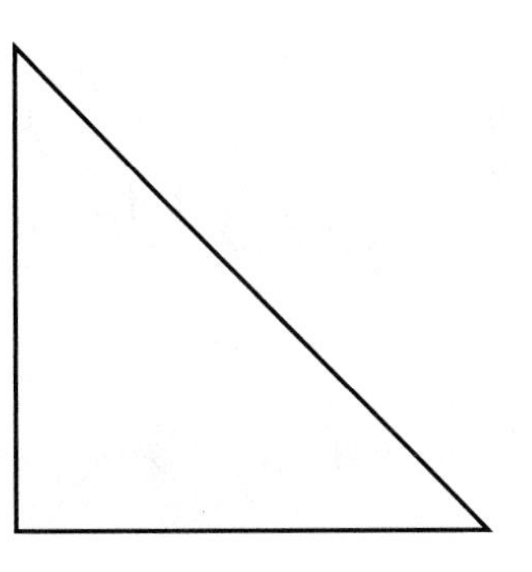

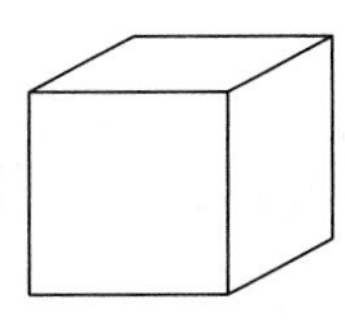

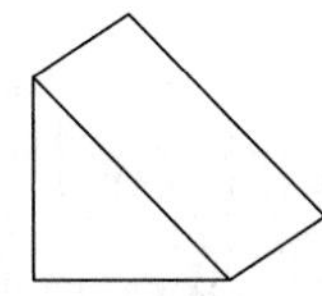

3.

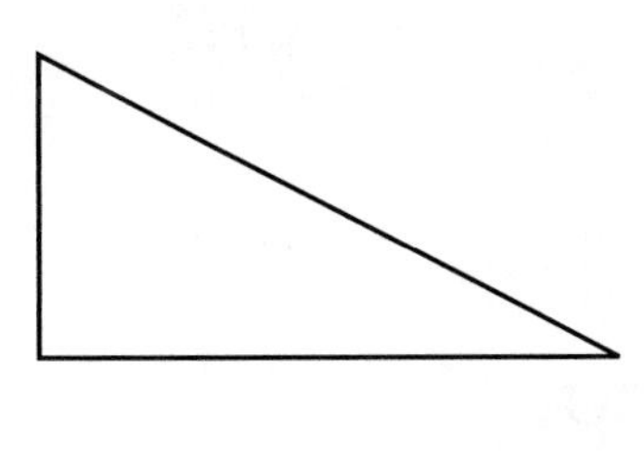

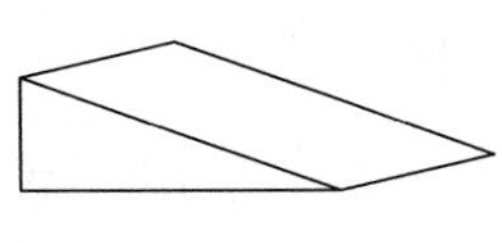

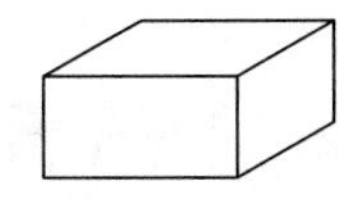

Name Date

Blocks and Boxes

Quiz

Choose the correct answer.

1 block

N

W						E
		Library		Dentist	Hospital	
	Zoo			Movie Theater		Post Office

S

1. Start at the zoo. Turn east. Go forward 3 blocks. Where are you?

(A) (B) (C) (D)

2. Start at the library. Turn east. Go forward 3 blocks. Where are you?

 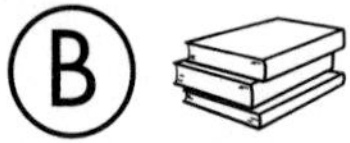  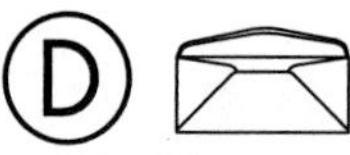

(A) (B) (C) (D)

3. Start at the post office. Turn West. Go forward 5 blocks. Where are you?

  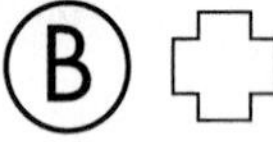    

(A) (B) (C) (D)

4. Use 3 to 5 Geoblocks to build a building. Then draw a picture of your building.

Name Date

Find the Blocks

Look at the building shown.

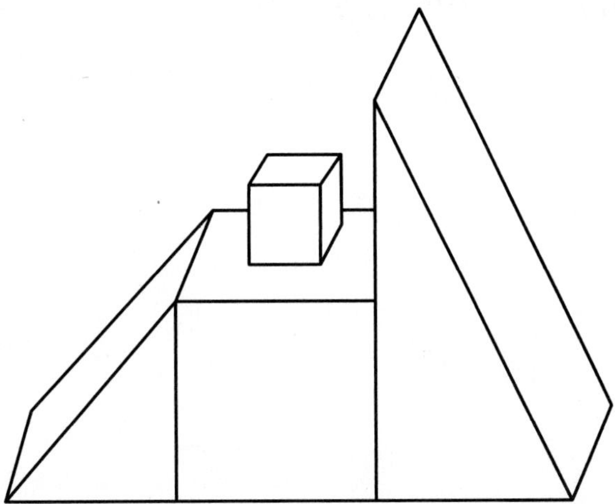

Draw the building.

Name Date

Blocks and Boxes

Drawing My Building

Create a building using 6 to 8 blocks.
Then draw a picture of your building.

Use anytime after Session 2.1.